Affairs, as he beadily eyes library after library as a "prime retail opportunity". The hottest ire is saved for Tony Blair . . . In the media, Bennett is invariably described as 'Eeyore-ish' but much of this diary sees a zest for life that's a little closer to Tigger . . . Few diarists could offer such a consistently funny and touching authorial voice as Bennett. Long may he keep on keeping on.'

Ben Lawrence, *Daily Telegraph*

'Bennett's status as one of Britain's leading playwrights of the past half-century has not diminished the acerbity of his pen or the sharp-ness of his wit. Reading Bennett's diaries is a fascinating exercise in modern history . . . *Keeping On Keeping On* is a superb collection, written from the unique perspective of an octogenarian at the top of his stylistic game, with a keen eye towards the past we have lost and the future we may yet inhabit.'

Charlotte Heathcote, *Express*

'A beautiful, humane and honest collection.'

Rachel Reeves, *New Statesman* Books of the Year

'Don't give a copy to your neighbor unless you want the soundtrack of Christmas Day to be dominated by muffled laughter coming from next door.'

Robert Douglas-Fairhurst, *Spectator* Books of the year

'I love him for his funny stories and his beady observations (starlings, he says, are 'slightly sweaty birds'). He can also make you think again about things you have always taken for granted, as when he points out that the paintings of Leonardo are 'a bit creepy'. And, despite himself, he is as on the ball as any ambitious young stand-up: of Lady Gaga's costume, made entirely of meat, he writes: 'It's not a dress in which you would want to walk the dog.'

Craig Brown, *Mail on Sunday* Books of the Year

'Companionable, inspiring, likeable, generous, funny. One feels lucky to have him. And lucky, too, that despite sometimes feeling "washed up", he has the strength – and the will – to keep on.'

Matthew Adams, *i*

'To settle down on a darkening evening with a new volume of Alan Bennett is to be in the company of an old friend. Someone you don't see as often as you'd like but with whom you immediately pick up where you left off . . . It's Bennett's deep well of compassion that marks him out, his morality and his righteous anger – qualities that run through his life and his work like letters through a stick of Scarborough rock . . . There are wonderful character sketches and random thoughts and witty aperçus fill the book, the serious and the silly cheek by jowl . . . In sum, an endlessly rewarding read by a man for all seasons and one who occupies a unique place in our culture and affections.'

Liz Thomson, *Arts Desk*

Keeping On Keeping On

ALAN BENNETT

FABER & FABER

P

PROFILE BOOKS

First published in 2016
This paperback edition first published in 2017

by Faber & Faber Limited
Bloomsbury House
74–77 Great Russell Street
London WC1B 3DA

AND

by Profile Books
3 Holford Yard, Bevin Way
London WC1X 9HD
www.profilebooks.com

Typeset by Faber & Faber Ltd
Printed and bound by CPI Group (UK) Ltd, Croydon, CR0 4YY

A CIP record for this book
is available from the British Library

ISBN 978-1-78125-650-3

FSC
www.fsc.org
MIX
Paper from
responsible sources
FSC® C020471

2 4 6 8 10 9 7 5 3

Contents

Illustrations

Introduction

Since diaries make up the bulk of this book a diary entry is an appropriate start:

> *10 December 2015*. Trying to hit on a title for this collection I
> pick up Larkin's *The Whitsun Weddings* . . . a presentation copy
> inscribed to me by Larkin at the request of Judi Dench back
> in 1969 when she and I did *An Evening With* . . . for the BBC.
> Looking at Larkin is a mistake as I am straight away discouraged:
> his poems are full of such good and memorable stuff that to
> plunder them just for a title seems cheap. Though it's easier
> for Larkin, I think, as at eighty-one I'm still trying to avoid the
> valedictory note which was a problem Larkin never had, the
> valedictory almost his exclusive territory. I find nothing suitable
> though *The Long Slide* is a possibility, which seems valedictory
> but isn't . . . *The Long Slide* is to happiness not extinction. Would
> *Pass It On* do, Hector's message at the end of *The History Boys*?
> But pass what on . . . I'd still find it hard to say.
>
> Nothing else done today except a trip over to Profile Books
> to sign copies of *The Lady in the Van*. The driver who takes me
> there is a big nice-looking young man with close-cropped hair
> and curling eyelashes. He is also a noticeably courteous driver.
> When we get to Clerkenwell I compliment him on his courteous
> driving but not (the subtext) on his eyelashes though it's
> something at eighty-one I'm probably allowed to do. No danger.
> Not that I ever have been.

In one particular respect the valedictory is not to be sidestepped as
it was in 2006 that Rupert Thomas and I said farewell to Gloucester

Crescent, the street in Camden Town where I had lived for nearly forty years, moving (though only a mile away) to Primrose Hill. It's said that newcomers to London often settle near the point of arrival and this was certainly true of me, who could be taken to have arrived from Leeds at King's Cross and been a denizen of North London ever since.

I started off my life in London in 1964 when I had a top-floor flat for £10 a week in Chalcot Square not far from where we have moved to. I was nervous about the move. In Gloucester Crescent I'd worked in a bay window looking onto the street where there was always enough going on to divert me in the gaps of my less than continuous flow of composition. In Primrose Hill I was to look out over a tiny back garden where the only excitement would be the occasional squirrel and I was nervous lest the spell of the Crescent such as it was, would be broken. Could I actually work there? This was such a real concern that for a month or two I kept office hours, cycling back to the old house and the table in the window that I was used to. But this soon palled so saying a reluctant farewell to the vibrant street life of Gloucester Crescent (drunks, drug dealing, snogging by the wall and the occasional stop and search) I embraced the tranquillity of the back garden in Primrose Hill and just got on with it.

In another respect, too I was hoping it would be a new beginning. Having failed in our old house to turn back the rising tide of paper I looked forward to a new start. I wasn't yet ready for a computer but I resolved to make fewer notes, not write so many drafts and generally keep paperwork to a minimum. This has not happened and having fled one nest I now have made another. I am not proud of being computer-illiterate and this too I hoped to alter so we did get a computer. However its sojourn was brief as it was the single item stolen in a break-in one afternoon and in this respect Primrose Hill proved hardly more law-abiding than Camden Town: my bike, chained to the railings outside was soon stolen, a would-be burglar tried to con his way into the house and a neighbour was badly mugged on our actual doorstep. Still it's a friendly neighbourhood and a socially mixed one and even if I can't quite cosify it as 'the village' as some do, most people speak or pass the time of day though whether it will survive when HS2 senselessly rips the guts out of it remains to be seen.

Shortly after we moved house in 2006 we entered into a civil partnership. Rupert and I had first got together in 1992 though we didn't live in the same house until 1997 after I was operated on for bowel cancer as is related in *Untold Stories*. We had now been together for fourteen years, our partnership domestic long before it was civil, so the ceremony was hardly a landmark. And even less so, thanks to me.

It was a rainy morning in Camden Registry Office, with the registrar performing the rites in the presence of Rupert's parents, his brother and a few friends and with scant ceremony, so scant in fact that even the registrar felt it a bit of a let-down, with the happy couple and everyone else doing nothing more celebratory afterwards than adjourning for some coffee on Great Portland Street. This was entirely my fault as, never keen on parties, had a more festive occasion been envisaged I might have jumped ship. It was only later that I realised how closely our ceremony mirrored the early morning marriage of my parents which is also described in *Untold Stories*. They, too, had had only a few relatives present with my father immediately afterwards dashing off to work where he was a butcher at the Co-op. Their only concession to the occasion was a visit that evening to the Theatre Royal and *The Desert Song*. We didn't even do that (or its equivalent). It's something (if only occasionally) that I am never allowed to forget.

In the ten years covered by this book politics has impinged more than I care for and like the woman in the fish shop the day after the 2015 election I fear that there will be a Tory government for the remainder of my life. And with it England dismantled. As the government continues to pick the state clean one marvels at its ingenuity in finding institutions still left unsold. And why should it stop? If there is money to be made out of the probation service why not still exhibit the insane? How long before even the monarchy is sponsored and government itself put out to tender? Is there any large corporation nowadays which one wholly trusts and which doesn't confuse honesty with public relations?

Some of these sentiments I more moderately voiced in King's College Chapel in 2014 in the sermon printed here. I could have suggested then that taking a leaf out of the government's book the Church of England too should be run solely for profit, parsons given targets and made to turn up at Epiphany with statistics of souls saved. Except that the trouble with such jokes is that they are a joke no longer and in this senseless world in which even the bees find government arrayed against them, moderation is hard to hold onto.

Eschew the valedictory though one tries to do, anything one writes at this age is bound to be to a degree testamentary, with the writer wondering what of anything he or she has written will survive and for how long. I can't say I much care since I shan't be around to see it though I hope that any posthumous assessment will at least be comprehensive, taking in not just what I've written but what I've said about it myself and this collection includes the preface and programme notes for four plays – *The Habit of Art* (2009), *Hymn*, *Cocktail Sticks* and *People* (all 2012). The introductions to my plays often say as much as the plays themselves, including as they often do cherished passages cut from the playing text, generally on grounds of length. But I have always written too much and one of the reasons why my collaboration with Nicholas Hytner has been so long and fruitful is that he is among other things a ruthless surgeon with no hesitation about wielding the scissors or pressing whatever key it is on the computer.

I have also been fortunate in my writing life that the *London Review of Books* has been prepared to print what prose I have written and the National Theatre produce my plays. I have been edited by both but rejected by neither and seldom put under pressure. Of course I might have written more had I been less complacent about finding a market for my work but I wouldn't have had such a good time.

One of the diary entries for October 2015 is about doing *Private Passions*, Michael Berkeley's always excellent programme for BBC Radio 3. It was nicely edited so that after my final choice, 'Softly and gently', the final passage from Elgar's *Dream of Gerontius*, I was allowed a little coda. As a boy at concerts in Leeds Town Hall I used to sit behind the orchestra. The music I heard seemed to hold out a vision of love returned, of transcendence and even triumph. But that was just the music and life wasn't like that. What was to become of me? Could I slip into the seat behind I would put a hand on my young shoulder and say, 'It's going to be all right.'

And it has been all right. I have been very lucky.

Alan Bennett

The Diaries 2005–2015

Preface to the Diaries

I am not a conscientious diarist. I don't sit down every evening, say, and review the day as all too often nothing of note has occurred. Except when I'm rehearsing or, more occasionally, filming I don't stray far from my desk and even if from time to time I record a breakthrough in something I'm working on, the diary is generally a tale of frustration and dissatisfaction which, though it may help me, is no fun to read. Still a diary does have a point. Nothing is ever quite so bad that one can't write it down or so shameful either, though this took me a long time to learn with my earliest diaries reticent and even prudish. I remember when I first came across Joe Orton's diaries in the eighties marvelling (and being depressed) at how while he was still in his teens he was unabashed at himself and unshocked by his fellows, a faculty he seems to have been born with but which took me half a lifetime to learn.

Diaries involve waste with much of what one records perhaps of posthumous interest but tedious to read and often bad-tempered, the diary getting one's ranting and resentment literally at first hand. Publishing an annual diary as I have done for thirty years in the *London Review of Books* I still find it lowering how little of what I have written in a past year is worth printing. It's never a good ratio. Still, there is more in this book than was printed in the *LRB*. Once upon a time I used to think that the paper edited my diary to chime in with their preconception of my character, a form of benign censorship designed to save me from myself. Thus I seldom got away with anything gay or particularly self-revealing, whereas nowadays no one seems to mind, the staff of the *LRB* so young and bright they probably have better things to think about.

3

I do rant of course, chiefly about the government so I make no excuse for that. We maybe go into too many old churches for some readers and country houses as well, though it was traipsing round the latter which led to me writing *People*, my play about the National Trust. These sightseeing trips often used to involve sandwiches which I lovingly delineated and even dismembered in the diary (especially after Christmas). I say 'used to' because my partner is now gluten-free so that's put a spoke in the sandwiches. This won't displease some readers who felt that we ought to do more to patronise local retail outlets. 'Why do you bother to take sandwiches to Byland Abbey?' wrote one reader. 'There's a perfectly good pub opposite.' A more serious casualty than the sandwiches is that in this volume we say goodbye to the Gers, that out-of-the-way part of France between Condom and Nérac where our friend Lynn Wagenknecht had an idyllic house, the demise of which is recorded in June 2008. There is nowhere abroad with the possible exception of New York where I have been as happy.

'Yorkshire' is the village in Craven to which my parents retired in 1966 and where Rupert Thomas and I still have the cottage. Unless otherwise stated most other entries are in London which, as I explain in the Introduction, used to be Camden Town but in 2006 became Primrose Hill.

2005

9 January. To Solopark near Cambridge, a vast but highly organised architectural salvage depot where (with unexpected ease) we find four suitable blond flagstones for the hallway. Something of the abattoir about such places and still there are the half dozen pepperpot domes from Henry VII's chapel at Westminster which we saw when we were here last and which were taken down by Rattee and Kett in the course of their restoration of the chapel in the 1990s. They are, I suppose, late eighteenth-century or early nineteenth-century and so less numinous than their predecessors would have been – though even these will have witnessed the fire that destroyed the House of Commons and the original Palace of Westminster.

13 January. Papers full of Prince Harry who's been to a fancy-dress party wearing a Nazi armband. Not a particularly bright thing to do though what I find sympathetic is that he can no more draw a proper swastika than I could as a child, none of my efforts looking other than a lot of silly legs chasing one another in a rather Manx fashion and not the chilling symbol one saw on the pitiless arm of Raymond Huntley or Francis L. Sullivan's over-filled sleeve.

18 January. To lunch at the Étoile with Michael Palin and Barry Cryer, nice and easy with Barry telling innumerable stories and jokes and Michael reminiscing about *Python*, particularly Graham Chapman. I contribute less in the way of jokes or reminiscence, though we talk about the Cook–Moore play, something similar now threatened for the Pythons. We're all of us very different. I'm the oldest by a couple of years but all of us still have a good head of hair with Michael as handsome as he was when younger though his face more leathery and Gary Cooper-like. Both of them say how utterly dependent they are on their wives, Michael's routine currently disrupted because Helen has had to have a knee replacement so his household doesn't run as smoothly as he would like. God knows what he would make of our routine but I tell them they're very lucky.

Michael is fascinated by Graham Chapman and his sexual boldness. Tells how booking into a hotel somewhere, Graham hadn't even signed in before he disappeared with one of the hotel staff and like Orton in his capacity to detect or to generate mischief.

Says G. was probably the best actor of the group, his performances often utterly serious however absurd the dialogue and instancing Graham's meticulously named 'Vince Snetterton-Lewis' telling how he used to have his head nailed to the wardrobe in a performance of documentary straightness.

28 January. Fly to Rome for a British Council reading. It occurs to me that a lot of the camp has gone out of British Airways and that as the stewards have got older and less outrageous so the service has declined. This morning there is scarcely a smile, not to mention a joke, the whole flight smooth, crowded and utterly anonymous.

The British Council reading is packed, with two hours of radio and TV interviews beforehand. All the interviewers are well-informed, with sitting in on the proceedings a simultaneous translator, Olga Fernando. She's astonishingly clever, translating aloud while at the same time taking down a shorthand transcript of what is being said, a skill she normally employs in much more exalted circumstances; next week for instance she is accompanying the Italian president to London to meet Jack Straw and she also translated for Bush on his visit to Italy last year.

The library at the British Council is busy and full of students who only leave when it closes at 8 p.m., and seeing these young Italians reading English books and magazines, watching videos and generally finding this a worthwhile place to be is immensely heartening. The British Council can still be thought a bit of a joke but like the BBC World Service it's a more useful investment of public money than any number of state visits, or, in Blair's case, holidays with Berlusconi (who, incidentally, I never hear mentioned throughout).

29 January, Rome. Seduced by its name, first thing this morning we go to look at Nero's Golden House, or such parts of it as have been excavated. It's a mistake. Walking through these tall narrow chambers, none with natural light and few with more than the faintest fresco, I feel it's no more inspiring than a tour round a nineteenth-century municipal gasworks, which it undoubtedly resembles. Most of the party wear headphones and follow the cassette guide and so become dull and bovine in their movements with sudden irrational darts and turns dictated by the commentary. Deprived of one faculty they become less adept at the others, and when they talk do so in loud unregulated voices. Wayward and dilatory in their responses they are seemingly without purpose, though of course they are the purposeful ones. What to us are featureless alcoves of scrofulous masonry (and with no evidence of gold) presumably echoed to the orgies and barbarities which are even now being detailed on the cassettes to which everyone else is listening intently.

On Saturday evening to the Campidoglio where the Capitoline Museum opens late, if to very few visitors and we are virtually alone in the vast galleries, though there are more people looking at the pictures which we skip in favour of the sculpture. I stroke the back of the Dying Gaul and would have done the same for the Boy taking a Thorn from his Foot, but the attendant is there. Afterwards we brave the wind and go round the corner onto the terrace to look across the Forum but it's too dark to see much and what one can see means nothing – the biggest handicap in Rome as in Egypt or China that I have no perspective on its history.

Eat at a friendly little restaurant down the street from the hotel, and recommended by the British Council – and twice, Saturday lunch and Sunday dinner, at La Campana, off the Piazza Nicosia not far from P. Navona – a lovely old-fashioned restaurant recommended by Matthew Kneale, and reminiscent of the old Bertorelli's – tiled floor, blond wood, old waiters and a huge menu. Note how unobtrusively friendly the Italians are, both neighbouring tables, to which we had not spoken during the meal, say good night to us when they leave. We tip, which perhaps doesn't do here and which probably does us no favours but one wants to reward the waiters (and the restaurant) for still being as they are.

Our waiter could well be played by Michael Gambon, though what a monologue by an old waiter could be about I can't think.

4 February. Condoleezza Rice announces that the US has no plans to attack Iran at the present moment, the implication being that we should be grateful for such forbearance.

One forgets what a vile paper the *Telegraph* still is. Last Sunday I was sickened by a vicious profile of Clive Stafford Smith, which implied that he was unbalanced and that his (to my mind saintly) efforts on behalf of those on Death Row in America were an unwarranted interference in the democratic process – and that if the people of Texas want to condemn their fellow citizens to death, justly or unjustly, they should be allowed to do so.

9 February. I use proof sheets as scrap paper and today it's one from *Afternoon Off* (1978), a TV play we shot at Whitby with a scene in a café and a long speech by Anna Massey. Stephanie Cole plays the other part, but it's hardly a conversation as she only has one line with Anna doing all the talking. And I realise, as I haven't until now, that I was writing monologues long before I specifically tried to, only in the earlier plays they were just long (long) speeches. *Afternoon Off* has several, because the leading figure is a Chinese waiter with very little English so everybody talks at him.

13 February. As with Havel once, I seem to be the only playwright not personally acquainted with the deceased Arthur Miller and with some line on his life and work. Many of his plays I still haven't seen, though years ago when I was reading everything I could get hold of on America and McCarthyism I came across Miller's novel *Focus*, in which a character begins to look Jewish when he takes to wearing glasses. It's a powerful piece and in retrospect rather Roth-like. No one quite says how much of his street cred came from his marriage to Monroe, though paradoxically more with the intellectuals than with Hollywood.

19 February. Shop in Settle, calling in first at Mr Midgley's antique shop at the end of Duke Street. It's closed and as Mr Midgley has been ill we assume it's that and are going away when Mrs M. comes to the door to say that John died yesterday. Both of us much affected by this, partly because we were fond of him but also because it will alter the landscape, visits to the shop always part of our Saturday morning routine.

Mr Midgley was originally an architect, trained at Leeds but who had had an antique shop in Settle as long as I can remember. His stuff was good and not dear, ceramics and glass mainly and over the years I must have bought dozens of rummers and heavy Victorian tumblers, the latter £2 or so for many years and even today only £10 or so. Whatever you bought from him would have a meticulously written label attached describing exactly what the piece was and its date and whether it was damaged – though he was such a skilled repairer you often couldn't tell where the chip or the crack had been. These labels were almost scholarly productions particularly when relating to the umpteen nineteenth-century potteries south of Leeds and I've kept some of them on the objects concerned lest the information be lost.

Once upon a time shops such as his were a feature of any small town but as rents have risen actual antique shops are seldom come across – dealers showing at fairs or having stalls in antique centres like Brampton. But what I think of is how much expertise has died with him – Victorian plates just plates, pretty or handsome enough, but unassigned now to a particular pottery or to Leeds or Castleford – John Midgley, antique dealer.

21 February. Snow arrives on cue around four but alas doesn't lay; 'It's laying!' one of the joyous cries of childhood.

22 February. To the private view of the Caravaggio at the National Gallery. Crowded, but because only the paintings are lit and not the rooms the crowds melt into the gloom, or form a frieze of silhouettes against the pictures. Only sixteen paintings on show and whereas in some of the earlier paintings that we saw in Rome one was struck by how clamorous they were – boys howling, heads screaming – here the pictures are much calmer and it is character that prevails. Some of the expressions are so subtle as to be beyond interpretation: in the *Supper at Emmaus* (1606) from Milan, a more tranquil picture than the same subject in the NG, the figure to the left of Jesus has a look both of interest and concern far more intriguing than the mere wonder and astonishment evident in the NG's 1601 version. And right at the end of the exhibition (and Caravaggio's life) there is Goliath's head, which is supposedly Caravaggio's own, and whether it's that but the look on the young David's face is so troubled and so overwhelmed he seems only to regret what he has accomplished.

24 February. To a Faber meeting for their sales reps at the Butchers' Hall, which is just by the back door of Barts, bombed presumably and rebuilt in undistinguished neo-Georgian some time in the 1960s. Doorman sullen and no advertisement for the supposed cheerfulness of the butchering profession. In good time so have a chance to look at the occasional paintings, including a couple of nice early nineteenth-century old masters (of the Butchers' Company, that is), besides various ceremonial cleavers including the one used to cut up the first New Zealand lamb brought to England and served to Queen Victoria in 1880. Nicest though are two Victorian or Edwardian toy butcher's shops. They're bigger and grander than the one Dad made for Gordon and me *c*.1940 but whereas these joints are nailed into place, Dad's were all made to unhook so we could serve them to our imaginary customers at the counter.

25 February. A propos civil liberties the government spokesperson most often put up, particularly on television, is the junior minister at the Home Office, Hazel Blears. With a name that combines both blur and smear and which would have delighted Dickens the lady in question has always shown herself to be an unwavering supporter of Mr Blair, though lacking those gestures in the direction of humanity with which her master generally lards his utterances.

1 March. On Saturday to Cambridge and the Fitzwilliam Museum. I used to regard the first room on the right at the top of the stairs as a shrine to recent literary celebrity, an anteroom to fame. Here were Thomas Hardy, G. B. Shaw, William Nicholson and many more. Now they are all scattered – Shaw and Hardy I spot on the gallery of the room next door and no sign of William N. at all. But still full of delicious paintings – like a sweet shop so many lovely things – and so un-grand, half the contents (I like to think anyway) left to the university by generations of dons, whose treasures they once were.

Pay our usual visit to Archbishop Laud wickedly placed next to another Van Dyck, of the voluptuous Countess of Southampton at whom Laud plainly cannot bear to look. You can practically hear his impatience and irritation.

12 March, Yorkshire. A cold bright day and I sit briefly at the end of the garden, watching a plane cross a vast sea of blue sky, leaving a single unfurled trail behind it. A plane such as this moving across virgin space must be more of a treat for the spectator than the pilot; it puts me in mind of myself as a child longing to be the first to jump (never dive) into the still swimming bath at Armley. The pleasure there was in disrupting the calm but also in being able to see through the undisturbed water to the murky end of the bath.

15 March. To Rousham in the morning to look at the gardens then to Daylesford Organic Farm Shop for lunch. The colour scheme is that greyish green one was first conscious of forty years ago when Canonbury and Islington took it up and then the National Trust: 'tasteful green' it might be called (it's the colour of the coalhouse door in Yorkshire). It's a definite spread – shop, restaurant, a cloister cum herb garden, together with barns, farm buildings and, one presumes, living quarters for the many employees. It's cheering to think that, if Nigel Slater is to be believed re residential catering establishments, the young people who largely staff the place will be screwing each other rotten. Not that there's a hint of that front of house, which is chaste, cheerful, middle-aged, middle-class and above all well off, the car park full of four-wheel drives, Pioneers, Explorers, Conquerors, Marauders, all of which have blazed a fearless trail across rural Oxfordshire to this well-heeled location a mile or two from Chipping Norton where the best is on offer in the way of lifestyle choices: delicious, wholesome food, multifarious cheeses, fifteen different types of loaf. 'Look, darling. Look what they've got,' calls one loving middle-aged wife to her browsing husband and then to the assistant: 'He's a real cheese man.'

Odd how I could take such a place without question did I come across it in New York, say, or California. But here it's so bound up with class and money and all one's complicated feelings about England I hold back. Like Saga, another rich and popular establishment catering to an obvious demand, it's so successful it becomes slightly sinister – the Daylesford Experience like the Saga one a perfect front for subversion of some kind, with the Daylesford philosophy that sort of bland and smiling philanthropy which in thrillers always masks elaborate villainy.

16 March. To St Etheldreda's, Ely Place for the funeral of my neighbour Anna Haycraft (aka Alice Thomas Ellis) who died a week or so ago in Wales and whose body had therefore to be brought down for the funeral and then presumably taken back to Wales to be buried beside Colin, her late husband, at their Welsh farmhouse. This, I gather, is pretty remote and the track to it hardly hearse-friendly so the grave when she eventually achieves it likely to be something of a relief.

The church is interesting, though only the shell is the thirteenth-century original, with the blind arcading and crocketed pinnacles particularly pleasing. Nor is there a lot of garish statuary and the images of English Catholic saints standing on medieval corbels round the walls are soberly painted and quite secular. Note how these occasions flush out the devout, the fluent genuflection before entering the pew the first indicator. Charles Moore sinks to his knees straight away and prays for a considerable period of time, and Piers Paul Read similarly. Some admiration for this, men who pray in public not uncourageous, though more often met with at Catholic rather than Anglican services.

The service is conducted by Father Kit Cunningham who talks about Anna, saying how she had summoned him to the bedside of her husband, Colin, who had died just as he was coming into the room. He thereupon anointed the body with Anna's blessing, though Colin was not a believer, Anna saying 'with the shadow of a wink': 'Now he will know who was right.' That this should be treated so lightly is mildly shocking – or would be if I had more conviction in the matter. The crucial scene in *Brideshead* turns on just such a situation, with the readiness of Catholics to reel you in at the last moment an issue with Charles Ryder. And Fr Cunningham seems every bit as kindly and understanding as the family priest of the

Marchmains. R. is not at the service but points out how shocked one would be by the reverse – a passionate atheist denying a dying or dead Catholic the consolations of religion.

Coming away I see Richard Ingrams, swathed in a black anorak, trudging along the pavement. He has a brief word with Fr Cunningham, much as, one feels, Oxford dons used to have with the train driver at Paddington when he'd brought the Cathedrals Express in on time.

18 March. That there should be an etiquette on the scaffold (tipping the headsman etc.) says everything about human beings, their savagery and their delicacy.

22 March. Christopher Strauli tells me today that for the last few years he has been employed at Addenbrooke's at Cambridge, impersonating patients for examination by students. He has to familiarise himself with various conditions and (putting on the necessary symptoms) is then interviewed and examined by the medics. He enjoys this, finds it interesting and says it is well paid. Like the book on the Casualties Union I read a few years back I can see this has many dramatic possibilities – not that I'll ever get round to realising them. [It figures in my short story 'The Greening of Mrs Donaldson', 2010.]

25 March, Good Friday. Supper at our friends Madge and Michael's not Saturday as it would generally be because tomorrow Jack Straw is expected for the weekend. James and Charlotte there with the children and Florence (10) tells a joke, having gone out of the room in order to rehearse it.

'There's these three boys in the class called Zipp, Willie and Wee and they're very badly behaved. When the teacher comes in Zipp is standing on the desk and the other two are playing about so the teacher says, "Zipp, down! Willie out! Wee in the corner!"'

There's always a credulity threshold in a joke and in this one it's the likelihood of there being a boy called 'Wee'. Except, as R. says, these days he could be Chinese.

Such a difficult year in prospect: concerts and readings, moving house, the film of *The History Boys*, the book *Untold Stories*; plus we're supposed to go to New York in May.

> I don't think I will sing
> Any more just now,
> Or ever. I must start
> To sit with a blind brow
> Above an empty heart.
>
> JOHN BERRYMAN

2 April. To Knole this Saturday morning, a not entirely pleasurable expedition as journeys down to Kent seldom are. South London has to be traversed first of all, beginning with that slow and stopping journey along what's left of the Old Kent Road and through New Cross and Lewisham, areas of London that have depressed me all my life.

Nor does it significantly improve once you're in open country as Kent never quite is, crossed and carved up by more motorways than even South Yorkshire. We come off one of these too soon or too late, it's hard to tell, then have to trek across the garden of England trying to find the largely unsignposted Sevenoaks. Still, it's the world of Denton Welch and places like East Peckham and Oxon Hoath have some of the romance with which I invested them in 1952 when I first read his *Journals*. At one point we find ourselves driving past the Gothick tower he painted as *The Coffin House*, now renovated and bijou-d as indeed most of the county seems to be – I've never seen hedges so manicured or cottages so desirable, as if lived in still by Betsey Trotwood rather than some Medway commuter.

Knole Park where we eat our sandwiches is packed, though the house much less so. I'm not nearly so keen on it as R. who gets more pleasure out of the upholstery and ancient embroidery than I do, not to mention the priceless silver suite which just seems to me like fairground stuff. Favourites with me are the painted staircases and the galleried second courtyard but it suffers, I think, from having been over-romanced by Vita Sackville-West and over-written by Virginia Woolf in *Orlando* – the MS of which is on show in the great hall.

Still, a good day and, having wandered round the house as ever both put off by the crowds and puzzled by what they get out of it (and indeed what I get out of it), sitting in the café it occurs to me it's one of those insoluble problems that I have tended to write plays about. So maybe this is another. And looking down at my napkin in the tearoom I see a possible title of 'The National Trust'. Actually a good title altogether and regardless of what it's about. Well we shall see. [This eventually becomes *People* (2012).]

9 April. Going up and down on the train to Leeds over the years one comes to know the conductors, who (with one exception) have always been friendly. One who regularly chats to me has literary aspirations and also a gift for languages, Finnish is his latest achievement. I'm translated into Finnish and last time we met on the train he promised to try and bring me back something of mine from Helsinki. Today he reports that all the bookshops had sold out – which is, I suppose, good news though I wouldn't have thought I rang many bells in the Arctic Circle. As the train draws near to Leeds he makes the usual announcement then follows it without any prior warning with the same announcement in what I presume is Finnish. One or two passengers look up, and someone raises his eyebrows in a 'what are the trains coming to?' mode. Whereas to find that the railways are still a haven for odd individuals and eccentrics seems to me a cause for celebration.

10 April. Killing time en route from Ilkley to Leeds where I meet R. off the eight-thirty train, I stop in a lane near Weeton. It's half past six, the sunshine still bright though bitterly cold at the end of an afternoon of snow showers and icy rain. There are rabbits in the field and two of them climb the wall and run across it so deftly I think they're squirrels. A pair of robins hop from post to post along a fence, in what is presumably some sort of territorial display, and then above the farm at the top of the ridge I see one of the kites from Harewood lazily circling round. This spot is just on the outskirts of Leeds – crest the hill and there are the beginnings of suburbia – but it seems, as it has always seemed to me since I was a boy, more intensely rural than the depths of the country.

15 April. In his review of Truman Capote's letters in the *LRB*, Colm Tóibín lists Capote's many dislikes, including *Beyond the Fringe*, which he thought 'rather dreary'. I never could think of much to say to Kenneth Tynan or he to me but whenever we met in the early 1960s he'd make a point of telling me that of all the stuff in *BTF* what 'Truman' had most liked was my solo sermon, I think because it reminded him of the sermons of his boyhood. Whether Tynan was just being polite to me or Truman to Tynan there's no means of knowing but in any case at that time I had no idea who Truman Capote was, the similarity of his name to Capone making me think he was some sort of literary racketeer, which wasn't far wrong.

25 April. Keep being rung by journalists asking how I intend to vote, information which I don't divulge not because I've got any principled notions to do with the secret ballot but because I like disappointing newspapers. If I were a voter in the Blackburn constituency my vote would go to Craig Murray, the ex-ambassador to Uzbekistan, who resigned from the diplomatic service over the foreign secretary's refusal to discount information obtained by torture in the prisons of Uzbekistan, a decision that means torture is likely to continue. If there is a market for the information why should it stop? Mr Straw claims to have lost sleep over his decision. Some of the tortured will have lost sleep, too, but that's because they will have lost fingernails first. I suppose I despise Straw more than Blair, thinking, perhaps wrongly, that he is capable of better.

26 April. Last performance of *The History Boys*. Rupert and I go down to the NT sitting in the audience though on the back row. Final performances are seldom good as everyone is saying farewell to their own lines so investing them with over much significance. They are also nervous and in the Hector–Hardy scene Sam Barnett as Posner has to fight back tears. Even the normally phlegmatic Frances de la Tour is affected and for the first time in the whole run for her or, I think, anybody else, she dries. It's in the mock-interview scene when she could easily be seamlessly prompted if Richard Griffiths or one of the boys had their wits about them. Instead they just stare at her and wait; perhaps taking it to be, as I do at first, a particularly effective pause. Eventually Frankie has to say, 'I'm afraid I'm going to have to ask for the line.' Normally a lapse like this would kill a scene stone dead but it survives and the laughs continue and the audience is unaffected.

29 April, Yorkshire. Settle is still a pleasant place to shop and though there are one or two empty premises it hasn't yet been given over to charity shops, which is the first symptom of a town dying. The spirit of the small shop still persists in Booth's, the local supermarket. At the cheese counter I ask for some Parmesan, which might be thought a relative newcomer to this out-of-the-way Craven town. But the assistant proudly reels off the names of the several Parmesans that they stock, ending up with a flourish: 'Or you may like to try the Reggiano, the Rolls-Royce of Parmesans.'

8 May. Much in the papers about VE Day, today the sixtieth anniversary. Several people who were in the crowd outside Buckingham Palace remember how they chanted: 'We want George,' 'We want

Liz.' I don't believe this. It's what they would chant now so they think it was what they did then. The King was never 'George' still less the Queen 'Liz'. That was in the future (though not for him). What I remember of that night and of subsequent public celebrations up to and including the Festival of Britain was the impact of floodlighting, light squandered as I had never known it before.

1 May. C. is a producer on BBC TV's *Songs of Praise* and in the run-up to the election has been having to interview various politicians including Michael Howard. He was less than forthcoming and when she asked him what was his favourite hymn, said it was 'I Vow to Thee My Country'. C. – with no irony or insinuation – asked him why. Howard simply stared at her and she got nothing further out of him.

Martha, Charlotte and James's youngest, has been slow to read but now aged eight is making great strides, particularly enjoying spelling. She is being given additional tuition by the father of a friend, a retired teacher who is also employed by Manchester United; the foreign half of the squad he is teaching to speak English, the English half he is teaching to read and write.

22 May. Reading Frank Kermode's review of John Haffenden's life of Empson makes me regret a little that Empson was cut out of *The History Boys*. In the first version of the play Hector sings the praises of Sheffield where he had been taught by Empson, then recounts to the boys wanting to go to Cambridge the circumstances of Empson's downfall at Magdalene. 'So when you say Cambridge University to me, boys, I say to you "A prophylactic in the wardrobe"' – this last delivered like a war-cry. Empson was not the only casualty in the play. Simone Weil got the boot, as did Nina Simone and Simone Signoret, Jowett (of Balliol fame), James Agate, Jane Austen, Molly Bloom, Hegel and Henry James, all of them biting the distinguished dust.

18 May. On Sunday evening I do a show at the Prince of Wales Theatre in aid of the Roundhouse (amount raised – *c.* £30,000). Michael
Palin comperes and we both take questions in the second half and the
theatre is full and it goes down very well – though I do nothing new.

I began by saying how my career had more or less begun and
almost ended at the Prince of Wales Theatre. When in early 1961
we were still debating as to whether to bring *Beyond the Fringe* to
London one of the interested managements was Donald Albery's.
He was one of the leading impresarios of the time, Binkie Beaumont
by then very much on the wane. Albery had put on – or at any rate
transferred – many of Joan Littlewood's hits and also Lionel Bart's
Oliver!. He hadn't seen the show but it was agreed that in January
1961 the set should be put up in the stalls bar of the Prince of Wales
and we put on a performance just for him.

Handsome and silver-haired Albery was a tall distinguished-
looking man made more so by a gammy leg which he kept straight
and heaved around in a characteristic swinging motion. It may even
have been a false leg but like many such disabilities (Douglas Bader's
another example) it was generally assumed to have been earned in
the war. Certainly Albery always carried with him an air of gallantry
in the desert, for which there was no justification at all, the injury
to his leg done when he was a child. But it was a famous handicap. Understandably in the theatre he always insisted on an aisle seat
and on first nights late-comers hurrying down the aisle often went
flying over this managerial limb, which was very much in evidence
at our command performance, one chair in the middle of the stalls
bar, Albery unsmiling sitting there. He remained unsmiling for the
duration of the performance, not a grin, not a laugh, though having
grown accustomed to more uproarious response we rapidly became
mildly hysterical. At the finish Albery rose and stumped out into the
corridor, followed by our agent. 'Well,' he said grudgingly, 'I'll put it
on, but at a very small theatre, and there is one condition: the blond
one will have to go.'

I wish I could say it was thanks to the unswerving loyalty of my three colleagues that this didn't happen but I think it was more due to cowardice: they were more prepared to face Albery than they were to face me.

Albery made a good deal of money from the show and always regretted putting it into a small theatre, the Fortune, rather than Wyndham's say, where he could have made even more. He retired to Monaco with a young Japanese wife and when I was there in 1984 for the Italia Prize awards, I ran into him swinging along the front. He greeted me with joy and enthusiasm, implying that I had come a long way since 1961 and that it was all thanks to him.

He may of course have detected that I was a less talented performer than the other three: I felt that myself but it occurs to me now that what made him single me out was one of the episodes in the sketch 'Aftermyth of War' in which I parodied a legless fighter ace, Douglas Bader again, stumping down the steps of the set stiff-legged much as Albery did himself. It would have been sensible (and sensitive) in the circumstances to have cut it out or toned it down but in those days I believed that candour and conscience mattered and what I had written I had to do. In the circumstances I was very lucky.

2 *June*. A situation on the margins of social interaction develops opposite. Working outside No. 60 is a handsome, though rather explosive-looking young workman who is emptying sand onto the pavement preparatory to mixing some cement, the bucket of water standing there in readiness. An eccentric older man, not quite a tramp but with too much luggage slung around his bike (a large umbrella, various carrier bags) to be an ordinary cyclist, stops by the cement-making young man, parks his bike and without, as far as I can see, asking permission proceeds to wash his hands in the waiting bucket. He washes them a little too thoroughly, while talking to the unresponsive young man who, if he is concerned about the usurpation of his bucket, doesn't show it – or indeed anything much, as he

scarcely speaks. Hands done the cyclist goes back to his laden bike and wheels it away while the young man empties some of the (now slightly polluted) water onto his sand and cement, the only sense that a liberty might have been taken or a boundary crossed being that he is now more pensive and as he mixes keeps gazing in the direction the tramp has gone.

8 June. 'That's something you don't see often nowadays,' I think as a woman passes pressing what I take to be a handkerchief to her mouth and so seemingly on the way home from the dentist. Or so it used to be. But of course she's not pressing a handkerchief to her mouth at all and has been nowhere near the dentist but is just on her mobile phone.

27 June. Willie Donaldson dies. Best known, I suppose, for the *Henry Root* letters, back in 1961 Willie, in partnership with Donald Albery, put on *Beyond the Fringe*. A deceptively gentle and kindly figure Willie was never condescending as Albery invariably was and seemed as much at sea in the world of show business as we were. By the time he came into our lives and though he was not much older than us he had already lost one fortune, I think to do with shipping, and if he made another out of *BTF* he soon lost that too, Albery, I'm sure, driving a hard bargain and creaming off most of the profits.

On the eve of the show opening in the West End Willie took the four of us and the producer John Bassett to a discreet brothel in Bond Street (the building now supplanted by Burberry) not for any hands-on sexual experience but to watch some blue films. The madame was French (or reckoned to be so), tut-tutting that I seemed so young (though I was actually the oldest of the four), and we perched rather uncomfortably on the edge of the bed while a whirring cinematograph ran off some ancient French films. They were silent, jerky and with nothing subtle about them at all, the participants anything but glamorous, one of the men resembling a comic villain in a Chaplin film. Still, we managed to find the films exciting. It was certainly the first proper sex on the screen I had ever seen and although at the start there were a lot of nervous jokes ('My least favourite shot' of some vaginal close-up) as time went on the atmosphere became almost strained, though with Willie his usual smiling vague self. At the finish the madame was insistent that we should not all leave together so we separately filtered out into an empty Bond Street with me wondering if this at last was 'living'.

7 *July*. It's perhaps the quality of my acquaintance but I have yet to speak to one person who is enthused about the Olympics. If the scenes of ritual rejoicing ('Yes!') were not enough to put one off there is the prospect of seven years of disruption, procrastination, excuses and inconvenience and all the usual drawbacks of having the builders in. It's supposed to 'revitalise' the East End: i.e. it's a heaven-sent opportunity to knock down what remains of it, much as Prescott is trying to do elsewhere, and either build over open spaces like Hackney Marshes or tart them up with tasteful garden furniture. A general fucking up, in fact, and for this we must rejoice. All one can hope is that there's a stadium somewhere on the Northern Line.

8 *July*. Shocked that after the initial horror my first reaction to the Tube and bus bombings should be 'How convenient' and at how little of what we are told I now believe. As Blair lines up in front of his sombre colleagues at Gleneagles it's hard not to think how useful this outrage is and how effectively it silences the critics. And as Bush and Blair trot out their vapid platitudes about 'the War on Terror', give or take a few score of dead it's hard not to think things are well under control. No one as yet suggests or speculates that this new front in 'the War on Terror' might have been avoided had the country not gone to war in the first place. Only yesterday the *Guardian* reprinted an *LRB* piece revealing how Iraq had been fleeced of billions of dollars via Paul Bremer's so-called aid programme – the figures those

of US auditors whose reports have passed without notice. Except that they're maybe even now being read by some burning-eyed youth planning more and worse.

9 July. I bike home then find I have dropped our Council Tax book en route and have to cycle back and find it which, luckily, I do. So when I sit in the garden to have my tea (toast and bilberry jam and a piece of peach and almond cake from Melrose and Morgan) I am whacked. I doze off and then come round to find the hen blackbird is hopping about. I give her some crumbs which she pretends not to notice before coming back to collect them – sometimes within a few inches of my feet. Puts her head down before a low scuttling run, then pauses on one leg. Find, suddenly I am perfectly happy at this moment, with the sharing of my tea with the blackbird a part of it – somehow a rightness to the trust which gladdens – and settles – the heart.

10 July. To Leeds in fiercely hot weather to film part of the *South Bank Show* at Methley, south of Leeds, the drive the same as those sad Sunday evening bus rides that took me back to the York and Lancaster barracks at Pontefract after a forty-eight-hour leave in 1952. There's still some stately countryside in South Yorks, the road lined with graceful trees, but Methley, which I remember as a pleasing eighteenth-century place, has spoiled itself since: the early nineteenth-century red-brick house by the churchyard now kitted out with lattice windows and the seventeenth-century hall pulled down in 1963.

Do various pieces in the church, much of it from autocue and, despite some misgivings, tell the story of how Henry Moore used to come to this church when a boy and that it was seeing some of the grotesque sculptures on the corbels that turned his thoughts to art. This may well be the story Moore told himself but it's so like the tales often told of artists and their beginnings that I have reservations (no need to have worried: it was cut). The tombs, though, are a delight and I stand addressing the camera while caressing the fifteenth-century Sir Robert Waterton and his wife, Cecily. At my back is Lionel, Lord Welles with his bruiser's face, pudding-basin haircut and elaborate armour, which did not save him from being cut down at Towton on Palm Sunday 1461. Unnoticed on previous visits is a sad little stand in the south-west corner, a sample of the tools and equipment of the last working mine in Methley, laid up here twenty years ago. The first mines in the parish were recorded in 1340 and the names of the mines since are listed: Parlour Pit, Mulberry, Garden and, the last to close, Savile Colliery. Here are a dusty pair of miner's boots, a shovel, a pick, a miner's lantern and two great cobs of coal: 'These tools and equipment hung to rest here at Harvest Festival 1985.'

Then to film in Leeds itself, at Allerton High School where, en route, we pass a tableau that I have never actually witnessed but which is nevertheless familiar: in the back garden of a council house a small pavilion has been set up and two figures in the white suits of forensic experts are lumbering in and out of the house. It's a crime scene, though Jamie, the cheeky grip, suggests it could be quite a small wedding. When we reach the school they tell us it's a thirty-year-old man, an old boy of the school, who has been charged with murdering his father.

There is much family history round the walls of the old-fashioned classroom, with photographs of relatives brought in by the class, and mounted on card with an account of the person pictured. Quite a few are of personnel from the Second War whom I take to be the children's grandparents, though as often as not they're their great-grandparents. This is a Jewish area so there are photographs from the ghettos of Poland and tsarist Russia and stern patriarchs from India and Pakistan. One child ends an account of her grandparents: 'They have been married for 48 years and still get on like a roof on fire.'

13 July. What captures the imagination about the four bombers is that when they split up at King's Cross only minutes before they knew they would be dead they were, according to the tapes, chatting and joking as if off on holiday. It's this gaiety and unconcern which makes all the talk of a War on Terror and the nation's resilience seem beside the point. It's Thomas More joking on the scaffold, except that More wasn't taking anyone else with him. But how can mere self-preservation prevail against such unconcern? This debonair going to their (and our) deaths beyond understanding and made so, too, because it would, in any other circumstances, be admirable.

Blair addresses the House of Commons where there is not a dissentient voice and thus it is inevitably described as the Commons at its best. It's actually at its most solemn and cowardly with no one daring to step out of line or suggest that without our subservience to Bush we would not be in this mess. George Galloway, for whom I otherwise don't have much time, tries to say this on *Newsnight* but is shouted down by an almost frenzied Gavin Esler, though the point Galloway is making – that while nothing can be done about the perpetrators themselves, the circumstances that have fed their fanaticism have to be addressed – is a perfectly sensible one and ought to have been raised in the House of Commons. Instead MPs are far too busy rising to the occasion, which for Blair is: 'Let's pretend it's the Blitz and bags me be Churchill.'

Meanwhile contrast our leaders cowering behind the barriers at Gleneagles with HMQ who, two days after the bombings, drives down the Mall in an open car.

28 July. It's now reported that the dead Brazilian boy Jean Charles de Menezes was not wearing a bulky jacket, did not jump over the barrier, but went through on his travel card. Who made these excuses – which is what they were – at the time of his shooting? Was it the police? And if so will the inquiry reveal it? (It has, after all, three months to do its work when it could surely have reported earlier.) But some of the papers, which print these corrections pretty obscurely, feature on the front page photographs of nail bombs supposedly found in the bombers' car. So what one finds oneself thinking is that if the death on Stockwell Station can be deliberately misrepresented why should not also the existence of the nail bombs? It's the Blair lies factor again. And, of course, 'the adrenaline was flowing.'

4 August. One has grown accustomed to – inured to would I suppose be nearer the truth – T. Blair's use of supplementary adverbs, 'I honestly believe', 'I really think', which diminish rather than augment his credibility. It's always sloppy but sometimes offensive. A propos the shooting of Mr de Menezes the prime minister says: 'I understand entirely the feelings of the young man's family.' No ordinary person would put it like this. The only way Mr Blair could 'understand entirely' the feelings of the young man's family would be if Euan Blair had been hunted down Whitehall, stumbled on the steps of Downing Street and he, too, had been despatched with seven shots to his head. Then Mr Blair would have had that entire understanding to which he so glibly lays claim, the claiming, one feels, part of his now developing role as Father of the People.

7 August. Jonathan Miller is a good neighbour, if only by default. He often ranges the Crescent on the lookout for someone to talk to thus incidentally noticing anything untoward. Today it is two men who go into my garden while their companion, a woman, waits outside the gate. They are actually having a pee and when J. remonstrates on my behalf, they turn out to be Australian. One of them apologises but the other is unrepentant, complaining that 'you Poms' are too fixated on the penis and what does it matter urinating in public? As for the garden it will act as fertiliser. J. unwisely tries to put the discussion on a higher plane, pointing out that there are issues of public decorum here and saying that so far as his genitals are concerned, the Australian in question presumably wouldn't be happy walking down the Crescent with his trousers down. 'Oh yes, I would,' and to prove the point he drops his shorts to reveal a substantial dick which he displays to the Doctor and anyone else passing. 'And what', persists J., 'would your girlfriend think?' 'Oh, I'd be quite happy,' says the girl – the dick in question presumably the source of some happiness already. Jonathan considers taking the argument about public decency a step further, and instancing the work of Norbert Elias, but thinks better of it and the Australians, who are possibly in a bad mood because (unknown to J.) they have just lost the Test Match, go on their way.

Hunting is killing for fun, e.g. Ronald Blythe in *Borderland* recalling Bewick stoning a bullfinch as a boy:

'I felt greatly hurt at what I had done and did not quit it all the afternoon. I turned it over and over admiring its plumage, its feet, its bill . . . This was the last bird I killed.'

Let the hunter reach the fox before the hounds get at it and hold it in his/her arms and read from its dying eyes, 'Why have you taken away my life?' 'For fun' is their answer.

30 August. I sit here in the shade on a boiling afternoon waiting for the bike to come from Faber with the first copy of *Untold Stories*. Dinah W. at Faber says it's as big as the Bible, which dismays (and which I wouldn't have thought would help sales). Still, it's only £20 (*Writing Home* ten years ago £17.50), which seems reasonable. The doorbell goes and when I open the door I find on the doorstep not a cycle courier but an angel out of Botticelli's *Primavera*, white-robed, garlanded and with ropes of flowers in her hair. It is Tracey Ullman, who is making a film down Inverness Street ('The way one does'), and who is just calling to show off her costume, the function of which in the film is never satisfactorily explained. I offer to escort her back, as even today such a figure walking through Camden Town might cause comment. But she has come the two hundred yards or so by car, the studio chauffeur waiting with the Daimler to ferry her back. Tracey gone I resume my wait and the book arrives about four.

10 September, Yorkshire. We blackberry along Wandales Lane, the (possibly pre-) Roman track below the fells on the eastern side of Lunesdale. The blackberries on the sun-facing side are now so ripe they are quite hard to pick, but the bushes on the other side are laden with heavy, moist but not overripe fruit, so we soon gather enough for three or four jars of thick juice – 'coulis' posh restaurants would call it. We end up, though, with our hands stained red, which brings back a film of the 1940s which scared me as a child. Jennifer Jones has been involved, perhaps unwillingly, in a murder, a situation any-way in which her hands are covered with blood. This sends her off the rails ('traumatises' her as would be said nowadays) and the mem-ory is buried. She then comes into the care of, and possibly marries, Joseph Cotten and seems fully recovered and leading an ideal life in the country. Then – fatal move – one day she goes blackberrying and the predictable happens: Joseph Cotten finds her screaming and hysterical with her hands covered in blackberry juice. What happens in the end I can't remember, maybe the incident is 'therapeutic', though it wasn't for me as I was terrified (though not as much as I was by *Jane Eyre*).

22 September. Nice elderly cashier at the check-out in M&S. 'I did agree with what you said in the paper about the shops closing in Parkway and it being all estate agents.'

I thank her and say how much I miss the Regent Bookshop, there being nothing at all now to enliven the upper reaches of Parkway or tempt one to go that way home.

'Oh, I agree. And I always had a soft spot for that bookshop. It was there my little granddaughter had her ears pierced.' And it's true they did used to do ear piercing, though quite why I'm not sure.

24 September. Good à propos Kate Moss's alleged cocaine abuse to be reminded of the cowardice of commerce. The Swedish firm H&M, one of several fearless enterprises that have distanced themselves from Ms Moss, declares itself proud to be in the forefront of corporate morality. That most of its clothes are said to be made dirt cheap in China is beside the point.

Actually I wouldn't know Kate Moss if I fell over her.

29 September. Among several things that the ejection and charging of Mr Walter Wolfgang from the Labour Party Conference demonstrates is the danger of endowing the police with any more powers than they have already. For shouting out 'Liar' he is charged under the Terrorism Act. The silencing of hecklers was hardly the act's original purpose but it is just the handiest blunt instrument available. This should be remembered in the next session of Parliament when the police are asking for yet more powers – three months' detention for instance – while at the same time solemnly assuring the public that they will only use such powers when the occasion demands it. This is a promise soon forgotten. If they have the powers they will use them – young Muslim or Jewish old-age pensioner it makes no difference. 'You're nicked.'

30 September. Keith M. tells me of a TV script that is currently doing the rounds in New York in which four Muslim bombers are holed up together and keep receiving orders from their al-Qaeda superiors to carry out suicide missions. They are terrified of their bosses but are all cowards and most anxious to avoid committing suicide. It's apparently very funny but no TV company has dared to buy it and they are currently trying to set it up in England. I wish I'd thought of it and if it's done properly it's likely to do far more for Muslim understanding than any number of well-meaning homilies from the Home Office.

4 October, L'Espiessac, France. Staying at the house for a couple of days is Scott Harrison, a young man who once worked as a barman for Lynn Wagenknecht but is now a photographer, working on a hospital ship which plies up and down the coast of West Africa where it berths at various ports and treats the local population, particularly those suffering from non-malignant tumours. The ship's movements are known and thousands travel to meet it and to be seen and with luck operated on by the ship's team of surgeons. Many are hideously deformed and outcasts from their tribe or local community on that account. Though the tumours are not in themselves life-threatening their sheer bulk will sometimes throttle or overcome their hosts. The operations, however, are often relatively straightforward, huge protuberances cut away, which instantly restore a hideously distorted face to relative normality, with those operated on requiring only minimal after-care. To the sufferers (and to those who have cast them out) the transformation seems miraculous and thousands of the afflicted await the ship's coming in the hope of treatment.

Scott has taken pictures of all this, some of which he has recently shown in New York and which tonight we (slightly reluctantly it has to be said) sit on the sofa in this French farmhouse and look at. They are, of course, heartrending, particularly painful the stricken, shamefaced aspect of the afflicted, who think themselves cursed: else why is one eye stuck out on a balloon of flesh twelve inches from its fellow; what is this huge creature growing out of the side of their neck; why can they no longer speak? The delight when they are relieved of these monstrous burdens is wonderful to see, particularly when they go home to show themselves to their families. All this Scott has photographed and plainly thinks of nothing else: he is entirely single-minded, obsessive even, nothing else interests him or engages him and though he's handsome enough he seems almost monkishly set apart. Maybe, too, he now wants to be a doctor. Several times when commenting on his photographs he says of some dreadful-seeming tumour that it was easily cured. 'It's a simple operation. I could do it.'

On another level entirely these photographs are interesting as many of the facial disfigurements recall the paintings of Francis Bacon, who is said to have been fascinated by medical textbooks and the pictures of such tumours that he found in his father's library when a child. This has never seemed to me to detract from his art: it explains some of it at best but doesn't, as it were, explain it away. Some of the photographs of these African patients, though, are so strangely reminiscent of Bacon's paintings that his pictures seem almost a documentary record of what can happen to the human face and this does seem if not to diminish his paintings, at least to demystify them and make them more comprehensible. So that one almost thinks like Scott, though of the painting: 'It's a simple operation. I could do it.'

Though the quality of the artwork is different these thoughts about Bacon apply also to Jack Vettriano, the Scottish painter (what once would have been called a commercial artist) who this week has been shown to have composed his paintings from figures taken directly from a manual of figure painting. This is no different from what Bacon did, though his paintings are shot through with disgust and despair as Vettriano's are with cheap romance.

2 *October.* Some drunken lads in the buffet bar as we are queuing to get off the train at King's Cross, one of whom was trying to explain to the others who I was.

'Really? He's tall for a playwright.'

Difficult to tell whether this was wit or drink, but quite funny nevertheless.

17 *October.* No newspaper that I've seen discusses the police in institutional terms or sees them as subject to the same compulsions as govern other large corporate organisations. The need to grow,

for instance, and accumulate new powers and spheres of influence comes as much from within the organisation as from any demands that are being made on it. Ninety days' detention suits the police not so much because thereby more evidence is forthcoming and with it an increased likelihood of convictions but because it will result in them having more power: more staff, more premises, more funds. This has nothing to do with justice, civil liberty or the preservation of order and the prevention of terrorism. It is the law of institutions. Like Tesco the police must grow.

18 October. Robert Hanks, the radio critic of the *Independent*, remarks that personally he can have too much of Alan Bennett. I wonder how he thinks I feel.

22 October. Mention in a piece by Caryl Phillips in today's *Guardian* of a school in Leeds. 'When I was a boy, we used to play football against a secondary school with the somewhat hopeful name of Leeds Modern. The joke, of course, was there was precious little that was modern about Leeds, including that school. This is palpably not the case now.' That was my school, the old boys of which were called Old Modernians, and I've always thought that this was a pretty fair description of that blend of backward-looking radicalism and conservative socialism which does duty for my political views. I am an old modernian.

25 October. Today is the first time I have been into Romany's the builder's merchants formerly in Camden High Street, which now inhabits a converted tram shed in Arlington Street. Visiting Romany's used to be a humiliating experience as the (mainly white) staff always managed to imply that one's ignorance of the gauge of screw you wanted reflected on your manhood. No longer. Now the staff is largely Asian and one's incompetence becomes a reason for sympathy and also high-pitched amusement. Where previously there was an ill-concealed impatience now there is compassion, sympathy and even giggling. I never thought buying a tarpaulin, which I did today, could be such a pleasure.

26 October. An interesting letter this morning from Claire Tomalin about the Drummer Hodge scene in *The History Boys*, saying that, contrary to what Hector specifically asserts in the scene, Hodge was not in the ordinary sense a name but like, as it were, Joe Bloggs, a generic name for a common and unthinking agricultural labourer. Hardy had protested against such stereotyping in an earlier essay, 'The Dorsetshire Labourer' (1883), so his use of the name Hodge in the poem was an ironic reference to those assumptions about such labourers he had earlier criticised. This in its turn explains why Tom Paulin – never one to leave a brick unthrown – said I had got the poem 'wrong', which at the time I took to be perverse but now see the point of. Since only a few Hardy scholars would be aware of this reading of the poem I'm happy I didn't know it myself lest it had stopped me writing the scene, or writing it in this particular way. As it is, and in the continuing life of the characters, I think of Posner going up to Cambridge and in his interview bringing out Hector's take on the poem only to be pulled up short by a don who puts forward the Tomalin interpretation. So when Posner goes back home with his scholarship he puts Hector right on Hardy.

1 November. A handwritten letter today from Carlisle, in capital letters, thanking me for my stuff and for speaking up for the shit at the bottom of the pile. Pleased by this as I've always thought I'd been speaking up for the shit just a bit further up.

Our Algerian road sweeper, oddly named Antonio, comes inside the gate, takes off his shoes and kneels down to pray. This is observed by Nora, who is downstairs ironing and who, more up in religious affairs than I am, announces that it marks the end of Ramadan.

3 November. Arriving in Harrogate with time for tea I go out to Betty's but there is a queue so I buy something to take back to the hotel and have it in my room. The something I buy is what Betty's call a Fat Rascal, a large flat fruit scone, a piece of confectionery which is marketed as a Yorkshire speciality and so unwilling am I to collaborate in this trumpery exercise that I find myself unable even to pronounce the name – instead pointing and saying, 'One of those curranty things.' R. regards it as moral weakness that I buy it at all.

5 November, Yorkshire. I have failed on several occasions to order in more coal with the result that the coal shed is almost empty, with piled against the back wall a large heap of slack – wet coal dust – well mixed in among it a lot of small coal and the occasional large cob. I sieve this out, saving the burnable coal and putting the coal dust into (extremely heavy) sacks. I wish the village still had its bonfire on the recreation ground as it could have gone straight on the pile.

But it reminds me how when stocks of coal were low during the war we used to sift the coal dust then and how for some (though not in Armley) that was their living, scratting on slag heaps for occasional cobs of coal which they would pile in an old pram and wheel home.

Just after the war, it must have been early in 1946 when we were living at Grandma's, Aunty Myra, Gordon and me went with a pram to a place down Armley Road where we queued for logs which we pushed back up over past Armley Gaol and down to Gilpin Place.

All these thoughts going through my head this Saturday afternoon as I sift the coal in the shed and sweep it out, and so pleased am I by the emptiness of it, and by the fact that I have cleaned up thirty years' accumulation of slack that I go back two or three times to admire my handiwork. Once, I suppose, it would have been an opportunity to whitewash it.

We have mice, the result of R. leaving a bag of grass seed in the cupboard under the stairs and tempting in some migrants from next door. Occasionally in winter we've had field mice and even on one occasion dormice, but have taken care to restore them to their natural habitat. But these are dark small house mice and so fast-moving they're hard to see – there's movement, but what of?

So 'mice' goes down on the Settle shopping list where there are two hardware shops. Practically Anything in the marketplace is just that, an Aladdin's cave of household goods, pots, pans, buckets and brushes and gadgets of every description, all very low-priced. But no poison. Tom, who keeps the shop, doesn't approve, but doesn't have any humane traps in stock either so that sends us to Ashfield, the more ordered and professional hardware store on the car park. While this is the shop for the dedicated carpenter or DIY enthusiast and is also a farm shop, happily absent is that blank-faced flat-voiced male expertise such shops often purvey, particularly in London. Indeed when I ask for a mouse-trap, the oldest assistant, now in his eighties, says, 'Follow me to the mouse department,' and we are taken to three shelves stacked with every type of rodent eliminator. We get a humane trap and some poison on the principle that if the mouse doesn't take the sensible option and allow itself to be caught and transported, it deserves all it gets.

'Does this put them to sleep?' I ask.

The assistant pats my hand. 'We like to think so.'

And of course what it is, with no overtones whatsoever, is sheer camp. That's what makes it a nice shop to go into and which oils the commercial wheels. Camp.

18 November. I'm reading *Nature Cure* by Richard Mabey, an account of a bout of depression and leaving the Chilterns, where he had always lived, for Norfolk. It's astonishing the range of knowledge he has at his disposal and humbling, too, though I find myself more interested in his life in nature around his home than when he takes off in the second part of the book for the wildernesses of America.

John Clare figures a good deal and Mabey quotes Clare's Enclosure elegy 'Remembrances' and these lines on a gamekeeper's gibbet:

> O I never call to mind
> These pleasant names of places but I leave a sigh behind
> While I see the little mouldywarps hang sweeing to the wind
> On the only aged willow that in all the field remains
> And nature hides her face while they're sweeing in their chains
> And in a silent murmuring complains
>
> Here was common for their hills where they seek for freedom
> still
> Though every common's gone and though traps are set to kill
> The little homeless miners.

I tip this into the script of my first television film, *A Day Out* (1972), in which there is a similar scene when some cyclists on an outing in 1911 come upon a farm gate festooned with dead moles and rooks.

I suppose the Clare passage would be referenced 'cf.' (i.e. compare), these annotated copies of my scripts often fat with stuff I've subsequently read but didn't know at the time of writing. They are not a patch though on Tony Harrison's handbooks to his plays, which are almost works of art in themselves, with notes on the text and drawings of the set and its associations, lovely objects altogether. Mine are more reassurances to myself that, as in this case, at least I've got something right.

19 November. Drive out to Oxfordshire where we have our sandwiches above Wheatfield Church near Adwell. It's a misty day, the sun just beginning to come through and the delicate apricot-coloured church slowly emerging from the mist is enchanting – like the opening scene of a film.

We go on to Tetsworth where R. buys some cutlery for the house then to Waterperry for some tea, then back home to London by five.

Later on we send out for a curry. A lovely day though I'm still not up to much.

In the car have an idea for a story in which, rather late in life, HMQ becomes an avid reader and how this affects things. [This becomes *The Uncommon Reader*, 2006.]

28 November. It wasn't until Dudley M. got into *Beyond the Fringe* that he realised you were supposed to have an inner life and when he finished in *BTF* and started on *Not Only But Also* he set about acquiring one, thus considerably irritating Peter Cook who preferred him as he was. Peter's drunkenness had a lot to do with them eventually breaking up but it was also that Dudley's not entirely mistaken notion of self-fulfilment made further co-operation impossible.

1 December. In America there is now no taking evolution for granted. What was (and still is here) a universal rational assumption, in the US has become a *position*. 'Are you an evolution*ist*?' Jonathan M. recounts an argument he has had with a woman in the New York Natural History Museum who asked him just this question. Later, talking to his students, he says he wishes he had answered the question 'Are you an evolutionist?' with 'Only in the sense that I'm a gravitationalist.'

3 December. Find an old note from Morrissey, *c*.1995.

Alan Bee

Yesterday you decline, but today your agent says you accept. Oh joy! If you fancy giving your cycle clips an airing I'll be in tonight at 7, 7.30, 8-00, with cloth on and pot of.

Most loyally,

a snooker pal of Kathleen Harrisons

4 December. Clearing out the study half of the sitting room (name of the room never settled in forty years of living here), I come across some notes made in 1996 on Sebastian Faulks's book *The Fatal Englishman*, a study of the (short) lives of Christopher Wood, Richard Hillary and Jeremy Wolfenden. The notes are confined to the section on Wolfenden whom I scarcely knew, though the last time I saw him, in Oxford in 1961, he stopped to talk.

Reading this memoir of Jeremy Wolfenden feels a foretaste of what is to come; there will be a lot more of this, one thinks, times differently remembered/events diversely recalled/perspectives that don't tally with one's own, though the first impression that comes to mind is of National Service and the JSSL camp at Bodmin, tumbling out of the Nissen huts and running in nailed boots up the paths to the parade ground at the top of the camp.

The lowliest arm of service was the army with soldiers bigger, clumsier and altogether *earthier* and we used to speculate sometimes whether, if we didn't know, one could guess just from the look of them whether conscripts were army, navy or RAF. And I still carry in my head some Platonic notion of what each arm of service typically looked like. Norman Tebbit is RAF. John Prescott is army, Robin Cook RAF, Tony Blair navy, John Major is one of nature's aircraftsmen. Kenneth Clark in the infantry, a corporal perhaps or a rundown second lieutenant.

The naval cadets tended to be chummier with the instructors, particularly the most highly coloured of them, Dmitri Makaroff. They took part in play readings, edited a magazine, *Samovar*, and even had little suppers with the instructors, evidences of sophistication slightly jeered at, I remember, by their coarser army and RAF colleagues. Set down in the back of beyond, for the instructors Bodmin was like some coda to Chekhov with London as longed for as Moscow ever was.

It was at Bodmin that I first became aware of Jeremy Wolfenden, though I think I knew, possibly from gossip when we were on the

Cambridge stage of the Russian course, of his fabled cleverness and also that while the son of Sir John Wolfenden, the provincial vice chancellor who was heading the commission on homosexuality, he was himself a homosexual.

This cannot have come through Eton gossip as significantly there were no Etonians in the army or RAF whereas the naval contingents included several. However on finishing his National Service Wolfenden was going up to Magdalen with a demyship in history and one of my closest friends on the course, David Marquand, was a demy too, so it may have been through him. But one tended to know about one's clever contemporaries. Kenneth Cavender, a boy at Bradford Grammar School, had got a scholarship to Balliol and then had hoovered up various other local Yorkshire scholarships, one or two of which I'd unsuccessfully competed for myself. Looking back I suppose I saw Cavender as Marquand and his friends saw Wolfenden, as The Competition, though to me it hardly seemed so as they were so much more advantaged they were all in a different league anyway.

The naval cadets I remember seeing at Bodmin – I don't remember speaking to any of them – included Wolfenden, who with his floppy hair and dark glasses was hard to miss. Others were Robin Hope, with whom he was thought to be having an affair, Robert Cassen and David Shapiro. They were all in their ways distant creatures – Cassen, Shapiro and Wolfenden because of their intellectual superiority, Hope because of his elegance and social assurance. Not to mind his association with Wolfenden being known seemed very daring at the time, though maybe not as bold as Hockney, say, who (though it was ten years later and in a very different milieu) always made homosexuality part of his style.

Since I never spoke to any of them, what the intellectual superiority amounted to I was in no position to judge but I suspect that a reputation for intellect at that age often consists in knowing how to talk like men of forty – not prodigies so much as prematurely middle-aged, grown-ups already. This grown-upness is perhaps one of the things Eton bestows on its boys with the bill to be paid later. Wolfenden's grown-upness seems to have included a sense that nothing is really worth doing, which comes to most people, if it comes at all, at the end of life.

Wolfenden as an undergraduate looked not unlike the young W. H. Auden and going to bed with either must have been much the same – both kippered by chain smoking and as likely as not pissed. Still, both of them managed it on a regular basis however unappetising it may have turned out to be with their partners, I imagine, flattered to find themselves not so much fancied as *rated* – being thought worthy to go to bed with such great minds.

Faulks needs W. to be handsome and fetching, which he wasn't except in a B picture sort of way, his appearance always seeming self-consciously decadent . . . black shirts, the dark glasses, the drooping cigarette, though by this time existentialism was just beginning to run out of steam. Nor do I remember him as being six foot tall, in my mind's eye stockier than that.

David Marquand saw a good deal of him at Oxford, and confirmed how clever he was – sitting next to Wolfenden in a lecture he found that he was simultaneously taking notes on the lecture, writing an article for *Isis* and putting together an essay for his tutor – and none of it, seemingly, a performance put on for Marquand's benefit.

I sat the same All Souls examination though don't remember Wolfenden leaving as Faulks says he did after half an hour. I was probably too busy wondering what had persuaded me to sit the examination in the first place. Having scraped a first by what I now regard as virtual subterfuge, I had perhaps briefly convinced myself that I was All Souls material. What the topics were or what I wrote I have mercifully no recollection; I just hope that the papers were destroyed and no record kept.

As with Guy Burgess, with whom it was said Wolfenden later had an affair, there was a good deal of drink, nicotine and dirty fingernails though, unlike Burgess, Wolfenden doesn't seem to have been big on charm. Whether they had an affair I doubt. The same assumption was made about Burgess and Blunt, less on the actual evidence than on the algebraic principle of getting everybody of the same sexuality on the same side of the equation and in one bracket.

When Wolfenden spoke to me, possibly for the first time, it was on St Giles, that little stretch between Broad Street and the Martyrs' Memorial and would have been in 1961 or '62 when, though I was appearing in *Beyond the Fringe*, I was still teaching in Oxford – though this didn't give me much of an edge, at any rate in Magdalen. 'Who are you?' said my neighbour at Magdalen High Table one night. 'Oh, I'm nobody,' I said and meant it. Which is bad enough both on his part and mine except that it was repeated word for word with the same don the following evening.

So more priggish then than I hope I am now I thought Wolfenden, to whom I'd also been nobody, stopped to chat because I was in *Beyond the Fringe* but I've no memory of the conversation except I came away thinking he was perhaps kinder than I'd thought.

There's some speculation in the book about his death and whether it was connected with his work for the secret service, but the cause of his death and the post-mortem report seems more or less the same as that of another alcoholic, Peter Cook, though Peter lasted longer.

Another aspect of this book is how unlike Oxford things were at Cambridge where Wolfenden's and my contemporaries have made something of an effort to pass each other off as some sort of *jeunesse dorée*, and drum themselves up into a generation with *Granta*, Footlights, Leavis and the late Sylvia Plath some of the chief ingredients.

The other ingredient which is even less appealing is the Apostles, the self-conscious, self-congratulatory and self-perpetuating group of supposedly the brightest or most coming men in the university meeting to admire each other's brains. I don't know whether it still exists, but though there are many reasons why I would have liked to have gone to Cambridge, the Apostles is not one of them.

Also mentioned in the Faulks book are the history teachers at Magdalen in Wolfenden's time, particularly A. J. P. Taylor (with whom, says S.F., Wolfenden would spend the night drinking) and K. B. McFarlane who with Harry Wheldon were W.'s tutors. Bruce is, as always, set up against the fluent and prolific Taylor as the costive and careful non-publishing medieval historian. What is seldom said – and isn't said here – is firstly how concerned and conscientious a tutor McFarlane was and secondly – and more generally – how of the three of them, Taylor, Wheldon and McFarlane, it was Bruce McFarlane who was valiant for truth. For both Taylor and Wheldon, history was a skating rink on which they could show off their techniques, turn their paradoxes, their sudden *voltes-face* with what actually happened in history not something that troubled them a great deal, argument the real part. It was McFarlane whose first concern was what really happened and whether it was to Henry V himself or to an insignificant fifteenth-century squire on his little estate of equal consequence: the truth had to be teased out. For Taylor and Wheldon truth was a different kind of tease altogether.

Tucked in with the Wolfenden stuff, I find notes on another memoir (privately printed) of David Winn, who was drowned as a young man and a contemporary, I imagine, of Francis Hope. It was one of the books I got from Francis Hope's library when Mary Hope was disposing of it some time in the eighties.

It's not a book intended to be read by anyone who did not know him, still less meant to be reviewed or subjected to analysis – but in its assumptions and its artlessness it says something about a kind of life that one thought had vanished with the Edwardians – 'Still going on', as Larkin says, 'Still going on'. Families so well placed that the easiest way to find their son digs in Oxford was to buy a house.

For me university was a bus I had to catch. For them there would be one along presently or some other form of transport through life – the higher civil service, the diplomatic corps. Culture was not something that had to be acquired but could just be put on like an old coat, hanging in the hall.

It would be comforting to think that all these young men (and they were all men in those days) who led such charmed lives were stupid, but of course this is far from being the case: many of them took firsts, several became fellows of All Souls, senior demys at Magdalen – a lazy and elegant progress in comparison to which my education I see in retrospect to have been a desperate scramble.

7 *December*. Yesterday we gave lunch to Norman Scarfe and Paul Fincham at Sotheby's which neither of them had ever set foot inside – either in the old set-up or its revamp. Good food, though, a bit draughty and since both of them are deaf not sure how much gets through.

Norman remembering how taking E. M. Forster out for a drive they passed Angus McBean's moated Suffolk house (lately featured in *World of Interiors*) and on a whim called. Angus overwhelmed and overawed but when they got inside they found Quentin Crisp was a guest. He was correcting the proofs of *The Naked Civil Servant* and reading out long extracts in the process. Whether it was that Forster was used to being the centre of attention or didn't care for such flamboyance it wasn't a successful encounter.

Norman also recalls when they were living at Shingle Street he had been working one day over at Snape Maltings preparing some lecture or exhibition for which he'd been doing all his own electrics. Late that night a neighbour phoned to say that if they went to the door and looked across the estuary they would see the Maltings burning down. They got in the car and rushed to Snape, Norman all the time thinking the fire might have been caused by an electrical fault and he was responsible. When the fire was investigated the blaze was shown to have started in the projection room, the one area in which he had not been working.

Norman now eighty-one or two, Paul in his late seventies and both vigorous and energetic, going to concerts, exhibitions and socially always in demand – not our lives at all.

8 December. I buy a bottle of organic wine at Fresh and Wild and looking at the label see that it says 'Suitable for Vegetarians and Vagrants'. Momentarily I think, 'Well, that's thoughtful, someone admitting that winos deserve consideration like everyone else,' before realising, of course, that it says not 'vagrants' but 'vegans'.

15 December. I am trying to clean up the front room, going through old files and papers dating back thirty and even forty years. I find this immensely depressing as many of the abandoned or unfinished pieces have good and funny lines, or are interesting situations – a boy in a First World War country house that has been turned into a hospital for instance; a TV play, *Gay Night at Bangs*, which I remember being very taken with in the eighties and many, many more – none of which I throw away, just dust and put in fresh folders with a new label describing their contents.

I wish I could think that all this unfinished stuff mulched the stuff I did finish (and which by comparison seems quite meagre). But I fear I just forgot most of it, the hours I spent labouring over these pages all wasted. Had I finished everything I started I would be, if not Shakespeare, at least as prolific as George Bernard Shaw – and a bit jokier.

16 December. Roy Keane has the face of a mercenary. Meet him before the walls of fifteenth-century Florence and one's heart would sink.

17 December. 'The Oxford Final Schools and the Day of Judgement are *two* examinations, not one.' Sir Walter Raleigh, Merton Professor of English.

This is a quotation I knew of, but had forgotten until I found it in Janet Adam Smith's memoir of her childhood and time at Oxford – all she'd got round to doing of a full-scale autobiography – and which Andrew Roberts (not the historian) has sent me. She lost two brothers in the First War, one of them wounded and sent home to Aberdeen to convalesce. She was learning the violin at the time and her hands were too small to do the proper fingering. He was watching her and one particularly high note he did for her, with a finger of his injured hand. When he recovered he was sent back to the front and killed.

2006

4 January, Yorkshire. A heron fishing by the bridge this morning as I walk down for the papers. No one else about. It takes off and flies down the beck to where the dippers normally patrol so walking down to the village I draw level with it and it waits motionless then, feeling itself watched, flaps off up the beck again. Herons are not rare but their size is never less than spectacular and, grey and white though they are, still seem exotic.

Bitterly cold with snow forecast later so we get off early up the M6 to Penrith and Brampton, hoping to have a look at the Written Rock, a quarry by the river at Brampton with an inscription carved by the Roman legion that cut the stone here for nearby Hadrian's Wall. But it's too cold to go looking for it and it's said to be over-grown and eroded now, though somehow to see the place that supplied the stone and the mark the men made who quarried it seems much more evocative than the actual wall itself. Instead we buy a couple of George III country chairs very reasonably in an antique shop before going round the much larger antique centre in Philip Webb's parish hall.

Still the promised snow doesn't materialise – or despite the dire and repeated warnings from the forecasters, just a wet quarter of an inch. Weather forecasting, which one wants to be as detached and impartial as medical diagnosis, is nowadays infected with the same longing for drama that shapes television and journalism in general. Like the War on Terror or the prevalence of cancer these Cassandrine predictions are meant to keep the nation in a state of disquiet, or 'on their toes' I suppose they would describe it. But weather should not be exaggerated: an inch or two of snow is not a 'white-out'; having to

47

drive at 50 mph rather than 70 is not 'the nation ground to a halt.' It's just *weather*.

6 January. Papers full of Charles Kennedy being, or having been, an alcoholic. I'd have thought Churchill came close and Asquith, too, and when it comes to politics it's hardly a disabling disease. Except to the press. But less perilous, I would have thought, to have a leader intoxicated with whisky than one like Blair, intoxicated with himself.

16 January. Sitting after supper by the table downstairs (books and papers crowding the meal into a narrow strip) I airily wave my hand and knock a glass to the floor where, of course, it shatters. But not just a glass, a lovely nineteenth-century rummer that I have had all my life. It was bought when I was living in Worship Street doing *Beyond the Fringe* in 1961, at a junk shop up the Kingsland Road and cost maybe 1/- – or 5/-, I can't remember – but nothing, even then. And it has been with me ever since, through my early time in Gloucester Crescent, Chalcot Square and Gloucester Crescent again and for these last ten years or so has been the glass Rupert has for his one glass of wine at supper every evening. Until tonight.

21 January. On the way down to the National I find Waterloo Bridge crowded with onlookers all gazing down at the river where the stray bottlenose whale has been manoeuvred onto a barge and is travelling in state down the river, the banks lined with spectators – whose concern for this distressed creature seems more honest, less mawkish and altogether more heartfelt than for any celebrity, say – and a collection of individual concerns not mass hysteria.

Alas it is sailing towards its death, which happens about seven though if it reminds people of the interdependence of us all as creatures it will not have been in vain. I should have stopped the cab to look as I have never seen a whale, dead or alive and as maybe no one has ever in the Thames, certainly not in my lifetime.

25 January. Have my hair cut, my barber a slight, dark haunted-looking man, I think a Kurd, in his thirties and if I understand him (he has very little English) living at home with his mother – though not gay, I would have thought. He has in the past asked me if I want my eyebrows trimmed, something I've always resisted on the principle that this will make them grow even more and I shall end up like Bernard Ingham. Nevertheless it's a point of principle with the barber that he should try and trim them just a little. Thus when he is shaving my sideboards with the electric shaver he will bring it back across my forehead, running it lightly across my eyebrows as if by accident – and leaving them, since he's not allowed officially to touch them, looking like a badly mown verge. He does this today and in another what he knows is a potentially impermissible move, rapidly runs the razor round my ears. My nostrils and the lobes of my ears are so far inviolate but I'm sure he will have his eye on them in the future. I, of course, say nothing, partly from embarrassment, and from not caring enough – and also to do so would be to impinge on what I'm sure he sees as his professional duties. So after a lifetime of avoiding such supernumerary attentions I am now at the barber's mercy. [Though I managed to postpone the inevitable for a further nine years; see 23 September 2015.]

31 January. A friend of John Williams, who died eight years ago, sends me a copy of one of his letters he has discovered, dated August 1968. It ends very characteristically (and with a drawing), 'In the garden there are sunflowers eight feet high, in bloom. The heads tilt over, look down at you standing below them. It is very refreshing to have a flower looking down at you.' [See *Untold Stories*, 4 December 1997.]

4–5 February. A weekend in London, much of it spent at the new house where I've made up a colour that seems to go on the walls, 'a pigment of my imagination' – a greenish yellow made up of a slug (exactly what it looks like) of Winsor yellow oil paint, half a slug of

Naples Yellow and a touch of dark grey. I mix these up in turps then add some matt glaze. I've been putting this on with a sponge but now have taken to applying it with a brush. Either way it goes on rather brown and uneven so that until I got used to it, I thought I'd ruined it. But then it dries out to a yellowish green, thin enough to reveal the grain of the plaster and which – once gloss varnish goes on – will look a deep and interesting surface. It's a pity the plaster itself isn't a surface that's more interesting – nothing like the various blemishes and changes of texture here as there are at Gloucester Crescent for instance.

10 February. Letters, letters, all praise not a breath of criticism and yet the feeling is of being pelted with small stones – fame a species of pebbledash.

16 February. Having of course, wholly forgotten that yesterday at 11 a.m. we went down to Camden Town Hall and signed the form prior to going through the civil partnership agreement, which is fixed for some time in March. No more splother or ceremony than renewing one's parking permit. Then we had a cup of coffee in the BM cafeteria and R. went off to work. And so, I imagine it will be when we do the actual deed.

20 February. One of the pleasures of painting, even if it's only the wall which I'm currently engaged on, is to be able to visit Cornelissen's shop in Great Russell Street, which sells all manner of paints and colours and where I go this morning in order to find some varnish to seal the surface of the plaster.

After I'd finished putting on all the greenish-yellow colour yesterday I did some trial patches of varnish on it. I knew, though it's twenty years since I last stained a wall, how this transforms and enlivens the colour but I am astonished all over again at the depth and interest it gives to even the most ordinary surface. There's no literary equivalent that I can think of to this *vernissage*, no final gloss to be put on a novel, say, or a play, which will bring them suddenly to life. Today when I go down to Cornelissen the assistant suggests that as an alternative to the gloss I try shellac, which has even more of a surface. It's one of the pleasures of the shop that you're served by people who know what they're talking about and who, one gets the feeling, go home from work, don a smock and beret and go to the easel themselves. Which reminds me how when I first stained some walls, back in 1968, I had no need to come all the way down to Cornelissen. Then I just went round the corner in Camden Town where Roberson's had a (long gone) shop in Parkway. They were old established colourists and had in the window a palette board used by Joshua Reynolds. Whatever happened to that?

Further to the painting, though, for which I scorn to don the Marigolds, I am buying bread in Villandry when I see the assistant gazing in horror at my hands, the fingers stained the virulent yellow-ish green I've been sponging on during this last week. As a young man my father smoked quite heavily and his fingers were stained like this by cigarettes – and a nice brown it was, and one which I wouldn't mind seeing on the wall; if he were alive still and the man he was when I was ten I could take him along to Cornelissen where I'm sure they could match his fingers in water, oil or acrylic.

And it stirs another memory from the 1970s, or whenever it was that the IRA conducted their 'dirty protests' at the Maze prison, smearing the walls of their cells with excrement. Occasionally one would see edited shots of these cells on television when I was invariably struck by what a nice warm and varied shade the protester had achieved. 'Maze brown' I suppose Farrow & Ball would tastefully have called it.

3 March. Oh to live in the world one sees from the train – empty, unpeopled, only a horse in the field, one car at the crossing, and a woman at the end of a garden taking down washing.

4 March. We stay the night at Lacock, as R. is doing a shoot at nearby Corsham Court. In the morning we walk round this picture-book village wholly owned by the National Trust since 1944. It's not yet ten o'clock but there are already cars in the car park and visitors strolling about; the bells are ringing for matins and, mingling with the visitors, a family, prayer books in hand, makes its way to church. Except is it a family, or is it like everything else in the village a dependency of the National Trust? It's not that the place is manicured particularly, though there is no stone out of place, just that its beauty and its settled tranquillity are in themselves slightly sinister.

7 March. A wet morning and we go down to Camden Town Hall for the formalities – I'd hardly say solemnisation – of our civil partnership agreement. Owen T. and Kate M. are the witnesses; Tom comes along too and Diana and Graham. The two registrars aren't too gushy, one of them not unlike Frances H., the other cheerful but keeping it all low-key, the only droll note when, as part of her brief, she talks about us 'now embarking on our life together', whereas that started fourteen or at any rate nine years ago. Afterwards we adjourn for coffee to Villandry which is nice and easy, Kate and Tom both very taken with Owen, R.'s brother, whom Kate had last seen when he was a toddler.

Now home where Nick Hytner has just rung after the opening night of *History Boys* in Sydney, which has been a great success and the boys hugely enjoying themselves and being pursued by droves of busty Australian charmers.

8 March. Biking back from the paper shop this morning I see the oldest of the market men bring produce from his truck, a sack of carrots in one hand, sprouts in the other and laid over the top of his head an open string bag of onions. It's only a small sack, which lays across his head like a wig and what he looks like is some oldish

Northern lady bringing home her shopping, with her hair still in Carmen rollers ready for her evening out.

15 March. After the murder of Mr de Menezes, Tony Blair claimed that he 'entirely understood' the feelings of the young man's parents. Today it is the eighty thousand people who, following the government's urgings, subscribed to their employers' private pension schemes. When the firms went bust or were unable to pay, their workers unsurprisingly turned to the government to make good their lost annuities, except that now the government claims it's not its responsibility. However in the Commons today Mr Blair reassures the aggrieved eighty thousand, telling them that he entirely understands their indignation. Is there any limit, one wonders, to the entire understanding of Mr Blair? Heaped naked in a pile on the floor of an Iraqi prison it must be comforting to know that you have the entire understanding of Mr Blair. Hooded, shackled and flown fourteen hours at a time across continents do you reside in the entirety of Mr Blair's understanding? No, presumably, because of course this does not happen.

17 March. I wish it were the Freedom of Camden I'd been offered rather than the Freedom of Leeds. Then I could write back saying, No thank you. All I want is to change my parking permit – a procedure that in Camden is virtually impossible to accomplish within a single working day. I cycle down in a bitter wind to the office in Crowndale Road with a folder containing enough documents and validations for an entry visa to Turkmenistan. The assistant, whose accent is so thick I find it very hard to understand (or even hear as the microphone is faulty), seems satisfied with the array of documentation I produce but then decides I need the windscreen permit currently in the car. I ask how I can bring this in without getting a parking fine. This she cannot solve but insists that she must see it. This has never been necessary before, nor is it on the list of documents the renewal document stipulated as being required so, thinking she is just being obstructive, I cycle on to Judd Street where the assistant is similarly unhelpful though at greater length. Before I come away I lean across the counter and say, 'Listen. I got married here last week. Compared with getting a parking permit it was a pushover.' Not a flicker. Easter Island.

1 April. To Mrs Hill's at Kirkby Stephen where Mr Hill has given her permission to sell us the pan stand, a fixture of the upstairs window, for £15, and we also buy a little flower jug (£5) and a cast-iron hob.

18 April. To New York for the opening of *The History Boys*. The plane is not full and unexpectedly comfortable but I miss the now archaic ritual of transatlantic flights in the days before videos and iPods: the coffee and pastries when you got on, the drinks and the lunch before the blinds went down and they showed a film. Once that was over you were already above New England and there was tea and an hour later New York. Now there's no structure to it at all, just choice – choice of programme, choice of video and no tea either, just today, a choice of pizza or a hot turkey sandwich. I browse through Duff Cooper's diaries and, dosed up on valium, am unalarmed by what little turbulence there is. But so miss R. – at every stage of the journey, setting off, getting there, half the person I am.

An odd incident at Heathrow. There is a long queue to go through security and a boy of eighteen or so comes down the line asking if he can go to the front as his plane takes off in twenty minutes. This he's allowed to do, my own flight not due to go for well over an hour. I am among the first off at JFK when I see this youth again, now hurrying to be ahead in the immigration queue also, so his claim to be on an imminent flight must have been a lie, and had anyone else spotted him who had previously let him through there might have been words spoken. Just in T-shirt and jeans he doesn't look as if he's been in First or Business so he must have parlayed his way off the plane ahead of everyone else just as he did earlier. But he has luggage and there is no avoiding that, and as I spot my name on a card and see a driver waiting he is still hanging about restlessly at the carousel. Disturbing, though, and it leaves me wanting an explanation and a notion of his life.

21 April, New York. Persisting with the Duff Cooper diaries, which, though they're more than frank about his innumerable liaisons, are utterly silent on more interesting topics, the cruise of the *Nahlin*, for instance, in 1936 when Duff Cooper and his wife accompanied the King and Mrs Simpson around the Mediterranean. Years ago Russell Harty had supper with Diana Cooper and she told him that she and her husband had had the adjoining cabin to the royal couple (or rather one royal, the other not) and that she had had her ear pressed to the wall half the night in case there was any action, but heard not a thing. The other guest at supper was Martha Gellhorn, both of them getting on and quite pissed, so that Russell spent the meal rushing from one end of the table to the other as each in turn slowly toppled off her chair.

Duff Cooper's philanderings are often quite funny. Having rekindled an old flame, Lady Warrender, he adjourns with her to his Gower Street house, now emptied of furniture and up for sale. Suddenly, while they're at it, there's a loud banging on the door downstairs which Duff Cooper eventually has to answer and it's the estate agent with some prospective buyers wanting to see the house. It's made funnier (and rather Buñuelesque) by Duff C. and Lady W. being so middle-aged and ultra-respectable. John Julius Norwich puts his father's sexual success down to his ability to write bad sonnets to his lady friends but one wonders if it was a more basic attraction. The moustache is hardly a plus, the photograph on the book jacket making him look like a 1940s cinema manager.

22 April. I do the rounds of the TV and radio arts programmes prior to the opening of the play on Sunday, accompanied by Jim Bik, our young low-key PR man. At one venue we are met in the lobby of some huge new communications emporium by the TV call boy who takes us through various gleaming and coded doors until we get to one where the code he punches in doesn't work. Not, I think, making a joke he says apologetically, 'Guess this is kind of lo-tech,' and knocks on the door.

23 *April*. The theatre where *The History Boys* is playing, the Broadhurst, is as dull as New York theatres mostly are, painted battleship grey and on this opening night packed with a slow-moving crowd of playgoers reluctant to take their seats. Beforehand, we go round and see the boys, who are a bit excited, though it's not a first night on which much depends as most of the critics have already been during the previews. The play itself seems to me to go too quickly and is a bit slurred, the result not so much of it being a first night as that the cast have been doing it on and off now for two years. When James C. drops his head on his desk it's with an almighty crash and he gets up looking a bit pale, but there are no other slip-ups. The response at the end is tumultuous, the audience (though I think this is nowadays obligatory) rising to their feet en masse. We go round backstage to find them all getting ready for the party; some of them have allowed themselves to be styled for the occasion in suits and big plain-coloured Windsor-knotted ties so that they look more like footballers than actors.

Then to the Tavern on the Green, a stupendously vulgar venue where we have to proceed past a gallery of photographers and TV cameras. Whether this is what always happens to a greater or lesser degree I'm not sure but there's not much doubt it's been a success, proved apparently by the readiness of the guests to remain at the party. I scarcely eat simply because I have to keep getting up to greet the boys' parents and, in Sacha Dhawan's case, his sisters and his cousins and his aunts, who have followed the production across the world through Hong Kong, New Zealand and Australia to this first night on Broadway. Back at 16th Street by 11.30 happy that it's all done with.

25 April. En route from New York to Boston by train Lynn W. has booked us onto the quiet coach, which is where we often sit when going up to Leeds. It isn't always quiet, though, and in my experience is probably the most contentious coach on the train. This is because, in England at any rate, the prohibition against the use of mobile phones is often ignored or not even acknowledged so that the occasional bold spirit will then protest and a row breaks out, and even when it doesn't there's frequently some unspoken resentment against offenders, who aren't even aware.

This morning our coach is quite subdued, no one uses a mobile, though the three of us talk quietly and occasionally Lynn laughs. I notice one or two stern heads bobbing above the seats without realising why until one pale, wild-eyed Madame Defarge-like figure advances down the carriage and gestures mutely at the Quiet Coach notice. We stop talking (though find it hard not to giggle). However another couple, possibly German, not realising they are committing an offence continue to chat whereupon Madame Defarge confronts them, too, and then goes in search of the conductor. As she passes me I say, mildly: 'It's only a quiet coach. It isn't a Trappist one.'

'Yes, it is,' she snaps and returns a few minutes later with the conductor who gives the new offenders a mild lecture. I pass Madame Defarge again as I tiptoe down to the loo and see she's working on some sort of thesis, her ideal mode of transport I suppose a cork-lined carriage. The 'Marcel Proust' might be a good name for a train.

29 April. On our way to a friend's sample sale on 18th Street we are held up at Broadway by a protest march. It's an alliance of all the various protest groups – Stop the War, Save Darfur, the victims of Katrina – with bands, banners, blacks, Bush haters and blue-suited ladies marching side by side. Somewhere among them, I'm sure, my

Amherst friends, the Elbows. To get across we have to mingle with the marchers and let ourselves be carried along with the flow until we hit the far side of the street and each time, going and coming back I find it brings me, entirely unexpectedly, to the edge of tears. Americans, as Rupert says, are capable of the best and the worst and this is the best – serious, humorous and determined – young couples with babies in strollers, old men in parkas, priests and Muslims, gays, veterans all testify that America is not just the ignorant red-necked bully half the world currently perceives it to be.

Compare though how much there is about America in our serious newspapers and how much there is about the United Kingdom in the *New York Times*: often not a thing. What we think and what we do is of no interest to most of America and even to New York. They are about as interested in our affairs as we are in the affairs of Portugal, say.

The march snarls up traffic all over New York, gathering at Foley Square before breaking up. We are in a patisserie in Tribeca and sit at a table with three of the marchers, two from Boston and the other an old lady (i.e. my age) from Westchester. They're serious solid middle-American ladies, radicals they ain't. But if I were George Bush I'd hope never to meet them face to face as their patience and conviction would show him up as the fool and trickster he is.

12 *May*. To Leeds where this evening I am to be given the Freedom of the City. The actual ceremony takes place in the council chamber, the leader of each party having the right to say their piece so it's quite a lengthy business. The acoustics aren't good and some I can't hear but keep a grateful smile on my face just in case, meanwhile spotting my relatives and guests who are scattered among the councillors. When it gets to my turn I slightly lose my way in the speech I've written out (but don't read) though do it well enough. It's only the first of two speeches I have to make, the second one after the dinner that follows:

To be given the Freedom of Leeds is a great honour, indeed the greatest the city could pay me.

I don't think, though that it diminishes the honour if I say that I feel I was given the freedom of the city more than fifty years ago, thanks to the education bestowed upon me here.

I went first in 1939 to Upper Armley National School, now Christ Church C. of E. Primary School, briefly to West Leeds High School and then to Leeds Modern School, now Lawnswood School, from which, thanks to a Senior City scholarship I went eventually to Oxford.

My parents set great store by education, which they had never had, both of them leaving school at twelve or thirteen and they were determined my brother and I should have the advantages that had been denied to them.

Leeds set great store by education, too and it was, of course, entirely free and thanks to the City they never had to pay a penny for our education from start to finish. So if I'm passionate about free education now and against loans and all the other ways in which it now has to be financed it's because I still believe that the way Leeds educated its children then was the best.

And it wasn't simply education in the schools. Just down the road is George Corson's School Board Building, the solidity and grandeur of which expresses the city's faith in education. And beyond it is the library building and at the top of the library, what was then the Reference Library, a superb piece of high Victorian architecture and a wonderful library where I regularly used to do my homework or work in the vacation along with many of my contemporaries.

Libraries don't have honours boards but if they did that of Leeds Reference Library would have a distinguished list because of the boys and girls who worked there in my time alone at least eight have become judges.

And next door to the library is, of course, the Art Gallery which was another part of my education, and across the road the Town Hall where every Saturday night throughout my adolescence I went to concerts and learned to love music.

So you see that when I say I was given the freedom of the city many years ago, that is what I mean.

I haven't had much to do with honours. They tend to be bestowed, come from above and maybe I have an ancient Northern distrust of being beholden. But this is different. As I understand it, it was voted on by all the parties unanimously, so I see it not as coming down but as coming up – and coming up from the people of Leeds. And that makes me very happy. Thank you.

16 May. Philip Roth's face in a photograph by Nancy Crampton on the jacket of his new novel, *Everyman*, is as stern and ungiving as a self-portrait by Rembrandt.

30 May, Yorkshire. Not one in fifty people knows how to restore or convert a house. A familiar fault round here is to strip off the stucco to reveal the supposed beauty of the stonework, which is often not beautiful at all and which, badly pointed as it then invariably is, becomes a garish patchwork besides letting in more damp than it did before. We pass such a house in Lawkland today, a tall dignified place it's always been, plain and rather Scottish-looking. Now, stripped of its weathered stucco it sports a suburban front door from a cheap builder's merchants, and coming round the corner and seeing it transformed I involuntarily cry out. But it's just one of hundreds in the neighbourhood to be similarly vandalised, the suburbanisation of Craven much worse than anything that has yet happened in Swaledale or Wensleydale. There's scarcely a barn within reach of the road that hasn't been kitted out with brown-framed windows and a little bit of Leeds or Bradford installed on its greenfield site.

1 June. Gilly P. who comes on a Wednesday evening to do our reflex-
ology also looks after various disabled people, including Jim, who
was blind and has just died. She went to his funeral at Kensal Green
on Saturday where the chapel was full of guide dogs, crouched in
the pews or lying in the aisle, Jim's dog one of the congregation, too,
though as ever not paying much attention, always looking round and
never concentrating. It was quite absent-minded with Jim, so that
he often got black eyes through bumping into things, this negligence
Gilly thinks to be put down to the fact that these days there are fewer
training centres for guide dogs and they're not schooled as well as
they once were.

After the service there is a wake in a local pub where many of the
blind get quite drunk, blind drunk in this case not just a phrase.
Several of them try tipsily to touch G. up and when she tells one of
them off for groping her he says plaintively: 'But I can't see what I'm
doing, can I?' According to G. this is a regular get-out.

2 June. Heard someone saying today instead of 'all the time', the now
pretty common phrase '24/7' – an American import, 9/11 its first
introduction here.

Wonder about the small feeling of satisfaction someone gets by
saying something as linguistically *modish* and up-to-the-minute as
24/7 – a small thrill at being at the cutting edge of language (or
using a phrase they've got off the TV).

3 June. To Wendover, where we have coffee and look round an
antique centre in the Old Post Office, the building with its lovely
banisters and painted sixteenth-century beams as interesting as the
stuff in it. We find a cheap blue-and-white plate (and resist several
others). R. buys some plants at a shop down the street and then we
go in search of Acton Turville which has a good church and where we
plan to have our sandwiches. But it's a spring Saturday and the bells
are ringing and of course there's a wedding. Still it's a lovely spot and

we sit on a seat at the far end of the churchyard and have our lunch as the bells eventually stop and the sound of the hymn drifts out over the grass where the bell ringers are having a picnic, too. Behind us is a wide medieval-looking field, new mown with the grass left strewn about to dry and a horse is sitting with some cows in the shade of the churchyard trees. It's a lovely spot and we are both very happy and know it – even though the church (where the WI will be offering cream teas at 3 p.m.) will alas have to wait. Then, after a bit of a trek, we find Chearsley Church which is a disappointment but make it to Waterperry by the back road from Long Crendon in time for a nice tea on the lawn and more plant-buying.

11 June, New York. Back for the second time in six weeks, this time for the Tonys and again to Lynn W.'s 16th Street apartment, which is the penthouse of a small 1930s skyscraper with a terrace all the way round and views uptown to the Chrysler Building and Central Park and to the west the Hudson and the Jersey shore. It's warm and windy and sitting in the bedroom with the door open I can see the Empire State Building reflected in the mirror opposite. Planes cross the blue sky unheeded as once before they did one sunny morning and, to someone here as seldom as I am, never without fell implications. We have a long brunch at the Odeon then walk back to 16th Street to prepare for the Tonys this evening.

The cast have all been styled for the occasion but nobody has taken on the challenge of styling me, my major contribution to fashion an Armani suit and a red spotted bow tie which, though it's tied and retied several times in the course of the evening, never manages to achieve the horizontal. It's also a magnet for well wishers, beginning with the doorman at Radio City Music Hall who opens the limo door and then adjusts my tie and it's still happening five weary hours later when we come away.

In the event of our winning the Best Play award we had agreed beforehand that the boys should all come up to receive it, which indeed they do. But so also do a collection of people whom I've never seen before, and in such numbers that David Hyde Pierce, who is presenting it, is practically elbowed out of the way. These turn out to be the backers who, of course, have every reason to be pleased and indeed one of them duly adjusts my tie.

I am then bundled out through a back door and across the street to Rockefeller Plaza where a whole floor has been given over to the press. I'm thrust blinking onto a stage facing a battery of lights while questions come out of the darkness, the best of which is: 'Do you think this award will kick-start your career?' News of my lacklustre performance on this podium must have got round quickly because I'm then taken down a long corridor off which various TV and radio shows have mikes and cameras and there is more humiliation. 'Do you want him?' asks the PA at each doorway, the answer more often than not being 'Nah,' so I only score about four brief interviews before I'm pushed through another door and find I'm suddenly back in the street in the rain and it's all more or less over.

16 June. Having seen the TV programme on which it was based I've been reading *Britten's Children* by John Bridcut. Glamorous though he must have been and a superb teacher, I find Britten a difficult man to like. He had his favourites, children and adults, but both Britten and Pears were notorious for cutting people out of their lives (Eric Crozier is mentioned here, and Charles Mackerras), friends and acquaintances suddenly turned into living corpses if they overstepped the mark. A joke would do it and though Britten seems to have had plenty of childish jokes with his boy singers, his sense of humour isn't much in evidence elsewhere. And it was not merely adults that were cut off. A boy whose voice suddenly broke could find himself no longer invited to the Red House or part of the group – a fate which the boys Bridcut quotes here seem to have taken philosophically but which might be potentially far more damaging to a child's psychology than too much attention. One thinks, too, of the boys who were not part of the charmed circle. There were presumably fat boys and ugly boys or just plain dull boys who could, nevertheless, sing like angels. What of them?

I never met or saw Britten, though he and Peter Pears came disastrously to *Beyond the Fringe* some time in 1961. Included in the programme was a parody of Britten written by Dudley Moore, in which he sang and accompanied himself in 'Little Miss Muffet' done in a Pears and Britten-like way. I'm not sure that this in itself would have caused offence: it shouldn't have as, like all successful parodies, there was a good deal of affection to it and it was funny in its own right. But Dudley (who may have known them slightly and certainly had met them) unthinkingly entitled the piece 'Little Miss Britten'. Now Dudley was not malicious nor had he any reason to mock their homosexuality, of which indeed he may have been unaware (I don't think I knew of it at the time). But with the offending title printed in the programme, they were reported to be deeply upset and Dudley went into outer darkness as probably did the rest of us.

18 June. The boy in Crosshills seen once giving a girlfriend a lift on his wheelchair as it were on the crossbar of his bike, seen again yesterday snogging another – or possibly the same girl – she sitting on the steps of some office beside which he had parked his chair, so that both being on the same height they could as it were kiss on a level.

Both occasions the same time, the dead of Sunday afternoon.

23 June. To a reading of *A Question of Attribution* which Sue Roberts is doing for radio in a studio down Broadhurst Gardens 'behind John Lewis' as Lindsay Anderson always used to describe the location of his flat. I go reluctantly but Edward Petherbridge as Blunt and Nicky Henson as Chubb do it beautifully, light and airy, and though some of it's a bit 'fine writing', several times I have to stop myself laughing at my own lines and think there's no reason to be ashamed of it at all. Whether it'll be comprehensible on radio is a different thing, it's such a visual play – but then it wasn't always comprehensible on stage.

24 June. Today is the last day of the British Museum Michelangelo exhibition, which, because of demand, is open until midnight. For all we go quite late, it's still crowded out, paintings hard enough to look at under such circumstances and drawings well-nigh impossible. One straight away abandons any attempt to look at them in sequence (not that the sequence helps) and makes for any drawing that is not being looked at, the people with earphones the real menace as they all move at the same speed and cause the jams.

More mystified than I usually am at exhibitions I can never take in the finer points of drawing and the bulging thighs and backs pebbled with muscle soon pall. R. notes, though, that women (who far outnumber men) seem to find them both moving and satisfying whereas I find them neither. Of course, Michelangelo is a star and so whatever he does is acclaimed, from the anatomical exactitude of the preliminary drawings for the Sistine ceiling through to the blurred and almost impressionistic figures of the three late Crucifixions with which the exhibition ends. It's hard not to think that there is an element of the sacred in everything to which he put his hand: it must be reverenced because this is by the hand of Michelangelo.

A propos the hand, the most famous image is, I suppose, that of God giving life to Adam but the only (easily overlooked) drawing for this is low down on a sheet of other drawings. There is a line drawn round the fragment, as at one stage it was cut out of the sheet before being later reinstated, but it's so formal that there is little remarkable about it and it's not unlike the stylised eighteenth-century hand on the signpost on Elslack Moor.

I wonder, looking at all these thighs and torsos, with the dicks never closely anatomised, whether Michelangelo ever did any pornographic drawings, as all artists must at some time be tempted to do, and if so what happened to them. I wonder, too, if they had survived and were exhibited here, a couple unabashedly making love, for instance, a boy getting it on, whether these would attract this same Saturday night crowd who would subject the sacred porn to their wholesome, safe, art-loving scrutiny, making them just as hygienic as the rest.

29 June. R.'s office outing yesterday when they go on a minibus to Scotney and Sissinghurst. The house just survives the droves of visitors but the gardens don't. As R. bluntly puts it, 'People spoil things' – a line in a play you could only give to a child or a licensed eccentric. But it starts me thinking again of the play, *National Trust*, I thought of when we went to Knole.

1 July. Watch the commentary and round-ups (they could hardly be called highlights) after the England–Portugal match. One Shakespearean moment at the start when Cristiano Ronaldo comes up behind his Manchester team-mate Rooney and nuzzles him, saying something that seems to be kind but almost certainly isn't as Rooney then swings round to watch him go. It's like an impossibly beautiful Iago goading a simple lumbering Othello, an impression confirmed when, after Othello gets the red card, Ronaldo comes away with a tranquil smile.

2 July, Yorkshire. Two rather dull fawny-coloured birds are nesting in the creeper just outside the kitchen door. Watching them (and looking them up in the bird book) I find they are flycatchers, one keeping station on the garden wall then looping round over the lawn until it collects a packet of insects in its beak which it takes back to the nest thereby releasing its mate to do the same. They winter in Africa and summer here in Craven, a circumstance I find – what? – both pleasing and, in some undefinable way, encouraging.

Working in the garden we are watched in the heat by the toad, which is just a slight bump in the water in the corner of the trough, its eyes on a level with the surface taking in the proceedings, then when the garden gets too *mouvementé* he/she turns its back and stares instead at the less taxing wall.

4 July. Talking to George Fenton about the football and about Ronaldo, George saying that watching the Latin teams in particular you see how these are boys whose mothers have loved and cherished them and who have all the confidence and swank that comes from that.

5 July. Last week I met David Walliams in Melrose and Morgan, our new posh local delicatessen. Big, handsome in a slightly Tartar way, he and Matt Lucas must currently be the most famous people in the country. Today he swims the Channel, seemingly without much effort and with very little ballyhoo. When I was a boy a young swimmer from Leeds, Philip Mickman, swam the Channel and the preparations and the weather and the pictures of him plastered in grease were front-page news in the *Yorkshire Evening Post* for weeks beforehand. Now, like Everest, people do it all the time, no problem.

7 July. Six o'clock and Antonio the Algerian road sweeper comes into the garden, shuts the gate and has a sit down in the basket chair by the front door while eating a banana. Now he gets part of a cardboard box out of his dustcart which he puts down as a prayer mat and begins his devotions . . . a procedure not quite as elaborate as the devotions we saw performed by a Hasidic Jew at JFK earlier this year but with some similar components . . . the angle of the body for instance, leaning forward, the touching of the arms and the face in a way that did one see it in a different context would seem obsessive. Now he finishes and on this day, supposedly the hottest ever, he comes and has another sit down and makes his phone calls. Meanwhile I wait for Gilly, the reflexologist.

8 July, Yorkshire. As I'm getting some money out of the cashpoint on Duke Street in Settle I feel a tug at my jacket. I look down and it's little white-haired eighty-five-year-old Onyx Ralph, who just about comes up to my waist. 'Hello, Mr Bennett. Did you think I was a mugger?'

11 July. Baroness Scotland is put up to defend the government's shameful capitulation to the United States in the extradition treaty. She makes much of the rule of law in America and the independence of the Supreme Court, citing its stand (after four glorious years) on Guantánamo but says nothing of the next person likely to be extradited, the hacker who got into the Pentagon computer. Whereas the three NatWest bankers can at least afford some defence, what will the next victim be able to afford? Nor does Baroness Scotland say anything of the plea bargaining that goes on in the US's nobly independent courts where the US accused cut their own sentences by putting the blame on their foreign associates who are then shipped across the Atlantic in shackles. *The World at One* gives the baroness an easy time as does Joshua Rozenberg, both blandly dismissive of this diminution of the subject's rights. The plain fact is that to be extradited on a charge the evidence for which has not been heard before an English court, is unjust.

16 July. Palmers, the old-fashioned pet shop in Parkway, which has been there as long as I can remember and from the look of the place much longer than that, has now closed down. The signs on the shop front (which I hope Camden Council has had the sense to list) read: 'Monkeys. Talking Parrots. Regent Pet Stores. Naturalists'.

In 1966 Patrick Garland and I filmed some poems to include in a comedy series we were doing, *On the Margin*. The standard form of comedy sketch shows then demanded a musical interlude between items, Kathy Kirby, say, or Millicent Martin. Boldly (as we thought) we opted for poems instead and were considered very eccentric, but Frank Muir, then head of comedy, and David Attenborough, the controller of BBC2, said it was all right and so we filmed Palmers to illustrate Larkin's poem, 'Take One Home for the Kiddies'. Another of his poems we used was 'At Grass'. Whether Larkin cared for either I don't think we ever heard.

I walk by today and in the window of this empty pet shop is a sad bedraggled pigeon, not, one imagines, a remnant of the stock but which must have got in through the already decaying roof and which sits there now, forlornly on offer. It's another poem.

17 July. The Met is to be prosecuted for 'failing to provide for the health, safety and welfare' of Mr de Menezes. Naive, I suppose, to have thought that the police would be brought to book for the shooting. They never have been in the past so why now? The longer and more protracted the investigation the plainer this has become, the boredom of the public now presumably part of the strategy. The truth is that on the relatively few occasions that the police kill they do so with impunity. The only reason this is not enshrined in law is that if it was they would do it more often. Still, if the police were authorised to shoot to kill it would at least make the law 'fit for purpose', in the home secretary's noxious phrase, and so gladden his heart. Meanwhile, one wonders what has happened to the policeman who did the actual shooting. It's to be hoped he's not still out there defending our liberties.

[*1 November.* It turns out that he is and in exactly the same way, though cutting down at least on the number of shots, seven in the case of de Menezes, one in yesterday's shooting. Presumably his strike rate has improved as a result of the 'retraining' he has received and, of course, the counselling.]

One criterion for judging this (or any other) government is how often it makes one feel ashamed to be English. Today ratchets up the score. I don't think it's quite up to Thatcher's level but it's getting there.

20 July. Work on the Queen story and get a little further to the extent that tomorrow when we go north I will put it in the fridge – something I haven't done since I was writing *History Boys*.

21 July, Yorkshire. To Leeds by train then the back way to Ilkley through Askwith and Weston, taking the turning down to the church at Weston past Weston Hall; meaning to sit in the churchyard for half an hour. I'd forgotten how odd the church is, the west front particularly. 'Picturesquely irregular W front', Pevsner calls it, 'with bellcote and cyclopic asymmetrically-placed buttress.' The bellcote is topped with what looks like an inverted Victorian footstool, with four bulbous legs. I'd vaguely remembered a seat in the churchyard but on the noticeboard is a warning, 'The Churchyard has been sprayed with weed killer', and indeed the seat is fenced off with chicken wire presumably to protect the few non-weeds that grow around it. Genuinely shocked by this method of churchyard maintenance. Our own church in the village is in effect a nature reserve, mowed or scythed but never sprayed, God, I'd always assumed, thought to be on the side of ecology.

22 July. The village street market is all set up by nine thirty, the cake stalls, the jam, the tombola, the duck race and (R.'s target) the junk stall, on which he has spotted a very run-down Ernest Race Festival of Britain chair which, as soon as the market is declared open (by the ringing of the church bell), he buys for £1. Pretty battered and minus its ball feet it's still got the original wooden seat, and is one of many thousands of such chairs that were scattered throughout the Festival of Britain on the South Bank that summer of 1951.

We also buy an almond Madeira cake and some delicious raspberry jam, the cake and the jam stall always the first to sell out. When events like this are depicted on television (e.g. in *Midsomer Murders* or *Rosemary & Thyme*) it's always as occasions for vicious backbiting and murderous (literally) rivalries. There's none of that here, I'm happy to say. Everybody speaks and the topography of the village, a long straight street backing onto the beck, is ideally suited to the row of stalls. The chair is taken through into the garden where R. spends the rest of the day restoring it.

24 July. A card from a friend in New York prompted by the invasion of Lebanon.

> Please go to the US Embassy and throw stones. S.
> (Say I sent you.)

30 July. Tony Blair addresses Rupert Murdoch's conference of newspaper editors and tells them that there is now no more left and right. In view of his audience he would have done better to tell them there is no more good and evil.

31 July. The same myth attached to Mrs Thatcher as it was to Stalin: neither of them ever slept.

5 August, L'Espiessac, France. Installed contentedly in the Pigeonnier Est, utterly silent, the tall windows filled with the bluest of skies and with a soft breeze that stirs the sheet as I write. On the mantelpiece Lynn has put a large schoolroom-size bottle of Waterman's Ink in its original, unopened box, the lettering and the design of the box putting it in the early 1950s, just after the Festival of Britain. The logo is in the shape of a television screen, which was the coming thing in 1952, the box, I suppose, meriting a place in the Design Museum.

I am reading *The Man Who Went into the West: The Life of R. S. Thomas* by Byron Rogers, whose book on J. L. Carr I read here on holiday last year. R. S. Thomas, the poetry of whom I scarcely know, sounds as bleak as Larkin pretended to be.

A huge hawk hovers high above the house. It doesn't fly off but just drifts upwards, and is gone. A hawk can hide in an unclouded sky.

'Grieving' used at home to mean vexing, or upsetting: 'It's griev-ing' (if something was spoilt, say, or broken). One of the instances where I'm not sure if it's a dialect usage or standard English.

8 August. The garden and the countryside already shaggy and unkempt, August the middle age of the land, shambling, pot-bellied, in need of a haircut. Some of the sounds escape me now (though I did manage to hear a cricket last night). Now sitting at the open window with Rupert still asleep there is just one pigeon, hitting the same note again and again like a piano tuner.

10 August, Toulouse. An unexpected queue for the 10.30 BA flight, the only clue a leaflet being handed out, saying that no hand baggage is allowed and all belongings must go in the hold. Everyone begins to repack their bags, which we would be happy to do, except that our hand baggage includes the aforesaid bottle of Waterman's Ink. This can hardly be put in the hold lest it break, inundating not only our luggage but everybody else's. When we reach the check-in we explain this to the harassed woman, who eventually caves in, partly helped by consulting our details on the computer. More impressed by my status than anyone else, my travel agent always gets 'VIP' put on my ticket. '*Pourquoi*,' they say at the check-in, '*vous êtes VIP?*'

'*Je suis un écrivain.*' It's a statement I'm readier to make in French than in English, but it causes hysteria among the check-in girls.

'*Ah, oui. L'encre!*' and then everyone goes into peals of laughter.

'*Non, non*,' I say lamely. '*C'est un cadeau excentrique.*' More hys-teria and on the strength of it we are waved through. It's only when we get to Gatwick (which is about to be closed) that we find that the 'plot', such as it is, centres on suspect liquids. Presumably nobody at Toulouse yet knew this and the sniffer dogs at Gatwick don't seem to know it either, as not being ink-sensitive they twice turn their noses up at our bags.

14 August. A year or two ago the National Parks were complaining that their visitors were predominantly white and that the Asian population of Leeds and Bradford, for instance, left them largely unvisited. In this morning's *Guardian* it's claimed that would-be terrorists learned some of their skills in camps in National Parks in the Lake District and the Yorkshire Dales. So some improvement there.

16 August. Good news that the defence secretary, Des Browne, has bowed to public opinion and pardoned the young men shot for cowardice in the First World War. Our fearless home secretary Dr Reid didn't have the nerve to do this when he was at the MoD, nor his ineffable dauntless successor, Geoff Hoon. No mention that I see anywhere of John Hipkin, the Newcastle pensioner who has made the pardoning of these young men his particular mission – good for him. Decency is what one asks from governments and occasionally at least it happens.

21 August. Political Correctness:

> [I am not going to affect] the livery
> Of the times' prudery.
> R. S. THOMAS

24 August. I am reading *The Secret Life of Cows* by Rosamund Young, a delightful book though insofar as it reveals that cows (and sheep and even hens) have far more awareness and know-how than they are given credit for it could also be thought deeply depressing. Though not if you're a cow on Young's farm, Kites' Nest in Worcestershire, which has been organic since before organics started and where the farm hands can tell from the taste alone which cow the milk comes from. Young makes the case against factory farming more simply and compellingly than anyone I've read and simply on grounds of common sense.

One curiosity about the book, though, is that while the author goes into much detail about the behaviour of cows and their differences of temperament and outlook she never mentions any idiosyncrasies when the cows go with the bull and whether their individuality, which she has made much of elsewhere, is still in evidence. Are some shyer than others? More flirty? It may be of course that this reticence is a measure of her respect for her charges, feeling that cows are entitled to their privacy as much as their keepers. But it's a book that alters the way one looks at the world and one which all farmers would do well to read.

2 September. Making the supper and idly listening to Radio 4's *Saturday Review* the only speaker I recognise is P. D. James and none of it anything to do with me until some Scottish woman in the course of telling off the novelist Mark Haddon accuses him of 'Alan Bennettish tweeness'. It's not a serious injury to my self-esteem but rather as if someone passing me in the street has just turned back to give me a flying kick up the bum and then gone on their way. I hope for some mild objection from one of the other participants but none is forthcoming so perhaps I'm now tweeness's accepted measure.

8 September, Yorkshire. On Saturday around the same time we blackberry up Crummock Lane, the stream full and loud over the other side of the wall on one side, a herd of friendly cows on the other – now that I've been told they have inner lives I ought to adapt my behaviour accordingly (though how?) instead just letting them lick my hands – and two lovely horses higher up the lane the same. Rupert if anything more nervous of the cows than the horses, which wear fly-masks, transparent blinkers across their foreheads that make them look blindfolded. We were planning to walk up to the clapper bridge but R. is uneasy about walking through the field with such attentive cows so instead we drive round on the Crummock road, park and walk down. No one about, utterly still and over the wall a ring of huge pearly white mushrooms. We pick about four, which is more than we will eat and then go down to the clapper bridge in what is now named Wash Dub Field, a National Parks notice explaining how the sheep were penned here to be washed. That and an iron seat apart, it's no different from what it was when I first came here forty years ago. But a lovely evening and we go back to a fire, beans picked from the garden and a salad niçoise with the mushrooms – never as nice to taste as they are to pick – for Sunday lunch.

11 September. There are buds in plays, points where other plays can branch out. I can see, for instance that this story about the Queen began as a bud in the scene between Hector and Posner in *The History Boys* when Hector is talking about reading.

I can see that one of the buds (because there can be several) which grew into *Habeas Corpus* was in the last speech of Act 1 of *Forty Years On* and I hear John Gielgud's voice saying, '"This time," I always thought as I tied my tie. "Perhaps this time." But there would be other times and time yet, I thought.'

And so one could go on, hopping from play to play, one budding out from the next, swinging from one to the other like Tarzan through the jungly fronds.

12 September. Read Nicola Lacey's life of H. L. A. Hart – the Sacred Hart as J. used to call him. The core of the book skipped – namely the jurisprudence and the philosophy, all I carry away from that the confirmation that I could never have been a don; still daunted by the sheer brains of e.g. Hart himself, Ronald Dworkin and their pupils and followers. 'I have no mind,' I think as I read, 'and never have had.' Not this sort of mind anyway. Hart's want of self-assurance is appealing, particularly in view of his great renown – as also is his difficult sex life – married but gay, with hopeless passions for heterosexual men continuing into his seventies.

I remember seeing him about Oxford in the fifties and knowing he was a star, just as one knew Lord David C. was a star – Rowse, Lord David Cecil and C. S. Lewis once seen walking down towards

Magdalen, just as conscious of their reputations and their glamour as any actor appearing at the Playhouse.

14 September. Jonathan M. very funny about Archbishop John Sentamu's front teeth, saying that he felt the gap was just the continuation of the centre aisle.

16 September. Listen to Sue Roberts's production of *Single Spies** on Radio 4. I'm particularly struck by Edward Petherbridge playing Anthony Blunt in *A Question of Attribution*. Although I played the part myself I've forgotten a good deal of it, particularly the lectures on art history in general which in the stage play Blunt gives directly to the audience. Petherbridge gets so much more out of these than I did that listening to them I can scarcely believe they've come from my own pen, infusing them with so much sadness and irony one feels Blunt's whole life is there. The same with Prunella Scales as the Queen, which was a joy to write and is still a joy to listen to. Nicky Henson is very good as Chubb, the man from MI5 – less breezy than he normally is and between the questioner and the questioned (which is also pupil and teacher) a relationship more flirtatious than Simon Callow and I ever quite managed.

I go on with painting/staining the walls of my study, doing an experimental strip of wall with cerulean blue which, on top of the yellow, turns it green. It would just about do but I feel I can do better – though what or how I've no idea.

18 September. 'There shouldn't be any religion. There should just be people being nice to one another.' This is check-out women at M&S discussing the Pope's remarks at Regensburg with an equally vapid customer while I fume in the queue. The conversation ends, almost incredibly:

---

* The double bill of *A Question of Attribution* and *An Englishman Abroad*.

'What about the Spanish Inquisition?'
'Exactly.'

21 September. The Bush–Blair attitude to war:

'A War' by Randall Jarrell

These set out, slowly, for a Different World,
At four, on winter mornings, different legs. . .
You can't break eggs without making an omelette
– That's what they tell the eggs.

Found in John Bayley's anthology *Hand Luggage* (Continuum, 2001).

28 September. At the outset of the Iraq war Tony Blair was deter-mined not to be another Chamberlain. Now as he slowly prepares to leave office one can see that Chamberlain is exactly whom he has come to resemble. In the 1930s Chamberlain put through some enlightened social legislation, but all anyone nowadays remembers is Munich and Appeasement. Tony Blair, too, has achievements in the social field but no one will remember those, only Iraq. I suppose this says something about history.

29 September. I call in at the Farmers' Market which now takes place every Saturday in the playground of Princess Road school. It's a friendly occasion, but whereas in Union Square in New York, the only other farmers' market I've been to, I take it as simply a nice (and useful) collection of stalls – meat, veg, bread, cheese – and am unself-conscious about it, here, on my own patch as it were, I'm aware of the middle class (and it is predominantly middle class) hugging them-selves in self-congratulation at the perfection of their lives. I know this is unfair and grumbling and I wish I were more open-minded and didn't care. But as it is I queue to buy two slices of delicious-look-ing pork pie but am put off by the vendor's over-cheerful butcherly demeanour (and his brown bowler) and come away empty-handed.

Ahead lies two to three weeks of promotion for the film of *The History Boys*, the opening with Prince Charles on Monday then visits to Glasgow, Leeds and Manchester talking to local schools and doing Q&A in cinemas.

One of these Q&A encounters at a school in Leeds is to be filmed by Channel 4 and looking through the schedule I find the school they've chosen is Leeds Grammar School. Now LGS is not a state school, indeed it's about as far from a state school as you can get in Leeds and I suspect it's still the same snobbish emporium purveying education that it has always been. Tony Harrison has bitter memories of it as a boy and when I made the mistake of opening their new theatre in the 1980s I was shocked by how much flummery there was – gowns and tassels on caps etc. like something out of Frank Richards or *The Magnet*. So I rule out LGS and they are now finding a state school that will fit the bill and not offend the writer's awkward sensibilities or trespass on the memories of his youth. [We eventually do the Q&A at City of Leeds High School.]

30 September. When, passing the house, someone lights up a joint they straight away look at the lit end, something they never do with a straight cigarette.

1 October. Watch *Bremner, Bird and Fortune* which nowadays we generally miss since it's been shifted forwards to eight o'clock. It contains a pun so terrible it ranks with those John Bird, John Fortune and I used painstakingly to construct for the (live) performances of *Not So Much a Programme* and *The Late Show* back in the 1960s.

In tonight's programme they are talking of someone who is 'not fit for purpose' and J.F. says that this leaves out of account the hapless employee of the Brighton Dolphinarium who was recently sacked on similar grounds.

J.B.: I didn't hear about that.

J.F.: Oh yes. Not fit for porpoise.

Back in the 1960s Bird and Fortune were playing detectives, one of whom was called Farley.

J.B.: It's a risk, Farley.

J.F.: No. It's a rusk, Farley.

The puns were deliberately introduced, sometimes without prior warning in order to break each other up, which in Fortune's case was always signalled (as it still is) by his opening his eyes very wide and shaking his head, a process known as 'boggling'. It doesn't happen this evening but it brings back the exquisite agony of trying not to laugh in full view of two million people.

9 October. Bike past a skip on Gloucester Avenue in which are three whole and undamaged Belfast sinks, thrown out of a house being 'renovated' presumably by East European workers who now undertake much of the building work round here. The sinks would easily fetch £40 or £50 second-hand but unschooled in the aesthetics and the economics of old-fashioned culinary kitchen revivalism the Croats or Bulgarians or whatever have just ripped them out and dumped them. In similar circumstances a few months ago a nineteenth-century marble fireplace was dumped from a window in Gloucester Crescent and smashed. If nothing else it's sheer waste but short of putting the builders through a crash course on the economics of architectural salvage it's hard to see what's to be done.

Of course the blame really rests with the new owners of the houses – nowadays likely to be young turks from the City with too much money and no knowledge of what to do with it. So decent nineteenth-century houses get ripped apart and turned into the modish and featureless dwellings that figure in the glossy brochures that daily clog the letterbox. Some houses in this street have been 'reno-vated' three or four times over so that there can't be an original fea-ture left. Trees are taken down, massive conservatories erected and with the cornice in the skip and the surrounds all gone, every house will have the same dull white-walled interior.

11 October. R. still ill when I leave at nine fifteen to introduce the film to an audience of sixteen- and seventeen-year-olds and afterwards do Q&A. There are good questions from the audience and James C. soon has them laughing. One question is about what scenes had to be cut and would I like one day to have a Writer's Cut of the film. A Director's Cut and (if there is such a thing) a Writer's Cut implies that there has been some disagreement or pressure exerted before the finished film reaches the screen – the Director's Cut a kind of rearguard action, 'This is the film as I'd really imagined it.' With us there was no such disagreement. What cuts there were – before shooting and afterwards – were all discussed and agreed on with no one producer, director, writer or actors pushing their own version or cut. The scenes I miss weren't the ones that were cut before shooting but odd bits from shots we had intended to include.

One is the toothy art mistress, Mrs Bibby (beautifully played by Penelope Wilton), who after trying in vain to get the scholarship boys interested in art is left chuntering to herself:

'The best way to teach art would be to ban it. Put it out of bounds. That way they'd be sneaking in here all the time. Art is furtive, unofficial; it's something on the side.'

She puts a bowl of hyacinths viciously on the table –

'The mistake is to put it on the syllabus. Yes, Hazel, thank you very much.'

Another casualty was a scene where Wilkes, the evangelical PE master (Adrian Scarborough), has all the boys hanging upside down on the wall bars except the plump Timms who can't manage this feat.

'Frame yourself, lad,' says Wilkes. 'They won't want you at Oxford unless you can hang upside down on the wall bars.'

15 October. In the course of an interview last week Andy Knott was asked if he minded that there was now another company taking *The History Boys* on tour.

'Well, put it this way. We're in the Dorchester. They're in Dorchester.'

25 October. 'It's good to talk' is the most specious and misleading injunction since 'All you need is love'. It has prompted millions of opinionated and empty-headed people to take to the internet and regale the world with their fatuities. It is not good to talk. Most of the time it's better to keep quiet . . . and that includes playwrights.

8 November. To Oxford with Bodley's librarian emeritus, David Vaisey, to look at the muniment room in New College. It's in the tower above the hall and chapel, with access by a spiral staircase so narrow that the two huge ten-foot chests which used to house the deeds and documents must have been built in situ in the fifteenth century. There are also two complete medieval tiled floors. Down the road we toil up another spiral staircase to the muniment room in the Bodleian, where there is no medieval floor but a delicate early eighteenth-century ceiling that might have come out of Claydon House, part of the fall-out after Gibbs built the Radcliffe Camera, a building which still astonishes me now as much as it did when I was a young man.

That young man turns out to have records here, too, as Simon Bailey the archivist shows me my original October 1954 application for a reader's ticket, my best twenty-one-year-old handwriting making me wince even fifty years later. I have other records, too, which ought to make me wince but don't, as here is a character assessment of me written by G. D. G. Hall, the law tutor and sub-rector of

Exeter who was later president of Corpus, a document originated when I went, as everyone did at the beginning of their third year, for an interview at the University Appointments Board in order to be placed for a job. Derek Hall's remarks on my character seem wholly fair and very perceptive: 'amiable, funny but not a first-class mind'. He ends up, ambiguously, 'not yet ready to play about with people', meaning, I think, that I wasn't fit for an appointment that carried any sort of authority. Though if there'd been more 'playing about with people', not just falling hopelessly in love with them, I might have been more fitted for Life back then in 1957. It's a source for Jake Balokowsky, and, under the Freedom of Information Act, an available one, apparently.

11 November. Catch part of the Festival of Remembrance from the Albert Hall but find myself switching over less from inattention than because it's more vulgar, sentimental and, inevitably, hypocritical than I can ever remember. The problem facing the producer is to find a way of commemorating the most recently dead without getting into the rights and wrongs of the circumstances in which the deaths occurred. If in doubt, he cuts to World War One and Two where we're on safe ground. After the messy roadside bombs of Iraq it's almost a comfort to be back among the tombstones and immaculate graves of Flanders.

Unsurprisingly there is not much room for jokes, but these days audiences need to be diverted, the Palladium and the Royal Albert Hall not all that far apart. So some elaborately dishevelled youth sings his heart out, along with another dewy-eyed group, and Chris de Burgh leads the nation in 'Abide with Me'. It's the Royal Sobriety Show.

As the various contingents march in and fill the arena, one longs for some representatives from Families Against the War, which would at least bring a breath of honesty to the proceedings. As always at such ceremonies, the dead don't get a proper look-in and having made their sacrifice are now taken to be somehow on the reserve, endorsing the continuing wars of the living. Overseeing it all is the bishop of Manchester, who has the face of a rugger forward and presumably the skin to match, because the ironies of the ceremony are inescapable. No wonder the Queen looks grim throughout, though as the royal party rises the one whose thoughts one would like to share is Princess Anne.

20 November. Two young men sit on the sand box by the wall and roll a joint, and a pretty large one too. They get down out of view and I see the smoke rising for a while. Then the younger one stands up, is mildly sick in the gutter and, wiping his mouth and laughing, he and his companion go off down the street.

24 November, Rome. Sitting on a bench in the Pantheon while R. and Lynn fight their way round through hordes of schoolchildren (and it isn't even half-term) I get talking to a young man who turns out to be a stonemason at Ely, working on the restoration of the cathedral. He has been redoing some of the medieval carvings and says that the higher up the carving the more lewd the carvers' imagination. One capital he has had to restore had a devil biting off someone's balls, and he needed the chapter's permission before he could reproduce it. He thinks the medieval carvers enjoyed such licence because the scaffolding on which they worked was so rickety the architect or the master mason was reluctant to risk much hands-on supervision and just let them get on with it.

25 November. The last day of a Caravaggio exhibition in Santa Maria del Popolo and the queue goes right round the church. We don't wait, but notice that the people queuing pay as much attention to the preparatory display of screens and moving images leading up to the actual paintings which, when they eventually reach them, they're rapidly hustled past. Come away depressed but are then cheered when, turning down a side street, we pass what looks like the back of a shabby garage. Except that the walls of these seemingly industrial premises are studded with architectural fragments – bits of moulding, tracery, the broken sculpture of a head or a hand and of all periods. The supposed 'garage' turns out to be the one-time studio of Canova.

26 November. On, on. Which is one of the things Simon Sainsbury used to say, I think – his memorial service last Tuesday (21 November) at Christ Church Spitalfields.

Knowing it was likely to be socially very grand makes me not look forward to it, particularly since I scarcely knew Simon – and only through sitting next to him at the NG Trustees. But it turns out unexpectedly enjoyable and even uplifting for all sorts of reasons, some of them incidental. I'm put right at the front and so have a close view of the quintet who are playing and able to see, as I was with the Medici, the undercurrents and tensions between the players and the signals that pass between them, particularly from the first violin. Another sort of direction evident with the choir, brought over, I think, from the Royal Chapel at Windsor who, there being no choir stalls at Spitalfields, stand in a circle in the manner of carol singers. Some are tiny, several are odd but all so serious and concentrated they seem oblivious of any other consideration but the music, and indifferent almost to that – just opening their mouths and out it comes. Wholly absorbing to watch at close quarters, though the setting lacks atmosphere and however meticulously restored the church seems dull and, perhaps inevitably, on the corporate side.

I sit next to Neil MacGregor who delivers an outstanding address – reads it, which is unusual for him, but so well and naturally with most of what he has to say about Simon – his multifarious and countrywide philanthropies for instance – entirely unknown to me.

I go part of the way back in a cab with Neil and I ask him about his job, which he revels in and which is not simply confined to the British Museum. He's practically a cultural ambassador or an UNESCO representative, just back from the Sudan where he's one of a group surveying the antiquities likely to be submerged by a new dam, currently being constructed on the Nile. The problems though are not simply to do with cultural artefacts and he talks of the villagers the dam will displace, who, although they have been told what is to happen and for whom alternative accommodation has been provided, have nevertheless no idea of what this being uprooted will mean. The human and the antiquarian problems in Sudan are mirrored in Iraq where the Director of Antiquities, a Syrian Christian, single-handedly defended his museums against the depredations consequent on the invasion and the war. Now in the aftermath he has had to ransom his two sons who have been kidnapped and despairing of carrying on in such circumstances has left Iraq for Damascus, ultimately hoping to get to America. As Neil pours this out, the words tumbling out of him as they do I feel both inadequate and ill-informed and it's perhaps as well he doesn't travel all the way but gets out at St Pancras to go to the Museum – looking, as he always looks, absurdly young but, I would have thought, one of the most remarkable men of his generation.

2 January. Catching up on the literary round-ups at the year's end I'm struck as so often by how cantankerous the world of literature is, and how smarmy, both backbiting and back-scratching much more so than the theatre or show business generally. I'm sure this is because actors don't moonlight as critics in the way novelists or writers do. Few writers are reviewers *tout court*, most having other jobs as novelists, historians, biographers or whatever, and writing reviews simply because they need or want the money. It's harmless enough but it makes literature a nastier world.

8 January. Reading Zachary Leader's biography of Kingsley Amis, though not with much relish. She was 'a good drinker', Leader says of the Swansea original of Mrs Gruffydd-Williams, and while one feels this is very much an Amis-type judgement, it's not one Leader dissents from – or dissents from sufficiently, drink and good fellowship equated throughout. Never having been able to drink much, partly through not having been brought up to it but also having had a duodenal ulcer as a young man, I suppose I feel disqualified, or somehow got at, as I did when I had to do a poetry reading for Amis in 1976, though then it was his self-consciously chappish manner I found hardest to cope with, never knowing if it was piss-taking quite.

It's stated in the book that Denis Brogan, fellow of Peterhouse, broadcaster and expert on the USA, used to boast that he had fucked in forty-six of the fifty states. I wish I'd known this in 1952, when in my first weeks of National Service Basic Training I was in the next bed to a boy called Huggins, a steelworker from Sheffield whose frequent boast was that he had 'had his hole' in six or seven towns and cities, which he would then list. At the time I was less than impressed and probably rather prissy about this conflation of lust and topography – had I known about Brogan (a regular with Alistair Cooke on *Transatlantic Quiz*), I might have treated Huggins with more respect.

11 January. Picture in the *Guardian* of an American soldier manning a gun in Baghdad, stencilled on the front of the gun a death's head. That's why the war is lost.

14 January. I'd written in my diary in this month's *LRB* about the puns John Bird and John Fortune are addicted to in their TV show, instancing the employee of the Brighton Dolphinarium who was sacked as 'not fit for porpoise'. John Bird rings this morning to say the audience narrowly missed getting an even worse one: the woman who went off to start a crèche on an Indian reservation in Canada but was sacked as 'not fit for papoose'.

25 January. I've taken to eating the occasional date, though it's not a fruit I wholly like. Mam used to eat them when we were little, bought in small compressed bricks, one of their attractions being that they were not on the ration or even on points. It's the texture I've never altogether cared for, too mushy and spreadable. Also the sheen on some of them. Very good for one, of course, which is why I eat them now, and it reminds me how ahead of her time my mother was in the food she ate herself and tried to pass off on us – the Allinson wholemeal bread she got from a confectioner's on Armley Moor, the prunes that were often in soak on the draining board, fads as I thought even as a boy of ten, picked up from Miss Thompson, a herbalistic lady living in the Hallidays who used to give Dad burdock and suchlike 'for his blood'.

1 February. To Westminster Abbey for Michael Mayne's memorial service. Though I'm not reading I still get in a fluster lest I'm late and whether I shall want to pee, so in the finish I'm glad I'm not contributing as that would have made it worse. Happy to see the nave is cleared of its new and dreadful chairs, though whether it's simply for this occasion not plain. Seated in the front row in the choir next to P. Routledge (who is reading) and James Roose-Evans. Patrick Garland arrives and lastly Rupert.

The choir is superb, particularly in the opening, Walton's 'Set me as a seal upon thine heart' which I don't ever remember hearing. The hymns are to me as unknown as the ones at Michael's funeral with the possible exception of 'Tell out, my soul, the greatness of the Lord', the tune I see written by Walter Greatorex (1877–1949), presumably the same Walter Greatorex whom I was this very morning reading about in Humphrey Carpenter's biography of Benjamin Britten. Greatorex a master at Gresham's School, Holt and who was a comfort and an ally of S. Spender when he was a pupil, was at first anyway no fan of Britten's though he ended up being influenced by him. Routledge reads and Timothy West and Pru S. and there's a good address, an encomium really by Canon Sagovsky whom I don't know. Alison M. gives me a little smile as she comes down the aisle by which I'm absurdly pleased (and I'm sure it shows on my face) – it's like being thrown the bride's bouquet – but in all R. is far more impressed by the service than I am who feels shut out – but R. always feels shut out by religion anyway.

Good eirenic verse by Frederick William Faber in one of the hymns and an implied rebuke to the evangelicals.

> For the love of God is broader
> than the measure of man's mind;
> and the heart of the Eternal
> is most wonderfully kind.
> But we make his love too narrow
> by false limits of our own;
> and we magnify his strictness
> with a zeal he will not own.

I owe it to Michael M. that I know – or knew – so much about the Abbey but queuing at the end to say hello to Alison and the family, I am looking at the monuments in the nave and find I don't know where anything is any more and that it's all gone from my mind like a script from a play one was in once and has now forgotten.

7 *February*. Reading Humphrey Carpenter's life of Benjamin Britten, I imagine you could write a pretty scandalous play about Aldeburgh – which at times doubles as Moscow under Stalin. One of the many to fall out of favour was Eric Crozier, one of the founders of the Festival. When its history came to be written by Imogen Holst (who was always besotted with Britten) any mention of Crozier's part in the enterprise was omitted – as were the other 'corpses'.

The Amis and the Britten biographies are in different ways demonstrations of the allowances that are made for talent; or in Britten's case, genius. Neither is particularly edifying and with Britten especially one wishes the many decent people with which he was surrounded had stood up to him more than they did. As it was they bade sad farewells to the ones who fell out of favour and huddled together to await their own turn.

20 *February*. There have been good reviews in the *Guardian* and the *Telegraph* for *Enjoy*, Chris Luscombe's production at Watford which I talked to him and his designer about before they started work but know no more about than that. He sounds to have made it work, which we didn't manage to do back in 1980 though M. Billington singles out 'Ms Craig' as the weakest link in the plot: 'there is no real tension between his dual role as scientific observer and family outcast'.

This is fair, though there is more to be said for the set-up than I made plain. I've always wanted to write *Oedipus* as a comedy and that was in my mind when I was putting together *Enjoy*. The father accuses the son of trying to kill him at Four Lane Ends – the name of an actual place in Leeds but also the setting for Laius' encounter with his son Oedipus. Oedipus is unrecognised by his real parents and this, as much as any advertisement for his sexual orientation accounts for Ms Craig's drag. He/she needs to be unrecognised when he/she returns home – though as in a dream, the mother knows this is her son besides his being someone else.

It's not well worked out – it was the first play I'd written when I didn't always quite know what I was doing – and I knew it was going wrong back in 1980 when the cast had long discussions about transvestites and transsexuals. 'He's just in drag, that's all' was my contribution but this wasn't thought to be helpful.

The notion of observing ordinary behaviour at close quarters which was thought to be far-fetched in 1980 is now, thanks to reality TV, a much more general concern and it's in this sense that the play has come into its own. Why it's called *Enjoy* I can't think – it was an exclusively American or a New York phrase in 1980. I think I just wanted the play to seem happier than I perhaps made it. 'Cheer Up' would have been just as good. It's on the same principle that *Lady of Letters* ends with Miss R. in prison saying 'I'm so . . . *happy*.'

21 February. On the hundredth anniversary of his birth a lot of tosh being talked about Auden as poet of Cumbria. Auden couldn't have inhabited his ideal landscape, however nurturing he found the idea of it. Everything about him was urban. He wanted opera, libraries, restaurants, rent boys – all the appurtenances of civilisation. You don't find them in Penrith.

Never underestimate the role of the will in the artist's life. Talent you can dispense with but not will. Some artists are all will.

1 March. To a fund-raising do for the National held at the Roundhouse. I'm next to a nice man, Ayub Khan-Din, the author of *East is East* who's a bit of a fan but for whom I think I may be a disappointment as I can't quite be the expatriate Northern boy he wants me to be. Also at our table is Helen Mirren whose entrance is greeted with a standing ovation, which she takes gracefully and does it well not overdoing the humility (as I would have done) or being over-grand, and in the course of the evening I very much come round to her – particularly a speech she makes about the kind of theatre matinées in the provinces (in her case Scotland); if there is one child in the audience entranced by the stage (as I was in Leeds and she in Scotland), that is what the funds they are raising are about.

And they do raise funds – bidding orchestrated by Harry Dalmeny, few items going for less than £20,000 – including the original script for *Cream Cracker Under the Settee* I'd sent, which fetches £30,000.

5 March, Lacock, Wiltshire. In cold bright sunshine this Sunday morning tourists are already arriving and as the church bells ring a family, father mother boy and girl, each with a prayer book, thread their way through the visitors on their way to morning service.

A heartening sight, a way of life still going on. Or are they, like the houses, dependents of the National Trust, conspicuous attendance at church a condition of their tenancy? [This and the related entry for 4 March 2005 led eventually to the play *People* (2012).]

Across the deer-grazed fields the honey-coloured Gothick front of Lacock Abbey home to the pioneers of photography, the first to catch life on the wing, their house, their family, this village – to which now people flock, the car park nearly full and it's not even half past ten.

A craft fair in the parish hall and in the wide high doorway of the tithe barn a trestle table with plants for sale. (Put your money in the box.)

Oh England.

The village shop, handily named The Village Shop. Subsisting on what you forgot to get/slipped your mind at Tesco; a half-timbered hotel, serving hearty meals with some of the authentic Tudor rollick; hearts of (limed) oak.

A red kite swoops cosmetically above the abbey ruins and seeing the car park emptying prepares perhaps to shut up shop when the visitors have departed.

Unusual among the employees of the National Trust in that he has a tattoo.

Nature red in tooth and claw, the red one of several subtle/discreet shades gloss or matt on offer by Farrow and Ball.

Gifted (as we say nowadays) to the Trust in 1944, the house/village and its appurtenances an emblem of that way of life (as pictured particularly on the railway posters of the time) that we were then fighting our way across Europe to defend – the big house, the tenant farms, the village with its tithe barn – England as it had always been, and which now the people – I'm sorry, the *community* – comes to savour.

In the park (but well out of sight of the house) is a village – or what seems to be a village, the street, the pub, the well-tended gardens, the village shop. Children wait for the school bus. A woman walks her dog as a man putting on some clothes bursts out of a house pursued by a woman who abuses him. The children at the bus stop are incurious as the man gets into a car and drives violently away, followed to begin with by the woman still hurling abuse. As the car accelerates out of sight she walks back, passing the children at the bus stop and saying, 'And what are you staring at? Have you never seen marriage before?' She goes inside the house, slamming the door.

9 *March*. Papers full of a row over casualties from Iraq dumped in NHS hospitals where they have been overlooked and neglected, the consequence, it's suggested, of there nowadays being no longer any military hospitals. I'm not sure when there were, that military establishments were that much better. I remember Stan, Aunty Myra's husband who was in the regular RAF. Diagnosed with inoperable lung cancer at the first-rate Midhurst Chest Hospital he was then transferred to an RAF hospital at Uxbridge where he lengthily died

in far more pain than he need have done – the philosophy of such places presumably being that part of taking the Queen's shilling was the suffering of more pain than pampered civilians could stand. Now Midhurst is a plush private hospital and Uxbridge, I hope, no longer exists though the indifference to military patients' welfare seems to live on.

16 March, Yorkshire. As age weakens the bladder I find myself having to pee more often, which, when I'm out in the country in a car, is no problem, though like a dog or a creature marking its territory, I do find myself often choosing the same spot. One regular place of worship is a lane on the outskirts of Leeds between Arthington and Harewood. It's a nice location and of some historic interest, as in the sixteenth century the land belonged to an ex-Cluniac monastery that was among the properties (they included Kirkstall Abbey) granted to Thomas Cranmer on the death of Henry VIII. It wasn't actually included in the royal will but was part of the general share-out that occurred then to fulfil the wishes supposedly expressed by Henry VIII on his deathbed. Not far away is Harewood House (where I do not pee). It's the home of the Lascelles family, an ancestor of which, John Lascelles, blew the gaff on Catherine Howard, the king's fifth wife, but was later culled himself in the purge of evangelicals during that dreadful monarch's last years. I watch two of the now well-established red kites tumbling about the sky above the Harewood estate, home these days to *Emmerdale*, that hotbed of the lust, murder and arson so typical of rural North Yorkshire.

22 March. Then via the M62 (a constant stream of traffic but moving at least) thirty miles to the Saddleworth turn-off where I'm met by David Makin, for whom I've agreed to do an evening to raise money to fund a public enquiry against a wind farm to be sited on the unspoilt moors above Denshaw. They're unspoilt certainly but so bleak and without cover or shelter I get perishingly cold talking to a journalist from the *Manchester Evening News* and having endless photographs taken, fatuously pointing at the threatened moorland. Saddleworth is less of a place than a federation of villages – Denshaw, Delph, Dobcross, Uppermill – the hall where I speak a largish place packed out. I read for three quarters of an hour then answer questions, sign books etc. and set off back at 10 p.m. David Makin's daughter and a cheerful Cézanne-like boy called Dante have agreed to lead me over the moors on a short cut to Oxenhope and Keighley. It's an extraordinary journey – the moors so high and bleak and deserted, the road along I suppose Blackstone Edge and far below the sprinkling of lights in the various houses and villages that cling to the folds and valleys of these mountains. It's Ted Hughes country and indeed we go through Mytholmroyd en route for Hebden Bridge – in a landscape that's but for the hills out of (the much derided by me) Sebald, i.e. not a soul about, the towns and villages deserted, no one to be seen and only the occasional car.

Tabitha leaves me at a point where there is supposedly a straight run over to Oxenhope – but, of course, I miss a turning and instead of heading across the moors find myself plunging down into the valley again – through Midgley and Ripponden on the road to Halifax. Knowing it's at least an hour and a half before I get home – and with no food in prospect and frightened of falling asleep – had I passed an hotel I'd have stopped there. But this part of the West Riding doesn't do hotels. Eventually I'm on the home stretch and phone R. from Coniston Cold – but don't actually get home till half past midnight.

23 March. Papers full of the sailors taken into custody by the Iranians for supposedly being in their territorial waters. Who knows what the truth of that is, though it gives the papers and the television a chance to rehearse the indignities heaped on similar sailors, taken prisoner a few years ago on the same charge (and one which turned out to be true). Then they were blindfolded and paraded in front of the camera before being taken under guard to Tehran – i.e. much the same (though milder) treatment than the Americans mete out to those who happened to be in the wrong place in Afghanistan – who were hooded, and taken not just to Tehran but halfway round the world, where they still are and waiting for trial.

No one makes this comparison of course – though the innocence of those taken captive is, in most cases, approximately the same. But one are decent, honourable British sailors with wives and children waiting anxiously at home. The others are brown men in robes who can't really expect anything better.

No one in the House of Commons uses the opportunity of the Prime Minister's statement on the 'kidnapped' sailors to draw attention to our own sorry record in conniving at similar kidnappings in Afghanistan or wherever the Guantánamo suspects were picked up or rendered. No one has the nerve, I suppose, as they would inevitably be shouted down. The papers full of pieces on the worried families, a mother separated from her children – all of which is true provided it's realised that this is worry and separation we are responsible for in exactly the same way – and have been inflicting for five years and more. 'Ah,' say the military and the H. of Commons, 'but our boys were in uniform.'

29 March. One unforeseen blessing of the war in Iraq is the settlement in Northern Ireland. Blair can hardly claim the credit, as it was only when the focus moved to the Middle East that there was real progress towards agreement in Northern Ireland. The spotlight tempts politicians to perform; shift it and they can just get on with the job.

31 March. Jehovah's Witnesses blitz the street and when they ring the bell I lie on the floor until the coast is clear. I imagine they're used to this sort of response and even when someone is unwary enough to open them the door the exchange is generally pretty curt.

In one house in the street, though, they are assured of a warmer welcome, as Jonathan M. is never wont to turn down the chance of a debate and likes nothing better than a brisk canter through the arguments against the existence of God and the literal truth of the Bible. Two hapless evangelists had just had half an hour of this and were staggering down the steps licking their wounds when they spotted, parked in the street, a Ferrari. In some relief they were admiring this superb machine, not realising the scourge of God still had his eye upon them. 'And you shouldn't be looking at that,' J. calls from the porch. 'That's Things of This World. You should be above that!'

3 April, Gatwick. 'You're not supposed to have this.' The tone is reproving. 'You can't take that.' What I can't take is a nearly empty tin of shaving foam, which the immigration officer triumphantly confiscates. It would hardly matter except it's the last of a series of setbacks, humiliations beginning at 6 a.m. in the Hilton, Gatwick where we are forced to stay as the flight goes at 8.30 – check-in time 7 a.m. The bedroom alarm rings early and cannot be stopped even when I dismantle the box and take out the battery. It's only then that I realise what is ringing is our own alarm. At the check-in we are told blandly that the BA flight is over-booked ('We often over-book' given as an explanation not an apology) and we are put on standby and so can't get any breakfast or even a cup of coffee. We are cleared half an hour before departure with massive queues at security and only get there along Gatwick's huge escalator bridge in the nick of time. It's only then at the final check-in that the attendant asks for an autograph and, having crammed us in right at the back, comes to chat about the car journeys my *Winnie the Pooh* have enlivened. Celebrity is never there when you want it.

4 April, Bologna. The recommended Anna-Maria trattoria being closed we eat at another establishment in Via delle Belle Arte, which might have been Sardinian or some ethnic version of Italian food but it's delicious and the waitress who's possibly the owner, delightful so this is a good start. Then we wander through the back streets largely occupied by the University of San Stefano, a superb series of linked churches. In the first church there's a typical Italian scene going on with a large TV monitor screen blocking the steep altar steps, an engineer doing a sound check in English ('Wan. Chew. Tree. Wan Chew Tree') interspersed with mad bursts of pop – this on (and perhaps helping to commemorate) the Tuesday in Holy Week. Through a little door is the adjoining church, vaulted in brick and almost wholly given over to a pulpit built above the shrine of St Petronius, and resting on wonderful lions. Outside is a quadrangle – the Cortile di Pilate supposedly a replica of the one in which Pilate washed his hands, but more remarkable for the elaborate inlaid and ornamented brickwork of the church wall – bricks treated like tiles and laid in diamond and herringbone patterns, with roundels and stars and chequerboards – all in lovely worn warm red brick. In the churches the columns are bound and belted in ancient iron. There is a museum we briefly look round though Rupert is put off by the young monk in charge of the books and postcards, who has an edge to him suggesting that religion is not the only thing in his life.

5 April. We make several journeys by train – to Ravenna, to Ferrara and at no point does anyone ask to see our tickets. Nor is there the barrage of threatening announcements that precedes the departure of GNER trains – that your ticket must be for this day and this train and if it isn't you will have to pay the full fare without benefit of any rail card or concession, the philosophy behind rail travel in Britain 'You're not going to get away with it'. In Italy nobody cares. Because the one-carriage slow train from Ferrara is crowded the conductor tells passengers to sit in First (which is indistinguishable from Standard anyway). And the fares must shame anyone from the UK – a third of what they would be here.

6 April, Good Friday. In the Museo Civico Medievale at the top of the wonderful (and utterly unheralded and unexpected) Via Galliera are various tombstones to medieval teachers and doctors, wholly secular in appearance in that they show the dead man teaching in the centre of a class of students. The students are reading, studying books under the direction of the dead master. It's not a scene one could imagine finding in an English church – though it might occur, I suppose, in an illuminated manuscript. Nor do I remember ever having seen these particular sermons in stone reproduced.

Later we go to Ravenna where in S. Apollinare, despite the queue of saints and apostles lining up down the nave what takes the eye is a little mosaic house at the north-western end, with a series of (almost French) windows, the last one a doorway of uninterrupted greenish-blue as it might be looking out to sea – which it probably was as Ravenna was by the sea then. But this depthless blue is like Larkin's

> deep blue air, that shows
> Nothing, and is nowhere, and is endless

and it's a huge window which (unlike the queue of saints, bearing their crosses) is of now.

16 April. Back in Camden Town and here on the trees in front of the house come the lime leaves which every year regardless of global warming unhurriedly shake out their little handkerchiefs to the day and almost to the minute.

18 April. In the clothes room I go through R.'s coats on the rack where there are generally one or two moths, particularly on his fur coat, and those out of reach on the dado I impale on a long brush. Moth-hunting has now become an obsession – though a useful one: yesterday I woke in the night and crept upstairs to kill two or three on the roof – the females, I fancy, fatter and darker than the males.

I talked last night to Debo about it who said it was Decca Mitford (I think) who called them 'Mawth' but had no other remedies to offer.

19 April. A handsome builder's boy waiting with a van just over the wall whiles away the time by practising some complicated dance step. It seems to involve a lot of little jumps, and in the beat before he does the jumps he snatches a look up and down the street to make sure nobody catches him at it. As he gets more confident, though, the steps get wilder and he dances to his reflection in the side of the van this bright warm morning. Now the rest of the crew turn up and he performs his routine for them, which they watch with indulgent smiles.

21 April, Yorkshire. I go out with my pail of salt and water looking for slugs. They don't require much hunting as there are dozens, huge creatures the size of turds, which, luxuriating in my absence, loll on the plants, sprawled on top of the poppies for instance while the rest wire into the alliums, so many of them that the poor plants are bowed under their weight.

22 April. Despite having (so far) survived a serious illness, when faced with real pain I tend to give up. I had gone to bed feeling fine but wake around six with what seemed to be indigestion which then worked itself down to my stomach with a real ache that came in spasms. A hot-water bottle didn't do much or cups of tea and I lay there for two hours quite happy to die. The cause, insofar as I could think of one was some stewed pears I'd had for supper, some hard and even though cooked not quite ripe. Then, straight afterwards I'd gone out into the garden slug hunting which involved a good deal of bending down with the torch searching the rhubarb and the alliums and putting the culprits into a bucket of salted water. Now I was paying for it and lying in bed, which I did most of the morning.

I couldn't see I would be able to get back to London. Slowly I come round but checking the train times before we leave find there are no direct trains from Leeds – 'planned engineering works' – though not planned sufficiently to warn passengers in advance, i.e. when they booked their tickets two days before as we did. Advised to go via Sheffield and a Virgin cross-country train to St Pancras instead we take the almost empty train to Peterborough, the guard having a good time because we are almost alone on the train. 'I don't want you two lads beating up the carriage. I know it's the ideal opportunity.'

30 April–1 May. To Essential Music in Great Chapel Street to record *The Uncommon Reader*, which Gordon House, former head of drama at BBC Radio, has adapted and is producing. What other readers are like I've no idea, but I always feel I am a sound editor's nightmare, breaking off in the middle of a sentence to start again, redoing paragraphs when there's technically no need and almost out of superstition, my technique (or want of it) so scrappy I must make work.

None of this will show, I always tell myself, and it doesn't but no thanks to me, and I'm sure if I weren't lazy and rehearsed the script properly by reading it aloud it would be both quicker to do and the result smoother and more satisfying. But I sight-read as often as not which, since it's mostly something I've written, doesn't much matter and I generally get away with it. Still, I always think my style, such as it is, is a compound of all my deficiencies, but maybe that's what style is anyway.

Gielgud didn't record like this, for all his skill, accenting and phrasing even the most trivial script in order to get the rhythm right. And Alec Guinness would work on a text for weeks, walking round the garden listening to the tape and saying the words out loud.

1 May. Unspoken dialogue: We are in the car when a pretty girl crosses too slowly. If I'd been bold (or insane) I'd have wound the window down and said, 'Listen. We're nancies. Big tits mean nothing to us.'

2 May. A delight to sit in the garden particularly at tea-time. I hope when I am gone no one will suggest that moving house was a shock still less a mistake. Though there is no room quite as beautiful as the ground floor of 23 G.C. with the evening sun slanting through the blinds, taken for all in all – situation, garden, the pleasure of the other rooms (e.g. kitchen and bedroom) this is a much more enjoyable house to live in. It doesn't look as nice from the outside, the garden gets less sun and the stairs are much steeper (and will get steeper as time goes on I'm sure) but there is no doubt in my mind that the change has been for the better.

3 May. Lord Browne disgraced largely thanks to the *Mail on Sunday* and the bribery of a Canadian youth. The newspapers painstakingly explain why we should feel no sympathy for him, but if the *Mail* chose to target Heinrich Himmler I would tend to be on his side.

The young man's name is Chevalier, which was the name of the man, friendship with whom helped to ruin Robert Oppenheimer's career. Chevalier was not gay but equally reprehensibly a Communist.

9 May. Seventy-three, which I find almost inconceivable, while feeling every minute of it. R. who was very put out by the clumsy details of the bookshelves currently being built in my study is much mollified this morning when Aaron, the young carpenter (who keeps a cow) is ready to adapt the design with no chuntering at all. For my birthday R. gives me two lovely tiles, a boy walking and pointing and another of a gardener, the book on Edwin Smith, which I expected and a group of tiles with a primitive design of a cat framed and supposed to be nineteenth-century Dutch but it could easily be a century earlier – and will suit the kitchen (where we already have a cow) very well. No calls other than from director Archie Powell, which gives real pleasure and I wish I had something we could do together.

11 May, Long Crichel. Yesterday as I was driving down to Dorset (with no radio) the prime minister had gone up to Trimdon and his constituency of Sedgefield in order to bring his term of office to a close, 'resign' altogether too un-positive a word. The newspapers have been quite kind, but his speech, while ostensibly looking at the state of England, is so self-centred it confirms what one has thought before, that to Blair the real importance of his premiership is as a stage in his spiritual journey. He tells the nation, assures it rather, that we are 'a country . . . at home in its own skin', that 'this country is a blessed nation,' even that 'this is the greatest nation on earth.'

This is virtually the opposite of what the last five years in particular have made me feel. It's only a few months since I was writing in my diary that sometimes being English it felt as if one smelled. To Tony Blair, though, it is of roses.

Note how in the south-west even the humblest hamlet nowadays seems to boast a business park.

An element of Morrissey's appeal, particularly for his Northern (or poorer) audiences is his *rawness*. Whatever success he has had has never given him any sort of veneer, no coating of wealth or sophistication. He still looks like a plasterer, or his mate.

12 May. Driving through rain-soaked Dorset we stop at Puddletown and the church there which is full of fixtures and character: a chantry chapel with alabaster tombs and the remains of what looks like its own reredos; there are good pews and lovely Laudian altar rails. But the most evocative of the fittings are high up on the west face of the chancel arch where hang two rusty bits of chain. On these chains, prior to the Reformation, was hung the Lenten Veil which was used to hide the sanctuary in the week before Easter. They're scarcely visible and of no picturesque appeal at all, but that these fastenings should have survived since at least the fifteenth century, a relic still of a ceremony that went out under Edward VI, is as vivid and evocative as any screen or wall painting (though there are those too).

Of course Puddletown figures in Hardy's history and there are names on the war memorial – Sparks, for instance – of his cousins and relatives, the church figuring among his inspirations much as Methley did for Henry Moore.

14 May. Another cold wet day and I flounder around with Auden/ Britten getting nowhere while feeling it is intellectually, musically and theatrically beyond me. If only one could be given a sign, or come to recognise a sign, that a work you are entering on will be seen to completion. As it is I fear these days of reading and taking notes, with occasional snatches of dialogue, will be like so many of the last forty years – likely to come to nothing and at best be mulch.

15 May. Richard Beer puts a postcard through the door with an overheard remark, 'What do you mean, you can't talk about Proust before breakfast?' I reply telling him that we've just been at Long Crichel, a house where in its heyday talking about Proust before breakfast was practically *obligatory*.

16 May. And this morning I make what I hope is a breakthrough with the Auden/Britten play when it occurs to me that what Britten would be coming to see Auden about is not just to say farewell or talk over old times but to ask him to do the libretto for *Death in Venice*. It brings all the difficulties they had with each other into focus and also gives the first part of the play with the two boys more of a point. But it's difficult – and I dare not start reading about it, still less listening to the opera. It's one of the plays that I shall have to write before I write it – or at any rate do the research for it. But go down to Parkway shopping for supper feeling so alive again and so not old and with that feeling I rarely get nowadays, of 'I hope I will be given the time to do this.'

17 May. Outside the bank I see the local vicar, his arms full of balloons and a Sooty teddy bear in the crook of his arm. 'It's Ascension Day,' he explains.

21 May. An absurd accident. I am cycling down Gloucester Avenue this morning when my raincoat catches between the brake block and the wheel and brings me to a halt. Normally when this happens a step or two back reverses the wheel and frees the coat but not this morning, and it's jammed. As a preliminary to loosening it I try to take the coat off but can't because I'm tethered to the bike, which now falls over, pulling me with it. I land painfully on my bum and lie there for a moment or two like Kafka's beetle, waving my legs in the air. Another passing pensioner, seeing my plight, goes to a friend's house for a pair of scissors in order to cut me free, except that the friend is out. So I limp home, lifting the back wheel and manhandling the bike, eventually managing to free the wheel without having to cut the coat. It's now ten thirty; my coat is filthy and so am I. I imagine that in the future there is going to be more of this.

23 May. Ros Chatto, my agent, calls to say I have been offered a role in the BBC Andrew Davies adaptation of *Fanny Hill*. She reads through this raunchy script finding no mention of the part for which I'm slated until she gets to the very final scene, where Fanny meets an old and respectable gentleman (me) whom she fucks to extinction, then inherits his fortune and lives happily ever after.

'I don't think so, do you darling?' asks Mrs Chatto. 'That's not quite how we see ourselves at this stage in our career.' The truth is I don't have much of an urge to act and I've always thought myself a bit of a fraud as an actor. Age, though, does make actors less choosy. When Gielgud was in his eighties he acted almost continuously, taking parts virtually on the cab-rank principle. Olivier did some of that, too, though restricted more by ill health. Alec Guinness definitely retired and took to writing, which was a pity as he would have excelled in small character roles if he'd allowed himself to play them. And I think he still wanted to but was held back, as he'd been all his life, by too strong a sense of self-preservation.

24 May. Reading Auden's *About the House* for the Auden/Britten play, I come across 'Accustomed in hard times to *clem*' (from 'Bestiaries Are Out'), clem meaning to starve, though I hadn't heard it since childhood when Grandma – and I think Mam – used to say 'I'm clemmed' meaning I'm starved or hungry. I thought it was dialect but it's in Chambers, origin OE.

26 May. Nowadays the road to Damascus would be called 'a steep learning curve'.

29 May. A biker delivers some proofs from Peters Fraser and Dunlop, and as I'm signing for them, asks what's my opinion of Cyril Connolly and why is it he's less well thought of than, say, twenty years ago. Because he's not long dead is the short answer and also, I suppose, because the literary scene has changed, with no one critic presiding in the way Connolly and (to a lesser extent) Raymond Mortimer did.

The only time I met Connolly was in 1968 – when my first play, *Forty Years On*, was in Brighton on its pre-West End tour. He was mentioned in the text, where it was implied he was quite short, as I'd thought he was – simply I suppose from his face, which was that of someone small and chubby. He came round to the stage door to show me that he was of average height. An almost legendary figure to me through my reading of *The Unquiet Grave*, he then sent a postcard asking me to lunch in Eastbourne but I pretended it hadn't arrived as I was too shy to go. I was thirty-four at the time and ought to have grown out of such silliness, another notable casualty of which was Jackie Kennedy, with whom Adlai Stevenson asked the cast of *Beyond the Fringe* to supper in New York in 1963. They went and I didn't. Never spelling it out to myself, I clung far too long to the notion that shyness was a virtue and not, as I came too late to see, a bore.

I don't quite spill all this out to the waiting courier, who is a graduate of UCL and shouldn't have to be biking round London delivering letters this cold wet May afternoon.

3 June. The air full of birdsong now in June as it never is in July or August perhaps because it's too hot or because the birds have built their nests, raised their young and gone. Now there is trilling and chinking and chirruping, a dialogue of persistence and variety that goes on far into the night.

5 June. My lunch owes a good deal to the Prince of Wales, whose beetroot soup I have and then his raspberry jam in my Yeo Valley yogurt. Jam and soup are both delicious, and in the middle of the yogurt I remember for no obvious reason the film *State Fair* and in particular the scatty mother. Decide she was played by Spring Byington (or was it Fay Bainter?). One or other of them anyway made some chutney that got unwittingly topped up with brandy, thus intoxicating the judges and winning the prize.

8 June (the day of Russell H.'s death, in 1988). With half an hour or so to wait before Rupert's train gets in I often go and sit in the foyer of the Queens. Once the most exclusive hotel in Leeds, nowadays it's a bit run down though the staff always friendly and no one ever bothering me when I sit in one of the alcoves answering letters.

Generally there's some function going on, a dinner dance, a wedding or a bar mitzvah and today the barriers are up outside against the arrival of Shilpa Shetty, heroine of *Big Brother* and star of some Yorkshire Bollywood film festival. Nobody questions me when I go through the barriers. ('Well, you're a celebrity yourself,' says the woman in the travel centre, 'or on the celebrity side anyway.') At the registration desk a bouncer is flirting with three pretty Indian girls taking the names of guests. 'They're all stood there waiting for Shilpa Shetty, whereas I know personally that Shilpa has been in this hotel for the last half hour.'

I go and sit on the station forecourt where an incoming clubber already slightly pissed weaves up to me. 'I bet there's lots of people've made this joke but you're not sitting on a cream cracker, are you?' Actually nobody ever has made that joke but he's gone before I can tell him and here is Rupert coming happily off the train and we go and have supper.

10 June. Dream that I am sitting outside somewhere in London when Stephen Fry comes by. He tells me that he is going out to supper with Alec Guinness. I am rather amused by this as it's a bit since Alec took me out. Alec (in a fuzzy black overcoat) now turns up and is slightly embarrassed to see me, covering his confusion by burying his head in a cashpoint where he draws some money. I then say to the ever amiable Stephen that I realise the reason why I haven't had supper with Alec myself recently is because he is dead. Stephen agrees that this would account for it and is a bit of an obstacle to their evening together but by this time Alec has disappeared, whether on account of embarrassment or sheer mortality isn't plain.

12 June. The Royal Festival Hall reopens. About a month after its unveiling in 1951 a party from my school in Leeds went down by overnight bus to the Festival of Britain where in the morning we went to a brief concert at the Festival Hall, such events taking place regularly throughout the day as well as at night, in order to show off both the architecture and the acoustics. I thought then, aged seventeen, that it was the most exciting building I'd ever been in, playful, inventive, the only experience that compared with it in wonder when I went as a child of five round the grotto at Hitchen's department store to see Santa Claus.

The music we heard that morning was pretty undemanding, kicking off with the overture to *Susanna's Secret* by Wolf-Ferrari followed by Holst's *St Paul's Suite*. Through the concerts I regularly went to in Leeds Town Hall I was a fairly sophisticated music lover and when the master in charge, the aptly named Mr Boor, said that he didn't go for all this highbrow stuff, it was a small lesson that older wasn't necessarily going to mean wiser. The next time I was in the RFH was eighteen months later when I was already in the army. Then it was Brahms's First Symphony, and one came out afterwards not onto the enchanted esplanade and playful promenades of 1951 but to acres of mud and destruction: Churchill, in a for him rare instance of political spite, had had the whole site razed to the ground. Socialism must not be seen to be fun.

13 June. On the few occasions I saw other boys naked when I was young I just thought the uncircumcised ones were poor – which they generally were. If they were not poor then why would they not have been tidied up?

15 June. A propos the conviction of the half a dozen would-be bombers this last week, no one that I have seen has commented on the fact that they all (I think) pleaded guilty. Why is this? Have they been told it will mitigate their sentence (it doesn't)? Do they think that, as with the IRA, the future will see some turnaround and they will be granted an amnesty (unlikely)? Or is it simply an expression of their desire for martyrdom? In a high-profile criminal case a clutch of guilty pleas would arouse comment. Why not here? Is it just the laziness of journalists (to which there is no bounds) – why is nobody asking?

16 June. Meet R. off the Cardiff train at Didcot and we drive through Berkshire's Edwardian countryside, red-brick villas behind high beech hedges, looking for Hamstead Marshall. An ancient buttressed wall with a stone panel dated 1665 suggests we are not far off. And here is the church above the road, the tower with an eighteenth-century look to it and a medieval chapel behind. But it's locked and no one about who could open it up. Fortunately, though, there is an opening in the wall and we look through to a huge field of barley. Marooned in it are six or eight sets of huge seventeenth-century gateposts in brick and stone, their summits crowned with urns, the posts themselves set with cartouches and carved orna-ments, a wonderful sight and all that remains, according to a guide on the noticeboard in the church porch, of the seventeenth-century mansion of Lord Craven and his architect, Balthazar Gerbier. There is a footpath across the field and we stroll through the high barley on this hot afternoon with swallows skimming low over the tops and it feels like a scene from the 1940s. It could be a Michael Powell film or a page from the diaries of Denton Welch. This isn't wholly imagination either, as it turns out that there was a camp here during the war for American airborne troops, which makes the survival of these wonderfully elaborate pillars, still here despite all that must have been literally thrown at them, even more of a miracle. The field would make a good *Brideshead*-like beginning for a film: as it is now and as it was then.

The gatepost in the middle of the barley is ringed with ancient iron railings, poppies among the barley and an elder in flower between the piers. 'Everything about this I like,' says R. 'There is nothing I would want to alter or improve. Unattended to, disregarded (though it's Grade 1 listed) it is just as the past should be.'

28 June, Yorkshire. Write to the Bradford Diocesan Registrar about a proposal to remove pews from St Andrew's Kildwick. The church is largely fourteenth-century, but a group of parishioners now wish to 'move forward' and are proposing the installation of flexible seating, a meeting room, a crèche, a kitchen, toilets and disabled access, because their 'style of worship' is not suited to the constrictions of a fourteenth-century building. I'm sure they're sincere, but the arguments being advanced are exactly the same as those of the equally sincere worshippers who wanted the stained-glass windows smashed in the seventeenth century or the rood loft removed in 1559. It didn't suit their style of worship either.

4 July. To Menwith Hill just outside Harrogate, where the veteran campaigner Lindis Percy has asked me to take part in an Independence from America demonstration on behalf of the Campaign for the Accountability of American Bases. Before I agreed (and in an effort to get out of going, I suspect) I consulted Norman Dombey who (as readers of the *LRB* know) is well versed in nuclear politics. Not that Menwith Hill – RAF Menwith Hill, as it is euphemistically called, though it's almost wholly American – is (yet) a nuclear base, only a satellite warning and surveillance station staffed entirely by US personnel and outside British control. Norman tells me that the base is currently given over to surveillance but while it probably played no part in rendition it would be vital to the US in any conflict with Iran.

So I make the journey north to nowadays not so genteel Harrogate and out into Nidderdale. It's wet and windy and the protesters, fifty or sixty in number (and also in age mostly) are corralled safely round the gate of the camp by approximately the same number of policemen, some of them grimly filming everyone in sight. The number of police shocks me, not merely because it's an implied threat to freedom of speech but also because I'm a council tax payer in this area of North Yorkshire and a hefty slice of my annual payment goes on the police precept, currently being squandered by a young policeman with big ears conscientiously filming some sixty-year-old ladies peacefully eating their sandwiches, as a second unit policeman (with smaller ears) films them from the rear. Most of the protesters (more women than men) wouldn't look out of place on a WI cake stall, though there are one or two eccentrics who may have called in en route home from Glastonbury, including an American dressed (or undressed) as a rather sturdier Gandhi; a young woman who claims to have walked all the way here from Australia; and someone else who periodically bangs a Tibetan drum. While none of this is quite up my street, I'm impressed by the general good sense and humour of the demonstration, which is not shared by the police who remain po-faced throughout. Even in the rain it's an idyllic spot, though, and standing on an improvised platform I can look across Nidderdale towards Pateley Bridge (where I was unofficially evacuated in 1939), a vista which the cluster of huge golf balls that constitute the base doesn't really spoil, they're so monumental and extraordinary. The place is seemingly deserted, with none of the 1,500 US personnel who work here showing their face.

Mark Steel speaks first and despite the rain and the cold manages to get the audience laughing, though not the policemen, who in fairness are probably cold and wet and resent having to be here at all. When it's my turn I say that I don't in principle object to the surveillance station and realise it may be necessary. But it's dirty work and if there is dirty work to be done we should do it ourselves. It's called RAF Menwith Hill and that's what it should be, under the control of the Ministry of Defence and thus (however notionally) of Parliament. As it is, though, this is sovereign America, a place in which Britain has abrogated all rights – a situation the US would never permit on its own territory. I finish by saying that after I'd agreed to speak I got another invitation for 4 July, to celebrate Independence Day at cocktails with the American ambassador. Regretfully declining the invitation, I felt that to tell him what I was planning to do instead might have seemed inappropriate.

On the train back I run into Jon Snow, who is returning from Bradford where he has been making a programme about the decline of the city. I note that at King's Cross, unlike me, he goes home by Tube, whereas after the rigours of Nidderdale I feel I'm entitled to a cab. Still, as Anthony Powell used sometimes to note in his journal, 'interesting day'.

7 *July*. The same week as I traipsed across North Yorkshire the *Guardian* has a piece by Terry Eagleton saying that of all the eminent writers and playwrights only Pinter continues radical and untainted by the Establishment. I'm not sure if this means that in Eagleton's view I don't qualify because of my absence of eminence or because such protests as I take part in are too sporadic and low-profile to be noticed. Either way if I had email I could send him or the *Guardian* a one-word message: 'Ahem.'

9 *July*. Going round some primary-school paintings:

Me: There's a good name. James Softely Haynes.
Maya (my guide, aged nine): Excuse me. Are we looking at Art or are we looking at Names?

12 *July*. Today look up my first word in the complete thirteen-volume *OED* in its new setting. It now occupies the nearest shelf in my new bookcase – and so is much more accessible than it has been in the forty years since I bought it. The word is *rankle*.

19 *July*. That TV production staff should have taken a hand in helping along the various competitions, phone-ins and charity pro-grammes is unsurprising. Back in the 1960s, when I had my first experience of TV studios, the audience went largely unmanaged. In comedy programmes there was a warm-up beforehand and a PA might cue the applause or start it, supposedly spontaneously, but the

response was otherwise unmassaged. In the late 1960s this began to change, and overenthusiastic PAs took to shouting approval in the final round of applause that ended the show. Then the applause before the appearance of the star – particularly on chat shows – got wilder and longer so that one had the nauseating spectacle of David Frost, for instance, standing supposedly touched and surprised by the audience's unexpected warmth, the shouts of the PAs now become whoops. This quickly became standard and a customary feature of live shows today, particularly Graham Norton's, with the audience readily entering into the subterfuge, knowing that they are part of the event as they would be at a pop concert. It's not a big step, therefore, from helping the show along in this way to manipulating competition results to suit the mood, and despite all the current breast-beating, not much more dishonest.

Even the sleight of hand over the royal documentary, with the queen sweeping in when she was supposedly sweeping out, won't much shock the public. HMQ was plainly cross and whichever way she swept doesn't alter that, even if it over-emphasises it. I am just happy to see the pretentious Ms Leibovitz properly discomfited, though I shouldn't think she'll remain so for long.

24 July, France. Walking through Lectoure with Lynn we go down a back street towards the car park. It's hot and already the lunch break; the houses are shuttered and the street completely deserted. We are passing a house that is being renovated with Lynn slightly ahead of me when a shard of glass falls or is thrown from somewhere up in the building, just missing my head and falling between us. It's half a window, jagged and sharp-edged, and had it hit either of us in the neck might well have been fatal. It takes a moment to realise what has happened, our first thought that it has been flung down by some heedless workman. We shout, but there is utter silence, whether because there is no one there or because the culprit has the sense to lie low. A woman comes out of a house, picking her way through the shattered glass, not looking at us and saying nothing. Absurdly, I kick the battered garage door but there is still this impenetrable and somehow malignant silence as we go on down the street, occasionally looking back to see if whoever was responsible is peering out.

28 July, Yorkshire. A warm and windy day for the street market where we stock up on homemade raspberry jam, a Victoria sponge and spend a fortune on the raffle and the tombola. It's a lovely friendly occasion, and wholly homemade, made more festive this year by a wedding in the early afternoon, the guests having to skirt the festivities to get to the church. We sit in the garden having elevenses while the Giggleswick Brass Band lays into 'Crown Imperial' and, with scarcely a pause, 'Finlandia' to follow. No floods in the village as the beck though full hurries the water down into the valley where some of the meadows get waterlogged but nothing to compare with what has been happening further east in Hull and York.

Do very little the rest of the weekend, except prune the various shrubs, the garden beginning to look shaggy a few weeks earlier than it normally does. Looking at the towering sunlit clouds I realise I have missed the anniversary of Bruce McFarlane's death, 16 July, which was just such a day as this when I ran Mam and Dad to Scarborough for them to have a few days' holiday before I came back to Giggleswick, where I opened *The Times* on the Monday morning to find his obituary.

It's getting near the day of Dad's death, too, and before we leave on Sunday we pick some flowers from the garden and put them on the grave where Gordon must have planted some bizzy lizzies, or begonias maybe. Think of Mam and Dad standing there smiling and think also of Anne next door whose chest is bad and has to go for an X-ray on Monday. Easy journey back with the same towering high summer clouds. Between Newark and Grantham I always strain to see the towers of Lincoln Cathedral on the eastern horizon but never do, the only time I have when we were unexpectedly bussed from

Retford to Grantham, when they were unmistakable in the last of the sun.

2 August. Chris Langham is found guilty of downloading child pornography and remanded for sentencing next month, having been told to expect jail. To imprison someone for looking at or making a copy of something makes me uneasy, even though, as in this case, the facts are not in dispute. And not merely with pornography. Last month some Muslim young men were imprisoned for, among other things, looking at or having in their possession a handbook with bomb-making instructions. That makes me uneasy too. Looking is not doing however much a police-led morality would like to equate the two, and would like the public to equate them also. Repellent though child pornography is, I don't find Mr Langham's conduct especially repugnant and am only grateful when I read about such cases that my own inclinations don't take me down that route. I don't know Chris Langham but I find the policy of targeting such high-profile figures deplorable, the relish with which they are pursued in the tabloid press chilling. I hope Mr Langham gets a short sentence and that he will not become the pariah the authorities would like, and that the BBC, not these days noted for its courage, will shortly re-employ him. R. does not agree and unusually we argue fiercely over this.

3 August. John Normington dies, an actor whose name didn't mean a great deal to the public but who was much loved in the profession and who seldom gave a bad performance. In *A Day Out* (1971) he played Ackroyd, the kindly nature-loving cyclist who railed against farmers who nailed up the carcasses of moles to deter their fellows.

In *A Private Function* he was the weaselly accountant Lockwood whose most memorable line was 'He's got us by the scrotum.' He had a fund of stories, chiefly of disasters he had been involved in, some of the funniest at the National to do with Howard Brenton's *The Romans in Britain* (1980) in which he played, among other things, an ancient Briton who has to pretend to wrestle with a wolfhound (stuffed), a feat that reduced the much raped and otherwise put-on cast to helpless mirth. On some nights he scarcely managed to get beyond the play's first line ('Where the fuck are we?') before he was on the brink of hysteria. He was the kind of actor who made you glad you were part of the same profession.

Overhanging this week has been the X-ray Anne had at Airedale on Monday, the results to be given her when she visits the doctor today.

She had called Gloucester Crescent but left no message so I ring her. She is still finding it hard to breathe and says slowly, 'It isn't good news. I've got lung cancer.' The doctor had apparently called at the house yesterday afternoon, a thoughtful gesture though one which indicated the seriousness of the situation. Now as I sit in the garden this hot afternoon she will be waiting at the health centre to be told more – though more, I feel, can only be worse – and she is due back at Airedale on Monday presumably for a scan.

7 August. A baby robin is about in the garden and each morning sitting out with tea, oats and raisins, I throw it a few oats. It eats one or two, almost out of politeness, then flies off, leaving the rest.

8 August. The date I went into the army fifty-five years ago.

Look at Ian Hamilton's *Keepers of the Flame* (over my lunch) into which I'd tipped the note he'd sent me after I did the piece on Mam and Dad's wedding for the *LRB*. I think he may have been ill already at that time when I was immensely touched, having thought he always disliked my stuff.

11 August. On Saturdays the *Guardian* is running a series on writers' rooms. Why any writer allows him or herself to be prevailed on to take part I'm not sure. Flattered to be asked, perhaps, though what would deter me would be, if nothing else, superstition: to allow a newspaper to photograph my desk runs the risk of never being able to do any more work there. None that I remember have been inspiring or even particularly pleasing: Colm Tóibín's today is all books, though said to look over rooftops, which could be nice; Margaret Drabble's faced the street, but with curtains so long and John Lewis-like I'd be frightened they'd get into the prose; Edna O'Brien's had some relics of Samuel Beckett, hardly likely to unchain the imagination or get the words flowing. Most have had awful fireplaces. Can we see where you work? No fear.

12 August. On Sunday, Anne comes in and sits quietly talking, first to Rupert and then to both of us, the only time she's been able to open her heart. She's so composed – or seems so – resolved not to worry until the full extent of the problem is known. When we go, she is sitting in the sun on the bench outside the café, looking so pretty and cheerful – the highest form of courage there is, it seems to me, to take away the burden of concern from friends and family who are departing, so that they can go away feeling better about you – and how bad you may feel meanwhile kept to yourself. I'm not sure I ever achieved this myself.

Back in London we have our usual Sunday supper of cheese on toast, bacon and a carrot and apple salad only with some broad beans we've brought back from the garden – and so delicate and delicious they're a different vegetable from the frozen variety and even the loose beans you get from a shop – so tasty I find myself rationing them as I'm eating so that I still have one or two left for my final mouthful. The inside of a bean pod, shaped to the bean and furred like the inside of a violin case has always seemed to me an instance of the prodigality of nature, a thing that is beautiful in itself and suited to its function. In Yorkshire the pods would go on the compost but here only into the bin.

15 August. When I was a child and we were living in the Hallidays I used to watch Mam going through the terrible ritual of blackleading the kitchen range, the finishing touch being when she cleaned the enamelled tin in the hearth with milk. Why I never knew, though it always seemed to me a wicked extravagance – a mealtime equivalent would be when Dad occasionally put sugar on his lettuce.

29 August. Rupert: 'You look like you're having some sort of *episode*.' (I think I was singing.)

30 August. When we met the Dowager Duchess of Devonshire aka Debo at Andrew Wilson's a few months ago I said I'd send her a copy of *The Uncommon Reader* when it came out. Today comes a letter (and a postcard for Rupert) thanking us both and bubbling over with enthusiasm and good spirits. She now lives at the Old Vicarage, Edensor and very much in the Mitford tradition she refers to it as the Old Vic, the ability and the delight in making up nicknames common to all the sisters. It was true even of the least lauded one, Pamela Jackson, who, when she lived next door to Hugh and Joan Stalker in Duntisbourne Leer, used to shop at the same Cirencester butcher, Mr Barron, nicknamed by P.J. 'Robber Barron'.

1 September. To Cambridge where we do all the things we usually do – taxi (grim unsmiling driver) to the Catholic Church where we go in Jess Aplin's shop opposite, then walk along past the Polar Institute and down the street and the (stone) plaque on the house where Darwin lived to the Fitzwilliam. A nice lunch of (very fat) mushrooms and cheese on toast then while Rupert looks at the ceramics I go to the first two or three rooms where I used to go when I was on the Russian course fifty years ago. I'd never walked round the top gallery of Room 3 where there are some lovely small pictures – the Henry Lamb of Lytton Strachey, a good Augustus John of one of his children but not his portrait of Hardy, which used to be here.

The woman attendant in the gallery below very pleased to see me and promises to look out for Rupert who I tell her 'looks very young but has grey hair' while I go and read under the portico before we go across the road to Gabor Cossa. Then along tourist-crowded King's Parade and through the back streets hoping to cut through Trinity Great Court but of course it's closed as it never would have been once and up the hill past Magdalene to Kettle's Yard.

As restful and reassuring as it always is, though I just sit in the available armchairs while R. does the proper round. Ideal though it is I see for the first time how some of it could be done better – or differently, always the enviable thing its low rambling rooms, the result of it being two or three cottages knocked into one. Judging from the visitors' book most people who come have been before, like a tall curly-haired boy, no older than an undergraduate who is showing it to his girlfriend. 'Come for a top-up?' says one of the ladies who oversee the rooms.

11 September. To the British Museum for the opening of *The First Emperor: China's Terracotta Army*. There are speeches in the Great Court – Neil MacGregor as always the best, no one that I've ever heard 'turning' a speech as well as he does and giving it a flick at the finish. There's also what is billed in the programme as a 'Special Guest'. This turns out to be Gordon Brown, who makes a decent speech too and one which, as R. says, must be impromptu as he repeats himself. Flattered to be gathered up by Neil and taken in past the explanatory displays ('You don't want all this foreplay, do you?') to the figures themselves. Though obviously the sheer size of the site must be staggering and can scarcely be imagined, what compensates here is being able to see the figures at such close quarters. The detail of them is extraordinary. No more so perhaps than in English alabaster tomb figures (1,500 years later) but those were often standard archetypes whereas these are individuals and perhaps portraits. The stance of the figures is so natural – a young man slightly slumped, a neckless wrestler and, as Neil points out, the generals always fatter than the soldiers. One damaged figure of an acrobat is like a Degas or a Marini and, maybe because it's damaged, is the only figure that seems not entirely naturalistic. And it's the humanity of the detail that is so touching. As we're coming out we pass behind the kneeling figure of an archer, whose meticulously modelled hair catches R.'s eye and the weave of his stockinged foot mine. Seldom have I felt so immediately satisfied by an exhibition or so unmystified. The social circumstances of the times and the nature of the whole society, that is a mystery, but not the objects themselves. It's Proust in plaster (except it's terracotta).

15 September. Discover a good bookshop, Crockatt and Powell on Lower Marsh, a street opposite the Cut near the Old Vic, where I buy Henry James's *The Lesson of the Master*. It's a short story in which Henry St George, a famous novelist, supposedly Daudet but resembling James himself, gives the benefit of his experience to a young writer, Paul Overt. St George, we are given to understand, has 'sold out', and in order to make money and keep up his position has fallen away from the artistic perfection to which he once aspired (and occasionally achieved). He now produces if not potboilers, then certainly inferior stuff – a declension brought about by too many worldly encumbrances, particularly his ambitious wife. He rather portentously advises Overt against marriage, whereupon the young writer sacrifices his love for the vivacious Marian Fancourt, goes off to Switzerland and writes a masterpiece. There's a twist in the tail (and in the tale) as St George ends up marrying Ms Fancourt himself, but the whole thing strikes me as a pretty formulaic exercise and not at all convincing, partly because it's suffused with such an extravagant notion of Art. Art makes both novelists throb with love and thrill with excitement, while at the same time (and of necessity) leaving what it is in their respective works that they're thrilling and throbbing about vague and unspecified. This is always the trouble with stories or plays about writers (or films about painters): the actual material that they produce can only be described; if it's shown or set down plainly for the reader to judge it invariably turns out to be poor or pretentious stuff. And why not? If one could write a story about a masterpiece and include the masterpiece why bother to put it in a frame in the first place? What I particularly don't buy is the notion of self-denial leading (in the story inevitably) to greatness.

16 September. Stuff cut from *The Habit of Art*.

A.: Do you pee in the washbasin?

B.B.: No.

A.: Everybody does.

B.B.: Not in Aldeburgh.

A.: Do they still adore you?

B.B.: (*considers*) The women do.

A.: I was in Milwaukee a few months back. They adored me.
     What about the boys? Do they adore you?

Britten smiles.

A.: I think that is what is known as a thin smile.

B.B.: You shouldn't despise Aldeburgh.

A.: I don't.

B.B.: I gave them a concert hall. Two.

A.: But they've given you much more.

B.B.: The sea, you mean.

Those I teach . . .

Do you teach? Not composing but conducting is teaching.
     Teaching the singers, teaching the orchestra. Teaching the
     chorus.

Teaching teaches – that's one thing I've learned.

Auden as prophet:

Struggling in vain to understand Auden's poem *The Sea and the Mirror* I come across a speech for Caliban addressed to the audience:

Ladies and gentlemen, please keep your seats,
An unidentified plane is reported
Approaching the city. Probably only a false alarm
But naturally, we cannot afford
To take any chances.

This was written in 1943.

20 September. I'm reading Robert Craft's memoirs, which are some-times almost comically bad and just a joined-up engagement book. At other times, though, he writes vividly and well. The book includes an account of the first night of *Beyond the Fringe* in New York in October 1962. Arnold Weissberger, the showbiz accountant, had procured seats for Craft and for the Stravinskys, with Craft not at his usual post by their side but sitting some distance away with Rita Hayworth (who was moderately pissed). There was much laughter, Craft reports, but with Hayworth laughing louder and longer than anyone else, much to Craft's embarrassment. Seeing that people in the audience were looking at them, Craft contrived to leave with Ms Hayworth at the interval. I never even knew Rita Hayworth was in the audience not to mention Stravinsky. Though Craft may not be the most reliable witness, as he also notes the presence of Charles Addams 'and his wife, Deborah Kerr' (*sic*).

24 September. Marcel Marceau dies. Much hated by Peter Cook ('Marcel Arsehole'), who couldn't stand the reverence with which mime was treated. Still it gave him a good joke: 'I was there,' he used to say, 'the night Marcel Marceau dried.'

2 October. Ned Sherrin dies who very much figured in the second period of my life after *Beyond the Fringe*, when he worked on the late-night shows *Not So Much a Programme* and *The Late Show*. He was an ideal producer in that no production problems or censorship difficulties were ever allowed to reach the performers – in this respect (and only in this) resembling another producer of mine, Innes Lloyd. Both of them protected the writers and actors from the BBC hierarchy. John Bird used to do a very good Harold Wilson and after one show Ned was summoned by Hugh Carleton Greene, the director-general, and told that the prime minister was threatening legal action. 'Tell him to go ahead,' said Ned. 'Say that just because he's prime minister he shouldn't feel he ought not to sue.' No more was heard of the matter. Ned was a gent, too, always sending you a note if you'd been on one of his programmes or he'd seen something you'd done. He made no secret of being gay or of the fact that he availed himself of the services of escort agencies and rent boys, about which he would teasingly drop hints in one of the several columns he wrote and at a time when the tabloids were going to town over similar celebrity shock horrors. 'Airily' is the adverb one associates with Ned and a refusal ever to be disconcerted, looking, with the top-heavy figure of his latter years, like a genial Lady Bracknell.

15 October. Talk to Peter Gill, who is bringing out a book on acting, *Actors Speaking*. He thinks that what has always been the shortcoming of American actors, namely, that while superb at naturalism they find artificiality difficult, is now the case here: and that paradoxically actors from lower down the social scale find it hard to imitate toffs (and so to play Wilde or mannered comedy) whereas Etonians, say, have no problem being ordinary or working class. It's partly that today's generation of actors are better at imitation (and so can do dialect) but what they lack is fantasy, with few of them able to indulge in what he calls 'the erotics of speaking'. He instances Edith Evans, an odd-looking girl and a shop assistant, who had a notion of herself as a beautiful and talented woman and who made her audience share that vision. And she was not alone: Peggy Ashcroft came from Croydon, Noël Coward from the suburbs and Alec Guinness was the son of a barmaid. But all of them had some sense of their proper position in life, a fantasy of what they wanted to be which these days would probably be disapproved of or discouraged, fantasy frowned on as some sort of escape.

21 October. One piece of slightly cheering news is the departure of the terrible Kaczynski twins in Poland. They had been child actors, a profession ideally suited to tyrants in the making, and the one photograph I've seen of them in character makes them look fittingly like cousins to the Children of the Damned. Years ago there used to be a set of twins in *Spotlight* called Imp and Mischief Champneys. They remained a fixture of that volume for years, it seemed, eternally young and in unfailing spirits, though I never saw a production in which they actually appeared. Thinking about it, David Cameron could have been a child actor. And Blair, who always had a 'Who's for tennis?' air about him.

24 October. To Bath where before going down to the Forum for a reading I sign stock at Robert Topping's new bookshop on the Paragon. Like his other shop at Ely, it's astonishingly well supplied and scholarly as well as popular, a series of enticing rooms – and plenty of chairs. The reading had originally been intended for the abbey, but though I'd done more or less the same performance in Ely Cathedral, it was thought to be too secular for Bath. The Forum is huge and the sound system dodgy, so I end up relaying my thoughts about HMQ reading into a hand mike, which since I'm reading from the text is a bit of a juggle whenever I turn the page. Afterwards there's a signing, which ends just in time to catch the London train.

The station is only a few hundred yards away but on the other side of a vast building site, another of Bath's ill-starred town planning ventures in the making, this time a vast shopping mall. Bath has been under siege all my life. When I first came here in the 1960s they had just set about demolishing streets and streets of early nineteenth-century housing, the service quarters for the grander buildings in the town. They were said to be of no architectural interest or significance, with no notion that they were part of an architectural whole. This, I think, was under the aegis of Hugh Casson, the deceptively mild-mannered and *bien-pensant* architect who in his time presided over many a planning disaster.

And so it has gone on since, with acres of indifferent modern buildings all carefully constructed in Bath stone as if that was all that was necessary to bind the city together. I'd hold a show trial in Bath, a Nuremberg for all the perpetrators of its architectural atrocities, the money-grubbing councillors who sanctioned it, the mediocre architects who did their bidding, winkled out from their wisteria-covered vicarages for proper retribution. Many of them are of course dead but like Cromwell they could be disinterred and their remains stowed under some sort of monument in the centre of this coming mall, a reminder of the crime they have committed. Apart from the demolished buildings themselves, the other casualty is decent architecture with otherwise pleasing designs: the extension to the Holburne Museum, for instance, now badly compromised because even fans of decent modern architecture are nervous of championing it in Bath where fingers have been burned so often. 'No more' is the understandable reaction. But it's too late. Under the arc lights the bulldozers grub away and the pile-drivers sink their shafts. On the flood plain one hopes.

As the train pulls out I think this is not a city I want to visit again. Before they are artists, before they are craftsmen, be they genius or mediocrity, architects are butchers.

29 October, New York. I almost bump into an aged New York lady as I come into the grocery store and she comes out. 'Oh sorry,' she says. 'I zigged when I should have zagged.'

30 October. At the Met (and largely thanks to a glowing account by James Fenton in the *Independent*) we visit the exhibition of tapestry.

'Well,' says one woman to another, coming out as we are going in, 'that was a real bummer.' While not quite as bad as that I don't get much out of it though Rupert takes to the Gobelins – too grandiose for me and no glow to the colours. The new classical sculpture court has more appeal, particularly a bronze hollow headless statue, the himation (i.e. the wrap or mantle) incised with fast colour still after 2,500 years.

The museum is teeming with visitors, a terminus of art, and what strikes one (particularly in the tapestry exhibit) is the stamina of older women, their worn-out men trailing in the wake of their wives still eager, still determined on self-improvement, still keen to know. 'Moses in the bulrushes? Well that doesn't look like Egypt to me.'

1 November. I have been reading Philip Roth's *Exit Ghost*, which I've enjoyed (insofar as I can enjoy a novel about an incontinent, impotent, irascible old writer who is two years younger than I am). One of the ghosts who is making his exit is, as I understand it, Nathan Zuckerman himself, Roth's eidolon or alter ego whose parallel life he has traced in half a dozen books. Another ghost laid to rest is that of Amy Bellette, who in *The Ghost Writer* was the much younger lover of the virtually forgotten writer E. I. Lonoff. In that book Zuckerman comes to identify Amy, mistakenly, as Anne Frank, who has survived the camp and lives on unrecognised. In *Exit Ghost* she turns up again and is now revealed not as Anne Frank but as a survivor nevertheless, only from Norway not Holland.

I had been reading this when we go into EAT on Madison and 81st for a cup of tea and a piece of (very unsatisfactory) coconut cake. An oldish woman in a red coat and beret (and looking not unlike how Enid Starkie used to look) beckons me over, having read and enjoyed some of my stuff. She particularly liked *A Question of Attribution*, the play that dealt with the Queen and Anthony Blunt. She has an accent which I don't identify, but she says she spent her childhood in occupied Europe and what she liked about the play was all the lies that were being told, 'Both of them lying. Him lying, her pretending. That was my childhood,' she says. She doesn't say whether she's Jewish or whether the lies were vital and necessary to survival, and in my typical unwriterly fashion I fail to ask, perhaps because it's so like a scene from Roth's novel. As we go she calls out: 'Stay alive!'

The whole episode is a reminder of what an archaeological site the Upper East Side is, with skeletal old ladies pushed (by their black minders) in wheelchairs up Madison Avenue, all with their stories to tell. It's like a long-lost city in some Middle Eastern wilderness where shards of history are lying about waiting to be picked up – or, in this case, talked to. But not by me, who is at a loss for words. 'He could have been a writer but he was at a loss for words.'

2 November. A young shop assistant in the (now differently located) J. Press: I had asked for one of their poplin shirts with the narrow collars, which he told me they didn't do.

Me: But they did once.

Assistant: Yeah. Back in the day.

4 November. Back from NY today and answering a bunch of letters I hear a programme on Radio 3 like the *Talking About Music* programmes Antony Hopkins used to do, dissecting a masterwork, in this case Tchaikovsky's violin concerto. I haven't heard it for a while so it comes back to me with almost the smell of Leeds Town Hall where I first heard it in 1948, played by the young dashingly handsome Alan Loveday – an Australian whom time has confused with another dashing Australian, Ken Rosewall the tennis player.

Very clear too is the feeling of transcendence such music inspired in me then: I knew I was never going to be happy but if the music was anything to go by I knew I would rise above it and lead a higher life and a more exalted existence than the happiness to which everyone else could look forward.

7 November. A young father and his son in the organic shop in Camden Town. 'This is a boy', he announces at the check-out, 'who prefers coriander to chocolate. Isn't that so?' And the boy – seven or eight, I suppose – confirms this unlikely preference, though more one suspects out of consideration for his father's feelings than any distaste for Kit Kats – or, as it would be in this context, Green and Black's.

10 November. Anne heartbreakingly pretty still, today in some spotted pyjamas and her floppy black raincoat and with her hair pinned up looking so lovely. I take her to her door and kiss her and hug her as about twenty cyclists come up the street. Finding the café closed they stop nonplussed, and call out to us, 'We've come from Burnley.' I say Anne is poorly though standing on the steps she looks anything but – just a beautiful woman – and of thirty not fifty-six.

15 November. Abu Hamza, the radical cleric, loses his appeal, the only obstacle between him and extradition to the United States the decision of the home secretary. The judge in the case, Judge Workman, admits that the conditions under which Hamza is likely to be held in the United States are offensive to his 'sense of propriety', thus briefly raising the hope that his judgement is going to be less workmanlike than it turns out to be.

Hamza is not an attractive figure and his case is difficult to defend, but it should be defended and extradition rejected on Karl Popper's principle that arguments should be rebutted at their strongest point. Nobody likes Hamza: his opinions are reprehensible and there is no question that he broadcasts them. But he is a British citizen and he should not be extradited to the United States under a non-reciprocal treaty which allows that country to extradite British subjects without due process. Let him be tried here and if found guilty imprisoned here, not in some supermax institution (offensive even to Judge Workman) where he will disappear without trace. Because next time the person the United States decides on may not have one eye and hooks for hands, disabilities which make him such a joke to the tabloid press. Next time the person chosen might be thought to be innocent and undeserving of such ridicule, and extradition might even be thought to be unfair. But it won't matter. The precedent has been set and gets stronger with every person so supinely yielded up to American so-called justice. Jacqui Smith, the vibrant successor to such champions of liberty as Jack Straw, David Blunkett and John Reid, is potentially a bigger threat to our freedoms than Abu Hamza has ever been. ITV News reports all this as 'Britain has won the right to extradite Abu Hamza'. Translated this means Britain has lost the right not to extradite anyone whom the United States chooses.

26 November. An obituary in the *Guardian* of Reg Park, the body-builder and sometime film star who (and this is news to me) was the mentor (if that is the word) of Arnold Schwarzenegger. Reg Park was at my school, though gone by the time I got there. However, at one point on my journey through the school I sat at Reg Park's old desk, his name carved on the lid. He'd been one of those boys who could do backflips and somersaults over the horse and was already famous, certainly in Leeds, as a body beautiful. Outside the pages of *Health and Efficiency* there wasn't much of a future for men in this, posing as an art still confined to the motionless statuesque nudes ('We Never Clothed') who regularly adorned the stage of the City Varieties. Leeds's loss, though, was Italy's (and eventually Holly-wood's) gain, where Park became a star of classical epics. And, oddly, he was not the only one, as twenty years later another old boy of my school, Martin Potter, played the lead in Fellini's *Satyricon*.

28 November. R. is reading *Brideshead Revisited* for the first time, my browning-at-the-edges Penguin that must be fifty years old.

'Tell me,' he says plaintively, 'is it *meant* to be snobbish or am I missing the point?'

Which is better than me who, reading it for the first time, in 1957, say, didn't spot the snobbery at all – I just took it as an entirely proper account of a world from which I was (rightly) excluded. Though I think I sympathised with Hooper (as Waugh probably did, too, not being much of a soldier himself).

1 December, Versailles. Having been informed by the hotel that we would be able to hire bikes to go round the grounds of the palace we find that this facility ceased on the last day of November. This turns out a blessing as we then decide to hire a sort of golf cart, an electrically powered trolley for four on which we trundle up the pleached alleys and ceremonial avenues of these vast grounds, a pleasure that recalls the first thrill of being able to drive. It's the ideal mode of transport and not merely it seems to me for the domain of Louis XIV. I would be happy to go at this speed (and in similar silence) about the streets of London. Indeed it surprises me that no city has been enterprising enough to declare itself a trolley cart zone.

6 December. During the war my father eked out his Co-op butcher's income by making fretwork toys which he sold to a smart toyshop down County Arcade in Leeds. His speciality was penguins mounted on little four-wheeled carts, of which during the war years he must have made many hundreds. Since then I've only come across two, one in the window of a junk shop in Harehills that was closed and when I went back it had gone; the other the property of someone who came to a reading I did in Muswell Hill but who, under the foolish impression that the toy was of immense value, refused to part with it.

Last week comes a letter from a woman in Mitcham to say that her husband, who has recently died, collected penguins and enclosing a photograph of one he'd found in an antique shop in Tickhill near Doncaster. Was this one of my father's efforts? She wasn't offering it for sale, just letting me know out of interest, but I write back confirming the attribution. Today cocooned in bubble wrap the penguin arrives, livelier in design than I'd remembered, but almost certainly from the Bennett atelier. It actually belongs to her son, Tom, who has waived all rights in it with a generosity that overwhelms me and out of all proportion to this simple little toy which now stands cheerfully on the mantelpiece, one of the few relics I have of my father.

20 December. I seem to have banged on this year rather more than usual. I make no apology for that, nor am I nervous that it will make a jot of difference. I shall still be thought to be kindly, cosy and essentially harmless. I am in the pigeon-hole marked 'no threat' and did I stab Judi Dench with a pitchfork I should still be a teddy bear.

24 December. Watch the *Service of Nine Lessons and Carols* from King's, broadcast on BBC2. Except that it isn't Nine Lessons any more but four or five maybe and the rest poems, devotional poems admittedly – Herbert, Drummond, Chesterton – and ones which 'echo the message of the Gospel' – but not the Gospels nevertheless and one suspects this is the point: it's an attempt to make the service less exclusive (or less exclusively Christian), more 'accessible' so ends up diluting it. Nor do the readers finish up by saying 'Thanks be to God' except when they have been reading from the Bible – which is, I suppose, correct but it's also a dilution. Aged eight or so, I once had to read a lesson in Christ Church, Upper Armley and was deeply embarrassed at having to end up saying 'Thanks be to God'. I pretended to forget it and came away from the lectern but was brought back in order to say the obligatory words – so ending up more embarrassed than ever, a connoisseur of embarrassment long before I got into double figures.

2008

1 January, Yorkshire. Having felt previously that John Bayley is too much 'in books', I am nevertheless cheered by the end of a piece on Larkin in *The Power of Delight*: 'His popularity, like that of many great idiosyncratic artists, rests on various sorts of misconception where the critics are concerned, and on the sound unexamined instincts of a more general public.'

A grey dark day and raining still, as it has been for the last week. Around four it eases off and we walk up by the lake. The waterfall at the top of the village is tumultuous, though the torrent has never been as powerful as it was in 1967 when (perhaps melodramatically) I envisaged the lake dam breaking and engulfing the whole village. The lake itself is always black and sinister, the further cliff falling sheer into the water. It was once more exotically planted than with the pines that grow here now, as the Edwardian botanist Reginald Farrer used to sow the seeds he brought home from the Orient by firing them across the water into the cliff with a shotgun. The church clock is striking five when we turn back, the waterfall now illuminated under its own self-generated power, the same power that once lit the whole village, and I suppose one day might have to do so again.

8 January. I spend a lot of time these days just tidying up and today I start on my notebooks. Around 1964 I took to carrying a notebook in my pocket in which I used to jot down scraps of overheard conversation, ideas for plays or sketches and (very seldom) thoughts on life. I stopped around 1990, by which time I'd accumulated thirty or so of these little hardbacked books with marbled covers. Today, barren of inspiration or any inclination to do anything better, I start to transcribe and even index them. In the process I'm reminded of one of the reasons I stopped, which was that so little of what I noted down ever found its way into print or into a play, the notebooks becoming a reproach, a cache of unused and probably unusable material and a possible testimony to the sort of thing I really ought to have been writing.

Some examples:

'She had a face like an upturned canoe,' said by the actor Charles Gray at breakfast in Dundee (though of whom I can't remember).

A.: I've been salmon fishing.
B.: It's not the season.
A.: No. I thought I'd take the blighters by surprise.

'Here we are. Fat Pig One and Fat Pig Two.' Said by my mother when she and my father were sitting on the sofa in front of the fire.

'They have one of them dogs that's never got its snitch out of its backside.' My father.

I get a kick out of my stuff being liked abroad . . . in Italy, for instance, where I always do well and in Germany. Of course the Queen story [*The Uncommon Reader*] did well everywhere . . . Taiwan, South America, Iceland . . . but that was because of the Queen not me.

It's always a bonus when young people like me. *The History Boys* obviously appeals and I can understand that but I wouldn't have thought *Talking Heads* would be much liked, though it was a set book for O or A levels, which mightn't necessarily be in its favour. At that time I used to get lots of letters from school students, questionnaires really, larded with compliments but actually wanting me to do their homework for them. I used to write back telling them to treat me like a dead author and so unavailable for comment. Make it up: nobody would know.

11 January. To Cambridge, where I talk to students about my medical history. It's part of a course run by Jonathan Silverman, director of communications at Addenbrooke's and himself a Cambridgeshire GP. As so often when I've spoken in schools I find I'm of more interest to the staff than I am to the students, and I don't do it very well, haltingly recounting the more noteworthy episodes in my medical life without drawing out many lessons from them. As usual girls ask more questions than boys, though once I point this out the boys kick in. One story I tell is to do with the importance of language. Years ago I saw a specialist about a troublesome knee. Having examined me, he asked whether I had any trouble with my stomach. I hadn't, but the question was alarming; my knee and my stomach: whatever I'd got must be more widespread than I'd imagined. What in fact the doctor was asking was whether I had a delicate stomach: had he said that, the answer would have been 'yes'. Given the all-clear he then prescribed Feldene, a vicious anti-inflammatory drug which there was later a campaign to ban after it had killed off numerous pensioners. It wasn't the doctor's fault: he'd just phrased his question wrongly. Still, it meant that as a result of the havoc wrought by Feldene I had to be put on the acid-suppressant pills that I've been on ever since.

14 January. Tom Stoppard rings my agent Rosalind Chatto to tell her that when in last year's *LRB* diary I quote an old lady in New York as saying 'I zigged when I should have zagged,' the original remark came from the American sports reporter Red Butler, who reported it as having been said by Randolph Turpin after his defeat by Sugar Ray Robinson. How my old lady came to know this is a mystery, and how Tom comes to know it, too, as I'm sure boxing isn't his thing.

17 January. Think this morning of making Auden's skin speak.

22 *January.* I'm reading George Steiner's *My Unwritten Books*, a series of chapters, some more autobiographical than others, on the books he wishes he'd written. The first section is on the Cambridge scholar and scientist Joseph Needham, microbiologist and expert on China, a man who fascinates Steiner and whom he wanted to write about in Frank Kermode's Modern Masters series, published in the 1970s. Steiner had first seen Needham at a protest meeting against Anglo-American intervention in Korea in 1950, at which the distinguished scientist claimed to have incontrovertible proof of the use of germ warfare by the American military. Admiring Needham as he did, Steiner was depressed by this but when he went to see Needham in his rooms in Caius they got on well until Steiner raised the matter of his testimony on germ warfare. Needham then became cold and angry, Steiner was dismissed and they did not meet again. Other than this telling and disillusioning encounter, the tone of Steiner's chapter on Needham is wholly laudatory.

At a much humbler level it reminded me of how as a schoolboy in Leeds in 1950 I went to a similar protest meeting at the old Mechanics' Institute, where one of the speakers was Mrs Arnold Kettle. The Kettles were well-known left-wingers, Arnold Kettle a Communist and lecturer in English at the university. They lived not far from us in Headingley and were eventually, though not I think at this time, customers at our butcher's shop. Like Professor Needham, Mrs Kettle denounced the invasion of North Korea by the Americans and their use of germ warfare, not a view I'd then seen put forward. I was at the meeting not because of any left-wing views, but because the war was of some personal interest to me, as in 1952 I was due to be conscripted and likely to find myself fighting in it.

What was so astonishing at the meeting – and also embarrassing – was to find Mrs Kettle weeping over the plight of North Korea and having to fight back the tears as she spoke. Never having seen anyone on a platform in tears before, I still wasn't convinced of the righteousness of the North Korean cause, only that Mrs Kettle was good but soft-hearted and probably self-deceiving. That she was toeing the Party line didn't occur to me, though it did to my companion, John Scaife, another budding conscript, who was much more scathing on the subject and cynical about the tears.

2 February. Ten days or so ago I did an interview for the *Today* programme in connection with the revival of *The History Boys* now playing at Wyndham's, in which I reiterated my unease about public-school education. This produced a mild stir and much silliness, someone in the *Independent* saying that if I object to parents bettering their children's prospects by paying for their education do I therefore object to parents sending a child to ballet classes. The *Mail* predictably labels me a hypocrite because I use both the NHS and private medicine, an admission I'd made myself on the radio, but with the *Mail*, as always, pretending it's information it's been clever enough to find out.

I've no relish for controversy, but what seems to me incontrovertible is that in the fifty years since I went up to Cambridge to take the scholarship examination there has been no substantial attempt to bring state and private education together. There have been cosmetic changes, an increased number of bursaries for instance and the (I would have thought very patchy) sharing of resources with which public schools have endowed themselves (swimming baths, squash courts etc.) but the core problem – namely, that most privately educated pupils regardless of their abilities are better taught and provided for than pupils in state schools – has not been touched. The situation is the same and in some respects worse than it was when I was seventeen. Is public-school education fair? The answer can only be 'no'. And 'Is anything fair?' is not an answer.

3 February. At moments trying to write this play (*The Habit of Art*) e.g. in a speech by one of the wrinkles on Auden's face, I tell myself it will be all right because it's what Edward Said meant by 'late style'.

4 February. More senior moments. I can't find my pullover and don't like the one I'm wearing because it has several moth holes. 'I had another pullover,' I say to R. 'I was wearing it this morning.'

'You still are. You've put the other one on top of it.'

Bike over to Gloucester Crescent and leave the bike there while I walk round to M&S. People often smile at me, but this afternoon nearly everyone smiles. It's only when I come back to Parkway to have my hair cut that I realise I'm still wearing my crash helmet.

8 February. A row over some remarks the Archbishop of Canterbury has made about Sharia law. They're perfectly sensible; the only thing for which he can be blamed is his underestimating the stupidity of the nation and its press. It's proof, as Dorothy Wellesley wrote, that as 'foreigners, especially the French, tell us, we have never acquired the adult mind'.

12 February. I am gradually assembling my papers that are to go to the Bodleian Library, resisting the impulse to catalogue them or even read them at all but just roughly sorting them into the various plays or books and leaving any further arrangements to them. This means, though, that there are a great many 'swaps' (or 'deaccessorising opportunities') – three or four virtually identical scripts of plays, for instance, the script of a TV play (in two or three versions), besides the shooting script and so much that is repetition. With the Bodleian being short of room I feel slightly shamefaced (and lazy) about this but if I did it in a more responsible (and time-consuming) way the papers would never get there. As it is I look at the 150 boxes I have so far accumulated and think that their bulk is in inverse proportion to their importance.

17 February. Anne (looking like Red Riding Hood and very pretty in a little knitted hat and red coat and boots) calls before going up to plant a tree on Trevor's allotment above Newby. Her bird table is always very popular and she keeps it well stocked except that a hawk has taken to hiding in a nearby bush and swooping on the unwary. At Gardenmakers near Wigglesworth where we often go for tea Andrew tells the same story only his bird table has two tiers, the lower one too small for the hawk which the other birds know and take refuge there when it's in the offing.

18 February. Ned Sherrin's memorial service at St Paul's, Covent Garden. A friendly service interspersed with songs, some from Sondheim, some from Sherrin and Brahms, but with none of them as tuneful as the hymns. The audience is very responsive, and it's the only occasion in my experience that the lesson (Timothy West and Ecclesiastes) is given a round of applause. The best speech, regrettably, is David Frost's, the best anecdote that Ned, questioned about the young man he had brought with him to supper, said: 'If pressed, I would have to say he's a Spanish waiter.'

Waiting at the lights this afternoon my bike slips out of my hands and slides to the floor, in the process tearing a piece out of my leg. Wendy, the nice nurse at the practice, tells me I should try and keep the dressing dry. The result is that when in the evening I have my bath I look not unlike Marat, except that whereas Marat has his arm hanging over the side of the bath, I have my leg.

14 March. Every day practically I bike past the two bored policemen who, armed and bullet-proofed, guard the house of the foreign secretary. I could give the address and, were I a Muslim and even had it in my possession, it would be enough to land me in custody. Passing the policemen so often, my natural inclination would be to smile. I never do because though I know they're bored and it's not their fault, I feel to smile condones a state of affairs (and a foreign policy) which necessitates ministers of the crown being under armed guard.

20 March. All the Leeds trains have been cancelled and I am wandering the station not knowing what to do when Rupert discovers me, having managed to get on to a Scottish train and change at Doncaster. Greatly elated by this we have a supper at La Grillade (halibut and chips) and then drive homeward in good spirits. Except that just after the Addingham bypass R. cries out and I see a grey shape in the headlights and he hits a badger – a young one, I would have thought and which, with its striped nose now lies senseless by the kerb. We drive back round the roundabout and then up the road again – and for one exultant moment it seems to have picked itself up and gone, but there it is, lying like an old rug by the roadside. We discuss running it over again to make sure it is dead – but neither of us can face it. R. is devastated; it's like Vronsky breaking his horse's back – a moment he can never call back – and feeling himself guilty and polluted by everything he hates – heedless cars, thoughtless motorists with him now one of their number. What particularly upsets him is that I have never seen a live badger – all the badgers I have seen like this one is now, a dirty corpse by the roadside. We drive on in sadness and silence.

10 April. A correspondence in the *Guardian* about eating apple cores takes me back to the perilous school playgrounds of my childhood, when eating an apple core, like wearing boots, was a social indicator. Poorer boys (wearing boots) spotting you eating an apple would say with varying degrees of threat, 'Give us your scollop, kid,' and then hang about until it became available. I never begged a core myself, partly because I wasn't that sort of boy, but chiefly because, like so much else in my childhood, it came under my mother's prohibition against sharing food or drink with other children, TB always the ultimate threat. That 'scollop' had another meaning apart from apple core I never knew until I was in my twenties and started dining out.

11 April. From my notebooks:

'I never fathomed the lav and we were there two weeks. It could never make up its mind when to flush. Well, you can't be stood there playing Russian roulette with it can you?'

Reading a letter:

    A.: Love and Kierkegaard?

    B.: (*snatching it*) Love and Kind Regards.

My life does seem right staccato somehow.

'Get the cattle prod and wake your father.' My mother.

When we say life we often mean risk.

12 April, Yorkshire. Snow in the night, which covers the lawn and clinging to the half-opened leaves makes the trees bulky and seemingly as laden with blossom as in a Samuel Palmer. In the afternoon we go over to Austwick and walk down the muddy lane to the clapper bridge. There are sheep and lambs everywhere and the beck is very full, gliding wickedly between the stones before flattening out over the fields. It's a perfect scene and R. is just saying how we must try and keep it in mind next week (when I have to go into hospital) when deep in the water comes the spectral body of a lamb. Though tagged, it's not long born, and must have slipped into the beck in its first days of life. I suppose we must try and keep that in mind, too, as pale and ghost-like, it is swept out now into the flooded meadows.

13 April. A boy running across the bridge this morning.

    'Ey, look. Crocodiles in t'beck.'

14 April. Regular check-ups for cancer sometimes turn up other problems: looking for one thing the doctors find another. Thus in February I was found to have a stomach aneurysm, and though it's my inclination to leave things as they are, it apparently needs to be seen to. Aneurysms these days are often quite straightforward, remedied with the fitting of a stent sometimes in just a one-day job. Mine, though, is not straightforward at all and will need an open operation, and the surgeons who see the scans and angiograms get very excited as they have never seen an aneurysm in this particular spot before. The operation is scheduled at UCH and arrangements made for other doctors to observe the procedure, the chirurgical equivalent, I suppose, of additional priests present at a funeral or memorial service being described as 'robed and in the sanctuary'. I am robed and ready myself today and indeed halfway to the operating theatre when we have to come back as the operation cannot begin until a bed becomes vacant in Intensive Care, in the same way I suppose, as Concorde was not allowed to take off from Heathrow until a landing bay became vacant at JFK. The upshot is that 'the procedure' is postponed until next Tuesday.

15 April. This afternoon Richard Ovenden, the Bodleian's keeper of special collections, comes round to load up a hundred or so box files and take them to Oxford. There will be more in due course, including all my notebooks and the annotated copies of the printed stuff, but I'm very happy to see the back of this first tranche. When I get home later on Richard Ovenden is calling. 'I thought you would like to know that this evening your MSS are reposing in Bodley's strongroom on the next shelf to the *Anglo-Saxon Chronicle*.'

17 April. George Fenton comes round with a present, an overcoat from John Pearce, the fashionable tailor in Meard Street who specialises in remaking or renovating old clothes. The coat is French, long, black and once had an astrakhan collar. It's a lovely thing, but what made George buy me it (and I don't like to think of the price) is that it was made by Proust's tailor.

18 April. A pre-operation session at the Elizabeth Garrett Anderson wing of UCH down Huntley Street, in which Siobhan, a nice, cheerful and silly nurse, takes me through the same questionnaire I answered twice last week. She then takes me in to see the anaesthetist, and he goes through the same questionnaire. He's Scots, so everything is 'a wee . . .' – a wee while, a wee op (which it plainly isn't). I'm coming away a wee bit depressed, though it's slightly alleviated when Siobhan says: 'I've just got one more question. Do you dye your hair?'

22 April. Before 'the procedure' (which ends up lasting seven hours) there is a slightly comic scene in which the nurse goes round the various wards gathering up the patients due to be operated on this afternoon. We are told to take a pillow with us so, clad in our hospital gowns and each clutching our pillow, we walk in single file behind the nurse across the bridge above the atrium that leads to the surgical wing. We look like medieval penitents on the way to public humiliation and an auto-da-fé. The technical description of the aneurysm is 'a dissection of the superior mesenteric artery'. Since its location is unique, before the operation I ask the surgeon if I can give my name to this particular spot. He is not encouraging, perhaps having thoughts of that for himself. It's a pity. 'Bennett's Dissection' sounds rather good I think as I drift off; it might serve as a description of (some of) my life's work.

24 April. I like uniforms. I preferred nurses when they looked like nurses not just ward cleaners. I found the sight of district nurses in their navy blue raincoats both reassuring and appropriate. White coats have gone too now, with doctors indistinguishable from patients except that the doctors are in shirtsleeves. I like white coats. But then I'm a butcher's son. White coats have no terrors for me.

1 May. Home, and my first outing is to the local community centre to vote against the dreadful Boris. I wear an overcoat over my pyjamas, something I'd never have the face to do if I was well. But I've been ill, I think, and now I'm getting better. Home to a nice supper of scrambled eggs and smoked salmon, followed by stewed apple and yogurt.

24 May. Clearing out some shelves, I find a note from Kevin Whelan dated Dublin 3 October '05. It's a poem headed 'Getting it off my chest'.

> I'm bruised inside
> from the
> punches I've pulled.

I'd have liked to have written that, though I've no idea who Kevin Whelan is.

2 June. What I might have said at Hay:
When people observe I'm very English, I might respond that I share Auden's hope in his 'Epistle to a Godson' (1972)

> to be
> like some valley cheese,
> local, but prized elsewhere.

8 June. John Fortune rings, just back from a gig with John Bird in (I think) Dubai. It's for a group of super-rich Arabs, few of whom speak English and who have to have the satirical barbs simultaneously translated via headphones. Unsurprisingly there are not many laughs.

The wives are startling, traditionally dressed in hijabs or veils etc. but in the costliest materials and styled by top Arab fashion designers. 'Oh,' I pertly quip, 'you mean like Yves Saint Laurent of Arabia.' Both Fortune and I are impressed by the promptness of this impromptu joke, but it comes about because when he rings I'm just listening to *Last Word*, the obit programme on Radio 4 which includes a section on the dead Yves, who, so his partner says, was born with a nervous breakdown.

14 June. Watch the TV coverage of Trooping the Colour, done this year by the Welsh Guards. The BBC in the person of Huw Edwards is at pains to point out that these are working soldiers, and to prove it there's a lot of film, some of it live, of the regiment in action in Afghanistan.

Whether there are Guards in action in Baghdad I don't know, but if there are, the forces there scarcely get a mention, or Baghdad either. Afghanistan, though a campaign every bit as futile and mistaken as the war in Iraq, has somehow become the acceptable face of war. It's maybe because Prince Harry was there (of which there's some discussion with the Prince of Wales). But I suspect it's more because we don't hear much of the civilian population of Afghanistan and that 'Johnny Taliban' (in Prince Harry's phrase) is more of an identifiable bogeyman than the factions in Iraq.

But it's a sunny day, the Queen is in a nice turquoise frock and appears to enjoy herself, even tapping her foot to some indifferent Welsh brass-band compositions before being driven back to the palace to watch the fly-past from the balcony and then have a spot of lunch. Nobody likes to ask any of the throng in the Mall if they know why we are engaged in Afghanistan or if they approve (as many would, I imagine). No grieving mothers, of course, and the deaths that have been mentioned have all been noble ones and not due to inadequate equipment, friendly fire, or anything ignoble at all.

15 June. And today comes George Bush paying a courtesy call on the Queen and Gordon Brown before having a cheering conscience-free get-together with his old mate Tony Blair. And here are the helicopters flying over Regent's Park to prove it.

26 June, L'Espiessac, France. I sit in the wicker rocking chair in the shade of the willow by the pool. Except that I'm slightly pestered by insects it's an ideal situation, with the lavender bank just coming into bloom and the trees and grass fresh and green after a week or two of rain. It's one of the perfect places of the earth, utterly silent and private, the twitter of a hawk the only sound. And it's the last time we shall be able to come.

It's a warm afternoon and with no one around I swim dutifully around the pool. I've never much cared for swimming (or known what to think about while I was doing it). I ought to be a better swimmer as I've got broad shoulders, but my arms were always too thin, I reflect, and I've never mastered the crawl. Today, though, I think of it less as swimming than as taking my scar for an airing, the long wavering pleat that now runs from navel to sternum. I reflect, as I labour messily round, that this will be one of the last swims I shall have here or anywhere else. I can't imagine ever finding anywhere as perfect or as private as this, and having swum in a pool bordered on the one side by a bank of lavender and on the other by fruit trees and a field of ripe corn, who could bear to swim *municipally*?

Tomorrow we leave as the house is now sold, putting me in mind of Francis Hope's poem about the holidays we had in rented villas back in the 1970s:

Goodbye to the Villa Piranha

Prepare the journey North,
Smothering feet in unfamiliar socks.
Sweeping the bathroom free of sand, collecting
Small change of little worth.

Make one last visit to the tip
(Did we drink all those bottles?) and throw out
The unread heavy paperback, saving
One thriller for the trip.

Chill in the morning air
Hints like a bad host that we should be going.
Time for a final swim, a walk, a last
Black coffee in the square.

If not exactly kings
We were at least *francs bourgeois*, with the right
To our own slice of place and time and pleasure,
And someone else's things.

Leaving the palace and its park
We take our common place along the road,
As summer joins the queue of other summers,
Driving towards the dark.

27 June, L'Espiessac. Last night in our room we find a huge four- or five-inch bright green cricket – perhaps a praying mantis – which we capture in the jug before putting it out into the rain. This morning hearing a couple of magpies raising a din I look out of the window and see a marten, possibly (the size of a large ferret) – ginger and brown fur, pointed nose coming out of the lavender field. It darts back in again but the magpies keep track of it and fly squawking over its head as it flounders through the mown grass to hide in the standing corn.

14 July. Wildlife this morning: one of Lisa's pet rabbits sleeps in the sun behind the fence on top of the gazebo; a jay flounders in the laburnum and a young robin so be-fluffed it's akin to a sheep in a half fleece, and a small brown bird that once would have been a sparrow but these days looks more distinguished nips across the garden, which R. spent all yesterday tidying and which looks lovely. R. who just about now is going to the eye specialist.

20 July. Although the East Coast rail franchise has now passed from GNER to National Express eccentricity happily persists: the trolley attendant this afternoon warns against too sudden opening of the sparkling water lest it be a bit 'Vesuvial'.

23 July. I'm pushing my bike through the gate of Gloucester Crescent this morning when a heron flaps up from the creeper on top of the pergola. It flies down the street getting all the seagulls agitated, and when I come out five minutes later the gulls are still making a din. The bird, having hidden round the corner, now takes off again and flies to No. 62 and perches on the fanlight above the door. The seagulls haven't seen where it has gone so it stays hunched up there in perfect silhouette (and in a setting not found in Audubon) while they scour the skies above the Crescent. I fetch a neighbour to see it and we watch it for a while, but the heron obviously feels this is getting a bit too what cameramen would call clubby and takes off again up the Crescent where we (and I hope the gulls) lose sight of it. It doesn't quite match R.'s experience when a heron mobbed by crows near Primrose Hill missed him by inches, but as with any evidence of urban rurality, I find it cheering. It confirms, too, my detestation of gulls, which I would happily see hounded out of cities and back to their proper stamping ground.

28 July. I'm just finishing the *Collected Stories* of John Cheever, all 892 pages of it. Full of casual profundities and lightly worn insights, few of the stories have the poetry of his novels or their leaps of language, but taken together they furnish an almost documentary account of what American East Coast society was like in the 1940s and 1950s. And not merely the society of the well-to-do. One of the most striking and unexpected insights is how precarious were these seemingly secure suburban lives, financially precarious and ridden with debt, and though they have cooks and maids, the loss of a job means ruin and departure; emotionally precarious, too, nothing in Updike that isn't in Cheever first. And these aren't just suburban lives in Cheever's enclaves of Shady Hill or Bullet Park. There are stories about elevator men, building superintendents and casual burglars, few of these apparently respectable lives that don't have a seamy side. As indeed Cheever's did. Plenty of drink, too, which is also close to home, though his homosexual double life would be harder to deduce from the stories than it is from the novels. Most of them were written to order, chiefly for the *New Yorker* (which never paid him enough), and he probably wrote better in the novels when he had more room to spread himself. But there are extraordinary tales: a casual office fuck leads to a woman being sacked, whereupon the culprit finds her stalking him until in the shadows of his suburban railway platform she makes him literally eat dirt. There's a story told by the belly of a man named Farnsworth and in Bullet Park a boy narrowly escapes crucifixion on the altar of his local church.

31 July. A depressing judgement in the House of Lords. This is the not unexpected rejection of the appeal against extradition to the USA of Gary McKinnon, the computer programmer who, for no other reason than that it was there, hacked into the Pentagon computer. Unless the European Court has more courage and more sense than the Law Lords he faces an American prison. And for what? Cheek.

11 August, Yorkshire. I put up the blind in the bedroom this morning to find a duck sitting in the middle of the lawn. Quite a plump one too, only the blind disturbs her and she waddles into the undergrowth. Comes back to sit on the lawn and as I write is in the gazebo at the top of the garden. R. delighted as Rob says he's never seen one in the garden before, though pheasants (and peacocks) quite common. Not sure whether we should try and shepherd it across the road and down to the beck or just let nature take its course.

A cool bright windy morning, the garden (and duck) looking lovely, the buddleia covered in great *snouts* of blossom. Ducks have always been R.'s favourite.

12 August. Over my lunch I often read or reread Richard Cobb, though not I'm afraid the monumental works on the Revolutionary Army and his studies on the French Revolution that made his name but rather the dozen or so autobiographical books and memoirs that he brought out particularly in the 1980s. On almost the last page that he wrote in *The End of the Line* (he died in 1998) he said, 'I am not a *belonger* . . . there could never be a Cobb cult.'

But I don't see why not. As he's one of the most vivid and particularising of writers, no detail too trivial. Perhaps sensing a possible rival, he claimed never to have read Proust but the memoirs of his childhood in Tunbridge Wells are as evocative as anything in Illiers-Combray.

Too anarchical for Oxford and a Jim Dixon before his time, I imagine he could be a difficult companion; he has his idiosyncrasies and I have learned to read him with a French dictionary to hand as his prose is peppered with French phrases, the unspoken assumption being that the French has nuances that the English version doesn't convey. Engagingly this is not always the case, there's no nuance at all, Cobb going into French simply in order to show off.

I can see how eccentricity (and the drink) might have made him an awkward colleague and this too makes me wish I knew more about him; I await with impatience the new *Oxford DNB* in which he will doubtless figure. That or a biography, which I can't see anybody writing.

14 August. On Thursday (hoping for *Dad's Army*) we caught a live broadcast from the Proms of Barenboim and his West-Eastern Divan Orchestra playing Brahms's Fourth. It was a terrific performance, broadcast in real time with no editing, so that one got a good deal of what Goffman called 'by-behaviour', the players off-duty, between movements for instance, or waiting for Barenboim to return to the podium for the encore. It helps that they are all young people, and some incredibly young, one violinist not much more than twelve, though Barenboim himself is now serious and unsmiling and looks not unlike Rod Steiger.

Tonight the broadcast is repeated and though it's edited it is still enthralling, one of the cameras fascinated with a particular wood-wind player who has a good deal to do, but who in his turn obviously fancies the flautist who's next but one. So at the end of his own contribution he'll often half-turn in order to pass the tune or whatever to this flautist, and she is equally attentive during his solos. There's a cellist with a cheeky face who plainly makes jokes, a bear of a violinist who throws himself about a lot, and next to him the child violinist with a face made tragic by concentration. It's hard to conceive how such a small figure copes with the great winds of Brahms, though he's more composed about it than his hairy and demonstrative neighbour.

It's moving, too, of course because of the moral stance of the orchestra, though the players are by now probably bored or at least matter-of-fact about this ethical burden. But as with similar experiences in the theatre (including I hope *The History Boys*), one longs to stay with them once the performance is over and they disperse. Who looks after the child, I wonder, whom does the cheeky cellist sleep with and are the flautist and the woodwind player as close as their performances suggest? So there's sadness too in being excluded from all this and longing, just as there is coming away from the theatre or for some people, I imagine, the football stadium.

24 *August*. J. is quick to reprove any misbehaviour in the street, sometimes recklessly so he was on fairly safe ground the other day when he spotted a resident of Arlington House urinating up against a car.

'What do you think you're doing?' said the Doctor (though it was pretty obvious).

'It's all right,' the old man said, 'I'm Irish.'

At which point the always straight-faced Julia O'Faolain came down the street. With more courage than it took to accost the Irishman, J. accosted her.

'What do you think of this? This gentleman is urinating in the street and his excuse is that he's Irish.'

With no alteration in her usual demeanour Ms O'Faolain took out her purse, selected a small coin and gave it to the urinater saying, 'Do not dishonour the green flag.' 'God bless you,' said the man and shook hands with Jonathan with the same hand in which he had just been holding his dick.

28 August. Unsolicited Nora brings me the review of the revival of *Enjoy* from the *Mail*. It was first put on in 1980, and while generally enthusiastic the *Mail* assumes, as did James Fenton at the time of the first production, that by putting the main young man in drag I am signalling my own (presumably suppressed) desire to get into a frock. It may be that the *Mail* assumes all homosexuals would like to be in skirts (or ought to be, possibly as a measure of public safety), but I've never had the slightest inclination in that regard, and even as a child would not have thought to dress up in my mother's clothes. But I wrote the play, so that proves I must harbour these unfulfilled longings.

The young man may not even be gay; I actually can't remember whether there's anything in the script to suggest this. He could be like Eddie Izzard or indeed Grayson Perry, both of whom prefer to dress as women without it being an indication of their sexual preferences, though in 1980 the audience wouldn't have understood that and nor, I think, would I.

29 August. A propos my supposed prescience in *Enjoy*, which has been much noted, where I do think I was slightly ahead of the times was with *Kafka's Dick*. If the play didn't entirely take Kafka seriously (which was heresy, even blasphemy to Steven Berkoff) it pointed the way to all sorts of stuff about Kafka that came after – Kafka as dandy, Kafka as cinemagoer and (reviewed today) *Excavating Kafka* by James Hawes, which is about Kafka and porn. I don't mean I saw this coming or even suspected it but the tone of the play and perhaps even more so the tone of the introduction to the play (*Kafka at Las Vegas* as it was originally called) have helped to loosen up Kafka studies, decalcified him even so that he got treated as he was in life not what he became posthumously, the prophet of the show trials and a candidate for Auschwitz.

31 August. Yesterday was warm and sunny, even hot. Today it's back to normal, grey skies and rain for the last day of the wettest August (and the greyest summer) that I can remember. Still, we'd decided to go out so after an early lunch we follow the M4 past Heathrow and take the turning off up to Langley to see the Kedermister Library. It's an old village buried now in suburban development, most of it post-war and the roar of the M4 never far away. Though we've been here once before ten or twelve years ago the church still takes some finding, but there are yew trees, a cemetery and two sets of neat seventeenth-century almshouses with between them the brick tower of the fourteenth-century church. R. has rung to check that the library will be open today but all the doors are locked and a notice on the board saying there will be tours of the library next Sunday. However just as we're turning away cross and disappointed a man gets out of a parked car who is the curator of the library to whom R. has spoken. Realising he'd given him the wrong Sunday he has come down to wait for the three hours he'd said it would be open in case we turned up. It's such a thoughtful and unlooked-for gesture it colours the whole of the visit, which is sheer delight anyway. I'd forgotten that library apart the church itself is full of interest, a magnificent royal coat of arms for instance, once on the rood screen and now just inside the door. It's dated 1625 and a wonderful piece of work, the lion's bristles made out of iron wire. There's an arcade of seventeenth-century wooden pillars, medieval tiles and umpteen plaques and monuments none of which I remember noticing on our first visit, when I think there was the aftermath of a service going on and we went straight up the stairs through another late eighteenth-century Gothick arcade to the Kedermister pew and the library itself. Today it's a more leisurely progress with the curator filling in the information not in a learned-by-rote way but full of enthusiasm and love for this extraordinary place. The pew *c.*1635 is painted and panelled, boxed in behind grilles and shutters with everywhere paintings of the eye of God (*Deus videt*). It brings back the wonder I had as a child going through the grotto at Hitchen's to see Santa Claus – painted, secret and full of surprises – panels that open for ventilation, and another panel which reveals the original holy water stoup inside the south door over which the pew was built. Even the modest benches that could be of any date are the original seventeenth-century furniture, the arms of Sir John Kedermister painted on the back.

The library itself is a small room off the pew and to the side – panelled and painted in the same way and like some casket or jewel box. The books, all uniformly bound are behind shutters, the backs of the shutters painted with blank-paged open books, in some ways the most odd and evocative of the decorations there. Though in a kind of frieze around the tops of the cases are paintings and landscapes – Windsor Castle, the Kedermister houses, and (with no *Deus Videt*) one small panel of a huge eye.

It's an extraordinary survival and so precious one fears for it, besieged by suburbia and with the M4 thundering by over the churchyard wall. In the cemetery is buried Paul Nash whose grave we visited last time, but it's spitting as we leave so instead we come straight back, through torrential rain, not stopping at Osterley as we thought we might. One component of the pleasure of such an afternoon is Rupert's delight. Without that (and without mine) the pleasure would be halved and there is always that thought.

1 September. A sunny morning and I wake thinking that forty years ago today was the first rehearsal of *Forty Years On*. It was at Drury

Lane and a much hotter day, I remember, and one that was to change my life. Though I write this living not thirty yards away from the flat in Chalcot Square where I was living then.

Appropriately, though not aware that it's an anniversary, George Fenton who as a boy was in the cast, rings first thing. Rehearsals began at ten and staying in Weymouth Mews George woke at ten and had to run the whole way to Drury Lane where Rupert Marsh was in the lobby with a watch saying, 'If you're late again, you'll be sacked.'

2 *September.* I seldom make a note of meals, particularly when I'm on my own, and today's lunch wasn't in any way memorable, but for once I'll record it. I'll normally have my lunch at one. Today it's a large granary roll that I slice up thinly for sandwiches, one side of which I spread with butter, the other mayonnaise. Then I put on some cos lettuce and smoked salmon, while in the centre of the plate is some carrot and apple salad left over from last night's supper. Sometimes I'll have a glass of water but today not. To finish I have a sliced-up banana topped off with vanilla yogurt and half a spoonful of blackberry jam. All this I put on the French tin tray R. bought earlier this year (when I was ill and having meals in bed) and bring it upstairs to my table, where I listen to BBC7's *This Sceptred Isle*, a history of England read by Anna Massey, Peter Jeffrey, Christopher Lee and Paul Eddington. Afterwards I take the tray back downstairs to get my midday pills: two Omega 3 tablets, one selenium and one saw palmetto plus a piece of dark chocolate and a cup of green tea.

It probably sounds nicer than I actually find it, which is rather routine, but some of the most memorable passages in Anthony Powell's *Journals* and James Lees-Milne's *Diaries* are to do with meals, particularly with Lees-Milne's meals during the war or the years of austerity. Somewhere he talks about a pudding of treacle pancakes and cream which even now makes my mouth water, though one of the revelations (to me anyway) of his *Diaries* is how much better the upper classes ate during the war than we did in Armley. Treacle pancakes and cream didn't figure with us, though the basics, particularly food in season like new potatoes and fresh strawberries, were far tastier then than they have ever been since.

4 September. A good deal in the *Guardian* about the Booker Prize and the experiences of those who have been its judges. I was once asked and had no hesitation in turning it down, the prospect of reading ten novels let alone a hundred quite enough to put me off. Later I read somewhere that Martyn Goff had said that no one had ever turned down the chance of being a judge, which confirms what several of the judges say – namely, that he's a tricky customer. Happy to see Rebecca West stigmatised as a bully as I've never understood why she was and is made such a fuss of – a sacred cow, I suppose. Roy Fuller gets some stick, too, which chimes with my remembrance of him when he was briefly a television critic. The whole thing reinforces what I always feel – that literature is a much nastier profession than the theatre.

6 September. In a shop in Petworth we are shown a chair that once belonged to Edward VIII and which came from Fort Belvedere. It's a monstrous thing, so decayed as to be undatable, the stuffing bursting out of the sides, the embroidery gone on the arms and with no character to it at all; it could have belonged to Henry VIII rather than Edward VIII. 'It's very comfortable,' the antique dealer says. 'Try it.' So I sit in it, this chair that the Duke of Windsor may well have sat in on the night of his abdication, though I feel no thrill on that score. And it *is* comfortable.

11 September. The sister of the divorce lawyer Mark Saunders, shot by the police in May, brings a case against the Independent Police Complaints Commission on the grounds that the officers involved were allowed to confer before giving their accounts of the incident. I hope she wins, and in her favour she's white and middle-class. If she were poor and black there would be no chance and not even a case. In Britain the police shoot people with impunity. They always have.

15 September. From my notebooks:

    A. They're very nice. They have a Brancusi in the bathroom.

    B. Do you mean a Jacuzzi?

    A. No. They have one of those as well.

'I've been to Australia. It was all I could do to be civil.' Ursula Vaughan Williams.

'Shall we remind ourselves of the earlier history of this picture?' Anthony Blunt with a group of nine-year-olds in the National Gallery.

Madman: If you ever want some good petrol, this is the place. I've had some really good petrol from here in my time . . . economical smooth-running stuff. They make a speciality of it. Just mention my name.

'It's like octopus pee.' My mother on a poor cup of tea.

20 September. Lovely morning in Settle, though for no good reason as it's as grey and wet as it has been for the last week and cold here too.

I take R. down to Phil Ward's in Giggleswick at eight thirty for him to have his neck manipulated. I come back, read the paper then collect him at nine thirty. We shop, which in Settle is always a pleasure as people talk. I'd got fed up of the old gate postcards they sell at the Information Centre but today they'd got a new selection including a good one of Ingleborough and I buy thirty. I must be easily their best customer. Then we go for coffee/tea and a flapjack at Car and Kitchen, then to the chemist. There's always been a seat in the chemist, on which I remember old people sat, as did the long-stay inhabitants of Castleberg Hospital. Now I sit there – as old as anyone in the shop – which next week, alas, is being taken over by Boots. Sign some books in the bookshop then collect my belt from Nelson's, the cobbler's on Duke Street in Settle. It's a belt I bought thirty years ago at Brooks Brothers in New York, the sort of belt that when I was a boy used to be fastened with a silver snake buckle. It doesn't have that, but with its blue and red stripe it's been virtually the only belt I've worn since the 1970s. The tongue gave out about fifteen years ago and old Mr Nelson repaired it. He was a lovely comfortable-looking old man, like the cobbler in *Pinocchio*, and his shop was old-fashioned to match, with a green glass 1930s shop sign that must once have been the last word and now I hope is listed. Today it's his son, who's equally characterful, his shop window full of assorted and sometimes eccentric boots and shoes for ladies and gents that he's made, one feels, just for the love of it. He wears a heavy linen smock, and when I say his father has mended the belt once already he says he hopes we'll both be around long enough to see it mended again. £8.

22 September. 'Elgar's *Nimrod* conducted by John Eliot Gardiner. It doesn't get much better than that. Or does it? Give us a call.' Classic FM.

28 September, Sweden. At the Design Museum on Sunday morning in Gothenburg I find myself sitting by a fire point labelled AB SKUMM but alas we have no camera.

Our lowest point in museum-going was one wet Saturday afternoon in Toronto when all we could find to do was to visit the Bata shoe museum. Gothenburg tops that with an exhibition of skateboards.

29 September, Gothenburg. I've just finished reading Philip Roth's *Indignation*. Marcus is the son of a butcher, the first in the family to go to university, but inured to the blood and guts of a butcher's shop;

he can draw a chicken, and I think makes sausages besides occasionally going out to customers' houses with the orders. It is so close to my own life that I wonder if I am not inventing these parallels. There are similar problems, for instance with the animal fat, Marcus's father cleaning it out of the bins, my father rendering it in the cellar and stinking out the house. His father is over-protective as I wasn't aware mine was until my mother said that on my first night in the army my father wept. But maybe butcher-fathers are a problem. Kafka's father may have sold fancy goods, but his grandfather was a ritual slaughterer.

In the novel Marcus cannot stand his roommate and changes his room twice. I couldn't stand mine and was interviewed by the head of my college much in the way Marcus is interviewed by the Dean of Men – a wonderful scene in the novel which is particularly painful to read.

Were I unbalanced in the way some of Roth's characters are unbalanced I might think these parallels were intentional but I do not flatter myself.

Today to Gunnebo, a late eighteenth-century country retreat of the Hall family, English who married into the commercial aristocracy of Gothenburg. The estate is an ecological showpiece with an extensive kitchen garden, pick your own flower beds and a restaurant serving the estate's produce. This is busy and obviously well known and a favourite haunt of Gothenburg's retired leisure. There are hordes of sabre-toothed Nordic pensioners who, knowing the drill, hoover up the best of the smörgasbord with ancient husbands ministering to the gobbling of their elderly cuckoo wives. The Swedes are generally considerate but age abolishes national characteristics, the only consoling thought that the French would behave worse.

1 October, Suffolk. Though Thaxted Church was delightful – and full of WI ladies (and gentlemen) clearing up after the Harvest Festival – far and away the most impressive is Long Melford, happily empty apart from an old man, Australian by the sound of him, manning the bookstall. He doesn't interfere with our looking round or play the guide, though there's so much to take in one could spend the afternoon there. All the Clopton glass for instance, a wonderful painted chapel with a hand inscribing a medieval poem intertwined with a vine that scrolls around the ceiling and between the beams. Separate from the church is a Lady Chapel, once the school and similarly painted with the benches used for the school still *in situ*: we take them to be from the 1930s, say, or Arts and Crafts reproduction but they are all 1630.

An old churchwarden comes and talks to us, there because lead thieves have taken away some pipes during the night. It is a face of such goodness and sweetness he might have been out of George Eliot – with lots to say about the church ('my full routine lasts an hour and a half') but not intrusively or wanting to buttonhole. A lovely place even down to the hollyhocks running wild between the buttresses and the gravestones, some slotted into the topiary yews that have grown up around them.

4 October. We go looking for Waterden Church, recommended by Richard Scott and said to be Osbert Lancaster's favourite. Not in the Shell Guide or the Collins *Parish Churches* book and no one in Little Walsingham Farm Shop has heard of it – or when they have, they can't explain quite where it is. We drive along the Fakenham Road and down an unmarked by-road where a farmer in a van points back over his shoulder. It's at the end of a rough track across a field next door to a run-down red-brick Victorian vicarage. The church, though, is medieval – the parish a lost village across the fields. It's got nothing of architectural distinction – box pews admittedly but of the simplest kind and in grained boxwood, a pulpit that has no pillar or plinth but standing on the floor, the font on bricks. The west window is an ordinary casement job but the view from the altar steps, through the chancel arch and down the nave is so atmospheric it makes me want to take a course in photography if only to record such places. It's a setting that would have delighted Edwin Smith.

The exterior bears more signs of its medieval origins than the interior – evidence of aisle arches, blocked windows and so on – but it's the utter simplicity that captivates.

Nor is it neglected. There are fresh flowers by the altar – and quite an elaborate bunch too and in the visitors' book someone else has called this very morning.

5 October. Pelting with rain, the smaller roads sometimes flooded and no light in the sky all day. The roads empty and we drive to Swaffham where we hope for some coffee but it's dismal and closed, the only café with its lights on a Chinese restaurant – a Chinese restaurant in Swaffham on a wet Sunday morning something of a yardstick.

Then on in the continuing rain towards Long Melford, turning off to Lavenham in the hope of some lunch. Like Swaffham it's largely closed and we're lucky to find a small back room behind an organic shop that does snacks. The other tables are taken – at one a woman and her daughter, at another a man and his daughter. I don't twig, as R. does, that they're all one family and since the child sitting with the man is making a bit of a din, which he indulges, I take it he's a divorced father out for Sunday with his daughter. I whisper this to R. who shakes his head, the child now actively disruptive, giving a running commentary on the game she is playing. I chunter a bit at this noise, unstilled by R. and I'm sure overheard by the woman at the other table – and it's only when we get outside R. explains that the child was obviously autistic. Obvious – though not to me, who's supposed to be the sensitive observer of the human condition. The thought that I have, however unwittingly, added to the mother's burdens (who must face this situation whenever they go out) is unbearable – and irretrievable. And I find it hard to dismiss from my mind for the rest of the day – and even now two days later it's hard to write about.

17 October. The new film of *Brideshead* seems to have fared badly. I've always thought the house in the original television series, Castle Howard, was ill chosen, though it's a mistake the new version replicates. I may have told this story before (I feel I've told most stories before), but when Derek Granger, the producer of the TV version, asked me to adapt it he admitted a little shamefacedly that they would be filming it at Castle Howard. I thought at the time that this was typical of the inflation a novel suffers when it's adapted for television and, priggishly probably, turned it down. I don't know that there was any suggestion that Castle Howard was in Waugh's mind when he was writing the book, though such identifications are anyway approximate, a back-projection as much by the author as by literary critics.

The new adaptation sounds cruder than the first version which, written by Granger himself, did at least retain much of the original text in the form of voiceover. John Mortimer no more wrote the script than I did, though he at least was smart enough to say he would write it and maybe even did a draft. That was really all Granger wanted, giving him a basis on which to write it himself. A nice man, he gave me supper in Rome on one occasion but took a long time before he could settle on a suitable restaurant, going into several, and walking round critically, coming out of one shaking his head saying: 'No good. Too many lampshades.'

24 October. For David Gentleman.

When I was a child I thought there was something magical about people who could draw. A boy in my class could do horses and this seemed to me at eight or nine a gift that was almost celestial.

I was reminded of this recently seeing David Gentleman drawing in Inverness Street market: not an uncommon occurrence as David is as much a component of the Camden Town scene as the market itself. On this occasion, a little Asian boy was stationed right at his elbow rapt in what David was drawing while standing so close to him that he was almost impeding the process. I can imagine artists who would find this intolerable but that David didn't is evidence both of how gentle and good-natured he is but also of his belief in the learning process and how interest and even skill is acquired and passed on.

Though he has ranged the world in his subject matter David Gentleman seems to me, despite his parents' Scottish origins, to be a very English artist. I first became aware of modern British pictures and painting when as a boy in 1951 I was taken to the Festival of Britain. David was just too young to be one of the artists featured and employed there but his vision seems to me to be linked to and grow out of that magical time. To read the list of artists and craftsmen by whom he was taught or with whom he associated at the Royal College is mouth-watering. Peyton Skipwith calls it a veritable roll call of the great and the good of the mid-twentieth-century British art world: in David Gentleman lives on the spirit of Bawden and John Nash.

And that's not all. Peyton Skipwith's account of David's career reminds us of his extraordinary range. My own experience teaches me that the British don't really care for range: they think of it as inconsistency or want of application. A single furrow is better. Happily that's never been David Gentleman's philosophy: postage stamp one assignment, a major Underground platform the next.

He has lived in the same street in Camden Town for the last forty-odd years during which time, in the intervals of depicting France, Italy or India, he has recorded his immediate surroundings much as that other Camden Town painter William Roberts did but from a different perspective (and without William Roberts's volleys of abuse!). And that's relevant. Art is never an excuse for bad behaviour. Talent isn't measurable by tantrums and I think again of his patience with that impromptu pupil in the market. I suppose what I'm saying is that David is a gentleman . . . or a gentleman twice over.

For myself I will always cherish the two sketches he did of Miss Shepherd, the Lady in the Van, a personage with whom he must have been almost as familiar as I was: we were all long-term residents of our Camden Town street. In her time Miss Shepherd went through several vehicles and on one occasion David did a quick thumbnail sketch of her watching as the tow truck prepares to take away her derelict van. He caught her in a familiar pose, feet splayed out in her version of ballet's first position and so exactly that when Maggie Smith played Miss Shepherd on the stage in 1999 I was able to show her the sketch so that she knew how to stand.

The other drawing is posthumous, done just a few days after Miss Shepherd died. I was working at my table in the window when I became aware of David casually leaning against the wall recording the van, now bowered in trees, which had been both Miss Shepherd's home and her catafalque. When he'd done he came in and gave me it.

26 October. With Lynn to the *Renaissance Portraits* exhibition at the National Gallery. It's a year or so since we've been and the thrill of walking through the darkened rooms is undiminished and as always the paintings are so enticing it's hard to stride single-mindedly past them en route for the exhibition in the Sainsbury Wing.

And it's a wonderful show which includes sculpture as well as paintings and drawings – the first room with a bust of the banker Strozzi (with leaden eyes) beside a painting of a windswept young man by Dürer that could have been painted last week (or last century anyway). Quite a few paintings by Antonis Mor which besides being photographically lifelike often have something ghostly about them. I know nothing about him but the paintings somehow suggest someone self-contained and almost sinister, a monochrome figure discreet to the point of immobility. The last room has full-length sculptures of Philip II and Charles V which manage to make Philip II handsome and even sexy (and in very fancy boots) – he carries a phallic baton resting on his hip, his armour with a small fluted

codpiece just peeping below the edge of his tunic – a figure so enticing I want to slip my hand under the tunic and behind the codpiece
to see how far the modelling goes and how lifelike it is.

On our way out we call in at Room 1 to look at the Titian on offer
from the Duke of Sutherland – an odd picture, Actaeon appealing
and rather public school, Diana with too small a head and all the life
and interest in the other nymphs at whom Actaeon is looking – not at
Diana at all. So maybe that was his real offence.

27 *October.* A lovely morning, and around eleven we drive out on
the M40, turning off at Stokenchurch and then along the Adwell
road, where we eat our sandwiches above the Georgianised medieval
church at Wheatfield. It's a church we've found open only once,
but it's a good picnic spot overlooking the flat lands below the Chilterns and around Thame. It's somewhat spoilt this bright morning,
though, because the church is now completely surrounded by ugly
timber fencing and three strands of barbed wire. There seems no
break in the wire (which pretends to be electrified), so there's no
entry into the graveyard still less the church itself, so how anybody
worships there is a mystery. Still, the sandwiches are delicious – lettuce, tomato, avocado, black olives and Parma ham – and we drive on
past Stoke Talmage to Easington, a church that is open and seemingly unchanged from when we last came fifteen years ago: two-decker
pulpit, moss-grown font, medieval tiles in the chancel, and a framed
account of how in the storms of 1992 the roof was badly damaged. It
has since been repaired, if not entirely by parishioners, certainly by
those who cherish this obscure little building – and a very grand lot
they are, including J. Paul Getty, Jeremy Irons and a Rothschild or
two, so that one just wishes they could take Wheatfield under their
wing.

All this, I have to say, is overhung by the thought of the reception
at Oxford this evening and the speeches, dinner etc. consequent on
the formal handing over of my manuscripts to the Bodleian Library.

This takes place in the Divinity School, where my praises are duly sung, the problem always on such occasions where to look, and how to look too: modest, sceptical, bashful, I can do all those – it's appreciative I can't manage. The credit for the manuscripts going to Bodley belongs to David Vaisey, who long before he was Bodley's librarian, asked me if when the time came I would think of depositing them here. Lest it should be thought there had been any sort of competition, this is the only enquiry I've ever had. Nothing from the British Library, nothing from Austin, Texas, nothing from Leeds. One offer in forty years makes me some sort of bibliographical wallflower. Finally, I tell the story of Richard Ovenden telephoning to say my manuscripts were resting that evening on the next shelf to the *Anglo-Saxon Chronicle*, adding that the only other time in my life when I'd been in such proximity to ancient memories was one evening in New York when I'd found myself sitting next to Bette Davis. And I add confidently that this will be the only occasion when the audience will ever hear Bette Davis and the *Anglo-Saxon Chronicle* included in the same sentence.

8 November. Listen to *The Archive Hour* on Radio 4, with Stella Rimington the ex-head of MI5 taking us through the material the BBC holds on the Cambridge spies, particularly the so-called fifth (or is it sixth) man, John Cairncross. It's all pretty factual, with Rimington banging the treason drum and making the mistake writers on the spies always make: that the whole lives of Burgess, Blunt, Maclean and co. were taken up with spying. Maybe they should have been and had they been dutiful Marxists ought to have been. But spies have lives too, and were (even Blunt) often quite silly and like everybody else out to have a good time. Arthur Marshall and Victor Rothschild (whose secretary Arthur Marshall briefly was) were the only sensible voices, with Marshall recorded as saying (on, I think, *Woman's Hour*) that just because someone you like and are fond of does something you disagree with doesn't mean you turn your back on them. Stella Rimington is shocked by this evidence of loyalty and good sense and asks us to be shocked too. A short extract from *An Englishman Abroad* ends the programme only, I think, because it points up how lost and lonely Burgess found himself in Moscow. Astonishing that the ex-head of such a disreputable organisation as MI5 can still expect anyone to *care*.

10 November. Did I nod or has there been any fuss about the Speaking Clock? I didn't much like 'The time sponsored by Accurist is . . .' but it was at least sober, and indeed English. Now it's a child who sounds like a fugitive from a John Waters movie who says, 'Hi! It's Tinkerbell! At the third bell the time will be . . .' and even the so-called bells sound silly. I had not thought of time as having a colour; now it is quite definitely pink and the texture of time fluffy. Why? And what other country in the world would submit to the time told in an American accent? What is happening to us? Or maybe all this has been said and I've missed it. But God rot the fools who thought it was a good idea.

One does try not to be an Old Git but they don't make it easy.

'All my life', Stravinsky complained to Robert Craft, 'I have been pursued by "my works" but I don't care about my works, I care only about composing. And that is finished.'

20 November. John Sergeant retires from the *Strictly Come Dancing* competition. I have no views on this but, having worked with Sergeant on a BBC comedy series in 1966, I can truthfully say that whatever he knows about rhythm and dance (i.e. nothing) he learned from me.

24 November. To Downing Street and a reception for Fanny Waterman, founder of the Leeds Piano Competition. The last time I was here was in Harold Wilson's time when he held a reception ('Do you know Buzz Aldrin?') for the astronauts. I was talking to Nicol Williamson as Lord Chalfont came up and said, 'This is Mr Williamson and Mr Bennett, Prime Minister. Actors.' Denis Healey was in the cabinet and here he still is, thinner but with the eyebrows intact, shaking hands with R. saying: 'And is this your Young Man?' The place is more corporate than I remember, and while in the other room a plump solemn Georgian boy gives a cello recital we take the hand-book, and wander round looking at the pictures. Andy Burnham, the minister for the arts, who with his heavy dark hair looks as if he's strayed out of an early Pasolini movie, makes a speech standing in for Gordon Brown, who's running late. Except that now here is Gordon Brown, young, tousled and despite the financial crisis almost care-free. It's a revelation. He straight away has the audience laughing, and makes an excellent speech, harder to do since these are not his natural supporters, rich North Leeds Tories rather than from poorer South Leeds, but they're completely won over. Later he shakes my hand, telling me I'm an institution. What he means, says the Young Man, is that you're not in one yet. We're both of us astonished at how different Brown is in private from the dour figure he presents in the Commons. Before coming away we look in the cabinet room, the lighting of which is pitilessly bright. 'It's like a night bus,' says R. to a lacquered Alwoodley lady who, never having been on a night bus (or possibly a bus at all), looks suitably blank.

26 November. Debo D. to supper. R. once having mentioned we often have cheese on toast, she claims that it's her favourite and begs to be invited. Warns that she will be 'dangerously punctual', and she is, nice Gerard her chauffeur delivering her prompt at eight o'clock. Not being able to see very well she comes with a small powerful torch that she keeps beside her at all times as people do their mobile phone. V. smart, in navy blue with a lovely white frilly blouse – at eighty-eight still glamorous and fashionable and an alert almost imperious look to her (though her manner not imperious in the least). Full of archaisms: 'Aren't you IT! Rupert, isn't he IT!'

We talk about her book and she retells some of it, how easy JFK was, the only time he paid the slightest attention to formality was when she was dining with him and two other members of the administration and going down to dinner they deferred, letting her go first – except that then JFK put his arm in front of her, saying, 'No, I think it's me. I'm head of state.' Says again as she says in the book how covered in hair Bobby Kennedy was, even when young.

Drinks a little but eats scarcely at all, even though it's the longed-for cheese on toast. But no awkwardness to any of it – chattering and laughing and always this extraordinary voice. Had once had to teach the actors (I think at Chichester) in *The Mitford Girls* and 'They couldn't even get the basics – lorst and gorn – hopeless.' The only actor who could do it perfectly had a Glaswegian accent so thick she couldn't understand *him*.

When she was running the farm shop at Chatsworth she felt she ought to know more about butchery so asked her local butcher up to Chatsworth. 'I saw him in my room, which has about three Velázquez, a Veronese and I don't know what else – very very grand. And I said, "Tell me about butchery." He looked round. "Well, Your Grace – imagine this is an abattoir . . ."'

30 November. A hard frost in the night, thick on the branches and the top stones of the wall furred (frost-furred) like the ears of a rabbit.

Something old-fashioned about a frost like this – just as there is with fog, the frost, though, always putting me in mind of Guildford in 1944 when Aunty Kathleen had come down to stay and took Gordon and me out for a walk to Bramley. It was a day like today, Aunty K. full of toothy enthusiasm – probably in her Persian lamb coat, Gordon and me in our navy gabardine raincoats and school caps. We were walking in woods or across a common where they had been coppicing or cutting wood and in the middle of this heath were the glowing embers of a huge fire. This, of course, delighted Aunty K. – as it probably did us – only with her it meant she had more of a tale to tell when we got back home to Epsom Road. And not just there but forever afterwards that walk across the common never forgotten by her or indeed by me – and Gordon probably remembers it too. I would be ten, Gordon thirteen. Mam and Dad would suffer the tale-telling, one of the many instances of the adventures their children had with the aunties which they were seldom able (or anxious) to rival.

Nothing else of the time remains except some books she and Grandma had brought us for Christmas one of which was an Edwardian tale of Cornwall, *Lost on Brown Willy* – the joke lost on me at the time. Another book they brought was by Cecil Aldin, which was of more interest.

Think of Aunty K. favouring everyone with her beaming smile and exaggerated diction, not in Leeds – wasted on tram conductors – but here in Guildford (and in the posher south of England) the bus conductor probably got it.

Bootees she would have been wearing, suede bootees.

The other white frost that I've never forgotten (and have several times written about) was at Cambridge in December 1951. Just such a day as this.

4 December. From my notebooks:

'. . . where we dedicated a glass of wine to Artemis and generally conjured up the spirit of things long ago. They also do a nice curry and chips.' I think said by John Fortune.

'I wouldn't want to be as bald as that. You'd never know where to stop washing your face.' My mother.

A.: I'm working on the structure of the cell.
B.: Oh yes. Whether it has bars on the windows, that kind of thing?

'It's one of those churches in the City like My Aunty by the Wardrobe.'

'If only one could do it with some clean part of the body, like the elbow.' Frith Banbury's mother.

'It's no good. The larger Florentine churches of pre-Renaissance date are not a success.' Roger Hinks.

2009

1 January, Yorkshire. Ill over Christmas I say to Ernest Coultherd, a farmer in the village, that my Christmas dinner consisted of a poached egg. 'Oh. Credit crunch, was it?'

Two dead salmon in the beck just above Mafeking Bridge, both of them huge creatures, nearly two feet long, so big that one wonders how the beck at low water can accommodate them, though there are a few deepish pools. It's thought at first that an otter is responsible, and as otters have been seen I suppose it's cheering that there are both otters and such large fish for them to prey on. However I talk to Dr Farrer this morning and he thinks the fish probably died after spawning and wonders if they're sea trout. Salmon have not been known to come up so far, as they can't negotiate the waterfall and the weir before the lake. I saw them in action at Stainforth forty years ago just after we had agreed to buy the house and it seemed at the time like a good omen.

3 January. En route for London we turn off the A1 into Rutland to look at the monuments in Exton Church – a splendid sequence from the fifteenth century through to the eighteenth century. The earliest, Sir John Harington and his wife, are curious. He died *c.*1525 but his armour is like that of someone killed at Towton or Bosworth, thirty or forty years out of date, a medieval knight not a courtier of Henry VIII. Another monument is by Grinling Gibbons and as R. says he can see why Gibbons generally stuck to leaves and garlands as his figures are squat and earthbound, possibly because they aren't designed to be seen from below. A lovely sixteenth-century monument opposite, the face of the recumbent lawyer (?) in cap and hood tied under his chin seemingly a genuine portrait – and looking more so as the marble of the face is flecked and pockmarked giving him a greater appearance of reality. A tiny trussed-up baby before him, his grandchild.

10 January, Yorkshire. I call in next door to have a word with the district nurses who are due to visit. It's after ten on a bitterly cold Saturday night and the two nurses are still on duty, washing and changing Anne, giving her her medication and settling her down for the night. And two nurses come again at nine the next morning, one of them the same nurse who had been on duty the night before. When one sees this level of dedication in the NHS it is both humbling and inspiring, and undertaken in such a straightforward matter-of-fact way, working round the clock not worth mentioning.

21 January. Working in the BBC Studio at Maida Vale I don't watch President Obama's inauguration and am astonished when I see on the news in the evening the vast concourse of people gathered in Washington. I don't read any official estimates of the numbers though it's to be hoped they estimate more accurately in the US than they do here, where any demonstration of which the police disapprove – the Stop the War marches, for instance – is routinely marked down whereas demos on which the police look kindly, the Countryside Alliance, say, are correspondingly inflated. If there had been a police presence at the Feeding of the Five Thousand there would have been no miracle. 'Listen, there were only a dozen or so people there. Five loaves and two fishes perfectly adequate.'

27 January. Christopher Hibbert dies. Unlauded as an historian because never on TV he was also marked down, I imagine, because so wide-ranging. His biography of Elizabeth I, *The Virgin Queen*, is by far the best account of her that I have read and I nearly wrote to him to say so. And now, of course, wish I had.

Find myself cheered this morning by the sun catching a silver scaffolding pole on a rooftop beyond the garden. The sea it suggests in the clean air. New York it could be, I think. Elsewhere anyway.

28 January. A photograph in the *Independent* of Picasso painting *Guernica* in 1937 in a collar and tie.

30 January, Yorkshire. My friend Anne's funeral and we are about to set off for the crematorium in the pouring rain when as we turn the car round a young pheasant skitters across the road. Nothing unusual in that except that this pheasant is pure white. I'm not given to a belief in signs or portents but it's nevertheless quite cheering to feel that she's still around.

The service in the village church in the afternoon is packed. I give an address but the whole occasion is wonderfully and unexpectedly rounded off by Ben, her middle son, who despite grief and nerves manages to say what his mother had meant to him and his two brothers. I couldn't have spoken impromptu as he did and the congregation quite properly gave him (and Anne) a great round of applause. The boys then take the flowers that have been on the hearse and decorate the front of her café.

1 February. Entertaining Mr Sloane, Orton's first play, is being given another outing, this time at the Trafalgar Studios. I saw the first production at Wyndham's in 1964 with Madge Ryan, Peter Vaughan and Dudley Sutton. Good in the part Sutton was already too old, as have been most of the actors who've played in it since. It's a play I would dearly like to have written, though these days for it to retain its shock value the young man should not be much more than a boy. As it is he's always cast as someone already well corrupted and who knows exactly what he's doing whereas from a boy of fifteen the flirtatiousness would be much more shocking. All productions put him in black leather and a little cap such as Orton himself used to wear.

Here too an outfit that is not so self-conscious would serve the play better. The more ordinary it is the more shocking it will seem.

3 February. One of the cards of condolence we get on Anne's death is unintentionally comical. 'Sorry to hear your bad news!' The exclamation mark is hilariously inappropriate though it's quite hard to pinpoint why.

14 February, Yorkshire. A red kite (I think) peering over a wall as we drive up the Feizor road later catches us up as it flies down over Buckhaw Brow. At this point it is mobbed by a crow – tackled would be a better word as one bird can't mob another – which harasses it until the kite presumably leaves the crow's air space.

If it was a kite it's the first I've seen round here and also (though I've often heard of it) the first time I've seen a bird harassed – though of course it was what R. saw when the crows mobbed the heron in Primrose Hill and in Gloucester Crescent the seagulls similarly (as in this year's *LRB* diary).

20 February. It's years since I was on *Desert Island Discs* but these days I'd find it much easier to choose the eight records I don't want than those that I do. I don't ever want to hear again:

Mussorgsky *Pictures at an Exhibition*
Rimsky-Korsakov *Scheherazade*
Schubert Fifth Symphony
Beethoven Pastoral Symphony
Mozart Fortieth Symphony

And it isn't that I've heard them too often. I just don't care for any of them.

7 March, Yorkshire. To Oxenholme, half an hour from home and on the edge of the Lake District, where we catch a Virgin train to

Yorkshire

On the beach at Sizewell

Tea with Anne in Café Anne

With Rupert en route to our civil partnership, 2006

Lynn Wagenknecht at L'Espiessac

L'Espiessac

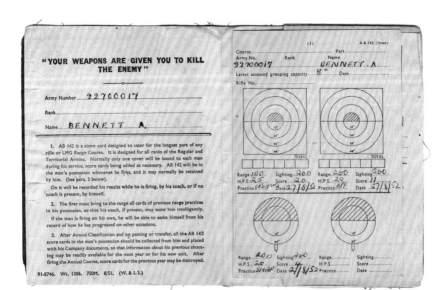

22700017 Private Bennett A.
Skill at Arms Book, 1952

Outside the Spider, Bodmin, 1954
Michael Frayn, back row left; AB back row right

Bruce McFarlane

With John Schlesinger, Caird Hall, Dundee,
An Englishman Abroad, 1983

Alex Jennings as Britten; with Nicholas Hytner;
Richard Griffiths as Auden

(*The Habit of Art*, 2009)

Jeff Rawle and Gabrielle Lloyd, *Cocktail Sticks*, 2012

George Fenton, *Hymn*, 2012

Filming *The Lady in the Van*, Gloucester Crescent, 2014

Glasgow. It's a brisk ride, only two hours and seems less than that because the scenery is so uninterruptedly rural and sometimes spectacular. Virgin trains, though, are designed on the American model with dark interiors and small windows and are nowhere near as comfortable as GNER. I've never had much time for the spurious populism of Richard Branson: his jolly japes and toothy demeanour can't disguise the fact that he is a hard-faced entrepreneur. These thoughts recur when we come back from Glasgow the next day and have to travel by bus two thirds of the way ('track repairs') and with a driver who has the radio on throughout. It rains, too, but the journey is redeemed when back at Oxenholme we drop down into Kendal and the Abbot Hall gallery, where there is a touring exhibition of Robert Bevan pictures. The shows at Abbot Hall are just the right size, and never more than three or four rooms. The Bevans are shown alongside other Camden Town paintings, the best of which is a lovely, glowing, slightly abstract picture by Spencer Gore, *The Beanfield, Letchworth*, which is from the Tate. There's a Gilman, *Mrs Mounter*, some Nevinsons and lots of Bevans of horses and their hangers on – horse copers, idlers and jockeys in civvies and large caps.

'I like Bevan,' says R. 'He wasn't afraid of mauve.'

What's interesting about the exhibition also is the various views it has of Cumberland Market, the great horse-market north of Euston Road where the 1950s Regent's Park estate now stands. It was bombed during the war, or so it's always said, though it was probably recoverable and from the various drawings on show in the exhibition one can see how these days it might have been a lovely place to live, a vast square surrounded by early nineteenth-century houses, a space comparable to the Marais if not quite so distinguished.

13 March. Red Riding by David Peace is much talked of and applauded, and it is powerful and sometimes hard to watch. Whether it's feasible or the assumptions about the police entirely plausible I'm inclined to doubt. 'The Leeds police kick mainly in the teeth' is the gist of it, plus an assumption that the force in the 1970s was thoroughly corrupt.

Though the circumstances were hardly as lurid, this was very much the assumption when I was a boy. Rationing offered increased opportunities for peculation and my father, a butcher, who was both Conservative and conservative, nevertheless always assumed that most policemen were 'on the take' and the magistrates, too. Still, though the police get away with extreme violence and even murder, I find it hard to credit (if I understand the plot) that masked bobbies could shoot up a club or batter and rape a reporter on the *Yorkshire Post* without there being some sort of repercussions. Comically, since in my memory the *Yorkshire Post* was always rather a genteel newspaper, I'd find it easier to believe if the reporter had been from the *Yorkshire Evening Post* – the newspaper Keith Waterhouse first worked on as a reporter.

So while *Red Riding* seems like gritty realism it is in this respect quite romantic, as romantic and fanciful as the stories told at the other end of the social and geographical scale in *Midsomer Murders*. In Midsomer the murders average three or four per episode but never seem to incur any comment in the press or ruffle the calm surface of the community. It takes more than the discovery of a mere body to stop the garden fête. *Midsomer* and *Red Riding* are not very different in this and alike, too, in that they're both, *Midsomer* particularly, a boon to actors.

23 March. A concert hall in Prague in 1942. A performance of Dvořák's Cello Concerto. The hall full, a group of German officers and their wives prominently placed, one of them a general. In the middle of the concerto the great door of the concert hall opens a little and three leather-greatcoated Gestapo slip into the hall. There are three aisles and an officer walks slowly down each one scanning the audience. One stops at the end of a row, another at the far end, and we see a young man in the middle of the row. There is some sort of disturbance, a shout during a quiet passage of the music maybe, so that the general turns round. He sees the Gestapo and waves them away and reluctantly they move to the back of the hall where they wait by the door. The concerto continues.

We are now at the third movement and during it a small paper bag is passed surreptitiously along the row where the young man is sitting. When the parcel reaches the young man he puts his coat over it.

The concerto ends, the applause is tumultuous, the Gestapo run down the aisle, though impeded by people leaving. They reach the young man's row and wait. At which point he takes a gun out of the bag and shoots himself. The general and his party leave.

24 March. Eleanor Bron, met outside Paul Scofield's memorial service at St Margaret's last Thursday, had said John Fortune was ill again so I call him. Not at first available as Emma says he's playing with their new Saluki puppy. Later he rings back in good spirits, having finished his chemo and been signed off, his doctor saying, 'This is an indolent disease, Mr Fortune. You and your condition are well suited.'

I have no good stories to tell him (the inanities of actors always a favourite). His social life has been limited to visits to Waitrose where the check-out girl asks him if he wants help packing. 'No, I'll manage,' he says, 'though it's one of the many things women do better than men.'

There is an old married couple behind him and the wife says viciously to her husband, 'Why can you never admit that?'

A similar couple in the store are at the greengrocery counter where the husband is undecided, on a cauliflower.

'What are you waiting for?' says the wife. 'Do you want it to sprout?'

John delights, he says, in these ancient couples who have spent a lifetime honing their skills at scoring off one another. Cheering call.

28 March. I go up the street to Sesame, the organic shop, slipping on a green corduroy jacket. I'm also wearing an old pair of green corduroy trousers so it looks like a suit. It makes me remember how Gielgud used to be excited – or pretended to be – by corduroy. 'Corduroy! My dear!' And his eyebrows would go up as if it were some kind of statement. Which it may well once have been, but was hardly the case in 1968.

4 April. News that this year's Royal Show will be the last ought not to impinge, and that it does is because back in 1948 the Royal Show took place at York and a coachload of us were taken over from school. Why I can't think as we were hardly sons of the soil and Leeds had no farming pretensions, few places less so, but I suppose events of any sort were thin on the post-war ground and this was thought to be one. I've no recollection of there being anything to do with farming, no prize bulls or sheepdog trials, and what stands out in my mind was that there was a good deal of free literature on offer. None of us schoolboys had ever come across this before and we dashed round the various pavilions stocking up on brochures about milking machines and silage pits, poultry catalogues and pamphlets about scrapie plus the latest in tractors and combine harvesters. Clearing out a cupboard a year or two ago I came across some of this material, now, I suppose, an archive though it was displaced a few years later by slightly more worthwhile giveaways from the Festival of Britain.

8 April. Fairly obvious that the newspaper seller who died in the G20 demonstrations was pushed over by a policeman. Equally obvious that even if the calls for a public inquiry are conceded no policeman will be charged or even suspended. According to the *Economist*, in the last ten years there have been more than four hundred deaths in custody, with no convictions for murder or manslaughter, the police always vindicated. This isn't simply against the laws of England; it's against a more fundamental law – the law of averages.

10 April, Good Friday, Yorkshire. Wet for most of the day, but towards evening it fines up and there is a strong sunset as we walk round the now empty village. In the fields above the back road there are two white horses, one in a pink jacket and the other blue. There's been an old and rather shabby white horse on this hillside for almost as long as I can remember with a rather Eeyore-like structure as its stable. That's gone and these horses are not shabby at all, rather smart in fact and they walk indifferently over to see what we have to offer – which is very little – a hand nervously offered, a pat on the nose and then off they go. Forty years ago to the day there were horses. *Forty Years On* was playing in the West End but in those days there were no theatrical performances on Good Friday and George Fenton and Keith McNally and I went down to Chislehurst to go riding – riding on the downs above Brighton one of the happiest memories of the tour of the play the previous year. It was a lovely day and I've remembered it ever since.

16 April, Yorkshire. En route home and with half an hour to spare we stop briefly at Kirkstall Abbey, which R. has never seen. After Fountains, Byland and Rievaulx, Kirkstall is a bit of a disappointment, though to me it was always a familiar relic, soot black with its niches and side chapels piled with meaningless masonry and stinking of urine.

Now it's all tidied up, the ancient Ministry of Works lead labels replaced by over-informative notices, illustrated with slightly jokey pictures of the jolly monks going about their monastic business. Still, I'm glad we've been as it confirms something I'd thought was a legend, namely that until the nineteenth century the main road (now the A65) ran down the nave of the abbey,[*] which to an unsuspecting traveller in the dusk must have seemed extraordinary, like a journey out of a dream.

Thinking of Byland and Rievaulx I remember the little sketches

---

[*] [Wrong: it ran very close to the nave.]

of beauty spots the cartoonist Thack used to do in the *Yorkshire Evening Post* and which Mam would cut out and put in the letters she and Dad wrote to me when I was in New York in 1963 with *Beyond the Fringe*.

18 April. Reluctant as one is to agree with Henry VIII, I find it difficult to believe that Prince Arthur, aged fifteen, did not consummate his five-month-long marriage to Katherine of Aragon. He would have had to be exceptionally innocent or lacking in lust or enterprise, though since he's said to have died of testicular cancer that might account for it.

19 April. I see I don't figure on today's *Independent on Sunday* Happy List, 'one hundred people who make Britain a better, more caring and contented nation'. It does include Ian McKellen (actor), Ray Mears (woodsman) and Sam Roddick 'for revolutionising sex accessories'. All of them 'representing values that need trumpeting'. Clinging on, that's what needs trumpeting, this Sunday morning (and not being swept away by the journalistic torrent). Keep on keeping on.

25 April. Listen to the (always interesting) *Archive on 4*. Tonight it's memories of Mrs Thatcher and a real feast of humbug with Lords Butler, Tebbit and Bell joining in a chorus of self-serving reminiscence of their old mistress with the equally fawning commentary supplied by Matthew Parris. Thatcher's was a court and her courtiers just as cowardly as the courtiers of Henry VIII, and one can imagine some sixteenth-century Lord Butler justifying his master much as Tebbit and Bell are doing this evening. 'It was unfortunate, of course, but the second wife had to go. She was impossible and yet, you see, His Majesty was genuinely fond of her, so much so that on the day she was . . . disposed of . . . he couldn't be anywhere in the vicinity and took himself off hunting. His Majesty was in many ways a very sensitive man.'

These days – i.e. after a lifetime – I am just about satisfied – or at least not embarrassed – by my handwriting. It's not neat but neither is it childish. It looks like the handwriting of an adult (and not yet of an old man).

This equanimity with regard to my handwriting vanishes when I look at the corrections I make to a script – and in particular at the present moment – to the fifth draft of *The Habit of Art*. Here my handwriting is big, childish, clumsy with no evidence of character or purpose and certainly not the handwriting of someone who has written the play. It's a mess. Nick H.'s handwriting in which he suggests improvements and points out omissions is neat, legible and of a piece with his other handwriting. Not so mine. Mine reverts to the all-over-the-place stuff I used to write while I was in the army and before I got to university – i.e. fifty years ago. Why I've no idea. But it is so.

8 May. A lot of fuss about the Prince of Wales, with a group of architects writing to the *Guardian* claiming HRH's objection to the Chelsea Barracks design is an interference 'in the democratic process'.

This is hypocritical rubbish. Architects have always had scant regard for democracy and as often as not have the planners in their pocket; anyone who stands up to them gets my vote, including the Prince of Wales.

11 May. We have a cat that visits, a big heavy-shouldered flat-faced black-and-white tom which can occasionally be found sitting on a rolled-up blanket in one of the cellars under the road off the front yard. If it's discovered in the cellar it leaves quickly but slows down on the steps and if one goes back inside, slinks downstairs again. It's grubby, unattractive and unresponsive to any words of affection. Indeed if one presumes to address it, it practically scowls. Rupert, who is allergic to cats, loves it.

24 May, Yorkshire. We stop for a cup of tea at bleak M1 service stations, the one after Leicester Forest – a vast hall, the atrium I think for a Travelodge, lined with shops, M&S, W. H. Smith, Costa Coffee but almost empty of people. The other, also empty, between Wakefield and Leeds.

I suppose we're both in a good mood and looking forward to the holiday so that these cheerless venues are not without charm – Indian ladies in saris squatting on the ornamental rocks eating a take-away beside parked cars; and half-naked, heavily tattooed, uncomely youths arsing about – and remind me of George F. saying forty years ago that there's no sense in holding aloof on bank holidays, better just to go along with the rest and (if you can) enjoy it. The emptiness of the place in the late afternoon sunshine and occasional new arrivals in the car park's vast piazza make it an unexpected idyll.

1 June. Clitter – a name for the bits of wax and old skin that gather in the ears, particularly as one gets older.

9 June. Reading *Enlightening*, the latest volume of Isaiah Berlin's letters, which has been rather grudgingly reviewed. One redeeming thing about Berlin – if he needs redeeming – is that he likes women. He likes talking to them, he likes writing to them, gossiping with them and, I suppose, though a late starter he likes sleeping with them. This is unusual. Most English men and fewer dons don't actually *like* women. They may like screwing them, but liking the women themselves, that's rare.

In the book there's an account of how Berlin lunched with the Queen and other eminent guests on 11 June 1957. At the lunch, Berlin tells us, he pressed the merits of Edmund Wilson's *Memoirs of Hecate County*, Nabokov's *Lolita* and the works of Genet, whereupon the titles were dutifully written down for Her Majesty by a courtier. So when in *The Uncommon Reader* HMQ questions the French president about Genet it has some (though fifty-year-old) foundation in fact. And it's sheer coincidence. In 2007 when I wrote the story I had no knowledge of Berlin's correspondence, the relevant volume of which was only published this year. I chose Genet simply as an author whom the Queen would be most unlikely ever to have come across. And to mention him to her even in 2007 might be thought bold, but much more so fifty years earlier when the home secretary, R. A. Butler, was rather cross with Berlin, implying his temerity might have interfered with his knighthood.

Like Auden Berlin seems to have had no visual sense at all and to have been uneasy in the countryside.

23 June. In the afternoon to Heywood Hill to sign books with Ms Debo. Not many books, thirty at the most, and we are soon through ten, even though D. needs a spotlight to be able to see the page. She writes along the top and I tuck in halfway down. Two Americans come in and ask to have their books signed, he claiming some sort of connection with Patrick Leigh Fermor in the SOE, though hardly in the war as he's young and quite full of himself. D. is very gracious and chats but they don't have much to say to me. Afterwards she gives me a lift ('Can I *split* at Lowndes Square') and Gerard her Irish chauffeur takes me back to Primrose Hill. He's a big fan and could go on *Mastermind* he seems so clued up about what I've written; nice voice and looks a bit like Father Ted.

Talking about Patrick L. F. Debo says he got into the bath (possibly at Edensor) and saw that both his feet had gone black. Thinking this was another affliction that comes with being ninety-one he called for help whereupon the butler came in and told him he'd forgotten to take off his socks.

27 June. Eugene, the New Zealand carpenter and Tree, his Thai wife have fitted up a lovely drop-leaf table in the utility room which lifts up to hold the laundry and the stuff coming out of the dryer. It's a plain old wood and looks as if it's been there forever and exactly the kind of thing that would catch one's eye in an old house as giving it charm. So nice that I start looking round for other drop-leaf table sites. R. entranced by it.

28 June. When we were staying at Kington in May we called at Presteigne, where the junk shop is a favourite of R.'s. In the window was a devotional jug with on it a picture of a hen and this verse:

> The Saviour of Mankind adopts
> The figure of the Hen
> To show the strength of his regard
> For the lost sons of men.

2 July. I am reading (or trying to read) Ivy Compton-Burnett's *A House and Its Head*, the result of dipping again into Hilary Spurling's superb biography. I encounter all the usual obstacles: the characters not distinguished from each other by their manner of speaking, forgetting which character is which with Compton-Burnett's description of what they look like not helping. And some of it (this is seldom said) downright bad. Still, there's more happening than one realises. In the first couple of chapters of *A House and Its Head* the eponymous Duncan Edgeworth burns a copy of a book, not named but what one imagines to be Darwin's *Origin of Species*, which has been given to his nephew for Christmas. Later that same Christmas Day the said nephew and his cousin re-enact an Anglican service, sermon included. Whether I shall manage to finish the book I doubt as I've never yet managed to read one of her novels right through.

6 July. But thinking I won't finish the book means that I can and do and find the novel ends with a flurry of marriages and (if I understand it correctly) the murder of a child being brushed under the carpet, money making all things right. I will try another one – *Manservant and Maidservant* is said to be good – but goodness, Dame Ivy is hard work.

7 July. The baby robin, now being fed by its mother on the fence, is the ugliest creature one could imagine: its feathers are scraggy and almost greasy, it has fierce black eyebrows and such a cross expression one wonders that even its mother can see any charms in it at all.

8 July. Two boys in Gloucester Avenue coming home from school, the same age but one boy big, the other small. The small one seeing a pile of dog turds on the pavement picks up a sprig of leaves and delicately garnishes the pile. While the big one claims to be disgusted (shouts, 'What did you do that for?') the other is hysterical with laughter and they go on.

28 July. To the National where we see half a dozen young actors for the rent boy role in *The Habit of Art*. None of them are quite right – one is too finished, another too tall – though why a rent boy shouldn't be tall I don't know, it just isn't a tall profession. There's one possibility but he looks a bit like a squirrel – and none of them can do the bravura speech at the finish.

Afterwards at home (and still, I suppose, hoping for Russell Tovey who'd now be too old – and too sought after) it occurs to me that the actor who plays the part could be too old and know it and spills out his insecurities to Kay, the stage manager, just as the others do. I could see how this could be funny – and add to the overall picture of a group of differently fractured people coming together to present something whole.

29 July. A piece in the *Independent* by Charlotte Philby, Kim Philby's granddaughter, prompted by the publication of Anthony Blunt's apologia released by the British Library. Not surprisingly she draws an unfavourable comparison between Blunt and Philby, bolstered by happy family pictures of her grandfather in Moscow. There's not much point, it seems to me, in apportioning guilt between them and anyway the treason side of it has never counted for much with me, though Philby does seem to have been responsible for the betrayal and presumed torture and death of a network of agents in a way that's never been proved of Blunt. What counted though, against Blunt, and Burgess too, was that they weren't journo-friendly. Journalists look after their own and Philby masqueraded as a devil-may-care drunken newspaperman and so was treated more indulgently by those in his profession. Blunt, who was an austere homosexual, a Marxist and a toff, got no such consideration. Though his character is still hard to fathom I've never had any difficulty believing Blunt and to a certain extent Burgess spent their lives paying for the mistakes of their Cambridge youth. Charlotte Philby thinks her grandfather was more honest, but it's a saloon-bar honesty. Philby was a chap. 'Let's have another drink on it, old man.' Good old Kim.

I August. This is Yorkshire Day, so designated apparently since the 1970s, though the festival had hitherto passed me by. This year I am rung by several newspapers for my comments on this joyful day, with them hoping, I imagine, for some jolly ee-ba-gummery. I suggest Yorkshire might be celebrating its distinction as the only county to have elected a fascist MEP, but nowhere is this printed.

5 August. This afternoon after a lengthy and wholly unsatisfactory visit to the English Heritage café at Belsay we intend to have a look at Warkworth and particularly its castle. But this week the Heritage has scheduled three days of medieval jousting at its castle so not fancying that (and the town very crowded) we walk instead on Druridge Bay sands which are less crowded and here at least the families look happy as they don't trailing round the town. Boys are skimming pebbles across the placid sea, reminding me of yet another non-accomplishment of my boyhood – the ability to throw stones whether across a pond, up in the air or at (not that I dared) other boys.

Then, for some reason I think of Updike – not long dead but a boy seventy-odd years ago who was skilled in all such boyish accomplishments – throwing things, hitting things and, in due course, fucking things but who yet managed to find in this intact and immaculate boyhood stuff that he could write about that wasn't just shame and failure – and maybe unlike with the rest of us it was even the shame and failure that was hard to find. Lying on the sand in the sun (still with my tie on) I think of Updike sunning his psoriasis which I would have found tragic or at least a stigma but which he what – triumphed over? No – maybe just discounted – didn't let it put him off his stroke. Such my thoughts aged seventy-five on this fairly grubby North Sea beach where the boys who were skimming stones are now building a sand castle.

20 August. Lucy, a donkey at Thistleyhaugh, the farm where we are staying, has never recovered from the death of her mate. We walk down the lane in the dusk after supper and see her ghost-like form glimmering in the trees; we call but she does not respond. One of the real regrets of my life is that I have never kept a donkey.

23 August. Penelope Wilton's just (last night) finished after thirteen weeks at the Donmar playing Gertrude to Jude Law's Hamlet. The production was going on (with Geraldine James in her part), first of all visiting Elsinore and then doing a season at the Broadhurst in New York. I'm glad I'm not a theatregoer living in Elsinore. All they must ever get are productions of *Hamlet*, while what they're probably longing for is *Move Over, Mrs Markham* or *Run for Your Wife*.

29 August. York as always a disappointment and each time I vow never to come again, the best bit the cafeteria at the Spurriergate Centre which is friendly, lively and not tourist-driven. Earlier as we walk from the station along by the river we call briefly at All Saints North Street to look at the glass. It's like a scene from a Powell and Pressburger movie with a group of amateur players getting into costume for a dress rehearsal of *A Midsummer Night's Dream*, various (very high church) chapels with their matchless medieval glass doubling as dressing rooms. Oddly there seems less glass than I remembered, though last time we came we had to rush round as they were setting up for another kind of performance, the midday Mass. Then, having eaten (our own) sandwiches in Spurriergate café – something I'm as nervous of doing at seventy-five as I was at seven in Harry Ramsden's – we make our way through the throng of shoppers and tourists to show Lynn Holy Trinity Goodramgate. Here, too, a performance is going on with a character in a battered top hat performing some monologue about the Black Death to a group of blameless tourists whom he has corralled in the pews. The performer has a loud sergeant-majorly voice compounded by his over-acting so that box-pewed though it is the church provides no escape. We give up on Holy Trinity and try the Minster – where nowadays there is no entrance at the west door or the north transept, everyone funnelled in at the south transept door opposite the Roman column at the top of Stonegate. We get just inside the door to a scene like Waterloo in the rush hour, the crossing packed with people, aimlessly milling about, some (like me) reluctant to pay and so not going through the turnstile, others staring vacantly round and the crowd robbing the space of all its wonder and (what I found as a child its particular attribute) the acoustic.

30 August, Yorkshire. Another ideal spot, empty of visitors this Sunday morning, is Jervaulx up beyond the head of Nidderdale and into Wensleydale. Some walkers using the café as a stepping-off point but the ruins otherwise deserted – nature and the building's decay having fashioned the place into a series of rooms that would have suited Vita Sackville-West.

No particular planting, though – valerian everywhere, crab apple trees and comfortable-looking sheep, the nicest detail the stone trough in the grass into which an underground spring burbles with the overflow disappearing back into the ground – presumably one of the water sources used by the monastery (whose last abbot Henry VIII had hung, drawn and quartered).

Remember at seventy-five Ariel Crittall's remark, 'What is it that I don't need to do any more now that I'm eighty? Oh yes, I remember, tell the truth.'

(She also, I think, answered the question differently: 'Oh I know. Wear knickers.')

From Jervaulx to Byland where the nice attendant in the kiosk shows us the few very faintly incised lines on the inside of the west wall, and which were presumably a guide to the masons building the rose window. Plus some more clearly incised lines down the alley with the carrels where the monks used to read.

With the abbey now at 5 p.m. wholly empty, we look at what to me is the most numinous object of the Dissolution, namely the green pottery inkwell, unearthed in the chapter house, which was presumably used when the monastery was signed over to the king's commissioners in 1540.

31 August. R. having spent most of the evening (and yesterday's) watching *Wuthering Heights* turns to me at the finish and says: 'You're rather like Heathcliff.'
Me (*gratified*): 'Really?'
R.: 'Yeah. Difficult, Northern and a cunt.'

2 September. I am reading the second volume of Michael Palin's diaries, which regularly feature the film producer Denis O'Brien. He produced *A Private Function*, which was made on a shoestring, the funds promised for the film regularly siphoned off for a more favoured O'Brien production, *Water*, which was set in the Caribbean and starred Michael Caine. O'Brien's partner was George Harrison, who didn't like the pig film either, and it's evidence of Michael Palin's generosity that he remained on good terms with the pair of them. At one point in the book my spirits rise when I read: 'Denis is in a very bad way.' Alas it turns out to be Denis the cat.

14 September. John Bird calls to ask where I found the phrase 'the habit of art'. I came across it in *Mystery and Manners*, a book of the incidental writings of Flannery O'Connor: 'The scientist has the habit of science, the artist the habit of art.' John, who is more widely (and rigorously) read than I am, had come across the phrase in the correspondence between Stravinsky and Jacques Maritain in the 1920s, making him think it came from St Thomas Aquinas. Since Flannery O'Connor was nothing if not Catholic that might be the link. I tell John Bird the story of Dudley Moore and me seeing Stravinsky and his wife Vera in the Hotel Pierre in New York in 1963, saying how the name Vera has always seemed to me to humanise Stravinsky. 'Not so much as Stockhausen,' says John. 'His wife's name was Doris.'

15 October. Across the river to the National for a rehearsal of some of the early scenes from *The Habit of Art* and in particular the crucial scene between Auden and Britten. In the afternoon Michael Gambon calls by, still full of regrets and apologies that he wasn't able to do the play. We all have a cup of tea and there's a lot of laughing, particularly as the actors from David Hare's *The Power of Yes* begin to drift out after their matinée. One of them is Simon Williams, a tall distinguished figure, handsome throughout his life just as was his father, whom I remember from a film I saw as a child, *One of Our Aircraft Is Missing*.

Simon is a Harrovian and says languidly: 'Yes. Character acting for me is playing an Old Etonian.'

20 October, New York. A limo picks me up at nine thirty to drive to Princeton, the driver (whose face I never see until we reach Princeton) looking from the rear like Lloyd Bridges in *Airplane* with lank grey hair, fidgety, shifting in his seat to the extent that as we speed along the Jersey turnpike I think he is about to have a heart attack and begin looking for where the key is located in the ignition ready in an emergency to switch it off. It's a hot morning, the industrial desolation along the Jersey shore shrouded in smoke and fumes, the real desolation of pollution not in New York – or not in Manhattan anyway – but in its surroundings. And even as we get beyond the worst of the industry it's still a desolate soulless environment with gas stations, hotels, out-of-town shopping centres, the occasional clapboard house just seeming to point up the tawdriness of what has developed around it. Princeton though is a different matter, a tree-lined road leading to a small and seemingly prosperous little town, too many boutiques and bijou restaurants maybe but a main street pleasant enough to sit out in and have coffee which we do until Carol Rigolo, head of French, arrives to escort us up across the road to the university proper.

And it's an attractive place, the architecture exuberantly Gothic with quadrangles flowing into each other, the buildings themselves as might have been drawn or designed by F. L. Griggs. Very few students and those we see quite laid back – a late Henry Moore sculpture on one of the lawns and curled up inside it (and fitting it perfectly) a boy reading. Friendly, too, some of them – an elegant black guy strolling through says (presumably having heard me speak), 'You don't get many days like this in England.' 'Yes,' I say. 'With us it's a rarity.' 'Quite. A rarity is what it is.'

22 *October.* Back in Manhattan, we sit on the terrace watching the sun go down over the Jersey shore – downtown skyscrapers against a sky that in the afterglow is almost green. Then there are buildings so tall and tumbled they might be in India, many-storeyed, many-windowed and with the cluster of water towers like turrets on the roof. Feel so privileged and lucky to be able to stay in this enchanting place that Lynn makes so comfortable – a twentieth-storey penthouse that

is cosier and yet more spectacular than the grandest apartment on Park Avenue or Central Park.

Lights coming on now with the last of the sun, two big office buildings flying the flag though what about I don't know.

A plane crosses the sky and dips down to Newark – all framed in the wisteria and creeper Lynn has grown over this many-arboured terrace – tables and loungers at every corner and the table outside the kitchen where we have breakfast and lunch.

Sky peach and warm still – this noisy, dirty heedless city one of the most blessed places of the earth.

The skyline now so spectacular it is almost vulgar, one of the posters on sale in a souvenir shop.

One of the moments that Cheever describes – the old lady in *The Wapshot Chronicle* standing to at the sun's setting. And – another recurrence – the urge in the presence of natural beauty to stay and to go at the same time.

24 October. A press release from the Bodleian Library:

> The author and playwright Alan Bennett is presenting his papers as a gift to the Bodleian Library, University of Oxford. This remarkable and comprehensive archive comprises materials relating to a distinguished literary career which began with the revue *Beyond the Fringe* in 1960 and has spanned nearly five decades.
>
> The archive includes original manuscripts, typescripts, handwritten notes and drafts for all his stage and television plays including the plays written for the National Theatre, the autobiographical books *Writing Home* (1994) and *Untold Stories* (2005) plus the manuscripts of his novellas and short stories, the latest being *An Uncommon Reader* (2007).
>
> What will also come to the library in due course are his own annotated editions of his published writing, together with letters and other materials arising and his own afterthoughts. There are

diaries in an unbroken series from 1974 onwards only a selection of which has already been printed.

Alan Bennett writes:

I re-write quite a bit so whatever I do tends to go into three or four versions all of which I keep and since I don't have a computer this does make for a fair amount of paperwork. The fact that a good deal of it is handwritten seems to delight the archivists at Bodley but it's always dismayed me and there's so much I'm quite glad to see the back of it. I just pity the poor research student who may have to make sense of it all.

More seriously I would like to emphasise that these accumulated writings come at no cost to the library or indeed to the tax-payer because I see the gift as an obligation repaid. I was educated at Oxford at Exeter College and I was fortunate in my time in that my education was entirely free. I say proudly that I had a state education, school, university . . . none of it cost me or my parents a penny. It's a situation which young people in higher education today can only dream of and this is wrong. I believe that free education is a right and would dispute the notion that unless one pays for one's education it will be undervalued. I hope I never undervalued the education I had here and though not to seem over-pious I see this gift such as it is, as some small recompense both to the University and also, though it is unfashionable to say this, to the state . . . or the Nanny State as it is disparagingly called. Well, as I say, I was lucky in my time and I'm grateful to have been nannied.

I think it's appropriate too that my stuff should be here in Oxford. My writing is nothing if not English and however universal and unboundaried scholarship may be these days I wouldn't want my stuff to be lodged in some Mid-Western university. At Bodley I shall be rubbing shoulders with Thomas Hardy and Philip Larkin. They might not be all that pleased but I am.

26 October. A *Francis Bacon Evening* on BBC4, i.e. Adam Low's excellent documentary and the (less excellent) film with Derek Jacobi as Bacon and a (much diminished) Daniel Craig as George Dyer – diminished, that is, from the hunk that emerged from the waves in the Bond film. Also glimpsed is Adrian Scarborough as one of the Colony Club crowd and in an unshown interview from 1965, a schoolboyish Julian Jebb – soft-faced, unlined and less the gnarled cherub he became later.

Briefly we switch over and catch some of *Flash Gordon* (1980) where hovering in the background while some sacrifice is prepared is in the robes of a high priest the unmistakable sardonic face of John Osborne – too long to wait for the credits to have his identification confirmed – but it is he – though whether as a joke or from dire necessity hard to say. [I ask John Heilpern – who confirms it is indeed Osborne.]

4 November. At one point during *The Habit of Art* tech, Nick Hytner asks how many of the score or so people in the auditorium have seen the play before. Only one person raises a hand. 'Good,' and he addresses the rest. 'How many of you realised that that was the words of Auden talking to the music of Britten?' All the hands go up and Nick is much relieved. This is one of his (endearing) habits: direction by plebiscite.

7 November. It's at this point, a couple of days into previews, that the author begins to take his or her leave of the play. It's nothing to do with a sense of work completed, which I seldom have anyway, or now the play is up and running a desire to get on with something else. Fat chance. No. While it's psychologically healthy (no sense in hanging around after all), it's because at this point the cast have been allotted their dressing rooms. Previously the rehearsal room has been the meeting place where besides work you gossip and have coffee and, if you're like me and are used to working on your own, have a nice, gregarious time. Now everyone except the playwright has a room to go to and a couch to lie on, the real meeting place henceforth the stage on which every night the actors rendezvous to do the play. For the author it's over.

8 November. On the front cover of the *Observer* Lewis Morley's photograph of me walking along the beach at Brighton in 1961. It's the only photograph I've ever had taken where aged twenty-six I could almost fancy myself. My look is both of yearning and disquiet and calls up the lines from *Henry IV Part 2* that Hector quotes in the film of *The History Boys*.

> The happiest youth, viewing his progress through,
> What perils past, what crosses to ensue,
> Would shut the book, and sit him down and die.

11 November. I seldom notice the two minutes' silence as I'm generally at home working, as I was today. On Sunday when there was the Cenotaph service and its two minutes' silence, R. was at an antiques fair in the Agricultural Hall in Victoria. As eleven struck there was an announcement and a hush fell, but one or two people seemed to think the silence meant 'Freeze!' and so they were not only silent but remained fixed in whatever attitude (handing over money, examining a vase) the silence caught them. Some of these positions were quite awkward, with the ending of the silence coming as a relief.

12 November. A hysterical afternoon at the National Theatre. The play is settling down and though we rehearse every day and have notes it's mostly a question of fine tuning. At one point in the first act Richard Griffiths as Fitz, the actor playing Auden, farts. 'That's Auden farting,' says Fitz. 'Not me.' This hasn't been getting much of a response so just as with a patch of dialogue that doesn't work, the fart has to be fine-tuned too.

We go through the repertoire of available farts transmitted from the CD from the sound desk and while not quite marking them with score cards the cast express their various preferences and we just about settle on two candidates, when Stephen Wight who plays Stuart, a rent boy, points out that the farts we are favouring are plainly farts made on a plastic or wooden surface whereas Fitz is sitting in a chair that is upholstered. A more smothered fart is required so the quest begins again. Having finally settled on the ideal fart it has to be played several times so that the cast, already hysterical, don't break up when they hear it for real on the stage. I can't imagine this scene taking place in a production directed by Peter Brook, say – or indeed Lindsay Anderson, 'Settle down' the reproving note.

17 November. A bit of noise outside last night and R. peered through the window and could see nothing, though hearing somebody laughing. This morning my bike is gone, the crime-proof lock still attached to the railings. This is only the second time I've had a bike stolen and so I suppose I ought to think myself lucky. The play opens tonight but it's the bike I'm thinking about and I keep going to the window to look at the place where it was.

30 November. We leave London with the weather still wet and tempestuous, making me dread battling up the Great North Road through the spray of the lorries. In the event though it clears up and it's a lovely day as we drive round Peterborough, have our sandwiches on the edge of a field near Wisbech, then not expecting much we turn off to look at a church in Walpole St Peter. Seen from the road, the large windows full of quarrel glass hint at its splendour but nothing prepares you for the perfection of the interior which is of a seemingly intact medieval church with nothing – *nothing* – to offend the eye. There are a full set of poppy-head pews (*c*.1600) – both in the body of the nave and at the sides. A pedimented screen (*c*.1631) that runs across the west end of the nave, a medieval brass lectern, the accoutrements of the church so many and so various one scarcely notices the painted chancel screen.

The oddest feature is the altar raised up high above the chancel to accommodate an external passage, vaulted with (among others) a sheep's-head boss to accommodate religious processions proceeding round the boundaries of the church. Nothing seems to have been lost, nothing spoilt and (a big factor with R.) no evidence of contemporary religion at all.

1 December. To Holt, which is as pleasant and friendly as we remembered from last time. At Richard Scott's shop we buy our Christmas presents for each other – various bits of stained glass, some of them thought to be architectural salvage from the French Revolution.

Then (this is the niceness of Holt) the pharmacist supplies me with some pills I'd forgotten to bring (ringing JP Pharmacy in Camden Town to make sure they were the right strength) and the NatWest is equally helpful to R. over some transaction he'd omitted to do last week. Then we have a nice lunch in an ordinary café before going down the Norwich Road to Salle. Two censing angels above the west door prepare you for the treasures within, the angels (and not just their wings) feathered. More unspoiled woodwork with huge brackets supporting a towering font cover, good misericords particularly one that R. finds of a frowning head of a man that may be Christ on the south-west side of the chancel stalls. Open are the doors to the spiral staircase, the two parvise rooms over the north and south porches, the north room particularly fine with elaborate bosses. Unusual these days to find such places accessible – health and safety having tamed many of the pleasures of looking at churches when I was a boy, when one of the particular attractions of a church was going up the tower – a treat even a Victorian church could furnish however dull it was otherwise. Still I never in the whole of my churchgoing youth saw anything like the feathered angels.

2 December. I am reading (backwards as usual with biographies) Selina Hastings's *The Secret Lives of Somerset Maugham* and much enjoying it. It's beautifully and *silkily* written with a good deal, though I've read at least two previous biographies of Maugham, that I did not know. It's also very sympathetic to its subject. But however understanding it is I find I withhold sympathy for him – not because of his cruelties or his sharp tongue, but because what he represents – and what I imagine he would be happy to represent – is worldly wisdom and that is a quality or a qualification to which I have never aspired or much admired. He's the author as Man of the World.

7 December. Write something and it happens. This weekend there has been a slightly relentless re-showing of some of my old plays and films on BBC2 and BBC4, with Archie Powell's documentary on BBC2 and a long interview with Mark Lawson on BBC4. Watching them both I note that, though I'm on different channels, I tell the same stories, make the same jokes and, while it's never quite a routine, I find myself falling into the same tedious repetition that I've written Auden going through in *The Habit of Art*.

15 December. My best Christmas cards are always from Victor Lewis-Smith, who lives in the Lake District, not far from Sellafield: 'I persist in telling visitors on the fell that the building they can see in the distance is in fact the Kendal mint cake factory, whose chimneys are emitting exotic mint vapour. It's for the best, it really is.'

31 December. Call Rupert to the back door to watch a full moon coming up behind the trees at the end of the garden. It's apparently a 'blue moon', i.e. the second full moon this month, which happens every two or three years. The next blue moon on New Year's Eve won't be until 2028 so it's the last one I shall ever see – and it's also the first that I ever knew about. The moon is strong enough to cast

sharp shadows, with the sky blue except for occasional reefs of cloud
so that with the snow still lying in drifts on the road earth and heaven
seem one.

2010

1 January. 'I'm happy doing what I'm doing. I'm not always happy with what I've done.'

13 January. Snow again this morning, soft and plump, snow out of Mabel Lucie Attwell softening the trees and coating the wires, though now the thin falling snow turns to drizzle and great clumps of snow slide from the trees and fall into the gardens.

19 January. D. Cameron's notion that the better degree the teacher has the better the teacher is so wrong-headed as to be laughable; except that he may shortly be in a position to put his cockeyed notions into practice. Somebody should take him on one side and tell him that to teach well you don't need a degree at all. I got a first-class degree and was a hopeless teacher. Russell Harty got a third-class degree and taught brilliantly. There was a great deal he didn't know but he knew how to enthuse a class and made learning fun, much as he could work a studio audience.

23 January. To the National where I watch the matinée of *The Habit of Art*. It's a sharp and energetic performance, matinée audiences often the best and today's helped because there are thought to be at least 130 blind people in the audience. Some of them have been up on the stage beforehand to familiarise themselves with the layout, handle the props and meet the cast, all of which helps to focus attention on the play and there's scarcely a cough. I wait in the wings for the actors to come off then go up to the canteen and have a cup of tea with them, something I haven't done since the play opened and have much missed.

24 January. Two boys from Doncaster have been sentenced for tor-
turing two other boys from the same village. In sentencing them the
judge gives them a stern lecture, though how much of it they understand must be debatable. It's a shocking story, with one of the victims
having been battered almost to death. David Cameron is quick to
move in and claim the crime is evidence of 'a broken society', con-
veniently ignoring the fact that Edlington, the village in question,
is smack in the middle of what was a mining community, a society
systematically broken by Mrs Thatcher. As with the Bulger case the
tabloids make a determined effort to find out the identity of the culprits, the crime frequently described as 'unimaginable'. I don't find
it hard to imagine at all. When I was eight or nine I used to play
torture games with two other boys at my elementary school up on
the recreation ground in Armley. I would pretend to whip them or
they me and with a forwardness that I never afterwards enjoyed was
always the one to instigate the games. At ten I went to a different
school and thereafter became the shy, furtive, prurient creature I was
for the rest of my childhood.

25 January. I find tattoos hard to understand, even to forgive.
Afflicted quite early in life with varicose veins I've always been
self-conscious of the greyish blue of the veins and found it a dis-
figurement and a stigma even, the blue of the veins the same blue
as that of a tattoo. That anyone would voluntarily do to themselves
what nature had done to me I find incomprehensible. Beckham, for
instance, had a nice body until he had it so extensively engraved.

30 January. Bitterly cold but bright blue day, a sprinkling of snow
during the night so that Cambridge looks much as it did when I first
went there in December 1951, gripped by a heavy frost but with
clear sunny skies – and with a beauty I've never forgotten. We have a
sandwich lunch in the nice café in the Fitzwilliam and walk through
the picture galleries, my eye taken by the same paintings, the same

sculptures every time – Nollekens' bust of Lord Savile, the lip curled and contemptuous (and not unlike Karl Miller), Van Dyck's provocative Countess of Southampton with her glass globe and of course Van Dyck's Archbishop Laud – of whom Lynn says, 'He looks like he'd benefit from a good massage.'

'– the third movement of Elgar's beautiful *Symphony No 1*.' That is what is wrong with Classic FM – the 'beautiful'.

10 February. Finish with some regret Frances Spalding's book on the Pipers, John and Myfanwy, the latter figuring in *The Habit of Art* where she is to some extent disparaged. I've always been in two minds about Piper, liking him when I was young with his paintings 'modern' but representational enough to be acceptable, a view I trotted out years later when Romola Christopherson was taking me round Downing Street. 'I suppose for Mrs Thatcher,' I sneered, 'Piper is the acceptable face of modern art,' not realising that at that moment the lady herself was passing through the room behind me. Some of his abstracts I like, particularly a collage, *Coast at Finisterre* (1961), which is illustrated in the book, and some of his Welsh landscapes. I don't care for his stained glass, though churches are always proud when they have a Piper window, the latest (and no more pleasing than the rest) glimpsed at Paul Scofield's memorial service in St Margaret's, Westminster. For all that, though, the book is immensely readable, drawing together so many strands of the artistic life in the 1930s and 1940s – K. Clark, Ben Nicholson, Betjeman and all the stuff to do with the genesis of the Shell Guides. Odd to think of Piper's gaunt figure sketching in my own Yorkshire village, the paintings he did there reproduced (not plain why) in Osbert Sitwell's *Left Hand, Right Hand* and now at Renishaw.

14 February. I am said in today's *Independent on Sunday* to be 'pushing eighty' with a photograph (taken at seventy) in corroboration.

The article is about the decline of Northern drollery, of which I am an example, though whether of the drollery or its decline I'm not sure.

I pass the house in Fitzroy Road with the blue plaque saying that Yeats lived there but with no plaque saying that Sylvia Plath also died there. I look down into the basement where Plath put her head in the gas oven. And there is a gas oven still, only it's not the Belling or the Cannon it would have been in 1963 but now part of a free-standing unit in limed oak.

It was this house where Eric Korn heard someone reading out the plaque as being to 'William Butler Yeast'. 'Presumably,' Eric wanted to say, 'him responsible for the Easter Rising.'

17 February. Stopped by a man outside the post office in Regent's Park Road who fishes in his wallet and shows me a note I sent nearly fifty years ago to Bernard Reiss, the tailor in Albion Place in Leeds who made me my first suit in 1954. The note is about two 7/6 seats which I'd booked him for *Beyond the Fringe*, the man showing it me Bernard Reiss's nephew. I tell him about the suit, which was in grey Cheviot tweed, the waistcoat of which I still have and which I took to show Mr Hitchcock at Anderson and Sheppard before they made me a suit last year. My first suit and probably my last.

2 March. R. back from Edensor where he and Simon Upton have been photographing 'the Old Vic'. Says the house is very busy with a lot of comings and goings – David Mlinaric to tea, Lady Vestey and another horsebreeding lady to lunch, Charlotte Mosley, the vicar – Chatsworth life but now crammed into the dower house. Debo (now ninety) in good form. Says that the Mellons used to pass on their discarded clothes to them – presumably during austerity and the days of clothing coupons – every now and again a great cardboard coffin of a box arriving full of couture clothes over which the sisters would squabble. Once she and Diana were in Jermyn Street both wearing one of the Mellon cast-offs (and she can describe the dress still, black with mink trim round the collar and lapels) when they saw Paul Mellon on the other side of the street. 'He mustn't see us,' said Diana, 'lest he recognise the clothes,' and then became hysterical. This idiosyncratic form of lend-lease persisting well after the need for it had passed.

When they go there's lots of 'Oh *must* you go? Can't you stay? What am I going to do when you've gone?' – R. doing a very good imitation.

3 March. Lunch at L'Etoile with Michael Palin and Barry Cryer, Elena Salvoni still presiding there at lunchtime and though she's ninety not looking much different from when I first got to know her at Bianchi's in the 1960s. Barry as usual fires off the jokes which are almost his trademark but today he also talks about how, when he was a young man in Leeds, he suffered badly from eczema and used to be swathed in bandages, face included. On one occasion he went out like this into the streets of Leeds but nobody stared at him, so correctly did people behave. He even went into a shop, looking, as he said, like the Invisible Man and the woman serving took no notice, just saying of the weather: 'Well, it's a bit better today.' I ask him how he got rid of it and he says it went soon after he met Terry, his wife, so that he attributed it to the stresses of being young (and, I imagine, with eczema, unloved) and living in a bedsit with all the hardships of his young life. While he was in St James's one of the patients on his ward hanged himself in the toilets, presumably driven mad by the intolerable itching. Michael P. is as kindly as ever and me as dull, three old (-ish) men having their lunch, next stop the bowling green.

10 March. To Durham where there are not many visitors this Wednesday morning and more guides than there are people to show round. See the line of Frosterley marble inset in the floor of the nave, the limit beyond which women were not allowed to approach the shrine of St Cuthbert behind the high altar with its wonderfully spiky Neville screen, which, when I came before, I took for some 1950s Coventry Cathedral-like installation and not a genuine four-teenth-century reredos minus its statues. Struck, though, as then by the marble hulks on top of the Neville tombs, which, as R. says, are more representative of dead and butchered bodies than their intact representations can ever have been. Previously these tombs, mutilat-ed and covered in ancient graffiti, were said to have been casualties of the imprisonment here of Scottish prisoners during the aftermath of the Civil War. The new notes in the cathedral's leaflet now specifical-ly disavow this without at the same time explaining how such radical mutilation occurred. This is somewhat mealy-mouthed, and rather than the fruits of some breakthrough study of the circumstances of the Scots' incarceration, their absolution sounds like political cor-rectness. A good example of changing taste is that Pevsner, writing in 1953, says of the nowadays perfectly acceptable rood screen by George Gilbert Scott, 'It should be replaced,' and the faux-Cosmati pulpit similarly. A propos guides we are using Henry Thorold's *Shell Guide to County Durham* written in 1980 which recommends a visit to Finchale (pronounced Finkle) Priory set in a bend of a river just north of Durham, of whose remoteness and unspoiled beauty Thor-old gives a lyrical description. No more – and when we eventually track it down on the far side of a housing estate it turns out to be on the edge of a caravan site that comes to within a few feet of the abbey.

Visiting Byland we'd remarked, coming away, on the variety of lichens growing in the ruins, the stones blotted with their grey patches. In Durham I notice similar lichens, particularly on the paths leading up to the south door, only later realising it wasn't lichen but chewing gum.

Back down the A1 and across country to Ramsgill and the Yorke Arms, the sun so low and bright I often have to stop as driving directly west, I can't see – exactly the sort of journey the late Roger Warner hated, the direction of his antique-dealing trips determined by having the sun behind him in the morning (so driving west) and behind him until evening when he's coming back driving east.

13 March, Yorkshire. Warm today for the first time and though I'm in my overcoat I sit out and read the papers in the bright sunshine. In the afternoon we drive to Ingleton where R. tries (and fails) to get a red Roberts Revival radio (it has to be red) from Tooby's; nor does he find one in the (increasingly boutiquified) Kirkby Lonsdale.

Then we walk along the Fell Road track above Brownthwaite, lambs in the field, a buzzard soaring about the sky. The walk is measured out in the sheep pen installations of Andy Goldsworthy – as far one way as the second of his pens, then as far the other way taking in two more. The sun comes and goes but coming out suddenly we see on the horizon, still snow-covered and like a vision of paradise, the Lakeland fells, lying like a great white whale across the horizon.

Lambs in the lower fields some so young and frail they must be tempting to the buzzard, the innocence and playfulness of lambs to me a recurrent mystery. We are about to stop the car and talk to half a dozen looking at us through the gate but then they get up and off, jerky and jumping and dashing about the field.

Tea in front of the fire now, Rupert reading Edmund White and me, I'm sure, about to doze off.

17 March. I'd forgotten until I was turning over some papers today that Stuart, the rent boy in *The Habit of Art* had had a previous incarnation in an early play that I began. He was still a rent boy booked by Auden but this was before the poet had returned to England, when he was living in St Marks Place in the East Village. The boy was more cultured than his English counterpart and may even have been at college, being a rent boy part of paying his way. Auden grows suspicious of the young man's background as he seems uncharacteristically well informed as to Auden's work and modern literature in general. It turns out that his previous clients make quite a distinguished list, numbering among them Spender, Isherwood, Thom Gunn and Truman Capote with fellatio or whatever really a more sophisticated (and arduous) form of autograph hunting. It's a less likely scenario in London than in New York where celebrities in those days anyway counted for more.

Tuft-hunting I suppose it would be called.

23 March. That Ted Hughes should have got into Poets' Corner ahead of Larkin wouldn't have surprised Larkin, though he must surely have a better claim. Two deans back, and not long after Larkin's death, I remember Michael Mayne saying that Larkin had earned his place on the strength of 'Church Going' alone. Though Hughes fits the popular notion of what a poet should be, many more of Larkin's writings have passed into the national memory.

26 March. A punk young blackbird, feather on its head stuck up and spiky, pecking about in one of the pots while a jay finds something – a snail maybe – on the fence.

31 March. Remember – I'm not sure why – when I was at school and doing the (somehow obligatory) amateur dramatics I was in William Douglas-Home's *The Chiltern Hundreds* with one of my lines 'That's the cross I've got to bear.' A devout Christian at the time I felt I couldn't say this line, my notion of piety having much more to do with dubious issues of conscience like this than with practical Christian conduct. Anyway I made my protest and the producer 'Charlie' Bispham, the chemistry master (dapper figure, pencil moustache), was gratifyingly sarcastic, thus assuring me I was a martyr for my faith. But I didn't say the line – and probably a lot of others as I was never very sure of the text. Twerp, I think now, marvelling at how I could survive the embarrassment, not my own (I was a Christian after all) but that of the rest of the cast.

2 April. Notes on Ian Hamilton's *Against Oblivion*:

Of Randall Jarrell: 'he had in 1952 – and with stunningly abrupt efficiency – exchanged an insufficiently worshipful first wife for one who was prepared to dedicate herself to Randall's adoration.'

'Insufficiently worshipful' such a good phrase and so apt:

The insufficiently worshipful wives (and families) of writers.

7 April. The open mouth of Chelsea's Frank Lampard, having scored a goal, is also the howl on the face of the damned man in Michelangelo's *Last Judgement*.

10 April. Make potatoes dauphinoise for supper to a recipe by Nigel Slater – and it's delicious, like proper cooking.

16 April. The row over Lord Ashcroft's non-dom status seems to have died down. Nobody, I think, noted that it was the reverse of the row that triggered the American War of Independence. In 1776 the rallying cry was no taxation without representation whereas with Lord Ashcroft (and the other non-doms) it is no representation without taxation, i.e. why should he or anyone have a voice in the making of legislation if he or she does not pay taxes.

18 April. I love the Van Gogh letters as objects partly because they're small, manageable and delicate. Some of the larger paintings, e.g. the Alpilles mountains near Aix, I still find hard to take, though obviously wonderful pictures. Similarly his boiling skies.

Surprised by his use of different techniques – dabs and hatchings in one picture, smooth matt application of paint in another – paintings that are virtually contemporary though the last pictures – in Auvers – one a day for seventy days – are, in a way, the most encouraging. He's painting so fast and so recklessly that any sense of painterly self-preservation is abandoned in the fever of getting it down. I feel – again absurdly – that this has a message for me at this late stage in my life – though Van Gogh was painting as wildly as this when, though near to death, he was still a relatively young man.

19 April. A propos the transport shutdown due to the volcanic cloud there have been the inevitable outbreaks of Dunkirk spirit, with the 'little ships' going out from the Channel ports to ferry home the stranded 'Brits'. It's a reminder of how irritating the Second War must have been, providing as it did almost unlimited opportunities for bossy individuals to cast themselves in would-be heroic roles when everybody else was just trying to get by. 'Brits' – so much of what is hateful about the world since Mrs Thatcher in that gritty hard little word.

29 April, New York. Picture taken for *Vanity Fair* in a bar on Greenpoint Avenue in Brooklyn, a desolate area now being colonised as most of lower Manhattan has been in the thirty years since I started coming here. Thus on Thompson Street years ago there was an establishment advertising live chickens for slaughter – an unlikely enterprise even in the poorest quarters of London. But there's one still on Greenpoint Avenue, which is a Polish quarter – rows of shut shops which are gradually opening up again, the shoot in one of the first of the smartened-up bars, plain huge-windowed, like a bar painted by Hopper. Opposite is a late nineteenth-century four-storey apartment block in granite and terracotta, with vast semi-circular studio windows. This is run-down too but is characteristic of its period and as grand as any Renaissance palazzo.

The photographer is easy to chat to saying how he learned photography by watching his father with the family camera and he was well into college before he realised that something he enjoyed doing could earn him a living.

As he photographs me, a huge truck laden with clapped-out cars slowly edges round the corner, followed by a community bus from a geriatric home.

Opposite is a tailor, the sign saying, starkly, 'Alter', and a few doors up a cash and loan facility open twenty-four hours. The car arrives to take me back, the driver thinking of going home to Hungary. 'This place, finished.' He switches on some rubbishy news programme. 'BBC World Service is the only one worth listening.' I don't say to him that come a week on Thursday (and the election), that may not be for long.

Normally in the late afternoon I'd walk over to Union Square to buy the *Guardian*. Today, having seen on the front page of the *New York Times* the row over Gordon Brown (quite properly in my view) calling a questioner 'bigoted', I give it a miss. Of course, if Rupert Murdoch gets his way there will be no more *New York Times* or anything liberal that matters. Murdoch here, Murdoch everywhere; Murdoch with the government in his pocket. Instead I sit outside in the sun, the sky empty of clouds and wind, watching the boats edging down the Hudson and the glitter of cars on the Jersey turnpike.

30 April. I'm sitting on the terrace – the north-west terrace I suppose it is, facing the monumental (thirty-storey or so) building in greyish-brown pleated brick, topped off with an Escher-like summit of ornamental-seeming staircases, the corner of which I have just walked round to find it is the Bell Telephone Building on 17th Street. It's blank-windowed and devoid of all life except that unusually an hour or so ago a man and two women came out onto one of the crenellated balconies seeming to be measuring something, occasionally looking over down the vertiginous front.

Yesterday I went into the almost featureless lobby where there was a cubbyhole and a barrier but with no clue as to what the building is for – whether it is indeed a telephone exchange still (built *c.*1930) or whether it nowadays has a more sinister purpose.

A hawk (maybe) flies across the cavernous air to roost (or nest) on top of the telephone building. I watch to see if it takes flight again but see only a plane high in the flawless sky.

1 May. The image of bliss as a child was on the Big Dipper at More-cambe when towards the end of the ride there were no more climbs and falls, the screams and suspense over and just the gentle coasting home.

2 May. Several of the obituaries of Alan Sillitoe who died last week mention how, when as a child he was being hit by his father, his mother would beg, 'Not on his head. Not on his head.' My father was a mild man and seldom hit my brother or me but when he did my mother would make the same anguished plea. 'Not on their heads, Dad.' It's a natural enough entreaty, though one that might be taken to have premonitory undertones: if these small boys were ever to climb out of this working-class kitchen and make something of themselves a good, undamaged head was what they were going to need.

10 May. For much of the day it has looked as if, inconceivably, the Liberal Democrats were going to fall in with the Tories and form a government – a prospect that so depressed me I felt (fanciful though this may seem) as some (though only some) people felt after Munich. Not having dared watch the TV news I knew nothing of Gordon Brown's resignation and the later talks between Labour and the Lib Dems and this at once raises the spirits. It's extraordinary to me that politics can so radically affect my mood. Now it seems to hang in the balance, the anger of Lib Dem supporters at their leaders even considering an alliance with the Tories surely one of the factors. The press and TV don't help. As in so many disputes the outcome would be easier if it coincided with a newspaper or a communications strike, a shutdown (and a shutting up) of the commentating voices. But a gloomy day.

Meanwhile every politician who speaks begins by making a ritual affirmation that their party's first priority is firm and stable govern-ment and the sooner that is achieved the better. Whereas it's all too plain that so far as stable government is concerned the politicians are largely superfluous and that the civil service can carry on with the firm and stable government just as they usually do – temporarily relieved of the interference from their ministers.

The metaphor is I suppose of the ship of state which, deprived of crew and captain, is rudderless. Except it isn't. Let it drift or ride at anchor. Who cares? The answer (in hushed tones) despite the experience of the last year still: 'The markets.'

12 May. For all the Lib Dems are in the cabinet I imagine there will be another cabinet somewhere which does not include them and where, once on their own, the Tories can come clean . . . or talk dirty. But then, this is what cabinet government has always been like: the cabinet and the real cabinet; it doesn't need the excuse of a coalition.

As always at signings when I'm faced with a seemingly endless line of nice, appreciative readers, most of them women, I come away thinking the writer I most resemble is Beverley Nichols.

14 May. Obituary in today's *Guardian* of Gerald Drucker, veteran double bass player and for the last thirty years principal bass of the Philharmonia. When I was a boy Leeds had its own orchestra, the Yorkshire Symphony Orchestra, which gave concerts every Saturday in the town hall. A group of us from the sixth form used to sit behind the orchestra (seats sixpence) and always behind the double basses. Drucker was a young man then but quite heavily built, a cross between Alfred Marks and the actor who played One-Round in *The Ladykillers*, he and his instrument well suited. According to the *Guardian* he'd already had a varied career before he landed up in Leeds, including playing for Xavier Cugat at the Waldorf-Astoria in New York. Cut to forty years later, when I saw him in the Festival Hall bookshop. I went up to him and stammered out my appreciation of that time in the 1950s, saying how much the orchestra had meant to me then. For someone who'd gone on to become principal bass of the Philharmonia and probably a good deal else, his time in Leeds can hardly have been a notable episode in his musical career, and thinking that this earnest middle-aged man babbling about Leeds must be wanting his autograph (though hardly a common occurrence in the lives of bass players) he took fright and fled the shop. I'll remember Drucker, though, together with other basses laying into the opening of Gustav Holst's ballet music for *The Perfect Fool*, one of the rare opportunities when they could briefly take centre stage.

15 May. We have robins nesting just over the wall and with a cat skulking around and a pair of magpies I invest in a water pistol. The cat so insolent and impervious to threats I feel it deserves it. Other birds include a pair of jays, two collared doves and a younger hanger-on, several blackbirds, a couple of starlings, who are newcomers, an occasional wren, and various blue tits.

16 May. Spend part of the afternoon hiding in the gazebo with a (water) pistol on my knee hoping to surprise the squirrel rifling the (squirrel-proof) bird feeder.

17 May. A week after Mr Hague is appointed foreign secretary the police presence (two heavily armed patrolmen) has not been withdrawn from David Miliband's house just up the road. I pass the house nearly every day and could have asked, but fear the police might shoot me in the interests of health and safety. It was never clear to me whether the force was protecting the property or the person, as Miliband could be seen, seemingly untailed, striding round Primrose Hill (and indeed the world) while the brace of bobbies still hung doggedly about his doorstep. When they do eventually depart the first casualties will be among the cyclists of whom, judging from the bikes leaning on the railings, there are many in the street. Having had my own (locked) bike recently nicked from outside my house (which has no police presence) I'd advise them to get their bikes inside sharpish.

23 May. I'm coming to the end of *Wolf Hall*, Hilary Mantel's novel, the first of two about Thomas Cromwell. Rich and vivid and teeming with life it's a monumental work and some, at least, of one's admiration is for Mantel's sheer industry. Presented as very much a modern sensibility Cromwell recoils from, or is anxious to avoid, cruelty, a restraint he learned in the service of his first master, Wolsey. He's particularly concerned about the penalties inflicted on those of his own reformist way of thinking. But cruelty is indivisible. Though he is repelled by Thomas More for the torture he personally inflicts on heretics, Cromwell is made to dismiss the Carthusians butchered at Tyburn just as 'four treacherous monks'.

More is the villain of this first volume. Mantel admits to being a contrarian, and is unwilling to give More any credit at all for moral courage so that one begins to feel the portrait of Cromwell is as skewed as Robert Bolt's (or Peter Ackroyd's) is of More and for the same reason, both men human and therefore venial when embosomed in their respective families.

Set against this massive work one's objections seem petty, and it's a tribute to the power of the novel that one discusses it as if it were history or at least biography, with one's misgivings elusive and lost in the undergrowth of the novel's intimate conjecturing. Still, one keeps coming up against inequities: Clerke and Sumner, two heretic scholars, starved to death in the cellars of Wolsey's Cardinal College; ten of the Carthusians who were not executed at Tyburn were starved to death in Newgate; Clerke and Sumner get a mention but not the monks. This is perhaps an author's privilege and one has to keep reminding oneself this is a novel, but time and again Mantel seems to let her hero (and so far he is a hero) down lightly. A little further along the road will come the punishment of Friar Forrest, roasted slowly to death in a gala ceremony at which Cromwell presided. One waits to see how Mantel deals with this.

I have to admit, though, that I find it hard to read about the middle years of the sixteenth century certainly with any pleasure any more than I can enjoy a history of the Third Reich, say, or a programme on Stalin's Terror. One element in *Wolf Hall*'s success is the regular and unflinching presentation of horror. There may be cornflowers on Cromwell's desk but this is a novel about torture, tyranny and death.

11 June. Drive round to Camden Town to shop and go to the bank where I draw out £1,500 to pay the builders. I put the money in an envelope in my inside pocket and then cross the road to M&S where I shop for five minutes or so. At which point two middle-aged women, Italian by the look and sound of them, tell me somebody has spilled some ice cream down the back of my raincoat. I take off my coat and they very kindly help me to clean it up with tissues from one of their handbags and another man, English, I think, big and in his fifties, goes away and comes back with more tissues. The ice cream (coffee-flavoured) seems to have got everywhere and they keep finding fresh smears of it so that I take off my jacket too to clean it up. No more being found I put my jacket on again, thanking the women profusely though they brush off my gratitude and abruptly disappear. I go back to the car, thinking how good it is there are still people who, though total strangers, can be so selflessly helpful, and it's only when I'm about to get into the car that I remember the money and look in my inside pocket to find, of course, that the envelope has gone. The women or their male accomplice must have seen me in the bank or coming away from it and followed me into the store. I go back to M&S, tell security, who say they have cameras but are not sure if they were covering that particular spot (they weren't). They ring the police while I go back to the bank, who also have CCTV which the police will in due course examine. I give my details, and my address and phone number, to a constable who, when I get back home, duly rings with the incident number. Ten minutes later, less than an hour after it has occurred, the doorbell rings and on the doorstep is a rather demure girl: 'My name is Amy. I'm from the *Daily Mail*. We've just heard about your unfortunate experience.'

I close the door in Amy's caring face, tell a photographer who's hanging about to bugger off ('That's not very nice') and come in and reflect that though the theft is bad enough more depressing is that someone in the police must immediately have got on to the *Mail*, neither the bank nor M&S having either my private number or the address. I just wonder how much the paper paid him or her and what the tariff is – pretty low in my case, I would have thought. The women are thought to be Romanians, and in any case were very good at their job and must have been pleasantly surprised at how much they netted and how stupid I was. Quite hard to bear is that I have to go back to the bank to draw out another £1,500 or the builders will go unpaid.

The con is a familiar one, apparently, and often pulled in Spain. It even has a name: the Mustard Squirter. Still it's the liaison between the police and the *Daily Mail* that is the most depressing. Years ago when Russell Harty had been exposed in the tabloids he was being rung in Yorkshire every five minutes. His solicitor then agreed with the local police that he should have a new number, known only to the police. Ten minutes later a newspaper rang him on it.

13 June. Yesterday afternoon the *Express* telephoned. This morning at eight o'clock the *Standard* is on the doorstep. Talk to Niamh Dilworth at the National about it and tell her that the police have asked me not to dry-clean my jacket and ice-cream-smeared raincoat in order to test them for DNA. She says that all they'll be able to discover is whether it was Wall's, Viennetta or Carte D'Or. The casualty, though, is trust, so that I am now less ready to believe in the kindness of strangers. But one has to be careful when one has been robbed. Like cancer it's one more topic on which it's easy to become a bore.

26 June. A propos Prince Charles's intervention in the Chelsea Barracks redevelopment Ruth Reed, the principal of RIBA, says: 'The UK has a democratic and properly constituted planning process: any citizen in this country is able to register their objections to proposed buildings with the appropriate local authority.' This is disingenuous. The planning process is and always has been weighted against objectors who, even if they succeed in postponing a development, have to muster their forces afresh when the developer and the architect come up with a slightly modified scheme. And so on and so on, until the developer wins by a process of attrition. Furthermore Ms Reed, in her role as trade union leader for her profession, ignores the dismal record of mediocre architecture which has ruined so many English towns and continues to do so. Anyone, even the sultan of Qatar, who stands up to this collection of mediocrities gets my vote. And all the talk of HRH exceeding his constitutional rights is tripe.

30 June. One of the umpteen competing narratives thrown up by my 'unfortunate experience' comes in the greengrocer's this morning when an Australian woman tells me how she had been at Glyndebourne, presumably somewhat dolled up, when what she describes as an 'over-effusive Latin type' (not, she thought, a fellow operagoer) had insisted on kissing her hand. Retrieving it she found he had in the process managed to grease her fingers with a view, presumably, to slipping off her rings – perhaps greasing her hand when he took it and, as he kissed it, hoping to take her rings off with his teeth.

5 July. A child in Settle is said to have asked what the Mafia was and his grandfather said, 'It's like the Settle Rotary Club, only with guns.'

9 July. In the rumpus over the cutbacks in school building, the errors in the schools listed and the (quite mild) humiliation of Michael Gove there's been no mention that I've seen about private education. I may have missed it, but since we're all supposed to be tightening our belts why not the public schools? Don't they have a contribution to make, subsidised as they are in all sorts of ways by the government? Soon after taking office Gove deplored the stratification of education in England, while managing to say nothing about the most obvious stratification of all, namely the public schools that form the top layer and will go on doing so.

15 July. Finish reading Adam Sisman's biography of Hugh Trevor-Roper, a wonderfully absorbing book. Seeing Trevor-Roper in Oxford in the 1950s I thought him extraordinarily young, so that when he was made regius professor in 1957 he still looked like an undergraduate. His face always seemed to me to have a flattened nose which gave him a slightly (and fittingly) pugnacious air. He was a lifelong sufferer from sinus trouble and at one point had his septum removed so this may account for it. Happy to see his predecessor as regius professor, V. H. Galbraith, mildly rubbished. I remember him as a small bullying man with highly polished boots; he thought the world of Maurice Keen (quite rightly) but took me for a fool and more or less said so. He'd apparently served with distinction in the First War and been decorated for gallantry by the French, the gallantry including driving his men over the top at the point of a revolver which, had I known it, would have made me like him even less. Another recurrent figure is that fugitive from Mount Rushmore Gilbert Ryle, who sounds, in his wartime days anyway, to have been very funny, saying of Trevor-Roper's supposedly tactful politicking, 'Many a bull emerging from a bloodstained china shop has congratulated itself on its Machiavellian diplomacy.' But as always when I read about Oxford I'm so thankful I never ended up a don.

25 July, Yorkshire. A week's holiday begins with an appearance at the Harrogate Festival. It's also a ninetieth birthday celebration for Fanny Waterman, the founder of the Leeds Piano Competition, one of whose ex-pupils is doing the first half of the programme. This is scheduled to last for forty minutes but, entranced by his own music-making, the pianist goes on for well over an hour while I fume in the dressing room. I don't mind curtailing my performance but this means I won't get my supper until well after eleven. Some of this truculence feeds itself into my stint, which begins with a speech in favour of the NHS from an early play of mine, *Getting On*. This is well received and encourages me to say how, whereas nowadays the state is a dirty word, for my generation the state was a saviour, delivering us out of poverty and want (and provincial boredom) and putting us on the road to a better life; the state saved my father's life, my mother's sanity and my own life too. 'So when I hear politicians talking about pushing back the boundaries of the state I think' – only I've forgotten what it is I think so I just say: 'I think . . . bollocks.' This, too, goes down well though I'll normally end a performance on a more elegiac note.

27 July, Yorkshire. To Mount Grace, the Carthusian monastery, visited once before fifteen years ago though today it seems much larger, the scale of it perhaps accentuated by the small size of the cells surrounding the cloister. The irrigation system still survives, with the individual closets connected by a channel running along the back of the cells and another channel watering the kitchen gardens which were a feature of each cell, the whole place delightful and making it understandable why they were queuing up to become monks here right until the eve of the Dissolution. The kitchen gardens are very much overgrown, some of them planted with authentic medieval herbs including tansy, which smells disgustingly of pee. It's an English Heritage site and R. suggests that rather than the medieval jousting and other olde japeries which are regularly laid on these days it would be far more of an attraction if all these adjoining cell gardens were run together and planted out as allotments. Something similar is currently being tried at one or two National Trust properties but it's what Mount Grace would be ideally suited for.

13 August, Yorkshire. When I go up on the train to Leeds I'll generally sit in the same seat, often in front of the same businessman, who must also be a creature of habit. We chat, though without really knowing one another, and today as we're getting out at Leeds he tells me that he's been staying with friends in East Anglia. He had mentioned that he often sees me on the train whereupon his hosts had looked rather sheepish. It turns out that at their work, office or whatever they have a sweepstake to which they contribute every month with the participants drawing various well-known names from a hat; the winner being the one whose named notable is the first to die. I am one of their names.

They haven't had a win for some time, their last bonanza coming with the death of Spike Milligan, who died in an otherwise fallow period so the pot had grown quite large, which it isn't always: if two names die within a month or two of each other when the pot hasn't had time to accumulate the winner will only get a paltry sum.

I laugh about this when he tells me, but I find it depressing to think that even in a light-hearted way there is at least one family in the kingdom waiting (if not longing) for my death. I don't know what the monthly contribution amounts to but were it substantial I suppose a game like this might even lead to murder – even if it's only a murder such as occurs in Midsomer.

It's also another instance of 'write it and it happens.' Towards the end of *The Habit of Art* Humphrey Carpenter tells the ageing Auden and Britten that they have reached that stage in their lives when even their most devoted fans would be happy to close the book on them: no more poetry, no more music. Enough. It's not the same but still, the thought of anyone who for whatever reason would be happy to see the back of you is disturbing even if it's a joke. Good plot (or sub-plot) though.

16 August. Annoyed that I didn't write down a quote from Camus that headed a piece on Tony Judt in (I think) Friday or Saturday's *Guardian* – something like 'The only party which I could join would be one whose members weren't certain they were right.' Though another quote appropriate to Judt and his life would be Simone Weil's 'One must always be ready to change sides with justice, that fugitive from the winning camp.'

Cf. Tennyson's line on the French Revolution: 'Freedom, free to slay herself, and dying while they shout her name.' (Read in *The Anthologist* by Nicholson Baker.)

One of the saddest things in architecture – a dilapidated greenhouse.

18 August. To the NT where Padraig Cusack chairs a meeting with a dozen or so journalists from some of the places that will be visited by the provincial tour of *The Habit of Art*. He also managed a similar tour of *The History Boys* and tells me that 'cunt', which Mrs Lintott has to say about the headmaster, in Plymouth was received in dead silence but as the production slowly made its way north it got more and more of a response so by the time the play got to Glasgow they were throwing themselves about. This may just be evidence of how easily shocked they are in Plymouth (and not at all on the Clyde) but other factors enter in. I think that I might not be allowed to say cunt in Plymouth but Jez Butterworth, say, would. In Leeds I'd get the benefit of the doubt and in Glasgow nobody's heard of me anyway.

22 August. Listen to the afternoon prom, wholly devoted to Rodgers and Hammerstein, particularly the filmed musicals. Thus there is *Oklahoma, Carousel, South Pacific, The King and I* and – of course – *The Sound of Music*, all of which, *The Sound of Music* excepted, I saw at the Cottage Road Cinema in Far Headingley in the late forties and early fifties. Not *The Sound of Music*, which was later, and has always been a joke.

The others, though, were – as the phrase is nowadays – the music to my life and particularly to my emotional life. In the darkness of that little cinema I would feel that 'If I Loved You' or 'Hello Young

Lovers' were songs addressed particularly to me and to whatever boy I was hopelessly infatuated with.

And it comes back to me this afternoon how I regarded such longings then as evidence almost of a destiny. Being in love unhappily singled you out, I thought, it drafted you into an aristocracy which set you apart. It was more than just a badge of being gay (which it wasn't called then anyway) but rather an ordeal you were called on to undergo if only to transcend it and reach a sublimity denied to other mortals.

24 August. To UCH for an X-ray of my hip. I leave home at 11.45 a.m. and am back there by one o'clock. This is because it's a walk-in facility which, on the several occasions I've had to use it, has been of exemplary efficiency. There is speed, privacy and one goes at one's own convenience – all of these regularly advertised as the benefits of private medicine. I have used both in the past and if need be will do so again but in this regard, as in so many others these days, the NHS is better.

30 August. Reading – but not enjoying Ion Trewin's biography of Alan Clark (borrowed, I'm happy to say, from the Sharpleshall Street Library, so I haven't contributed to the Clark fortune), who was no stranger to worries about his own health. I find him difficult to like or have much sympathy for even as a swashbuckler. The gentleman he seems to have thought himself he certainly wasn't, except in some outward particulars. He began life as a used car dealer and though with a silver spanner in his mouth remained one. Without the money he had from his grandfather and from his over-indulgent father he wouldn't have got started as even his career as a military historian was smoothed along by being K. Clark's son with the connections that brought him. Thus he could send his writings to Liddell Hart for approval and to Trevor-Roper; no door was closed.

He also skived off National Service, which one would have thought he might have enjoyed. And as a young man he looks a spiv.

There's a chapter about the publication of the diaries which reminds me of the conversation at my agents Peters Fraser and Dunlop (then at Chelsea Harbour) between Agent Jones and Michael Sissons. Sissons must have come into Jones's office when I was talking to Jones on the phone. Jones put the phone down but not properly with the result that I could hear Sissons telling Jones what dynamite the (then unpublished) diaries were and describing some of the elaborate security precautions they must put in place when publishers came to the office to read through them prior to making an offer.

I hope I wrote this down at the time, though short of going down to Faber and checking the transcript I've no means of knowing.

To begin with, I remember I kept shouting down the phone but in the end just gave up and did what anybody else would have done (Clark himself certainly) and eavesdropped.

Apart from his love of animals Clark's hypochondria is his most appealing – certainly his most human – characteristic.

31 August, Yorkshire. While we've been here I've read Chris Mullin's diaries (1999–2005), *A View from the Foothills.* There are dull patches e.g. African politics and jockeyings for position in the Labour Party but what comes over very plainly is Mullin's fundamental decency and honesty. He's so patently a good man that one feels he's taken on board the government simply because (and having voted against the war) he adds moral weight. He's glamorised by Blair (referred to throughout as The Man) and even at the finish when he knows Blair deserves to go he can't help but be sympathetic. Other impressions are of the relentless grind of an MP's job and the sense of futility that comes with almost any experience of politics, partly due to the iron grip exercised by the Whips and also by the unshiftable weight of the civil service, who turn in jargon-laden speeches that he has to rewrite or, worse, actually deliver, who bury initiatives they disapprove of and cling desperately to their procedures.

Mullin, I think, emerged unscathed from the MPs' expenses

scandal – which is unsurprising considering that his London base was a (frequently burgled) pad in Brixton, from which he travelled in on the 159 bus – and his home in Sunderland where cars are frequently vandalised or abandoned in the lane at the back of the house – and paradoxically one of the uplifting features of the diaries is the ordinariness of his complaints: he doesn't let his position, even when he's a junior minister set him apart from the common man. I hope I meet him one day if only to tell him how clearly his voice comes through and to say (though I don't think I would ever dare) never to underestimate the good he has done in his life.

3 September. Primrose Hill never fails to surprise. Today I am walking up Chalcot Road along the edge of Chalcot Square when I see an old lady having difficulty walking and just making it to a bollard where she rests for a moment. She's spectrally thin and has difficulty speaking, but she manages to gasp out that she's looking for Cahill Street and that her son is touring round in his car also looking. I offer to go home and fetch an *A to Z* while she sits on a seat, though the seat is already occupied by a young man who is taking no notice of this little drama. Suddenly the woman straightens up and starts speaking in a man's voice and I see that, having been wholly convincing as an old woman, she is actually quite a young man. Still, though, he claims not to know where he is, saying that he keeps having 'these dos' and that the last thing he remembers was being in Bromley and where is he now? Another passer-by has stopped to help and I decide it's getting a bit too complicated for me so I go on my way.

Ten minutes later I'm walking up the street and the old lady/ young man comes running up to me together with the one who'd been on the seat, who, it turns out, had been filming the encounter. Surprise, surprise they're actors, trying to put together a pilot for BBC3. This is a shame if only because it makes the whole encounter more ordinary. Afterwards I think back to my last unsought encounter in M&S when my pocket was picked, and had this been a similar scam it would have been just as easy to pick my pocket again as I'd helped the 'old lady' to the seat. This had never occurred to me. Streetwise I'm not.

5 September. The occasion of R.'s visit to Wales was a visit from Edinburgh by his Aunty Stella to stay with her sister, R.'s Nan, who lives in Penarth. The whole family assembled, R. given a lift from London by Owen, his brother. The grandparents live in a small council house into which were crammed R. and Owen, their parents Diana and Graham, Aunty Stella and the grandparents. This meant that R. had to share a bedroom with Aunty Stella who likes to recite Shakespeare to him. Last night before going to sleep this eighty-nine-year-old Welsh lady recited from memory the whole of the sonnet 'Shall I compare thee to a summer's day'. R. loves her.

9 September. Much of the afternoon spent in bed, gearing up for the evening and a further instalment of Debo week, tonight a reception at the Garrick for the publication of *Wait for Me!*. Not a large do – and quite grand, the lady herself wonderfully done up and with a huge emerald pinned to her front which even I who know nothing about jewels can tell is something special ('the size of a pigeon's egg' is the storybook measurement). With Jacob Rothschild on one side, I sit the other ('Oh, Nibs, you don't have to') before I make way for other grander suitors and talk to Ruth and Andrew Wilson and find myself in a group that includes (in order of height) Alan Titchmarsh, Tom Stoppard and Stephen Fry.

But now Debo is making a speech and it's a remarkable spectacle as, at her own request, this ninety-year-old lady is helped up onto a chair – and not a wooden chair – but an upholstered club chair, where she stands unsupported, reading ('I can't see you, of course') from hugely printed cards and being prompted by Charlotte Mosley and someone from John Murray.

'What do I say next?'

'Hurrah.'

'Oh, that's right. Hurrah!'

Currently in a state where I can scarcely climb the stairs let alone step up onto a chair I find this an extraordinary sight – and as memorable in its way as Saint-Loup running round the restaurant banquette at Proust's dinner, the proper adjectives being indefatigable, courageous, indomitable, the battleship virtues.

17 September. Standing and steps. That's why I could never have been a priest. Too much standing – too many steps. I think this today watching the Pope at Westminster Abbey – standing by while the choir sings some interminable anthem and the prayers that follow. The procession takes ages to form up though when His Holiness reaches the chancel he does at least get to sit down but then he has to haul himself up the steps to the altar where there's a lot more standing about (though kneeling must be pretty painful too). The service itself uninspiring – no rousing hymns, the only one I know 'O Thou who camest from above' (Samuel Wesley) whereas since the Westminster choirmaster is a Catholic he must know that there are hymns Catholics and Protestants share.

The camera seems to dwell on the most angelic boys in the choir though whether this is ironical or just mischievous is hard to say. Also a regular shot of His Holiness is shared with the youngest of the Abbey clergy who has a nice round grammar-schoolboy face and looks about sixteen. The Pope's secretary much in evidence, too, even sharing in the plaudits of the crowd as he and his master slide by in the Popemobile.

Good to see the Abbey, though, including the Cosmati pavement, uncarpeted for the occasion and more Cosmati work in the sanctuary where the shot of the Pope and the A/B. of C. kneeling at the shrine also takes in, in the foreground, the plain top of Henry III's tomb and in the background the effigies on the tomb of Richard II. As His

Holiness leaves the Abbey the A/B. of Y. nips in for a quick kiss.

I watch but had the procession passed the end of the street (unlikely) I don't think I could have been bothered to go out and wait.

The Abbey being full you don't get the horror of the conference seating.

18 September. Listening to Fritz Wunderlich singing Handel's 'Ombra mai fu' brings back Uncle George in the front room at Gilpin Place on a Sunday night singing his heart out with Aunt Eveline at the piano. I don't suppose I knew it then but it is more touching in memory because Uncle George would like most amateur singers only have the vaguest idea how the words were to be pronounced, just concentrating on getting the music right.

In retrospect these musical evenings seem immensely sad – though they weren't at the time – and for a child often just tedious. But in a film of my childhood the camera would track by the light of the gas lamps up Gilpin Place to the faint 'Ombra mai fu' or 'Where'er you walk', past the lighted windows of these red-brick back-to-back houses closing in on No. 7.

20 September. Nice occasion today. Several months ago Augusta in R.'s office had asked me on the quiet to keep this afternoon free as they were planning a surprise for R. However I didn't have to decide whether to tell him or not as he found out by accident in the office and that it involved the Dorchester. So a car picks me up at three to take me to Vogue House where we pick him up and go on to the Dorchester, the Pavilion Suite on the eighth floor, the set of rooms decorated by Oliver Messel. The occasion is to commemorate R.'s ten years as editor of *World of Interiors* with about twenty of the staff foregathered. It's far from being a formal occasion and touchingly clear how much he is liked and how happy they are working together. Some say this to me – Mark, the art director whose career R. has nurtured, Jessica H., Nat and Maria –

all of them so loving. We stand on the balcony with a vast view over London on this warm autumn afternoon with me wishing we could eat out there it's so delightful. Eventually we are called inside and sit down to an elaborate tea beginning, eccentrically with a goat's cheese salad and proceeding via dainty sandwiches in blocks to a mango and cream dessert in a glass before eventually arriving at the scones, cream and jam that constitute afternoon tea proper. Elaborate (and sometimes virulently coloured) cakes follow – the whole process taking nearly two and a half hours – though it's always enjoyable and much less wearisome than I would have found a dinner party.

Coming away we walk up South Audley Street when we are hailed from across the street by Morrissey who's sitting outside a pub with a friendly girl whom I take to be his agent. It's a slightly awkward encounter, Morrissey beginning by saying, 'Are you disgustingly happy?' R. says I make M. nervous and I'm certainly not at my ease, my main thought how nice it will be for R. to tell the people in the office about this odd conjunction. Struck by how big he is and how, in other circumstances (and I mean this as a compliment) he could be digging up the road.

Posh hotels – or the Dorchester at any rate – have improved with the waiters and the maître d's no longer the least bit condescending. After the tea they bring boxes for people to take home the cakes and scones they haven't eaten – something that wouldn't have happened even ten years ago.

28 September. One drawback of writing about Auden is that if one does hit on something striking to say or turn a nice phrase it's assumed by the audience that it was Auden who wrote it, the text just taken to be joined-up Wystan. Of course this works both ways and critics in particular are, I think, nervous of taking exception to stuff that I say in case I'm actually quoting the poet.

13 October. Good Forster quote, in Isherwood's version, 'Get on with your own work, behave as if you were immortal.' (*The Sixties: Diaries Volume Two.*)

21 October. Find in the bookshelf a copy of *The Private Art: A Poetry Notebook* by Geoffrey Grigson, which I must have read years ago and forgotten. Tipped in, as booksellers say, is a letter from a woman about Louis MacNeice, on whom I'd done a TV programme and who was a friend of Grigson's. She had known Grigson and he had told her how en route to Fawley Bottom to have lunch with John Piper one Sunday in 1939 he and MacNeice had stopped in a field to picnic and listen to Chamberlain's broadcast and the declaration of war.

The story seemed odd. If they were going to lunch with the Pipers why stop for a picnic, particularly when Myfanwy Piper was a noted cook? And why at eleven in the morning? Interest in Grigson rekindled I track down a copy of his *Recollections* (1984) to find that MacNeice had had nothing to do with it, but that on the eve of the declaration of war Piper had spent the night at Grigson's cottage in Wiltshire. In the morning they drove off to have lunch with John Betjeman at Uffington, stopping on the way and 'stationing a battery set on the yellow stubble in time to hear Chamberlain say we were at war. John Betjeman poured out sherry and with the Betjeman half-smile said, "For the Duration."' Grigson was always unpleasingly proud of his independence of mind and the memory didn't soften his attitude to the future poet laureate, whom he describes as 'a kindly and forgiving man; but I detested and still detest his verses, or most of them'.

The last time I heard the phrase 'for the duration' was in a sadder context. Merula Salaman, the widow of Alec Guinness, was already ill at the time of his death in 2000 and only survived him by a month or two. When I last saw her she had moved into the guest bedroom, because it overlooked the garden, and there she lay in state generally with at least one of the three dogs on her bed.

'I think I'll stay here,' she said, 'for the duration.'

22 October. Call at Mrs Hanlon's at Menston, one of the few antique shops in this area still functioning. She often has plant pots – today buy two, her first sale of the day – business very poor and she only keeps going by selling at Newark, one of the regular fairs.

On the floor is a flat white pottery dish with an inscription on it and it's only as I'm going out that I see what it is – a butcher's dish from Wilkinson's, the butcher's supply firm Dad used to go to down on the south (and slummier) side of Leeds Market – the only other reason for going down that street to go to Scarr's the big hardware shop or to catch a tram to Temple Newsam.

Wilkinson's was a regular port of call, either with Dad on his afternoon off or occasionally sent down on our own for stuff for the shop – the most disgusting of which were the salted giblets used as sausage skins. Mr Wilkinson a solid flat-faced unsmiling man in a grey dustcoat – so not dressed as a butcher in one of the blue-and-white striped aprons he also sold, one or two of which we still have, though very ragged.

Now though we have a dish – which R., for whom it has no such associations, is delighted by.

28 October. Reading Geoffrey Grigson (*Recollections*) again, this time on the Scottish poet Norman Cameron who had a girlfriend, a ballet dancer, but who was mildly troubled when she told him when they were in bed together of her activities with sixth-form boys and that 'nothing gave her such pleasure as the look in a schoolboy's eyes when she opened his fly buttons and manipulated him in a train, and he came over her hand' and that 'the last time she had pleasured a boy like that, it was in an empty carriage in the Cornish Riviera.'

Other than envying the sixth-form boys, one's struck by what a loss to literature, movies and indeed life was the demise of separate compartments on trains – a whole *mise en scène* made redundant. Films apart, one thinks of all the scenes in novels that take place in railway compartments. Indeed were this Another Literary Periodical (and not the *LRB*) it would provide months of copy from readers writing in with appropriate examples – suitable for the back page.

29 October. In *Poems and Poets* Grigson says of Robert Herrick,

> The amorous situations in his verse are what might have been, *if*. Not what has been. 'Wantons we are', he wrote in a two-line poem about poets –
>> and though our words be such,
>> Our Lives do differ from our Lines by much.

With Larkin it's the opposite. The person of the poet is lovelorn and not getting much altogether (e.g. 'which was just too late for me'). Larkin outside the poems, while not exactly having a whale of a time, certainly isn't going without, more sex out of the poems than in them.

6 November. I have been reading Bruce Chatwin's letters, which (unlike Larkin's letters, say) don't change one's previous impression of the writer. They reinforce the picture I had of him from Susanna Clapp's memoir and Nicholas Shakespeare's biography as of someone never still and endlessly on the move around the world – travel not an interval between work but a way of getting work done. He has bolt-holes everywhere, his world for all it takes in some of the planet's wildest places, nevertheless quite cosy, the Albany, an Indian fort, a Welsh tower, a Greek island, there is always somewhere to stay. And people put themselves out for him despite the fact that (on Diana Melly's evidence) he never does a hand's turn – just turning up for meals and expecting them to be ready, the notion never in question that his writing is the important thing. I suppose some of this is will, some of it charm – with his famous good looks a part of it, though on the only occasion I saw him in the flesh, at a party given (I think) by John Ryle in the 1970s he didn't seem to me to be good-looking at all. He was remarkable, there was no denying that but physically puny and his head too large and almost insectile, a visitor from another planet.

Other beefs – and they are beefs, making me feel small-minded and ungiving – are to do with his self-absorption, one of the most frequent topics in his letters the progress of whatever book he is working on, a topic I can't imagine concerns his correspondents to the degree it concerns him.

Money – which until the last years always seems to be short but never seriously so: when the rich are poor they are never poor like the poor are poor – and so it is with him.

9 *November.* The Ivy has been having some sort of anniversary pageant celebrating some of the famous who have dined there, including James Agate. I suppose it was a habit he cultivated in private but there would be some theatrical truth in presenting him seated behind a foaming bumper of his own piss ('Ah, Pissto!'). Perhaps this was a habit he learned at Giggleswick School, which has always been slightly nervous of acknowledging him. Or that the sometime headmaster's wife Madge Vaughan was a lover of V. Woolf.

10 *November.* A routine colonoscopy, though it never is routine, with no telling what's round the next corner. Today it's a little fairy ring of polyps, innocent enough but ruthlessly lassoed and garrotted by the radiographer lest in two or three years' time they grow up to be the 'nasties' he's on the lookout for but thankfully does not find. On the way down we pay a reverential visit to the site of my original operation before, as he puts it, 'cruising down'. Unaccountably this takes me back to the amusement park on the front at Morecambe in the first year of the war when Dad took my brother (nine) and me (six) on the Big Dipper. As Big Dippers go it was pretty tame, though far too scary for me, who never went on it (or any other) again, but there was just one bit I enjoyed: when all the ups and downs were over, the train briefly coasted along a high straight stretch behind the

boarding houses and with a view over the sea before it gently rattled down the long incline to the platform and the end of the ride. And that was what the last bit of the colonoscopy reminded me of seventy years later.

2 *December*. Thinking of the injunctions – they were hardly advice – that Mam used to deliver when we were young. When I went off to university she said (and often added as a postscript to her letters), 'Don't stint on food,' meaning that if I had to economise it shouldn't be on meals. I was never in such straits that I had to make a choice, but, had I been, food (rather than books, say) would have come first anyway, though not because she had said so. Another injunction that was almost a mantra was said whenever my brother or I were on the point of leaving the house: 'Don't stop with any strange men.' This was another piece of advice that I never had any cause to heed, though in retrospect I wonder if it helped to make my youth as hermetic as it was, as Mam would still be saying it when I was in my twenties and patrolling the streets of Headingley in the solitary walks I had been taking every night since I was seventeen.

There were other more mundane prohibitions, particularly in childhood, generally to do with avoiding TB. We were told never to share a lemonade or a Tizer bottle with other boys; we should keep the sun off the back of our necks nor were we allowed ever to wear an open-necked shirt until we were in our teens. We never ate prepared food from shops, so not the beetroot bubbling in an evil cauldron in Mrs Griffiths's greengrocer's down Tong Road, not the 'uggery-buggery' pies on sale in the tripe shop or the more delectable offerings in Leeds Market. Permissible was potted meat from Miss Marsden's genteel confectioner's or Prest's on Ridge Road, their respectability making them in Mam's eyes an unlikely health hazard.

Not that it follows on, but these days I am too old to be on my best behaviour. And I'm too old not to be on my best behaviour also.

14 December. To the Naval and Military Club in St James's Square and my annual lunch with Blake and Diana Parker. Rather (and unworthily) dreading it because their grandson Harry is coming, who, stepping on a roadside bomb in Afghanistan, earlier this year, lost both his legs.

Coming into the club I see a young man with two sticks but just about walking who (and it's a measure of how nervous I am) I straight away take to be Harry. I say, 'I imagine we're going to the same place.' 'Perhaps,' he says (glasses, good-looking and not unlike the young Richard Marquand). I show him where the cloakroom is where he collects an aged relative and I realise I have got the wrong man (slightly relieved as he's quite stand-offish). I apologise and, unsmiling, he says he imagines it will be a similar sort of occasion. As I suppose it will be, though he looks to have lost one leg not both – and having noticed him I then notice other young men, limping or on sticks and suppose this is where the military take their wounded sons and grandsons out to lunch. Not Harry, though, who has had a bad night and had to cancel, sending in his stead Tom, another grandson, a massive young man, one of the Olympic rowing team at Beijing and now a shipping broker plus (I think) Harry's sister, another grandchild of Blake and Diana (addressed as Granny throughout). I am sitting next to Penelle Bide, a friend from Chichester, whose late husband married C. S. Lewis to Joy Davidman on what seemed her deathbed. A nice woman, she brings me a signed (and uncut) first edition of A. A. Milne's adaptation of *The Wind in the Willows* which she has found in her late husband's library – I imagine quite a valuable book.

A propos letters, one from Debo enclosing a Christmas card she has made herself out of anything that comes to hand including sticking plaster and even corn plasters and a programme for some poultry show in Stratford on Avon which asks to be preserved under a glass dome like some Victorian wax flowers.

15 December. Andrew Wilson rings to tell me more about Penelle Bide whom he thinks was a pupil of Rev. Bide (his nickname almost inevitably Abide With Me), who was later in life chaplain of L.M.H. – and who was a modernist churchman whom in memory Andrew sees as having a volume of Heidegger open on his knees as he talks about 'the existential movement'. Bide chosen by C. S. Lewis to marry him and the divorced Joy after being refused by Bishop Carpenter (Humphrey Carpenter's father). Humphrey (as a child on his eternal tricycle) apparently remembering Lewis red-faced and furious bursting out of his father's study with Carpenter saying, 'It's no good, Lewis. Rules are rules.'

16 December. In his book *The Poetics of Space* (1958) the critic and philosopher Gaston Bachelard quotes the advice of a dictionary of botany: 'Reader, study the periwinkle in detail, and you will see how detail increases an object's stature.' 'To use a magnifying glass', Bachelard comments a little later, 'is to pay attention.'

(From *The Man with a Blue Scarf* by Martin Gayford.)

17 December. Finish Nicholas Shakespeare's biography of Bruce Chatwin, which I thought I had read but must only have bought – this copy borrowed from the Sharpleshall Street Library. Chatwin's charm is difficult to convey, though he undoubtedly had a great deal, some of it physical but partly also the aura of romance he spun around himself. Then, too, he seldom seems to have stopped talking and while this could be wearying (it would have wearied me) some people found him spellbinding.

Chatwin – like Sebald, Kapuscinski and Oliver Sacks – operates on the borders of truth and imagination, dodging over the border into fantasy as and when it suits and making them difficult to pin down. Defenders of Chatwin like Francis Wyndham dismiss criticism of this as 'English, literalist or puritanical' – in my case all three. One tells the truth or one makes it up, not both at the same time.

One tells the truth. It isn't just a whim. Or so I tell myself. Such characters trouble me.

20 December. Remember our sledge at Halliday Place, not the slim high-slung slatted toboggan I always envied, a real flyer, but a low flat three-boarded thing that Dad had probably run up (with rusty runners) and which for the rest of the year was kept in the coalhouse and always in danger of being taken for firewood.

28 December, Yorkshire. The roads in the village so icy that whereas I would normally walk down to the shop for the papers this morning I go by car. It's not cold particularly but filthy underfoot and grey besides. One of the few things about Primrose Hill I miss is walking round the corner for my small decaff latte which these days marks the beginning of my day's work. It occurs to me that, though it was not called latte – or called anything – I have been having milky coffee like this all my life. Mam and Dad didn't like coffee, natural or Nescafé, their way of making coffee to have a panful of milk and water which they boiled up and as it boiled scattered ground coffee on top. It was almost medicine in Dad's case as hot milk was thought good for his stomach but it was also part of Mam's morning routine. The coffee would come from Hopper's, the grocer's just up Weetwood Lane, the beans ground in a big red funnel-type coffee grinder at the side of the shop. The smell – like all the smells in the shop – delicious. Sometimes too to scent the living room cum kitchen at 92A Mam would scatter some ground coffee over the gas ring, the smell reminding her of 1944 and the Corona Café down Guildford High Street, the whole window of which was occupied by a coffee-roasting machine.

The cooking facilities at 92A were pretty limited, a range taking up most of one wall. It wasn't used for cooking, though, which took place in a gas oven hidden, like the sink behind thin hardwood doors to the right of the range, the doors seldom closed and a source of embarrassment to me as a boy on the rare occasions when I ever brought friends home. Mam had cosified the range by fitting a cretonne pelmet across it, with on the shelf some of her Staffordshire ornaments. It was a room that displayed all her humble aspirations to gracious living but which didn't live up to mine. We lived at 92A from 1946 to 1957, when we moved down to a flat at 8 Wood Lane, the sole survivor of that lost living room the walnut workbox Mam rescued from Dad's stepmother the Gimmer's dustbin and which is on the chiffonier behind me as I write.

6 January. The alterations we have been having done are now pretty much finished, thanks to Max, a young Latvian who's unsmiling but an excellent carpenter and Eugene, much jollier and from New Zealand who has supervised it all. Walking round the job this evening R. is shocked to discover in the bathroom above the bath a crudely made wooden cross. He takes this to be the work of Max who, scarcely out of his teens, already has two children and is, I imagine, Catholic. R., whose feelings about religion are more uncompromising than mine, finds the cross disturbing and is determined to ask Eugene to tell Max to take it down. I'm less exercised by it, seeing it as some sort of dedication, the sort of thing (though more crude) that a medieval workman might have put up at the completion of a job. We are both of us wrong as when Eugene is approached he explains it is not a cross at all but a makeshift coat hanger he has rigged up over the bath in order to dry his anorak.

14 January. George Fenton tells me of a memorial service he's been to at St Marylebone Parish Church for Maurice Murphy, the principal trumpet of the LSO, who did the opening trumpet solo in the music for *Star Wars*. The service due to kick off at eleven thirty, George arrives with ten minutes to spare only to find the church already full, the congregation seated, silent and expectant. It begins promptly at eleven thirty with everyone behaving impeccably and not a cough or a rustle throughout. And he realises it's because they are all musicians and orchestral players for whom this is like any other concert and where the same rules apply.

18 January. To see my GP Roy McGregor with a list of questions R. wants answered re my hip. Not in favour of an immediate op – which he thinks should wait until I'm actively incommoded, which I'm not as yet. Now has very few patients as he teaches all the time. In despair at the proposed changes, seeing it as the dismantling of the NHS. I quite agree.

If Cameron had made it clear such a radical reorganisation of the NHS was his intention before the election he must have lost – there was no indication of it in the manifesto. So that makes him a liar. And that he didn't dare say so makes him a coward.

21 January, Yorkshire. A creature of habit, en route home I generally stop and have some tea at Betty's in Ilkley where I also buy an organic white loaf. Today the assistant tells me that the café (and presumably the four or five other branches in the Betty's chain) no longer does organic produce as they've changed their flour miller. 'However,' she assures me, 'the flour is locally produced.' As are, presumably, its pesticide residues. When I ask why the flour could not be locally produced and nevertheless be organic she cannot explain. Money is, I imagine, the short answer with 'locally produced' a concession to the supposed cost (and carbon footprint) of transport. This is confirmed when I talk to the organic shop in our village who tell me that 'locally produced' is now the usual face-saver for firms wanting to economise on the provision of organic produce.

Years ago I might have been able to put my spoke in more effectively than I can today as at that time I was offered a non-executive directorship of Betty's. It was well remunerated and coming with as many buns as I could eat I came quite close to accepting. It was only when I found out that my duties would include sitting regularly in the café where I could be hobnobbed with by other patrons that I regretfully drew the line.

27 January. Difficult to say why or how but part of the Torification of life has to be put down to Classic FM – and some of it to the National Trust.

28 January. (Dad's 107th birthday.) Ring Angus M. at the National to arrange a Platform for when my two short stories contained in *Smut* come out. He has found himself in a dilemma because the National Theatre filter doesn't allow him to google smut as a word so he is having to get his information direct from the publishers.

31 January. Steve the electrician rings this morning, wanting Rupert who is still getting ready. He shouts that he will ring him back and I suspect he is on the lav. I say this to Steve and he rings off. I tell R. I have said to Steve he is on the lav, at which he very much objects ('too much information') – and also he doesn't like 'lav'. I ask him if he would have objected if I had said he was in the lav. No. That would have been acceptable. So what he is objecting to is just the preposition? Yes it is – but he is very pleased with the remark as illustrating my pedantry (or peculiarity) and one which can be added to the Sneeps Library of my more (as he sees it) absurd statements.

He is silent in the car, already – as he admits – planning to retail the exchange at the office and going off at the finish in high spirits, very happy with the entire episode which I'm sure I will not be allowed to forget.

Meanwhile he has not rung Steve.

4 February, Yorkshire. Train an hour or so late, 'a plastic bag on the overhead lines' just north of Wakefield means I must vary my routine and not have tea in Ilkley but try and find some in Leeds. Tea and toast is all I want but Harvey Nichols don't provide it in their Country Arcade café. Upstairs there is sushi and, did I wish to sit at the bar, toast. I don't so I go down to the café again and have a scone the size of a small loaf. It's now rush hour – Leeds is briefly thronged before it empties out for the evening. I walk haltingly through the streets, buying Sunday's train tickets then sit in an alcove in the Queens for a couple of hours during which time, so far as I can judge, two fancy-dress groups foregather and depart – one all male and dressed from the fifties, the other more eclectic – one girl a wasp, another young man Fred Astaire. All noisy but amiable and taking no notice of this shabby green-overcoated figure who is grappling with the *LRB*.

12 February. I take out the typewriter – my last working one, bought for £5 at Age Concern in Settle – and type out the first two pages of *People*.

13 February. An oddity. Yesterday in the paddock at Newbury several horses are electrocuted, two fatally, with the accident put down to a forgotten cable under the grass which had been damaged when the turf was spiked. A week or so previously I'd watched on TV an episode of an American series, *Diagnosis: Murder*, starring Dick Van Dyke, with the plot concerning three athletes in Florida, two of whom were electrocuted on the playing field in exactly the same fashion as the horses. No one else has noted the coincidence, but then I don't imagine there are many people so sad as to be watching the now rather aged Dick Van Dyke at half past one in the afternoon.

15 February. Not having a book on the go I take up again Larkin's *Letters to Monica* which I'd tried to read when it first came out but given up. It's more interesting than I'd thought then but not much more, with too many post-mortems on previous meetings, what he had said to her, what she had said to him and what they had both really meant. The letters date back to the late 1940s and early 1950s and bring back all the dreariness of digs and Oxford out of term, Sunday lunches in cafés up the Iffley Road and awkward evenings spent listening to records in the rooms of undergraduates one didn't really know or even like but who just happened to be marooned in Oxford out of term.

One black mark against Larkin is that he no more cares for the work of Flannery O'Connor than Amis did: 'The day didn't get off to a very good start by my reading some stories by "Flannery O'Connor" in the bath . . . horribly depressing American South things.' This is October 1967. I can't see how Flannery O'Connor (which he perhaps thought was a pen name) could be so easily dismissed by someone supposedly appreciative of language. The colours were too bright perhaps.

3 March. 'A health system that once acted against inequality is out to enshrine it.' My GP Roy McGregor in the *LRB.*

7 March. Read and enjoy *Edgelands* by Paul Farley and Michael Symmons Roberts about the lure of in-between places and the edges of cities and other communities. I feel I was on to this years ago in my play *The Old Country,* when Hilary, a spy in the Foreign Office, describes the venues where he met his Soviet contact; it's also the same sort of no-man's-land that figures in the film of *A Question of Attribution.* The authors of *Edgelands* are two Lancashire poets and there are frequent references to Lancaster and the estuary of the Lune including Salt Ayre, a huge landfill site to the west of the city now grassed over. The name takes me back to childhood when going by train from Leeds to Morecambe on holiday you knew you were nearly there when the porter came along the platform shouting the mysterious invocation 'Lancaster Green Ayre'.

9 March. I sometimes write stuff down because I don't think I will hit on the right word again: 'A man walks up and down the pavement opposite communing with himself but actually on his mobile.'

'Communing' is the (fairly ordinary) word I'm uncertain of coming up with again.

11 March. R.'s Aunty rings from Edinburgh. She was ninety last week and apologises that she hasn't learned a new Shakespeare sonnet to mark her birthday. However she again recites by heart, and with no mistakes, 'Shall I compare thee to a summer's day' and promises to learn a new poem for when she sees him in the summer.

13 March. Overheard. 'No woman was safe, even your Aunty Pat.'

24 March. Elizabeth Taylor dies which excuses re-noting what I've written about before, how at a party of Arnold Weissberger's at the Savoy *c.*1971 she perched briefly on my knee, though why I can't now remember. A solid woman she was wearing The Diamond and was (not in consequence) quite a hefty burden so I was relieved when she stood up – behaviour that was almost royal, i.e. so relaxed as meant to emphasise how unpretentious she was and so intended for remembrance in a Shelley Plain sort of way.

27 March. Fill in the census form to which I add this plaintive rider:

> I have completed the census form while strongly objecting to the agency, Lockheed Martin, that is carrying it out. Information of this nature should only be divulged to a government agency under the direct control of Parliament. Lockheed is basically an arms manufacturer and thus not the most scrupulous of organisations. This is an undertaking that should never have been outsourced.

That it was the last Labour government that outsourced it makes it even more depressing.

29 March. Dad's violin was always kept in the sitting room well away from the rough and tumble of family life. In the Hallidays it was in the front room that was never used, at 92A it was in Mam and Dad's bedroom but in the village in his last years it was always accessible, lying on a chair, say, or on the sideboard, the case often open, the fiddle ready to be taken up so he could play along to the wireless or even the television.

11 April. Profile in the *Guardian* of Niall Ferguson in the course of which he says, 'You know the play *The History Boys*, I remember realising that my American friends thought Irwin was the hero of that play! I said, why? They said, "Well, he got the kids into a great college, didn't he?"' I'm quite happy with that – and it was a point Nick H. frequently made in discussions about the play, saying that the touching up apart, given a choice between Hector and Irwin most parents would want their children taught by Irwin because he got results. But at the same time most parents would also know that the notion of education purveyed by Hector was a more durable and life-changing one than the more expedient stratagems put across by Irwin. The point is neither was *right* – or, as I think Hebbel says, in a good play everyone is right.

The trouble with Ferguson is that he sees plays, as with much else, in terms of polemic. They're an argument. And sometimes they are – but they're also (and certainly in my case) a tour round the subject in an attempt to unravel a contradiction. I got into Oxford as Irwin when at heart I was Hector. The interviewer (Decca Aitkenhead) says unequivocally that Ferguson was the model for Irwin. This isn't true. The similarity between Irwin and Ferguson and Andrew Roberts only occurred to me halfway through writing the play. The model for Irwin, insofar as he has a model, was me.

15 April. Some sense of being washed up this morning – or at any rate of not being a man of the world. Nick H. is on the radio talking about *War Horse* on Broadway, where it's been a great success and will be a Spielberg film. Had I adapted it as I was asked to do, it might have been neither but I should have had the wit to see that this was meant to be a simple tale and gone along with it. As it was I said to Tom

Morris that I didn't think there was much I could do. So goodbye royalties, huge in London and New York and goodbye the Spielberg film. Still I've done other things in the interval e.g. *The Uncommon Reader* that will last longer. But there's no disguising that I feel regret.

17 April. Seeing a banana skin on the pavement reminds me how when I first read the *Dandy* and the *Beano* the presence of a banana skin meant that inevitably it was going to be slipped on. No matter that at that time, in the early 1940s, few children had seen let alone eaten a banana, the skin was still shorthand for calamity. Other comic clichés were a fish, almost certain to be stolen by a cat and always represented as a perfect skeleton devoid of flesh but still with the head on; a string of sausages, destined to be grabbed by a dog, the sausages trailing from the dog's mouth like a scarf in the wind; a bull (beware of) in a field, a billy goat similarly, with a ladder another portent of disaster. The bump on the head which might be the consequence of one of these mishaps was generally described as being 'as big as a pigeon's egg', something else which like the banana I had never seen.

18 April. Why does the opening theme of the Tchaikovsky No. 1 Piano Concerto never return? What is that about? Everybody listening to it (at least for the first time) must always have expected it. But no.

26 April. Though it's now five or six years since it closed, much missed still is the junk shop in the marketplace at Kirkby Stephen run by Mrs H. It sold what these days is dignified by the name of kitchenalia – old crockery, cutlery, pots and pans – but reviewing what we have bought over the years the haul is astonishingly diverse: earthenware bread crocks which we use in the garden, a lovely thirties clock that chimes the quarters, innumerable rummers and heavy glass tumblers, a tin hearth surround (I don't even know what it's properly called), Tidy Betties, which are the brass shields that go in front of the fire grate, and the pokers and tongs to go with them. All our transfer-printed Victorian dinner plates came from there and tea plates besides, so many that they seldom get used.

Some customers found greater treasures including a sixteenth-century griddle embossed with the Tudor rose and if you were into armorial firebacks this was the place. We have a walking stick with a duck's head handle; our pigskin log basket once held fleeces in a mill. Apart from the odd stool there wasn't much furniture . . . no room in the shop for that . . . but there were old photographs, tea caddies and the occasional silver spoon. The stock was cheap, absurdly so sometimes in the light of London prices and it didn't alter much over the years, I suppose because the stuff consisted of the back end of farm and country auction sales. Crouched over her one-bar electric fire Mrs H. never seemed much interested in money and was openly sceptical of the enthusiasm of her customers. We came into the shop one Saturday afternoon just as a woman was leaving laden down with purchases and flushed with pleasure at the trophies she was carrying away. Scarcely had the door closed behind her when Mrs H. remarked, 'There goes a woman with more money than sense,' and I don't doubt she said the same of us. But we didn't mind and when she closed I wrote to her to say what joy we'd had from the shop over the years. True to form she never replied.

3 May. A distressing call today from Dr C., the oncologist who looked after my friend Anne during her last illness. He talks about hospital services being deliberately run down and the difficulties of ward care due to shortage of staff but it's only gradually I realise that what he wants is for me to try and write a play about it. I explain what a slow worker I am and how long the trek from conception to execution but it still sounds like an excuse. He's shy or I make him so and he plainly has difficulty in articulating his worries, but what comes over is his concern and indeed his despair. It's alarming that doctors should be driven to such desperate measures and leaves me feeling both disturbed and inadequate and wishing I could just say, 'Yes, I'll do it,' and forget everything else.

7 *May*. The 'No' (to proportional representation) vote, which I can't bear to read about; the best comment Vince Cable's who said it proves once again that the Tories are tribal and ruthless. He might have added tricky and dishonest and no different from what they have always been.

21 *May, Yorkshire.* A plumpish young man gets off the train at Leeds just behind me.

'Aren't you famous?'

'Well I can't be, can I, if you don't know my name.'

'It's Alan something.'

'Yes.'

'From Scarborough?'

'No.'

'So which Alan are you?'

'I'm another Alan.'

'Are you just a lookalike?'

'Well, you could say so.'

He pats my arm consolingly. 'Be happy with that.'

24 *May*. Tim Lott collects me at six thirty and we drive over to Kensal Rise where I am to do an evening to raise funds to help pay for a legal challenge to Brent Council's plans to close Kensal Rise Library (and five others). Tim is pessimistic about their chances, libraries for him as much a haven in his childhood as they were for me, though he's thirty years or so younger. The church is full, with *Newsnight* in attendance for which I give a rather scrappy interview before doing the reading, which goes well. Back home I'm in time to watch *Newsnight* and am depressed to see how scraggy I look, my neck in particular, with every shirt these days looking like a

horse-collar. There's a studio discussion between Tim Lott and some clown (Littlewood, I think, his name) from the Institute of Economic Affairs. He's an almost comical baddy, shifty and spivvily suited and maybe picked out by *Newsnight* because he's so unprepossessing. He ridicules my assertion that closing libraries is child abuse, in the course of which he describes me as 'this highly successful millionaire' and suggests I should buy the library myself. He also claims as did Eamonn Butler back in 1996 that there is nowadays no need for libraries, for which other uses should be found, describing them as 'prime retail opportunities', which says it all.

26 May. These days I'm not sure how children learn to read. I only know that the period immediately after you've learned is vital. That's when access to books or a computer is essential. Virtually every day I pass by the Chalk Farm library in Sharpleshall Street and after school and in the holidays it's full of children reading or looking at computers. Many of them I imagine are poor, the library the only place where they can keep up with their better-off classmates who have computers of their own.

And Brent says, well, we've got a spanking new central library. But that's no good to those children. Libraries have to be local, they have to be handy. They shouldn't need an expedition. But that early period in a child's reading life is vital. Interfere with that, hinder a child's access to books in whatever form and you damage that child probably for life. I have said it many times already but it's worth saying again: closing libraries is child abuse.

Enough ranting.

30 May, Yorkshire. Asked to provide a foreword for a book of oral history put together by the people of the next village to ours, Austwick, I'm expecting it to be a bit of a chore. But the histories turn out to be funny and interesting with the memoirs vivid and specific, particularly about the Second War, which for many of these villagers was the time of their lives. At the centre of the book is an extraordinary adventure when in the early hours of Monday 9 June 1941 the pilot of an RAF Whitley bomber returning from a raid over Dortmund got lost crossing the Pennines and, running out of fuel, had to make an emergency landing.

Though it was the height of summer and should have been quite light, there was fog and cloud and the terrain is hilly and indeed mountainous, with the only flat land in the valley bottom crisscrossed with dry-stone walls. Miraculously there was a gap in the cloud and the pilot brought his plane down safely, coming to rest at Orcaber Farm near Austwick. Thereafter it was like a scene from an Ealing comedy. Not knowing if the plane was British or German, one of the Home Guard with his rifle came running across the fields followed by a farmer with a pitchfork and, once the news got round, the entire village. None of the children went to school, ferrying each other on their bikes to the landing place, the village policeman, failing to rise to the occasion, riding after them shouting: 'Stop, stop. Two on a bike, two on a bike!'

Preparations went on all day to get the plane up again: dry-stone walls were taken down, trees felled and gates widened, and the plane was stripped out and refuelled. If it was a miracle that the plane had got down it was even more so that it got up again, taking off in the late afternoon and just clearing the trees at the end of the field. A plane crash might have meant a sad plaque in the village, like the several memorials to crashed aircraft that are up on the moors. Instead it was an idyllic and extraordinary day that Austwick has remembered ever since, and today at the annual street market I talk to two of the boys, now in their eighties, whom the policeman had chased for being 'two on a bike'.

2 June, Suffolk. A perfect day, though it begins with me feeling seedy in the junk shop at Yoxford where we buy a (very foxed) circular mirror *c.*1830 for £30 and one of Norman Scarfe's Shell Guides for £3.

Lunch at Walberswick, then to Southwold which is crammed with cars and people, a real breath of Brighton. However Ruth Guilding has recommended a junkish antique shop on the edge of the town, a lovely place where I buy a country table, a painted version of the little candlestand we bought years ago in Cirencester and some plant pots for R. Then tea in an unlikely health food shop in otherwise unremarkable Leiston where (again on Ruth's recommendation) we drive over to the beach at Sizewell. It's largely empty and spoilt, if you like, by the power station but the more attractive a place for that – full of the detritus of boats and fishing, black tarred huts and not picturesque at all – altogether uncrowded, a few families on the shingle and lovers in the scrub but a lovely spot. I fix myself up with a comfortable seat on the shingle with my back leaned against a pallet while R. goes for a walk along the shore.

Coming back over the dunes to the car we pass a war memorial, unceremoniously sited by the refreshment hut, to the dozen or so Dutchmen who escaped from occupied Holland and crossed the North Sea by kayak, only five of whom made it with three of them surviving the war, the memorial erected by the last survivor.

21 June. I dream I am back in the attic at Grandma's in Gilpin Place, lying awake listening to the sound of trains shunted into Holbeck. Though Grandma's was only two blocks from the railway line strange streets, particularly in Wortley, were always perilous and I never ventured over there to look at the railway. So the shunting was just a sound at night but one I was so used to that like the wind or the rain on the slates it was part of the natural world. And shunting, not that I ever hear it now, is a sound I associate with sleep and darkness.

24 June, Yorkshire. Day grey and overcast. The Leeds train gets to Wakefield at three when a touching old-fashioned scene takes place – waiting on the platform is a young mother and her son. When the train stops they look along the platform, wave and run out of view. A few minutes later as the train draws out I pass them, the father holding up the little boy to see the train go out, his wife holding his other arm. It's happened two or three times and again today.

3 July. A few weeks ago I caught on TV a few minutes of Zoltan Korda's *The Four Feathers* (1939), the film of A. E. W. Mason's novel. It's a film I remember vividly from when it first came out, the few minutes that I see the scene in which Durrance, played by Ralph Richardson, loses his pith helmet as he's climbing a cliff in the desert. The helmet bounces away down onto the sand leaving him exposed to the burning sun, which sends him blind. One other scene stands out. The hero, Harry Faversham (John Clements), fears he is a coward and having declined to go with his regiment to the Sudan goes native in order to prove himself by working unrecognised to assist his ex-colleagues who have sent him the feathers. To corroborate his disguise as a harmless native he has himself branded, the branding scene vividly depicted in the film, more so, I think, than it would be today.

Thinking about the film sends me to the book, which, published in 1902, is still in print as the most famous and successful of Mason's many novels. Happily he lived long enough to enjoy some profit and fame from the film, dying in 1948. The book, unsurprisingly, turns out to be less straightforward than the film, spending a good deal of time on who knew about the four feathers and whether the soldiers who sent Faversham the first three feathers knew about the fourth feather – sender, his erstwhile fiancée, Ethne. All this gets pretty tedious and repetitive and rather Henry James-like in its moral ramifications. It's gone through so often that one wonders whether the repetition is because the book came out originally in serial form. Each chapter certainly has a subheading: 'Durrance hears news of Faversham'; 'The House of Stone'; 'Colonel Trench assumes a knowledge of Christianity'. The branding scene that terrified me the most aged five doesn't occur at all, nor in the book does Faversham shepherd the blind Durrance across the desert to safety. Predictably the film ends more spectacularly than the book, with the Battle of Omdurman. So, unusually, it's a film that's better and more interesting than its book, which is altogether too languorous. The film also stars, almost inevitably, Sir C. Aubrey Smith who, as in many films before and during the Second War, stood for probity and honour (though with a twinkle).

5 July. Anna Massey dies. She was always fun and she got better as an actress as she got older, though I only worked with her twice. None of the obituaries mentions the performance of hers that I best remember, when she portrayed the painter Gwen John in a biopic. This included one of John's self-portraits in which she painted herself nude. Not unlike Gwen John in looks and figure, Anna did it nude herself though she would have been well into her fifties at the time. It was superb and also courageous, actors who are so often mocked for their sentimentality sometimes deserving the VC for their nerve. The last time I saw her was in 1997 on King's Cross Station. I'd just had an operation and was waiting to start chemotherapy, which I told her and then found I was unexpectedly in tears so hurried off to my train. What was heartening about her life was that quite late on she fell head over heels in love with a Soviet scientist whom she married and was very happy.

23 July. Home again via the Old Kent Road – the south (or west?) side of which is, despite all the horrors, still fascinating architecturally with some wonderful remnants of houses behind the kebab shops and Chinese restaurants – extraordinary capitals on these early nineteenth-century buildings, and wonderful tall brick Edwardian blocks of flats or a warehouse – so much still here that one feels that given dictatorial powers and unlimited resources one could rescue whole frontages and even quarters, though doubtless in the process destroying the vigour and vitality that is still so evident.

Much in the paper about Lucian Freud who has died at eighty-eight. The best (non-aesthetic) tribute would be a list of all the women (some little more than children) whom he has slept with. (Cf. Ted Hughes – though Freud's list, I should have thought, much longer.) Freud openly acknowledged that he believed all indulgences were licensed because he was an artist. But then all men think they are artists, in this respect anyway.

25 July. A man meaning to take some liquid Viagra by mistake takes some Tippex. There are no ill effects except that next morning he wakes up with a massive correction. (Barry Cryer.)

1 August. R. goes home to Wales for a family gathering. It's only a small house and again he shares a room with his Aunty Stella who, true to her promise made earlier in the year, has learned some new poems. So in the darkness of a Penarth bedroom this ninety-year-old lady recites Housman's 'Loveliest of trees, the cherry now' and Browning's 'Home-Thoughts, from Abroad'. And not a fluff in either.

2 August. I suppose one ought to be grateful to the *News of the World* for phrases like 'intimacy took place'.

4 August. Antony Crolla brings round the oval walnut table from Gloucester Crescent and sets it up in the flat ready for when R.'s family come to supper next week. I've had the table, I think, since I was at Oxford where it came from the antique shop the other side of Magdalen Bridge (£8). It was at 16 Chalcot Square and then stood for years in the bay window at Gloucester Crescent where it was covered with a greenish-brown chenille tablecloth. On it I wrote everything I did up to *George III* – or whenever it was I bought the late Victorian Arts and Crafts desk which I work on now.

It's far from perfect: the veneer has gone in one section which has been disguised with brown paint; the decoration on the (slightly rocky) pedestal is heavy and unpleasing. But it lasted me half my life and now this Thursday afternoon here it is again.

5 August. Note with these great men their occasional competence at menial tasks and the wonder with which this is greeted, washing up the stuff of fable.

8 August. It is the day after the Tottenham riots and waiting for a prescription in the pharmacy in Camden High Street I find that though it's only four o'clock it's already closing, with boards being put up against the windows and the nice young counter assistant, the daughter of the pharmacist who did *Talking Heads* for her O levels, hopes that I will be going straight home. For my part I've been looking round the shop to see what would come to hand should rioters burst in from the (utterly peaceful) High Street, deciding that something from a tub of walking sticks and fancy umbrellas would make the best weapon. Meanwhile a couple of addicts, indifferent to these adjustments to their routine, wait patiently for their daily ration of methadone as I wait for my Glucophage, which now comes, the door is unlocked and I'm again told to go straight home, which I don't think anyone has said to me since I was a child.

11 August. A film clip seen three times today on the television news shows at least ten policemen, most in full riot gear, kicking in the door of a council flat in order to arrest a suspected rioter. The cameras have plainly been invited along to see the police in action but there are so many policemen that, rather comically, they have to queue to get into the flat, occasionally giving threatening shouts while waiting their turn. Eventually a black youth is brought out, feebly struggling, and is dragged away. It's an absurd exercise and raises as many questions about the proper deployment of police resources as their inadequacy did yesterday. (It later transpires they got the wrong flat.)

19 August. In Karl Miller's *Tretower to Clyro* Seamus Heaney keeps putting in an appearance either in person or via his poems. 'Two Lorries' has to do with a 'tasty coalman' who fancies Heaney's mother, and another coal-hole poem, 'Slack', is about the coal dust used to bank up and damp down a fire, slack a feature of my own childhood as were the accessories that went with the sale of it: empty folded coal-bags, a set of iron scales and a leather-aproned coalman as familiar in Armley, Leeds as they were across the water in Derry. I don't remember our coalman being particularly tasty though I had dreams about him tramping through our spotless house in order, I suppose, to ravish my mother, not that in the dream she seemed to mind, or mind the dirt anyway (which would have been slack had there been more of it); he never got as far as the ravishing, probably because I didn't know what that entailed. I am five years or so older than Heaney and, it being wartime, our coal came not on a lorry but from a cart drawn by a Shire horse. This cart – it belonged to the Co-op – visited many of the streets in Armley, including the Hallidays where we lived and the streets around the elementary school where my education began, stopping on occasion just over the playground wall.

There were several variables in this stopping and the spectacle it sometimes provided. The cart had to halt at the top of Christ Church View where we could all see it and this had to happen during the morning or the dinner-time break when all the school would be outside. Third, and most essentially, the Co-op horse had at this time to want to do a piss.

News that this was happening would spread rapidly. Lowry is not to my mind a naturalistic painter, but his depiction of a crowd gathering as in several of his factory paintings catches it perfectly, the coming together of a crowd like an abscess or an inflammation. There were only ever two reasons for a crowd to gather in the playground: one was a fight and the other the pissing of the Co-op horse.

There was a difference, though, in these two crowds, with a fight drawing a raucous, partisan and often quarrelsome throng whereas the spectacle of the Co-op horse was observed in almost total silence. The pissing of the Co-op horse is not an occasion for any agglomeration of persons that figures in Elias Canetti's magisterial *Crowds and Power*. It may well occur in his fellow Nobel laureate Heaney's work, horses (and their penises) being more of a common sight I imagine in County Derry than they were in Canetti's Hampstead. But to us children the spectacle of the Co-op horse and its immense dangling dick inspired something like awe. It was not merely the dimensions involved but also the horse's noble indifference to scrutiny, even the scrutiny of the entire school. Sad it was if the whistle went for Lines before this magnificent member had been retracted and of all my memories of Upper Armley National the most vivid is the Co-op horse.

28 August, Yorkshire. Mid-afternoon and hikers trudge back from Ingleborough, some of whom will have gone down Gaping Ghyll. Now they pause on the bridge, straining to see if there are any trout in the brown water. Years ago I remember a child saying to its mother, 'Mam. Do fish have young?'

29 August. Hear a few minutes of the prom 'in holiday mood' devoted to Hollywood, which might have been quite enjoyable had not the music been dolled up in special arrangements. My prejudice against this goes back a lifetime to my father playing along on his violin to the wireless on a Sunday night and in particular to Tom Jenkins and his Palm Court Orchestra. Dad was fine if the numbers were performed as they had been written because, playing by ear, he could easily accompany the music since he knew where it was going. The problem arose when the music was 'arranged', generally by someone (first name forgotten) Hartley. No hope of following the tune through Hartley's flights of fancy and Dad would (mildly) curse and put down his fiddle. In *Sunday Half Hour*, which generally followed, the hymns were not arranged so Hartley was never a problem.

1 September. The papers slightly unexpectedly have reviews of *The Madness of George III* which opened in Bath on Tuesday. The *Independent* is good and factual but Billington in the *Guardian* gives it the same failed 'Play for England' notice he did twenty years ago. That it's not meant to be a play for England and can't be wrenched into being one doesn't occur to him. It's history not allegory.

5 September, Mells. I knew about Mells from reading Evelyn Waugh's biography of Ronald Knox and from all the First World War stuff which comes at the end of the first act of *Forty Years On*. The church closes off a short street of terraced houses which wouldn't be remarkable were they in Rotherham, say, but are more so here, in that like the Vicars' Close at Wells they turn out to be medieval. The church of course is medieval, too, with over the wall, and just visible in a traditional configuration of church and state, the manor house, home of the Horners. Opposite the church door is Munnings's equestrian statue of Edward Horner, its Lutyens plinth like a smaller Cenotaph, though how the dates compare I'm not sure. But it's only the most striking of First War mementoes in a church that is virtually a shrine: nearby is the white-painted wooden cross erected on Horner's first grave and another similar cross for his brother, who was also killed in France and is buried outside the east end of the church with a tombstone by Eric Gill. Gill did the memorial to Raymond Asquith, too, a lettered inscription that blends into the tower wall opposite the Horner tomb. Everywhere is palpably Edwardian and Arts and Crafts including a relief of a peacock by Burne-Jones. A film about the First War could begin here, the whole place redolent of the dead and particularly the illustrious dead. And, yes, there are memorials to the men of the village and others round about, but it is these famously unfulfilled dead of the Lost Generation that dominate.

8 September. A directive must have gone out from the National Trust high command that in future notices telling members not to sit on the heritage chairs should be eschewed in favour of a more subtle message. These days seats that are not to be sat on sport the head of a thistle or a sprig of holly. Other possibilities that occur would be hawthorn, nettles (though they would have to be fresh) or even a stuffed hedgehog. One wonders whether this genteel initiative had the prior approval of Health and Safety.

16 September. I occasionally pick up the *TLS* to read on the train and today it's a review of Ian Kershaw's *The End* about the last days of Hitler. I turn the page and there is a photograph of Joseph Goebbels inspecting some troops of the Volkssturm in Silesia in March 1945. He's shaking hands with Willi Hübner, a child of sixteen, which is unremarkable except that next to Hübner (and also in the Volkssturm) is Peter Cook. He is looking at Goebbels with the ghost of a smile and is much as he was around 1970, his face angular and handsome which it was before the drink took hold. Perhaps to someone who hadn't known him the resemblance would seem less remarkable. To me it's uncanny, though in an ideal world the child beside him would also look like Dudley Moore, than whom he is no bigger.

20 September. The papers full of Murdoch's rumoured payment to the Dowler family of £3 million or more, all the reports I've seen focusing on the inflationary effect this will have on other similar payments. Nobody comments that a settlement of this size simply reflects Murdoch's view of human nature. However mortally he or his newspapers offend or injure, the victims can always be bought off.

5 October, Yorkshire. La Grillade in Leeds is so much our favourite restaurant. It's where we always eat on a Friday night and equally invariably have fish and chips. But last night was Tuesday when fish and chips is not on the menu. I book a table at six fifteen and when we arrive at eight fifteen fish and chips is available, as usual, but cooked especially for us. This makes me feel like Proust at the Ritz.

14 October. The legal action to try and keep Kensal Rise library open fails in the High Court, much to the delight of Brent Council and by extension other library-closing councils throughout the country. Adding insult to injury Brent greets the news by emphasising how much improved its library services are going to be as a result, which is such a dreary and clichéd PR stratagem I'm surprised they bother. In the opening scene of *The History Boys* Irwin, who has progressed from teacher to TV personality to spin doctor, explains to a group of MPs that they should present an impending bill that will limit freedom as doing just the opposite. Even in 2004 this was such a hackneyed procedure I had doubts about including it. But Brent Council still thinks it's worth trying – as indeed does Mr Lansley. It worked for Goebbels so why not now?

Were I Liam Fox's associate Adam Werritty and going into lobbying and PR, I would have changed my name at the outset. Verity has the literal ring of truth about it, Adam Verity a dauntless fighter for justice, whereas all Werritty suggests is some anxious yapping dog which, whatever his faults, Werritty hardly seems to have been, but rather complacent in fact (and with a touch of Christopher Biggins about him). But so many Tories are now infected with the neocon ideology one wonders whatever happened to Tory pragmatism; wounded certainly by Mrs Thatcher but now wholly outmoded.

23 October. 'Big shout for you this morning,' says R., having been listening to the radio where on *Desert Island Discs* Mark Gatiss has been talking about growing up in South Yorkshire and watching *Our Winnie* (the name part played by Sheila Kelley, one of Mike Leigh's rep) and realising that his life could be worth writing about too – much as I suppose I did when reading Richard Hoggart's *Uses of Literacy*. Gatiss links it up with Hector's *History Boys* speech about a hand coming out and taking yours. Immensely bucked by this (which I'll write to Mark G.) coming as it does at a difficult time with the play, one of the shortcomings of which is that it lacks such human moments.

24 October. Judy Egerton sends me *Among Booksellers* by David Batterham. Batterham is a second-hand bookseller and the book a collection of letters to Howard Hodgkin from the places, some of them quite far-flung, where book buying has taken him. There are letters from Spain, Finland, provincial France and even Istanbul, with Batterham's picaresque adventures the connecting thread. There's something of John Harris's *Echoing Voices* about the book; a gallery of eccentrics, with Batterham himself the most notable, drunk, sometimes penniless, on occasion sleeping in doorways and always writing home about it. Lucky Hodgkin to have been the recipient of these letters and sensible Hodgkin for saving them.

26 October. In bed with a cold I'm rung by a television company putting together an obituary of Mrs Thatcher. I've not much to offer though mention the trip I made *c.*1990 along the M62 from Hull to Liverpool, a trail of devastation, decay and manufacturing slump that stretched from coast to coast, much of it the doing of the Iron Lady. It struck me then that no one had done such systematic damage to the North since William the Conqueror. This produces squeals of delight but they're not enough to persuade me to say it on TV.

Deaf with (and these days even without) my cold, I hear a mention of the Stone Roses on the radio as Cold Moses which, as the name of a group, would serve just as well.

31 October. I'm reading a volume of letters from Richard Cobb to Hugh Trevor-Roper and others, edited by Tim Heald. Seeing it advertised and having devoured everything Cobb wrote I get hold of the book straight away only to be slightly disappointed. It's gossipy without being particularly funny with Cobb rather sucking up to Trevor-Roper (and his wife), though in the absence of Trevor-Roper's replies (unsaved by Cobb) one doesn't know how this was received. Cobb is also a Tory in the Ingrams mode – a Tory anarchist I suppose Ingrams would say – and one of those middle-aged men (A. Powell, K. Amis, Alan Clark) who claimed to find Mrs Thatcher sexually attractive. The book is suffused with that self-conscious political incorrectness that the *Spectator* made its own in the 1980s and 1990s and a good deal of drinking goes on, not least by Cobb himself, and while the scrapes this gets him into are funny and appealing – tomato soup down his suit, an airline meal tipped into his neighbour's lap – the notion of the 'heroic drinker' is a bit hard to take. Still, Cobb was a great teacher and historian and an enviably good writer, never (possibly because of the drinking) as appreciated in England as he was in France. And (I'm two thirds through) the book gets better. Still, it's hard to warm to someone who lauds Pinochet (and even Botha) and is as much a bore about 'lefties' as ever Amis was.

5 November. Now the birds are still, light has gone from the garden and the life from the scene. R. is downstairs drawing – a lovely picture of my shoes he did in the week, just the kind of thing for the *LRB* cover.

7 November. In the afternoon to Hinton St George, a remote village south of Ilminster lost in a maze of deep and narrow lanes. It's absurdly picturesque with some terrific houses, Somerset better supplied with handsome buildings than anywhere I've seen and not universally knocked about or 'improved' as they would be in Yorkshire. The church is being repaired both inside and out and the Poulett chapel with its monuments, which we have particularly come to see, is under restoration and full of scaffolding. This turns out to be a blessing as the two restorers are here working and the senior of the two is delighted to talk about restoring a seventeenth-century Poulett monument. It's described in Pevsner as 'baroque' but it's much more peculiar than that, the fairground colours of Tudor and

Stuart monuments revealed only when the restorers removed the grey and beige paint with which it had been covered in the eighteenth and nineteenth centuries. The pillars are decorated in crude scagliola, marbled in black and white with the side panels in bright reds, orange and yellows. Waiting to be treated are two 'wild men', figures that have lost their arms and had them mended with crude clay implants, and on the floor of the chapel is a tray of what look like grey drop scones but which are samples of clays and mortars in different shades ready for the restoration. Both the restorers learned their craft at a college in Lincolnshire of which neither of us had heard, there being (apart from the Courtauld) just one other such institution, at Gateshead. Also in the chapel, opposite the monument being restored, is a fine alabaster monument to an earlier Poulett which originally stood in St Martin-in-the-Fields. To protect the effigy against damage during the restoration a blanket has been thrown over it, leaving the head visible, so that it just looks as if it's an old man happily asleep.

Having held up the work for too long we come reluctantly away, with both of us wanting to go back and see the completed monument. This may not be possible. All the monuments are in the Poulett chapel which is private (cf. the Spencer monuments at Brington and the Russell tombs at Chenies); many of the villagers had never seen this monument until the necessity for restoration gave them the entrée. Now we go on to Crewkerne where there is a good bookshop, though not good enough to have what I always ask for, any old copies of the novels of Ivy Compton-Burnett.

20 November, Yorkshire. Though he was ultimately headed for Scarborough, like Queen Eleanor, the wife of Edward I, Jimmy Savile's journey to the grave was marked by several resting places, one of which was the foyer of the Queens Hotel in City Square in Leeds. I am in there regularly myself, generally waiting for R. off the London train, but though I've seen Sir Jimmy in the hotel as I have Eddie

Waring and Don Revie, I missed the lying in state. This evening I head for the corner where I generally sit but am unsurprised to find an adjacent chaise longue occupied by a half-naked young man with his chest festooned in wires and electrodes. Not giving this another thought I sit elsewhere, the foyers and function rooms of large hotels regularly taken over by displays of orthodontic equipment, investment opportunities in Qatar or, as in this case, I imagine, demonstrations of resuscitation techniques. The wired-up young man is obviously promoting something. Later the manager passes, who points me out the exact spot where the Savile bier rested and I enquire about the cardiological demonstration. It turns out not to be a demonstration at all, the man having come in complaining of chest pains. Whether it was then an 'Is there a doctor in the house?' job or that the hotel makes cardiograms available on request I don't ask and in any case the pain has since abated and the young man has left. R.'s train is now imminent and with the foyer about to be taken over by a posse of middle-aged men in curly wigs and flares plus a couple of Alma Cogan lookalikes I leave too.

23 November. A cycle courier comes to collect my diary extracts for the *LRB*.

(Laughing.) 'This your doing?'

'I suppose so.'

Which I like because both in his question and my apologetic answer there is the notion of writing as an offence committed.

24 November. In Dorset, passing a signpost:

'That's where Hardy's buried.'

'Really?'

Pause.

'Laurel's in Ulverston.'

25 November. A week or so ago someone from Occupy London telephoned to ask me to come and speak to the campers outside St

Paul's. I'm mildly surprised by this because, though I'm wholly sympathetic, I don't normally figure on any roster of letter-signers or rally-rousers. One who does is Vivienne Westwood who, the following day, addresses the throng from the steps of the cathedral. We agree that reading is more my line and I'm given a time for this afternoon. However, when I arrive, I find they've forgotten I'm coming, so I wander down the colonnade, stumbling around among the igloos until someone spots me and takes me into the tea tent. Here I sign various books and reflect that, apart from the patchwork of notices plastered up everywhere, this supposed hotbed of terrorism doesn't seem much different from similar tented assemblies I've visited at Hay-on-Wye and the yurts of the literary festival at Edinburgh, though neither of those has posters warning of the plain-clothes policemen operating on the site together with their mug shots. Now I graduate to a slightly larger tent where I read and answer questions, most of them literary and none to do with the politics of the situation, though I do say that the Corporation of the City of London deserves very little sympathy and that its stance as a guardian of the environs of St Paul's is utterly hypocritical. Hitler generally gets the blame for the destruction of London, but by comparison with the demolition wrought by the banks and the City corporations the Führer was a conservationist. Though I know this isn't what the encampment is about, I remember in the 1970s long before these young people were born, writing letters to the *Times* about the destruction of the City at a time when I still thought letters to newspapers did some good. Camping out might have been more effective then; at least there were still remnants of Paternoster Square left to camp out in.

3 December. In the days when I wrote about spies, notably in *The Old Country*, *An Englishman Abroad* and *A Question of Attribution*, it was often assumed, though not by me, that being homosexual predisposes a person to treachery – a view implicitly endorsed by historians as diverse as A. J. P. Taylor and Richard Cobb, neither of whom believed homosexuals were to be trusted. This never seemed plausible to me nor did I feel my (as it would be called today) relaxed attitude to treachery was to do with my own sexual predilections. It was left to Genet whose *Thief's Journal* I am reading, to pin down what I felt when he says, 'It is perhaps their moral solitude which makes me admire traitors and love them.'

Long before his disgrace, Blunt was at one of the (many) parties at the Courtauld Institute where at one point a colleague saw him coming on to a female companion. Later on in the proceedings she saw him on the same sofa but now embracing a young man. He caught her eye:

'Oh Anthony,' she said, 'you're so fickle.'

'It's true,' said Blunt, 'but remember, many a fickle makes a fuckle.'

As the poet Gavin Ewart remarked, at least his jokes weren't fake.

Love is putting it a bit strongly and maybe admire too – but moral solitude is exactly right. Morals make you beholden – whether it's to God or other people. To be a traitor is not to be beholden and it is to be alone.

In the early days when I finished a play, I used to take extra care crossing the road lest I had an accident and wasn't around to see it put on.

24 December.

Dear M/S Debo

Christmas Eve and all

Through the house

Nothing is stirring not even a

Mouse, though

The Editor has just said I am going upstairs to wrap your (i.e. my) presents and, like Captain Oates I expected him to be some time, only he has returned almost instantly and having finished, so that doesn't augur well for the morrow.

We have received some pre-Christmas gifts including a parcel from S from a butchers in Dumfries. It is the most carnal parcel

I've ever had, containing venison, pheasants, partridges, rabbits and many smaller and lesser known mammals. If S has sent similar parcels to all her acquaintance the countryside of S. West Scotland must be wholly denuded of wildlife, so nothing stirring there either.

I don't suppose you keep up with the pop scene but one current leading songster is Lady Gaga and one of her outfits consists entirely of meat (true) and not just beef skirt but a sirloin stole, mutton chop sleeves, the lot, so that she could easily run up a dress or two from S's parcel alone. It's not a dress in which you would want to walk the dog. You always say your outfits come from the Bakewell Game Fair or wherever where I'm sure Lady Gaga's would go down a storm.

On Wednesday the Editor and I went to a private view of the Leonardo exhibition at the National Gallery. You probably have three or four Leonardos tucked away in the attic so the National Gallery's (rather meagre) show scarcely signifies. Not particularly star-studded though your friend Neal of British Museum fame was there looking older i.e. 18 rather than his usual 14½. Bamber Gascoigne of *Your Starter for Ten* fame and other personalities but nobs fairly thin on the ground otherwise. I actually don't like Leonardo much and think the paintings are a bit creepy particularly the all-in wrestler babies. I made the mistake of saying I don't find them very appealing whereupon there was an H. M. Bateman type reaction with art historians running screaming from the gallery and the editor of the *Burlington Magazine* having to be revived with a glass of Wincarnis.

I'm sorry this silly letter won't get to you by Christmas but we keep thinking about you and hope you won't be snowed in. No chance of that down here where it's positively balmy.

Much love from us both

Nibs

3 January, Yorkshire. En route to Leeds we have lunch at Betty's in Ilkley, packed with people stir-crazy after the holiday. We are sitting facing the car park and the row of shops beyond.

Me: What is that shop called?

R: Which?

Me: It looks to me like 'Hot Faeces'.

R: It's 'Fat Face'.

Between a shop calling itself Fat Face and one called Hot Faeces seems a difference of degree only, with both equally mysterious. Is it a shop where one gets a fat face (hence sweets and confectionery)? Or an outsize shop? Neither apparently, just a well-known fashion outlet. Still, the name seems quite odd to me, if not nearly as unlikely as what I thought it was. 'Keep up' I suppose the message.

4 January. Heartened by the verdicts in the Stephen Lawrence murder trial and by the consistently dignified behaviour of the parents, particularly the mother – a woman who has had to be a heroine before she could be recognised as a mother. Hard not to think that the highest honours in the state should be given to such as her, if only because she has made the nation feel better about itself and rekindled belief in the ultimate triumph of justice.

Both parents seem to have the ability to make people behave better around them; I've seldom seen plaintiffs so restrained and forbearing at the conclusion of a trial – and a trial that has gone on for seventeen years.

12–13 January. Watch the second of two programmes on grammar schools on BBC4. I was asked to take part but didn't, feeling my experience wasn't typical. I never thought of Leeds Modern, the school I went to from 1946 until 1952, as a grammar school though I suppose it was. It wasn't so self-conscious and pleased with itself as most of the schools that feature and the range of ability for which it catered seems in retrospect so wide it might well have been a comprehensive school before its time. Nor was it in the least bit snobbish as so many of the schools that figure in the programme seem to have been, though none as snobbish as the grammar schools that, on the introduction of comprehensives, turned themselves into direct grant schools as, for instance, Leeds Grammar School did. Another absentee from the programme is Tony Harrison, an old boy of Leeds Grammar School, the snobbery of which is pilloried in some of his poems. By rights all such schools should be free schools, as indeed in the light of their origins, should many public schools. The nearest public school to us in Yorkshire is Giggleswick which started off as the local grammar school. It's certainly not free today, though like many public schools its exclusiveness shelters behind what is thought of as a generous allocation of scholarships and bursaries. These points are just about made in the programme, but what is more noticeable is how ex-grammar-school boys like Roy Strong are sentimental over their teachers, which ought to be sympathetic did not the camera go in vampire-like to catch the tears.

Maybe my parents were just undemonstrative as I remember nothing comparable to the pride of the parents of Neil Kinnock, for instance, when he passed the eleven plus (and so wouldn't have to go down the mine). I can't even remember taking the exam except that my friend (and alphabetical neighbour on the school register) Albert Benson passed it with me but was too poor to go on to what we then called secondary school.

As it was put together, the programme tended to confirm Anthony Powell's thesis that documentaries aren't based on the evidence but are simply scenarios dreamed up by the director, the conclusions known in advance with the facts arranged accordingly.

I've never been particularly concerned about the end of the grammar schools, seeing it as nothing compared with the continuing offence of the public school. On this I'm as big a bore as (if less worthily) Hockney is on smoking. The only person in the programme waving that flag – rather uncharacteristically – is Edwina Currie, who is, as she puts it, a Scouse Tory who acknowledges the continuing unfairness of public-school education while knowing her party will do nothing to alleviate it.

Notes for Judy Egerton, *Last Word*, Radio 4, broadcast on Sunday 22 April:

Art historians can be quite snooty, their pleasure in pictures not always obvious with not much delight. Judy loved pictures and wasn't pretentious about them. She lived in a small two-storey mid-nineteenth-century house near the Oval rather like a Cambridge house, the walls of which were full of pictures with scarcely a space – and pictures of all sorts and periods, one or two quite good – she had an early Thomas Jones for instance – others by young artists who had taken her eye – and she *had* an eye, the house a lovely assembly.

She was a very good cook. I remember having three helpings of a Moroccan lamb dish she made though most meals I had with her were lunches at a little Italian restaurant in Store Street near her office in Bedford Square and where they always made a fuss of her. It was good but it wasn't posh.

When she was working on her definitive book on Stubbs, she used to tell me stories of visits to country houses where the owners claimed to have one of his paintings and how even in this day and age she was treated as a social inferior, no arrangements made to take her back to the station particularly when she'd given the horse-rider or whatever the thumbs down. At one point and through Stubbs she got interested in portraits of servants and when I used to find an example I'd draw it to her attention but she'd always been there first. Still she never made you feel a fool as art historians have been known to do.

The first time I remember speaking to Judy was in 1995 when we'd both been at a memorial service at St George's, Bloomsbury, for Charles Monteith of Faber and Faber. It hadn't been much of a service – some of the eminent speakers wholly inaudible and she caught me up as I came out and talked about this in a way that was typically Judy, how deplorably they had read, being unimpressed by the great and the good. I found this sympathetic. I'd just been made a trustee of the National Gallery, which I enjoyed but was rather overawed by and Judy was quick to show me there was nothing to be overawed by at all and cutting most of the board down to size.

I don't know whether she caught this sceptical tone from Larkin, whose lifelong correspondent she was, or whether it chimed in with something in both their personalities but it's what made her a lively person to talk to – and something of an outsider. If that's Australian, which she was, I never detected anything else Australian about her, even in her voice, though maybe those two most English of painters, Hogarth and Stubbs, had to do with this.

24 January. 'Well, love, the call's going on,' is what my mother used to say in the early 1960s when I phoned from London, meaning that telephoning to them was still a luxury. On the rare occasions when I was at home and wanted to make a private call it had to be on the shop phone, which was mounted on the wall with a separate mouth and earpiece. So some of one's intimate moments were played out amid sawdust and blood.

2 February. An environmentally sensitive bus named after me in Leeds. I just wish it could have been a tram.

16 February. What people were doing at eleven o'clock on the morning of 3 September 1939:

Humphrey Carpenter's *The Inklings* (Tolkien, C. S. Lewis and
    Charles Williams) – rowing down the Thames
Hugh Trevor-Roper and Gilbert Ryle – walking across
    Northumberland
John Piper and Geoffrey Grigson – en route for lunch at the
    Betjemans
The Bennetts – on a No. 16 tram going down Tong Road, Leeds 12

9 March. I am reading Colm Tóibín's *New Ways to Kill Your Mother*.
Of Hart Crane's suicide he writes: 'He walked on deck . . . took off
his coat, folded it neatly over the railing (not dropping it on deck)
. . . then suddenly he vaulted over the railing and jumped into the
sea.' This was in 1932. At Calverley on the outskirts of Leeds seven
years previously my grandfather folded his jacket neatly too before
stepping into the canal.

11 March. The crowded train from Oxford makes its last stop at Slough
where a Sikh gets on – in his twenties, tall, distinguished, black-suited,
black-turbanned. He sits there unsmiling, a princely figure, seemingly impervious to his surroundings, the aura only broken when at one
point he briefly texts. Otherwise he might be a head of state.

17 March. A new robin – hatched last year I imagine and much about
the garden. A very *dapper* little bird.

18 March. R. to Cardiff to see his grandmother on a potentially difficult day as it's also the day of the Grand Slam rugger match between
Wales and France. The train is very crowded and he sits in Weekend
First opposite a middle-aged French couple whom he assumes to be
fans, but with nothing in their behaviour that gives any clue. However, just before the train arrives at Cardiff the very proper bourgeois
lady takes out her compact and with her lipstick carefully draws the
French flag on both cheeks and colours them in. This is done so

unselfconsciously and without a smile R. feels that for this alone they deserve to win.

20 March. Tonight Lansley's bill passes into law and the NHS is effectively abolished. For a doctor or any sort of health professional it must be like the fall of France – a relief that it's done with and a pause before resistance begins to be organised. Though I doubt that it will.

12 April. See a way to begin the man and his mother story, though it has echoes of Mrs Forbes. Still it cheers me up and I have quite a productive morning. In the late afternoon I shop for vegetables to put in tonight's stew, including turnips which they often have at Yeoman's but nowhere else. Today Nigel the greengrocer has to get some from the cellar or, as it would have been called in Dad's shop, the back place. And I think what a good title *The Back Place* would be for an anthology of the – maybe quite unworthy – stuff that wouldn't make it into a more respectable collection. The back place at the shop was where Dad (and sometimes Gordon and me) made the sausages, shaped the rissoles and where (at 92A anyway) it was hung with beasts' heads. I suppose it was in the time of rationing what people meant by 'under the counter' – though Dad never kept anything much there except supplies of greaseproof paper. The back place was also the setting, at least in the imagination of the Widow Eliot, where I could have been seen studying Russian or stuff for my degree.

The words put into the mouth of Humphrey Carpenter in *The Habit of Art* are to do with how writers feel threatened by biography, their lives as they see it what they have put in the shop window, the rest – what's in the back place – their business. The stuff in the back place (emphasis on back rather than place) was not meant to be seen. It's the back places of writers' lives that they want left unexplored.

16 April. Wrens *bounce*.

25 April. At five a car comes to take me down to Silk Sound studios on Berwick Street to record a voiceover (of my own voice) for an episode of *Family Guy*, the story being that Brian, the dog, has written a play, premiering at Quahog, which 'all the playwrights' (i.e. Yasmina Reza, David Mamet and me) duly go and see – and rubbish. They had first of all asked if they could use me as a cartoon character to which I graciously agreed (not saying that I felt it was the highlight of my career). It was then they asked if I would voice myself. Yasmina and David had apparently not been tempted but I went for this too and it was only as I was signing the clearance afterwards that I realised *Family Guy* is a Fox (i.e. a Murdoch) programme and so not something I would normally do. Today was the day Murdoch Sr was on the stand at the Leveson Inquiry and en route to the studio I ask the driver who has been his most famous passenger. Without hesitation he says Muhammad Ali but then reels off a list of other celebrities he has driven, including the Murdochs. I take this just to be the driver keeping in the swim but a few minutes later the car phone rings with the message, 'Car for Mr Murdoch at eight thirty.' Which Murdoch it is I don't ask, though feel myself faintly brushed by the wings of history. The driver, incidentally, is the first person I've spoken to who is actually looking forward to the Olympics.

30 April. Outdated though some of them are, we still rely on the Shell Guides, particularly when searching out churches. Some, generally the ones with which John Piper was involved, are more idiosyncratic than others but they've always been easier to handle and broader in scope than the Pevsner guides and they don't make one feel a fool for not knowing what a soffit is (or gadrooning). Until recently, though, Yorkshire hasn't been well served by the guides. Then in 2001 came *North Yorkshire* by Peter Burton, a favourite photographer of Betjeman's, and today I'm sent *West Yorkshire*, one of the Heritage Shell Guides by William Glossop, a notable addition to the series and full of good things and marvellous photographs, some still by the now late Peter Burton.

The good thing about Glossop is that unlike me he doesn't wring his hands too much over what has been lost, particularly the wholesale destruction of Victorian buildings that has gone on all over the country, though even he finds the destruction of Bradford hard to forgive. He's also milder about church robberies than I'm inclined to be and the thieves who wrenched the original Norman bronze door ring from Adel Church he calls thoughtless. I'd feel like nailing them to the church door.

Bleak though it often is, I find the area round Halifax romantic and almost fabled. This is because my mother's family the Peels came from Elland and at family gatherings in Leeds the talk was always of places I'd heard of but never been to . . . Greetland, Salter Hebble, Ripponden, Sowerby Bridge. My aunt Eveline had been a pianist for the silent films, with Ivor Novello a staple of her repertoire. I bet she didn't know (this is one of Glossop's plums) that Novello wrote 'Perchance to Dream' in Barkisland's Howroyd Hall, the original stage set a copy of the sitting room. A lovely book.

2 May. Jeremy Hunt has the look of an estate agent waiting to show someone a property.

10 May. I sit in Rome airport while R. stands by the baggage carousel. We're only here for four days, and did either of us have bags on wheels we would not have to wait as most passengers these days seem to lug them on board. As he waits a flight arrives from Beijing and behind him a middle-aged Chinese woman leans forward and (with her fingers) blows her nose copiously onto the floor.

11 May. One object of the trip is for R. to see the room in the Vatican Museum devoted to Roman animal sculpture, a possible article for the magazine. He has got a special permit which enables us to bypass the queue – at 11 a.m. (and in baking heat) stretching down the hill outside. Inside our contact is waiting but there is no getting round the throngs of tourists pouring into the building, most of them I imagine set on seeing the Sistine Chapel ceiling. It is like a mainline station in the rush hour but with this difference, these people are all of one mind – tour guides in the van, gathering their flocks up as they scatter at the turnstiles, coach parties supporting their aged and their lame and, of course, their fat – some of them so gross one wonders they have the energy spare from just getting about never mind the sightseeing. Unsmiling, too, most people, grim even – or at least determined, pressing on and upwards along galleries lined with sculptures and busts, hung with thousands of ancient artefacts too many to be even casually appreciated, let alone properly – though instead they halt in an awed circle around a Michelangelo hulk – hunk, too, probably once upon a time – thighs and crotch that has lost its cock but kept its scrotum.

The animals we have come to see are not much looked at either and blessedly form a small backwater off the slow-moving throng. What do I notice? Probably not much more than anyone else – a mosaic floor, divided into panels of various vegetables, one panel a bunch of asparagus, the thought as trivial as 'They ate asparagus just as we do – and parcelled up in the same way.' A hedgehog. Goats, always a touch sinister, horses gouged by lions, a huge and wonderful camel's head, various boars – no domestic pets it occurs to me now writing this. Wandering to the end of the room where there is a view over the city I come round a corner on a nun, in uniform, gazing on a naked Venus.

We have a chance to go on and out via the Sistine Chapel but the throng is too great so we turn about and thread our way back and out into the now quieter street, the earlier queue having evaporated.

Best, so it's said, to come in the afternoon when all the tours have gone.

Lovely supper at the restaurant George F. recommended, the Da Fortunato, up a side street from the Pantheon. Decent, unpretentious, the food delicious, the waiters looking like dentists or professors of philosophy. At a table behind me a dozen or so Italian businessmen all in suits and eating a pre-ordered meal that looks tempting – whitebait, courgette flowers in batter, raspberries. In England they would have got rowdier as the meal went on; here they are genial and enjoying themselves but decorously so.

In front of me a prosperous middle-aged man and his wife or girlfriend. They both have steak tartare followed by – steak tartare again.

On the next table to them is an oldish man, white-haired with a fine, handsome face who looks like someone out of Cheever. Out of Cheever, too, in that he disposes of a whole bottle of white wine in the course of his meal (Jerusalem artichoke followed by grilled sole – the filleting of which he follows attentively and completes himself, carefully picking out any stray bones). He is entirely self-sufficient, taking no interest in anyone else dining and seems familiar to the staff. He could be an expatriate poet or, perhaps more likely, the distinguished retired head of a grand advertising agency – and it's not merely that the hero of Roth's *Everyman* is almost that – I fancy by the end of the meal he is quite drunk but our meal is over so I can't stick around to see. There could be no sharper contrast with this man than the other Americans dining – half a dozen big and overweight tourists who sit in the centre of the room – altogether out of place in such a fastidious establishment, though the waiters give no sign of thinking so. Another not untypical figure is the old proprietor, dark-suited and looking like a businessman but whose function seems now to be reduced to straightening the odd chair – and even at one point a table, which he carefully manhandles out of the room. It's a lovely meal, though, and we plan to go there again this evening, Saturday.

13 May. We pack our bags ready for this afternoon's plane then stroll along the street to the Palazzo Doria Pamphilj, passing on the way a covey of priests and earnest young laity en route for a pro-life demonstration. I feel sorry for these devout and less than butch youths (me, once), knowing the priests look down on them, while longing for sterner converts.

At first the palazzo seems closed and we have to circumambulate the whole building to find the entry door. This, though, is salutary, as it makes one realise what a vast place it is – virtually an entire city block and a small town in itself. The late Stuart Burge, the theatre director, was hidden here as an escaped POW in the war, which I took to mean he spent this perilous time in the bosom of the family. Stuart always played this down and now I can see why, as he may well have been lodged in some attic or vestibule of this vast complex, never setting eyes on the Doria-Pamphilj themselves. The museum itself is staggering, with rank on rank of paintings stretching from floor to ceiling so that when you look in a small side room and find the Velázquez *Innocent X* unheralded and on its own, it's almost by accident. One blessing of the palazzo is that though every one of the rooms on show is lined with posh seventeenth- and eighteenth-century chairs, none of which is to be sat on, and the upholstery protected by nasty see-through plastic, there are always in addition three or four canvas and metal chairs, so one never goes far without somewhere one can sit down and take in the room, sightseeing thus becoming almost a pleasure.

Security at Fiumicino seems quite relaxed, to the extent that one of the men on duty, a nice jolly fellow, makes jokes about it, saying (as he conducts the body search), 'No bombs today then?' and R. gets much the same treatment.

Things have changed, at least in Italy. A few years ago a friend of ours in Canada made a joke about bombs as he was going through security and was promptly hauled off to a cell where he was strip-searched and kept there for several hours and when he was eventually released had some incriminating entry made on his computer record. Even allowing for my nervousness about flying I think I still prefer the Italian approach.

23 May. A party for HMQ at the Royal Academy where around six we join a straggling queue of notables, the actors the most obvious, though Vivienne Westwood is her usual unobtrusive self. Talk to various people in the queue, one of whom seems to know my plays well but then congratulates me on my paintings of trees – she's the first of three people who confuse me with Hockney and though he too is at the party I doubt if he is ever confused with me.

Inside the place is less crowded than one had expected and with the rooms so tall it's almost airy. We're directed into one of the emptier rooms where HMQ is due to pass through but are then pounced on by some young man who asks if he may introduce the (slightly bewildered) Duke of Kent. We have an awkward few minutes but the day is saved by Clive Swift, whose son Joe has just won a medal at Chelsea. HRH knows about Chelsea and so brightens considerably. Meanwhile lurking by the door HMQ is due to come through is Kate O'Mara and, when I next look, lining up to meet Her Majesty are Ms O'Mara along with Joan Collins and Shirley Bassey, the impression being that anyone can get to speak to the monarch provided you're pushy enough. But it's all very casual, so much so that R. doesn't even see the queen, though she's distinctive enough, dressed in white and glittering with jewels, determinedly animated and smiling, which, since she's been at it for two hours already, is an achievement in itself. We go on through the rooms, talking to all sorts of people – Jim Naughtie, Nigel Slater and David Hare, who claims that the best conjunction he's seen so far is George Steiner talking to Joan Collins.

Come away at eight o'clock with HMQ still at it, and the policemen in the forecourt very jolly and eating ice cream.

24 May. A year or so ago and more I was a prize in a charity auction at the Roundhouse and drinks or whatever with me sold, I don't know how much for, to Guy Chambers – the songwriter (for Robbie Williams) and pop promoter. Dates have been arranged four or five times and one or other of us has cancelled but this evening a car comes to take me up to Lambolle Road in Belsize Park for what I imagine is going to be some sort of cocktail party. But not at all. Guy C. and his wife Emma have got their mothers round and some friends and their wonderfully behaved children, there's a big chair in the corner for me while they are on sofas or sitting on the floor from which they ask me questions about what I've written (particularly *Lady in the Van*). Though he's obviously v. successful in a world of which I've no knowledge, the set-up is nicely childlike and I feel like a teacher in a primary school. I talk and answer questions from seven thirty or so till nine fifteen and it's lovely and easy and no chore at all. I walk back over Primrose Hill, the evening hot still with couples strolling about the streets – a murmuring night with love in the air – the top of the hill busy and crowds outside the pub in a lively Regent's Park Road.

1 June. John Horder has died at ninety-two, who, after a succession of bad doctors at university and in New York, was the physician who restored my faith in the medical profession. It was partly because he listened, as doctors have learned to do since, I hope, but which in the early 1960s they hardly did at all. Kind and in some respects saintly, his care for his patients brought on regular breakdowns and he was no stranger to depression. Famous as Sylvia Plath's doctor, he always reproached himself that he did not see her suicide coming. What he thought of Ted H. is not recorded. Once examining (as he was often called on to do) my back passage he said: 'No. I can't find anything that concerns me here but' – his finger all the while up my bum – 'it's always nice to see you.'

4 June. In Yorkshire it's a lovely blustery blue day but in London the rain which soaked Sunday's endless Jubilee regatta has had a more melancholy consequence, as when we get home we find by the back door two dead baby wrens, drowned presumably in the torrents that poured down on HMQ. One thinks of all that work – the parents flying in and out every five minutes – all gone to waste. Now, without them, the garden seems empty.

19 June. Watch the last of Grayson Perry's TV series *In the Best Possible Taste*, which have been good programmes, though requiring the subjects – tonight it's the upper classes – to think about decoration and style, thus almost inevitably falsifying the answers, the unthinkingness of style of its essence. It put me in mind though of my second play, *Getting On* (1971), which I look up. It's not a good play (and far too wordy) but where it scores – and is almost documentary – is about class and style, and particularly the style of the young marrieds who were my contemporaries in 1970, with George, the verbose Labour MP who's its central figure, hankering after the style of the old middle classes, 'the middle-class family . . . the most exclusive interior decorator in the world'. He also hankers after unselfconsciousness in style and taking things for granted which, forty years later, I'm still on about in *People* – not that anyone will notice.

22 June. Funeral of my agent, Ros Chatto.

A typical phone call from Ros would begin: 'I don't think we want to do this one, darling' – and more often than not she was right.

'It's one of those e-mails, darling. It begins, "Hi Ros!" I've never met her in my life.'

And though if one did the job it would at least have made her a little money, that never came into it and once the tiresome distraction of work was disposed of she could get down to the real business – gossip, what she was reading, what you were reading, what plays she'd seen, what plays you hadn't seen – phone calls which came two or three times a week right until the finish with Ros refusing to recognise illness was anything other than a bore.

It's a small and unheralded sort of courage but courage nevertheless.

I thought of Ros as my contemporary though she was a decade or so older and had memories of the theatre that went back to the time when Peter Brook still directed plays on Shaftesbury Avenue and she was always giving little sidelights on her life before that. In *The History Boys* a boy seduces a master and there was some tut-tutting that this was unlikely. 'Nonsense,' said Ros. 'I seduced the art master when I was sixteen.'

Other regular features would be excerpts from the collected wisdom of Robert Morley. 'I've discovered the sovereign remedy for diabetes – meringues.'

How one will miss her. It's as if the whole landscape has altered.

3 July. Feel I should register the continuing excellence of Radios 3 and 4 prompted by two and a half hours of reminiscences on Radio 3 by the ninety-year-old John Amis, which included him talking at length to Myra Hess (whose voice I've never heard before) and also to Walter Legge, both of whom were fascinating and with no indication in Amis's voice that he himself is well past his sell-by date.

Consistently good, too, is *Last Word*, the obituary programme on Radio 4, and *The Archive Hour*, which on 7 July was about Harold Macmillan – the Night of the Long Knives. This was terrific stuff both in itself, Macmillan always a treat even when he's being a showman, but also in pointing up the driving down of standards in politics that has occurred since. Taken together with Sue MacGregor's *The Reunion* and Jim Naughtie's *New Elizabethans* these half a dozen programmes are alone worth the licence fee.

5 July. Speech at the Kentish Town Health Centre:

We are here to celebrate the 125th anniversary of the foundation of the James Wigg practice. No one now, of course can remember James Wigg who began this practice in 1887 but there may still be one or two people who remember his son John Wigg who succeeded him and was in practice at the start of the National Health Service in 1948.

Many of us, though, myself included will have fond memories of his first partner, John Horder who alas died two months ago at the age of ninety-two and whose widow and fellow practitioner Elizabeth is with us this afternoon.

I don't think any of them or any of the long succession of doctors who have worked at the James Wigg would be offended if I said that this has always been a practice that has served the poor and underprivileged.

Though there are areas of Kentish Town that have come up in the world it is still a relatively deprived area and the doctors who practise here and all the staff, driven by a calling that is both social and therapeutic and that has been a feature of the James Wigg throughout its long history.

Thinking of the period between the First and Second Wars which, in 1948, led to the foundation of the NHS, John Wigg said, 'The resentment of the dreadful injustices experienced by my patients will never completely subside and I would rather choke than vote for the party which sponsored them. The deprivations were bad enough. What was so intolerable was the carefully nurtured suggestions that only the indolent were victims of the economic battle.'

That was written in the late 1930s but it's a view that still hangs about and is made an excuse for economies and so-called reforms that are no reforms at all. And the doctors in the practice today still find themselves battling for the rights of their patients often against marketing philosophies which have very little to do with their welfare.

Still when we look round us at this health centre, achieved over the last decade not quite single-handedly but very much thanks to Roy McGregor and which, without his patience and boundless enthusiasm and energy would have been impossible, we can, as patients be grateful for what is both a centre of excellence and one of service.

And though this is a very modern practice may the day never come when patients are referred to or thought of as customers. The word patient means a sufferer and when someone comes to the doctor they are coming not because they want to buy something but because they want help. Structure and restructure the Health Service how you will doctors are not shopkeepers, patients are not customers and medicine is not a product.

Just as James Wigg back in 1887 went into general practice to alleviate the plight of the poor of Kentish Town so even in the vastly changed circumstances of today medicine at whatever level is still a calling and we should be grateful and proud that here in the James Wigg practice we have such a dedicated band of professionals: doctors, nurses, ancillary workers at all levels whose ideals are still those of its founder, James Wigg.

14 July. Drive in the now almost daily rain up the M40 to turn off in Oxfordshire for Middleton Stoney and Rousham. The rain has stopped as we drive into the stables courtyard where there is a gathering of what look like grand gardeners drinking champagne out of plastic cups. Spotted by R. in a shapeless hat and raincoat one detaches himself and raising his glass comes over. It is Michael Wheeler-Booth – my contemporary at Oxford and a friend and pupil of Bruce McFarlane. Their group now adjourns to the summerhouse at the western end of the front lawn while R. and I occupy its easterly twin and have our sandwiches, their much more elaborate picnic – salads, sausages – taking time to set out. Meanwhile we do our tour of the garden which, despite the rain and the occasional muddy path, is otherwise immaculate – the rill or cascade, always my favourite, running clear and steady out of the pond in which there is one flowery-tailed tadpole, possibly a newt. The river is high and fast, flowing brown and dimpled almost up to its banks. Now the sun is coming out and in the reeds are dozens of blue and black (mayflies(?). This is the third or fourth time I've been to Rousham but it has never before seemed so appealing. The kitchen garden in particular is a riot of colour, its plump cottage garden borders showing no sign of the months of rain we've had, the beds in the rose garden full of tall self-sown maroon poppies. Back at the summerhouse they are well into their lunch which the ladies urge us to share while the men ply the drink. I talk to a retired history don from Oriel, Jeremy Catto, friend and disciple of Trevor-Roper who as regius professor had been attached to Oriel without liking the college one bit. Nice and easy to talk to though my nervousness of dons is never entirely dispelled, however chatty they are. One sad bit of news he tells me is that Maurice Keen is now in a home in Banbury suffering from dementia. I have not seen Maurice Keen in sixty years but this does not make it less melancholy.

31 July. Shopping in Primrose Hill this afternoon I see David Miliband on the phone outside the bookshop. It's the first time I've seen him since the election (and his demotion) so I wave and he straight away comes off the phone and we talk. I'm not even sure if he still lives in Edis Street (which he does) but that apart he talks entirely about me – where do I live now, what am I reading, have I got a new play on but in that kind of half-attentive way politicians have, asking questions but scarcely listening to the answers – royalty, I imagine, similarly.

No reference to politics except to say he didn't think we are quite where we should be at this time but after the party conference it would be more clear. I say – and this isn't just politeness – that he is much missed as indeed he is. Even if not in his brother's place but in close association with him it would make all the difference – and not just cosmetically.

As I go, I say, 'Remember you are missed. So think on.' But maybe people say this to him all the time.

27 July. A flying visit to Norfolk, where I am to read at the Holt Festival. Rather than hang about all morning R. sensibly gets us off to look at two churches at Warham, both medieval but with one done up in the eighteenth century. As we look round the first church (which has three fonts) there is some sort of exercise going on in the air, with planes filling both sky and church with thunderous noise. 'The Olympics?' R. suggests, that unlonged-for day having at last arrived. Not particularly memorable, one church does have a note-worthy memorial:

RICHARD HENRY BURDEN CATTELL M.A.
RECTOR OF THE WARHAMS 1928–1947
CAPTAIN OF THE ENGLISH RUGBY FOOTBALL TEAM 1900
CHAPLAIN TO THE FORCES AT GALLIPOLI 1915.
THIS TABLET IS PLACED HERE IN REMEMBRANCE BY
HIS SEVEN DAUGHTERS.

It's a novel by Ivy Compton-Burnett.

1 August. R.'s latest joke is 'Team AB' – 'another medal for Team AB after his epic cycle ride for this morning's papers.'

2 August. A few days ago Daniel the American boy opposite tells us of a horrendous attack on someone in the Crescent in which two men in balaclavas in a stolen car stop and rob someone from Rothwell Street and another neighbour, intervening, gets robbed too and beaten up and is left on the pavement outside our house with a broken back.

No one seems to know much about it, the American boy, having been born in Detroit, astonished that such shocking violence can occur in the genteel surroundings of Primrose Hill.

R. goes off to work at nine thirty but is back in ten minutes having run into Beverley S. The man attacked and left seemingly crippled on the pavement was our neighbour Anthony S. Fortunately he was not so badly injured as the American boy thought, having broken a rib and a scapula – the result of an entirely gratuitous kicking given him by the mugger when he had already taken his watch. Their daughter, Catherine, also a doctor was in the house and when the police arrived they were told both by Catherine and by Anthony not to move him – which, of course, they promptly did making matters worse and more painful. Nor did the ambulance arrive, the force supposedly deployed at the Olympics, Beverley having to take him to UCH in the car. When he eventually arrives at UCH Casualty is as empty as everywhere else and he was promptly treated and is now much better to the extent that he has gone off to work, though not surprisingly somewhat shaken up.

6 August. All the Olympic stuff, I suppose, makes me remember when I was a boy and the series in, I think, the *Hotspur* or the *Wizard* about Wilson. Wilson was a tall sinewy man of indeterminate age, modest, taciturn, mysterious, who in a typical episode would bring off some amazing feat of endurance – running a vast distance in a seemingly impossible time, scaling an unconquered peak – an achievement which he would shrug off with his customary modesty. Then someone would come across an old document or a barely legible memorial stone which, when deciphered, recorded a similar feat also by someone called Wilson . . . only two hundred years previously. So each story ended with a troubled intimation of Wilson's immortality.

At one point in, I think, the 1980s Trevor Griffiths urged me to write a play about Wilson – or maybe said he was thinking of doing so himself. As it is the character of Wilson persists as an ideal of what an athlete ought to be. I can't imagine Wilson snarling in victory as, say, John Terry does, still less punching the air. You wouldn't have found Wilson brandishing his medals at the TV cameras in the way some of the athletes were doing on Saturday night.

8 August. The two boys who have won in the triathlon live in Bramhope, a village on the outskirts of Leeds which we often drive through. The only other notable resident of Bramhope is (or maybe was) Saddam Hussein's cousin.

11 August, Yorkshire. This afternoon we go as so often to Garden-makers for tea, where there is now an added attraction as Andrew and Hilary have taken to keeping hens. Seeing them last time we were here R. was besotted and sought ways of devising how we too could keep poultry – though where and how impossible to imagine. Today we pay the hens a second visit, Rupert feeding them, some-times from his hand or sitting on the bench in the middle of the pen just happy to watch them all. They're an odd mixture, hens – fastidi-ous in their footwork, pausing foot poised before delicately putting it down. Then at other times scurrying about with nothing fastidi-ous to them at all. R. coaxes a sick and retarded chicken into taking some corn (the other hens always trying to peck it) with Andrew and Hilary scarcely less in thrall than he is.

21 August. I am rereading as I periodically do all my notebooks – they're too unselective to be called 'commonplace books' but are just where I've noted stuff from my reading that I didn't want to forget or have some reference for. This rereading has been currently sparked off because of trying to find a quotation from Hebbel about the char-acters in a play all being in the dock and how all are found not guilty.

I generally put a book and page reference for all the entries, though my handwriting is often hard to read. There are other entries I think I wrote myself, such as this one dated December 1982, 'All nature and never a call for pity. Death and no compassion and no thought of com-passion, no expectation of it. None looks for mercy, but only escape.'

That impresses me though maybe it's because it's the kind of sub-philosophic stuff you get in the better class of commonplace book – like the 'That sounds exactly like literature' passages I occa-sionally smuggle into plays – I've never found a place for this one, though and it's thirty years old.

22 August. There are different ways of being English, one of which is not to want to be English at all. I doubt if anyone French is ever ashamed of being French – however deplorable the government might be. Disaffected though he or she may be, to be French is still the best thing in the world.

24 August. I've never found literature much of a community; books yes but not authors. I've always been happier with actors rather than writers.

26 August. When I was religious as a boy I used to envy Catholics who only had to say the words of the Mass and not have to mean them in the way that Anglicans did.

Hens (which we visit again today) don't repay affection. They don't *fawn* as, say, dogs do. And they *skitter* but are fastidious at the same time. But to feed them or to watch them being fed is unexpectedly restful. They soothe.

It was the opposite of restful when, evacuated as children, my brother and I went down the field with Mrs Weatherhead, the farmer's wife, to feed her hens. There were a lot of them for a start and the two or three cockerels who lorded it over them were noisy and fierce, flying at Mrs Weatherhead and trying to get at her bucket. She would have none of this, clouting the birds with the bucket or her big aluminium scoop in a scene of seeming pandemonium.

Once the hens were feeding my brother and I were put into the hutches to collect the eggs, a proceeding I hated. The hutches were raised up on wheels so they could be towed about the field, the wheels, I suppose, a precaution against rats. Sitting in the sun in the middle of the field they were intolerably hot and filled with the stink of hens so that the natural pleasure we got out of finding the eggs was diminished by the desire to get the eggs and get out as quickly as we could.

In children's books collecting the eggs, like milking the cows, was reckoned to be a treat but not for me; an early lesson that books said one thing but life was another.

21 September. To the City of Leeds School in Woodhouse, the head of which is Georgie Sale, a troubleshooting headmistress formerly at my own old school and who, though not a fan of Michael Gove, relishes schools like hers that have to be turned round. There are fifty or so nationalities here, including two boys who were child soldiers in Africa and are thought to have killed people, and two boys smuggled out of Afghanistan in a wooden box built above the axle of a jeep. They came to Leeds thinking they had relatives here but found they had moved on and so lived rough in Hyde Park, preying on students and stealing food until they were picked up by the police and brought to the school. None of these I see, but only a light airy secondary school, the children's art on the walls and a display of masks and costumes they wore at the bank holiday carnival. I read to an audience of parents and friends, though fetched up hard against Life as I am here, my usual stuff seems trivial and frivolous, with the purpose of the evening to raise funds so that these extra-curricular events can be maintained. Were the school an academy funds would be provided, so I must be grateful to Mr Gove for bringing me out on this Friday night.

25 September. Less enthusiastic than the newspapers about the Leicester disinterment of the supposed body of Richard III partly because it will be a feather in the cap of the Richard III Society. I take this to be quite a wealthy organisation, possibly with American backers because it played a part in the supposed restoration of Lead Church in Yorkshire.

Lead Church, which I have known all my life and to which I used to cycle out from Leeds when I was a boy, is a single-chamber chapel, fourteenth- or fifteenth-century, that stands a few miles from the field of Towton where the Yorkists won a great and bloody victory over the Lancastrians on Palm Sunday 1461. The chapel – or a previous building on the site – served as a dressing station after the battle, the many dead from which have been found in various mass graves in the neighbourhood.

Though not far from various conurbations Lead was always an idyllic spot, set in the middle of a field with sheep grazing up to the threshold of the church doorway. And so it remained until at least 2000 and might be thought to be immune from alteration as it was vested in the Churches Conservation Trust. Visiting a couple of years ago we found that the turf no longer grew up to the door. Instead a patio of reconstituted stone had been laid down presumably to host gatherings of some kind and at the east end of the church was a suburban garden, where the white rose of York figured prominently. Inside the church a banner proclaimed the 'restoration' was the work of the Richard III Society – a piece of vandalism so infuriating I took down the banner and hid it behind the altar – and would have burned it, had I had a match. I wrote to the Churches Conservation Trust to complain and received a placatory letter, saying the patio had been there for several years – which it hadn't, the whole I suppose quite trivial incident an illustration of the perils of a well-meaning voluntary organisation that couldn't leave well alone perhaps because the funds of the Richard III Society meant that it had money to spend.

26 September. In Yorkshire at the weekend where we pay our now ritual visit to Andrew and Hilary's chickens at Gardenmakers. We incidentally have lunch but the chickens are the big draw. One striking hen (dark-coloured feathers, a sprinkling of russet) is much more fastidious than the rest which, when R. throws them the seed, run frantically from one end of the pen to the other. The duchess-like hen disdains all precipitation; condescends to pick up the odd grain but remains definitely aloof from the cluckings and careerings of her sisters. It seems almost beneath her even to eat – though she looks well fed enough.

I know that Debo used to insist that her hens had characters though one felt at the time she had to be slightly indulged in this. Seeing this particular hen's behaviour there is no doubt she was right – the past tense sad but appropriate in that these days she is past telling, which I would otherwise have loved to do.

10 October. A. Titchmarsh rings to say they've booked for the play at the National which, since it's not due to open for another three weeks or so, makes me slightly nervous. Seeing the posters up similarly. He says they've gone to Grantham. I say I didn't know they were planning to move. They weren't. What he'd actually said was they'd got a grandson. Such mishearings are nowadays a regular occurrence.

15 October. I thought I would list the various names people have for me. In the local post office where I go every morning for the papers I am 'Mr Alan', though Zam with his filmstar looks just calls me 'Alan' (and occasionally pats my arm). The English lady (from Kent) in Shepherd Foods who wears a burqa calls me 'Mr Bennett' and because it's the way she's been brought up (and I'm older than she is) won't say 'Alan' ('My mother would give me a clip').

In the coffee shop across the road where I get my daily decaf latte it's 'Sir', though one of the (several) discussion groups outside refers to me as 'that man', as in 'Hello, that man,' which has an undertone of the parade ground to it. In the greengrocer's I am 'Mr B.' and to the elegant old lady who used to own it and who has lived round here longer than I have, I am 'My dear'.

To Sam Frears lower down the road I am just 'Bennett' and when I occasionally see another neighbour, Dom Cooper, I am called out to as 'A.B.', which is what he and the other History Boys called me. At the stage door of the National I am 'young man', which reminds me that the doorman of the Goring Hotel once called Alec Guinness 'young man' thereby forfeiting his tip – though he might have expected to have it doubled. Our fair-haired bin man always bellows 'ALAN' above the noise of the rotor. 'Still on your bike?' I am grateful to be so generally greeted and put it down to having that kind of face, as my dad was the same. Still I doubt anyone ever said to him, 'Hello you old cunt,' as is occasionally said to me.

16 October. The fiftieth anniversary of the Cuban Missile Crisis which, at the time, I never expected to live to see. We were in America with *Beyond the Fringe*, the first hint of trouble coming when the show was playing Washington. Some of the younger members of the Kennedy administration took us along to the press conference at the White House when the existence of the launch sites was first revealed. I remember nothing of that, struck only by how glamorous Kennedy was, how swiftly he came to the podium and how he flirted with the women journalists. I had never seen such charm. By the time we got to New York with the show the crisis had hotted up, with all four of us just wishing we were back at home – not that that would have done us any good. We also stayed together most of the day, with Peter Cook, always avid for news, following each new development and often on the phone to London. On the crucial night, as it was thought, I stayed with Dudley Moore in his Midtown apartment. This he later embellished for chat-show consumption as my having hidden under his bed which, since it was seldom unoccupied and often the scene of tumultuous activity, would hardly have been a sensible precaution. By the opening night it was thought the crisis had passed, whereas in fact it was just coming to a head. A siren went off in the middle of the show and dead silence ensued, but it was only a fire engine and the relief meant the audience laughed even more. None of this, though, was as memorable as after the assassination the following year when on Thanksgiving I remember walking through a Manhattan that was empty and wholly silent.

20 October. Another speaking engagement, this time at Settle College which is just down the road, to raise funds for their newly opened library. As usual I follow my reading with a Q&A, the first question being, 'Mr Bennett. In the light of the Jimmy Savile revelations will you be changing the plot of *The History Boys*?' No, of course not, is the answer, though the supposed parallels had not occurred to me. I point out that Hector's fumblings with his pupils are inept, to say the least, and that the boys are all seventeen or eighteen and far more sexually sophisticated than Hector, who is in many ways an innocent. The notion that the plot of a play should be modified in the light of subsequent events is also an odd one.

25 October. Joe Melia, who has died, was an intellectual actor. Clown though he also was he bubbled over with ideas. Regardless of the circumstances in which one met him – (in my case) generally walking on Primrose Hill – he always had a book on the go and was the only person I know who could read as he walked, though Pepys used to do it, reading all the way from his office to Greenwich. And maybe today it's less unusual in that people can walk nowadays while glued to their iPads much as Pepys (and Joe Melia) did glued to their books.

28 October. My first play, *Forty Years On*, was set in a school, Albion House, which was also a country house on the South Downs and a (fairly obvious) metaphor for England. My latest play, *People*, is set in a run-down country house in South Yorkshire whose owner expressly disavows its metaphorical status. It is not England. I don't imagine, though, this will stop both critics and audiences from making the connection. Taken together the two plays are a kind of parenthesis: *Forty Years On* (1968) open brackets; *People* (2012) close brackets.

29 October. Write it and it happens. *People* is set in a mansion situated on the edge of what was a coalfield and is now a business park. Today the play is in technical rehearsal, when the author is the last person anyone wants to see, so I have come with R. and Christopher Simon Sykes to Garsington on the outskirts of Oxford where they are photographing the seventeenth-century country house, once lived in by Ottoline Morrell. The house will be known to many people for its opera festival run by the late Leonard Ingrams, but I first read about it when I was seventeen in Stephen Spender's (then quite daring) autobiography *World within World*. Garsington is everything an English country house is supposed to be, the panelled rooms hung with pictures and fabrics and overflowing with books, which spill out onto the landings and bedrooms in a warm and comfortable disarray that no interior decorator could ever achieve. Ilex trees frame the view from the front over the valley towards Wittenham Clumps, the house itself just one of a complex of buildings – barns, a dovecote, a farm – that have grown up over the years. In *People* Dorothy, the lady of the manor, expressly disclaims any pretensions to metaphor her house might have. 'England with all its faults. A country house with all its shortcomings – the one is not the other.' In this perfect house such a disclaimer would be much harder to make. A metaphor for an ex-England maybe.

But I tell Christopher S. S. the story of the play and he is unsurprised by the descent of the porn film crew. He was at a stately home the other day and walked into a room to find a film crew and a naked girl spread-eagled on the rug, a shot they were filming for a calendar.

30 October. A forties sky, broad and blue and streaked with thin cloud and waiting for a dog-fight.

10 November. Read to an audience in York at the request of Graham Mort, the poet who used to live in our village. The audience is made up of chiefly teachers, teachers of English particularly. The meeting is full and very responsive though I don't read as well as I usually do, nor do they always laugh as much – this perhaps to be put down to their all being of one mind. All doctors would be the same as all teachers, or all anybody: audiences shouldn't be homogenous before one even starts; it's the performance, even of a reading, that should weld them into a unit.

The best moment of the day comes when I get out of the cab and cross Regent's Park Road, when crossing with me is a sleek rufous fox. It pauses on the pavement to watch me crossing before loping unhurriedly into the shrubbery round the old people's flats. There it pauses again and looks at me looking at it before going off across the forecourt.

11 November. T. S. Eliot I only saw once, some time in 1964. It was on the old Central Station in Leeds, long since demolished, which was the terminus for the London trains. I was with Timothy Binyon, with whom I had been at college and who in 1964 was a lecturer in Russian at Leeds University and was also teaching me to drive. In the early 1960s there had been a long overdue attempt to reactivate the slot machines which all through the war years and after had stood empty and disconsolate on railway platforms, a sad reminder of what life had been like before the war. Now briefly there was chocolate in the machines again and cigarettes too; it had taken twenty years but austerity was seemingly at an end. One benefi-ciary of this development was a rudimentary printing machine to be found on most mainline stations. Painted pillarbox red it was a square console on legs with a dial on the top and a pointer. Using this pointer, for sixpence or a shilling one could spell out one's name and address which would then be printed onto a strip of alumini-um which could be attached to one's suitcase, kitbag or whatever. Astonished to find such a machine actually working after decades of disuse, Binyon and I were printing out our names watched by a friendly middle-aged woman who was equally fascinated.

It was at this point the train came in and after most of the pas-sengers had cleared there came a small procession headed by the friendly lady, whom I now recognised as Mrs Fletcher, a customer at my father's butcher's shop, followed by her daughter Valerie pushing a wheelchair with, under a pile of rugs, her husband T. S. Eliot; all accompanied by a flotilla of porters. It was only when this cavalcade had passed that the person we were waiting for made her appearance – namely the current editor of the *London Review of Books*, Mary-Kay Wilmers, who at that time worked for Faber and Faber and whose titular boss Eliot had been.

T. S. Eliot died early the following year. Timothy Binyon, having produced a definitive biography of Pushkin, died in 2004 and now Valerie Eliot has died. I only met her a couple of times, though was persuaded to attend her funeral if only because, through her family coming to our shop, I had known her longest – if in some respects least.

She used to claim that she remembered me as a boy doing my homework in a corner of the shop – an unlikely recollection, and a slightly distasteful one, reminiscent of Millais's (fairly odious) picture of Christ in the carpenter's shop. Had I ever chosen to do my homework in the shop it would have got short shrift from my father who would have seen it as 'showing off'.

What Valerie Eliot did do, though, was to send me the notes her husband had made on the inside of his programme after their visit to *Beyond the Fringe*:

An amazingly vigorous quartet of young men: their show well produced and fast moving, a mixture of brilliance, juvenility and bad taste. Brilliance illustrated by a speech by Macmillan (Cook), a sermon (Bennett) and an interview with an African politician (Miller, who otherwise reminded us of Auden). Juvenility by anti-nuclear-bomb scene, anti-capital-punishment scene and the absence of any satire at the expense of the Labour Party. Bad taste by armpits and Lady Astor speech (?). Still, it is pleasant to see this *type* of entertainment so successful.

14 November, Paris. At five to call on Peter Adam who wrote something for *World of Interiors* a couple of years ago, subsequently sending us a beautiful drawing by Keith Vaughan.

Adam could stand as representative of European culture, British and continental over the last forty years – having known everyone, particularly the generation of writers and directors at the BBC in the 1970s – Tristram Powell, Julian Jebb, Jonathan Miller, Melvyn Bragg and the writers too beginning with Hester Chapman and including Selina Hastings, the Gowries – no one he does not know, though not in a name-dropping sort of way but as memories of a world in which he moved. And still does, having last week been at the funeral of Hans Werner Henze, where a massive wreath from Angela Merkel fell to the ground during the service provoking general mirth and, as the coffin was borne out, one of the bearers' mobile phones went off and he dropped out to answer it leaving the coffin dangerously lopsided.

In his eighties now probably, dressed in a rich black velvet smoking jacket and embroidered slippers – a noble presence and a congenial one. We stay for an hour or so, walking back along the Rue de Sèvres and up Cherche-Midi, past the apartments on Coëtlogon where Keith and Lynn lived in the late 1980s and to which I still have a key.

15 November, Paris. Write it and it happens. *People* begins with two old people sitting in a grand though dilapidated room when a young man comes in (he is virtually naked, but that is incidental). He puts his finger to his lips, indicating that filming is going on. Dorothy, the younger of the two women, says 'Are we dangerous?' meaning will they be in shot, and the young man shushes her again.

This afternoon I'm packed, ready for Eurostar and waiting in one of the hotel drawing rooms while R. does some last-minute shopping. A porter comes in and puts a log on the fire, at which point a young woman looks in, puts her finger to her lips, motioning him to forget the fire as they are filming in the next room.

I cannot see what it is they are filming, but it is a lavish crew of some twenty or so with half a dozen other technicians hanging about outside. Someone is being interviewed, I can tell that, which in England would warrant a crew of three or four at the most. Whoever it is has a low purling voice which, increasingly deaf as I am, I can't quite hear. This goes on for an hour or so at which point R. returns and with him our taxi. Standing up to go I have my first view of who is being interviewed. It is Salman Rushdie.

23 November. The dress rehearsal of *The Habit of Art* and Frankie parading in her *haute couture* reminds me of the relatively rare occasions in Leeds when we ventured into the café of Marshall and Snelgrove. In addition to the social atmosphere being rather grander than what we were used to, there was an additional hazard in the shape of mannequins who paraded between the tables modelling numbers that were presumably on offer in the Ladies' Gowns Department. Mam was very anxious not to catch the eye of these haughty women lest (on the analogy of the auction room) one was thought to be a prospective purchaser.

3 December. The basic London Library fee is now £445.00. My borrowings are so few this works out at £20 per book – and this is an underestimate. I suppose I have to think of it as a contribution to charity.

2013

3 January, Yorkshire. The year kicks off with a small trespass when we drive over from Ramsgill via Ripon and Thirsk to Rievaulx. However the abbey is closed, seemingly until the middle of February, which infuriates us both, and though at seventy-eight and with an artificial hip it's not something I feel I should be doing, we scale the five-bar gate and break in. The place is of course empty and though it's quite muddy underfoot, an illicit delight. It's warm and windless, the stones of the abbey sodden and brown from the amount of moisture they've absorbed. Spectacular here are the toilet arrangements, the reredorter set above a narrow chasm with a stream still running along the bottom. Unique, though (or at least I haven't seen another), is the tannery complete with its various vats, a small factory in the heart of the abbey and which must have stunk as tanneries always did. I remember the tannery down Stanningley Road opposite Armley Park School in Leeds which my brother and I (en route for the Western cinema) always ran past holding our noses. The site at Rievaulx is just over the wall from the abbot's lodgings, which smelly though medieval abbeys were, must have been hard to take. Coming away we scale the gate again, happy to have outwitted authority, but since all that stands between Open and Closed is a five-bar gate it's maybe English Heritage's way of turning a blind eye.

11 January. The doorbell goes around noon. I'm expecting Antony Crolla, the photographer, so don't look through the window and open the door to find what I take to be a builder with a loose piece of flex in his hand and what could be a meter. He says he's working at a house nearby but needs to check our drain which may have a hairline crack. He makes to come in, but I say that if there is any work needs doing we have a builder of our own and in any case my partner deals with all that. He then claims to have spoken to my 'boyfriend' who says it's OK. I shut the door on him and telephone R., the so-called builder meanwhile banging on the door. R. of course has never spoken to anyone, so I go back to the door where, as soon as I open it, the caller gets his foot in the door (literally). Our friend Bridget, who's downstairs, now comes up and at the sight of a third party he takes fright, retreating to a white van waiting opposite with its engine running which drives off so quickly I fail to get the number. Thinking about it afterwards, where he went wrong was in not being ingratiating enough or trying to explain what the 'drain problem' was and graduating straight to the frenzied banging on the door; 'your boyfriend' didn't help either. Like all crooks he was affronted when his honesty was questioned, if only because it implied a criticism of his performance.

19 January. Snow yesterday which makes Yorkshire out of the question with a particular cause for regret Friday night's fish and chips at La Grillade. Still snowy today though no more has fallen but rather than moon about the house all day we make an effort to go out and take a cab down to the Courtauld which I've not visited, or since it was remodelled at least. Though it's crammed with masterpieces it's not a gallery I find I like – as being too bare and uncosy with none of the genial clutter of the Fitzwilliam with its leather banquettes and occasional furniture. And with so many famous pictures there's not much chance of discovering anything for oneself. As it is I almost shy away from the best-known stuff – Cézanne's *Card Players*, various Van Goghs – as at a party one would avoid going up to a celebrity guest. We spend more time looking at Manet's *Bar at the Folies-Bergère*, unable to make sense of the mirrors and the perspective while noticing the odd little pair of acrobat's legs dangling in the top left-hand corner.

Still in a gallery my most trustworthy instinct is whether I want to take a painting away. *The Card Players* no. A tiny Seurat of a (blurred) man, yes.

4 February. I don't imagine that my old Oxford supervisor, the medieval historian Bruce McFarlane, would be much exercised by the discovery of the body of Richard III, though there would be some mild satisfaction in finding the king exactly where the sources said he was. McFarlane wouldn't have thought the body particularly informative as compared with the real stuff of history, some of the ex-Duke of York's receiver's accounts, say, or records of Yorkist estate management.

The TV programme on Channel 4 was a lengthy and slightly spurious cliffhanger, culminating in the always conjectural reconstruction of what the famous corpse looked like. No different from the fanciful portrait, it turns out, but with enough humanity to satisfy the convictions of the Richard III Society, who were stumping up for the whole exercise. Bracketed in my mind with the 'Bacon is Shakespeare' lot, the Richard III fans seem not without a bob or two and with some of their barmier members on parade in the programme. I also blame the Richard III Society for tarting up Lead Church. [See 25 September 2012.] So had the last of the Yorkist kings been left under the car park I would not have grieved.

14 February. Valentine's Day – Tuesday's expedition to The Lacquer Chest having proved fruitless – I have nothing to give R. He manages a lovely card of a tile that I can pin on my wall and three good ties which we can share. It's also twenty-one years since we first got together, an association durable enough to silence even the most voluble backbench Tory. It happens too to be the night Keith McNally has asked us to the previews of Balthazar where we go, me with some trepidation, R with more of an ill grace, redeemed though by our taking Dinah W. who (unaccountably to me) has no date. And predictably we all have a lovely time. It looks terrific, a huge lofty-ceilinged room, lively, busy with the staff – more women than men – friendly and funny and attentive. K. takes us through into the bakery next door, a shop that is on the street, and as enticing and delectable as the one in New York. He keeps stopping and introducing us to people working there, giving us their stories – one oldish guy at the fish counter whom he had flown in from NY but who had been stopped at immigration and sent back before being provided with a lawyer's letter at JFK and flying straight back again. You can see – as one always has, right back to the Odeon in 1980 why he is a good (and funny) boss to work for and very much on the floor.

Also at a table (wholly occupying it) is the biggest man I've ever seen – not fat, just huge, six foot eight and mountainous, a rugger player for the Harlequins apparently. 'I know,' says our funny Italian waitress wistfully. 'All the ladies, they think the same thing.'

16 February. Go down to the London Library, empty as always on a Saturday afternoon, to collect E. M. Forster's *Journals and Diaries* (in three volumes), having resisted buying them at £285. I am thankful I did as on the evidence of Vol. 2, which I read for the rest of the day, he is no diarist and doesn't really attempt to be one. Vol. 2 is temptingly described as *The 'Locked' Diary 1909–67* but only the most zealous policeman could detect wrong-doing here – though I suppose catching the eye of young men counted as wrong-doing until – well 1967 which was when homosexuality came off the ration. Like Larkin he doesn't seem to have done too badly, various gentlemen 'obliging' him as the ladies did Larkin. Like Larkin, too, his well-being is often bound up with that of his mother. The novels don't much figure, or work of any description though I'm handicapped by only having read *Howards End*, never having managed *The Longest Journey* or *A Passage to India*. Saw him only once, I think when I was in the army and coming round a corner at King's I nearly knocked him down – in his latter days quite easy to do.

17 February. I am a founding member of the Council for the Defence of British Universities and today comes a letter asking for a brief account of my time at Oxford, quotes from which they could use in support of their cause.

I never think my experience of university was typical but I send this:

> What Oxford gave me was time. Like many of my generation I didn't go up until I was twenty and had done National Service. I was young for my age so, though I worked hard, my first two years were pretty much wasted. It was only in what I imagined was to be my final year that I tippled to the (still to me) rather shameful fact that there was a technique to passing examinations which had less to do with knowledge than presentation and indeed journalism. This carried me through my finals and enabled me to stay on and do research and indeed to teach . . . even if I was not much better at teaching than I was at learning.
>
> In that time, though, I was supervised by someone whose passion for his subject, his care for his pupils and his moral rigour I have never forgotten and whose example has stayed with me all my life.

I am not sure this is much use to the CDBU but I hope it helps.

27 February. 'On your bike this morning?'
I nod cheerfully.
'God help us all.'

5 March. So cold this week that I do what I haven't done since I was in the army in Bodmin in 1954, get up and put on my clothes on top of my pyjamas.

14 March. Walking up to the bridge at Primrose Hill where once the station was, an oldish woman stops me, looks furtively around and says, in an undertone, 'I don't like Leonardo either' – this, I presume to a reference in my *LRB* diaries a couple of years ago. What makes it comic is her concern not to be overheard, her few words suggesting she is maybe German.

28 March, Suffolk. Turns out a good day partly because we didn't have any plans. First comes a ritual visit to Yoxford where we go round the junk shop and I buy a book of letters between Beth Chatto and Christopher Lloyd. Then coffee in the eccentric post office where an ancient customer recognises me and shakes me so firmly by the hand it's like being caught in a mangle. 'Say something whimsical,' he commands.

29 March. Richard Griffiths dies. We've been away for a couple of days so are spared the unctuous telephone calls that always come from the tabloids on such occasions, 'We're sorry to be the bearer of bad tidings' or 'We hope we're not intruding on your grief.' Outside his family the person who would have known him best as an actor at the National and who would have been most acquainted with the logistic difficulties caused by his bulk was Ralph his dresser. No one will think to ask him, and I've never known him gossip about the actors he's dressed (myself included), but he would have an angle on Richard and how he coped with his life that is unshared by any of the obituary writers.

Richard had an unending repertoire of anecdotes and an enviable spontaneous wit besides. I was working with him at the time when Henry VIII's flagship the *Mary Rose* was being laboriously raised from the depths of the Solent. This was being done by means of a cradle when suddenly a cable snapped and the wreck slipped back into the water.

'Ah,' said Richard. 'A slight hiccup on the atypical journey from grave to cradle.'

6 April. Were there a suitable forum I would put in my own word for Dennis Stevenson, currently being pilloried with his colleagues for the collapse of HBOS. In the early 1990s when I was a trustee of the National Gallery Stevenson was a trustee of the Tate and must have seen me arriving at one or other of those institutions on my bike. I had no helmet in those days really because it made me look such a twerp. However one day a car arrived at the house and the chauffeur knocked at the door with a box so light I thought it could only be an orchid. It turned out to be a white crash helmet with a note from Dennis Stevenson saying how his son (with no helmet) had been knocked off his bike and suffered epilepsy as a result, though happily not permanently. Since then if he saw anyone he knew without a helmet he bought them one. So in this particular instance I won't be joining in the howls of indignation.

8 April. The morning spent paying bills: British Gas (and electricity), Thames Water, Yorkshire Water, Camden Council, Craven District Council and Mr Redhead the coal merchant in Ingleton. Many of the bills are overdue, about which I am unrepentant. The only one I pay promptly and with no feeling of resentment is Mr Redhead's.

It wasn't always so. Before the public utilities were privatised one paid bills more readily, not just because they were considerably cheaper, which of course they were, but because one had little sense of being exploited. Now as I pay my water bills for instance, I think of their overpaid executives and the shareholders to whom the profits go and I know, despite the assurances of all such companies, that they are charging what they know they can get away with. Competition has not meant better service nor has it brought down prices, with some corporate behaviour close to sharp practice. British Gas, for instance, regularly omits to send me a first bill but only a reminder, which has no details about consumption. When challenged they say this may be because bills have been sent online. But how can this be when we have no computer? If one telephones and manages eventually to get through one is dealt with by someone always charming and even-tempered (and often Scots) who promises to look into it. But when in due course the bill comes again it is still with no details and coupled with threats of court action. So whereas once upon a time I paid my bills as Auden said a gentleman should, as soon as they were submitted, these days I put them off, paying sometimes only at the third or fourth time of asking or when I am assured (rhetorically, I know) that the bailiffs are about to call. I am no crusader but I wish there was a consumers' organisation which could co-ordinate individual resistance to these companies, setting up non- or late payment on such a scale that it would put a dent in the dividends of the shareholders and the salaries of the executives concerned.

This was written a few hours before I learned of Lady Thatcher's death and it's an appropriate epitaph.

12 April. Each day brings new revelations about those due to attend The Funeral. One inevitable invitee, now of course unavailable, would have been Jimmy Savile.

17 April. Shots of the cabinet and the ex-cabinet at Lady Thatcher's funeral in St Paul's just emphasise how consistently cowardly most of them were, the only time they dared to stand up to her when eventually they kicked her out. What also galls is the notion that Tory MPs throw in almost as an afterthought, namely that her lack of a sense of humour was just a minor failing, of no more significance than being colourblind, say, or mildly short-sighted. In fact to have no sense of humour is to be a seriously flawed human being. It's not a minor shortcoming; it shuts you off from humanity. Mrs Thatcher was a mirthless bully and should have been buried, as once upon a time monarchs used to be, in the depths of the night.

22 April. Some signs from his latest contribution to the *LRB* that Karl Miller is coming round to Mrs Thatcher now that she's safely in the grave. He quotes in order to disagree with it a remark by Jonathan M. (his brother-in-law) about Mrs Thatcher being vulgar. J. whom we saw yesterday was understandably miffed, not remembering the remark or thinking it in the least bit witty. He would have preferred Karl to recall his description of Mrs Thatcher's voice as being 'like a perfumed fart' and though I don't relish the role of Jonathan's Boswell I do think that is worth remembering.

If in the future anyone remarks on how young I look I shan't, as I generally do, mumble about having kept my hair; I shall say 'I put it down to/blame (or thank) the involuntary celibacy of my youth', which is nearer the truth.

3 May. I am reading Neil MacGregor's *Shakespeare's Restless World*. It's very good, even overcoming my (A. L. Rowse-generated) prejudice against reading about Shakespeare. I hadn't realised at Richard Griffiths's funeral in Stratford that Shakespeare's father had been buried in the churchyard, the whereabouts of the grave now unknown. So when, waiting for the service to start, I went out for a pee under one of the yews in a sheltered corner of the cemetery I may well have been pissing on Shakespeare's dad's grave. More decorously, Richard's massive coffin was resting where presumably Shakespeare's coffin rested, a notion that would have pleased him though at the service it goes unremarked.

15 May. Starlings. Slightly *sweaty* birds. Two in the garden at the moment. They have the look of a threadbare maitre d' who hangs up his tailcoat shiny with age in his cheap lodgings every night. Cocky, too, of course, a thumbs-in-the-lapels sort of bird.

20 May. One of the many depressing features of George Osborne is that his rhetoric about the poor and supposedly shiftless can be traced in a direct line to exactly similar statements voiced in the seventeenth century and thereafter. Osborne may well be proud of being part of such a long tradition though I doubt, his St Paul's education notwithstanding, that he's aware of it.

2 June, Wiveton. This morning we are having our breakfast outside the hotel room in warm sunshine when we hear a cuckoo, and a cuckoo so persistent it becomes almost a bore, though it's the first one I've heard in two or three years. Finish Ronald Blythe's *The Time by the Sea*, an account of the time he spent at Aldeburgh as a young man. A good book, it's uncritical of the regime, adulatory of Britten and Imogen Holst, though more muted about Pears. The fact is Aldeburgh was a court, and whether the ruler is Henry VIII or Benjamin Britten all courts are the same, with the courtiers anxious to indulge and to anticipate the whims and wishes of the ruler. So good or faithful servants are summarily dismissed or, if the king is prime minister, wars are found pretexts for because that is known to be the great man's (or woman's) wish.

3 June, Norfolk. In Salle Church the war memorial commemorates the dead in two world wars with, as is usual, the dead of the First War far outnumbering the dead of the Second. And particularly so in this case as there is only one local man who was killed in 1939–45. Perhaps because of this or just as a measure of economy the memorial reads, 'In grateful remembrance of the men of Salle who died in the Great Wars', the final 's' plainly added much later. Nowhere else have I seen the Second War called a 'great' war.

7 June. En route for Leeds I've just finished my sandwiches (smoked salmon with dill sauce) when Tony Harrison comes down the train looking for a loo that works and preferably not one of the revolving-doored jobs that are wont to expose you to the next entrant. He's on his way to Leeds for the Beeston Festival and also to take another look at his father's now (thanks to *V*) famous grave which these days is quite showily signposted as it gets so many visitors. He's easy to talk to and though I miss my nap (and doing the crossword) it's a pleasure to see him and gossip – though Dinah W., who's his editor as well as mine, keeps me up to date. On his new knees for instance, which he recommends, and the care the Brotherton Library is giving to his manuscripts, including a specially assigned (and apparently quite notable) bibliophile with whom he is working to put them in order.

10 June. I read somewhere that the Romans used to crucify tigers to discourage others of their species from preying on humankind. On much the same principle, though less epically, gamekeepers nailed up the carcasses of crows and moles. Nobody, so far anyway, has suggested nailing up the culled carcasses of badgers, though it might be as effective as what DEFRA is doing already.

21 June. Read the proof copy of Nina Stibbe's diary of her time as nanny at Mary-Kay's. It's fresh and droll with Nina's personality coming through very clearly. Sam and Will are funny (and funny together) as is Mary-Kay. I on the other hand am solid, dependable and dull, my contributions always full of good sense; I am said to be good at mending bikes (not true) and at diagnosing malfunctioning electrical appliances (certainly not true). None of this I mind much, though it is painful to be even so lightheartedly misremembered. I am the voice of reason, something of which I've never hitherto been accused. I'm also a dismal Jimmy who periodically puts in an appearance as like as not (and this at least is fair) bearing a rice pudding. Much is made of the charms of turkey mince which I never recall being offered and which, had I been, I would certainly have refused. Such is art.

22 June, Yorkshire. Around seven I look out of the window and there are six pheasants on the wall, two cocks, four hens, reminding me of the time when Mam, in the middle of a bout of depression, called upstairs to say there were three huge birds on the wall. I called back that she was imagining things and came crossly down to find that she was right, only in those days the birds were peacocks from the Hall. Today the pheasants don't hang about, two of them skidding down the sloping roof of the hut like ski jumpers and launching themselves into space before stepping fastidiously round the garden expecting to be fed.

8 July. I'd be happy if Andy Murray had to play his final every Sunday as on a perfect day of continual sunshine the village has been quiet, the roads empty the only similar street-clearing event the obsequies of Princess Diana and when in the late afternoon we go over to Wigglesworth to have tea at Gardenmakers we find Andrew and Hilary having their own solitary tea in the garden. Not that I'm a fan of Murray and it's depressing to find his grim grimacing determination has paid off, a triumph of grit over grace – not that anyone in tennis has much grace these days (as if I knew [or cared]).

14 July. To Stainburn where the church is unexpectedly open as it hasn't been in all the years I've been going up to sit in the churchyard. Simpler inside than I'd remembered as in memory I'd endowed it with a three-decker pulpit, whereas it's just cut down and on one level. Good simple seventeenth-century pews, three or four with finials but mostly with simply roll-top mouldings and marks on the simple king post above the Norman chancel which suggest there was once a rood.

The guide book claims the porch is seventeenth-century which it may well be but the niche for a statue over the door must be older, as seems the moulding with blurred heads below it.

Sit on the seat for twenty minutes or so with just one swallow for company. Then to Leeds where R. is on time and we have delicious fish and chips.

16 July. A book review in the *LRB* by Jonathan Coe of *The Wit and Wisdom of Boris Johnson* edited by Harry Mount kicks off with some remarks about the so-called satire boom of the early 1960s. It recalls John Bird's *The Last Laugh*, the Cambridge Footlights revue of 1959 (which I saw) and while recognising that it was too radical to be very funny, claims 'it was undoubtedly a strong influence on Peter Cook (one of the original cast members)', implying, I think, that in *Beyond the Fringe*, staged the following year, Peter was pushed in the general direction of satirical comedy. I don't think this was quite the case, rather that John Bird's show confirmed Peter's reluctance to have anything to do with any subject, be it satire or not, which was not funny. Coe instances Peter's lines in 'Civil War', the sketch that opened the second half of *Beyond the Fringe*. When Moore 'voices disbelief that a four-minute warning would be enough' – in the case of a nuclear attack – 'Cook drawlingly retorts: "I'd remind those doubters that some people in this great country of ours can run a mile in four minutes."'

I feel both small-minded and obsessive in being able to recall this after more than fifty years, but the four-minute joke was not Peter's but mine. Peter's more characteristic contribution to the sketch and its uproarious ending was when, in accordance with official instructions on what to do in the event of a nuclear explosion, he got into a large brown paper bag.

Coe also says that in *Beyond the Fringe* 'the tensions and contradictions inherent in the movement were already visible.' This is certainly true, and I learned early on that one had to be quite defensive of one's own material lest it be usurped by colleagues. Peter, who was by far the most prolific of the four of us, was already in 1960 established as a successful sketch writer for revues in the West End. This meant that at that time he had no wish to offend an audience and shied away from sketches that did. It was only later in his career that, as his humour became more anarchic and audiences in their turn more fawning and in on the joke, he ceased to care. Showbiz dies hard and in these toothless stand-up days I think Peter might just have liked Jeremy Hardy but would have drawn the line at Stewart Lee.

19 July. Depressed by the latest government privatisation as the NHS-owned company supplying safe blood plasma is sold off to a US firm which is ultimately owned by Mitt Romney and so likely to be asset-stripped and disposed of. The clowns who have come up with this wheeze in the Department of Health, including the simpering Jeremy Hunt, have presumably no knowledge of the history of the NHS and the part played in it by the blood transfusion service. Richard Titmuss's *The Gift Relationship* (1970) demonstrated conclusively that voluntary and unpaid blood donation was in itself the greatest safeguard against the contamination of blood such as occurs in the US where blood is a commodity and so sold by anyone anxious to make a quick buck. While this sell-off by the Department of Health hasn't yet negated the voluntary principle it's the beginning. And what reassurances are there that the supply of plasma will continue to be as free as it is under the NHS? When will fees be introduced and, when they are, whom will the hapless Hunt blame? The NHS.

21 July. Now find myself enrolled in the campaign to save some of Smithfield Market from developers, the culprits the planning committee of the Corporation of London. Who are these people? Where do they live that they so blithely sanction the wrecking of yet another corner of London? Their names and addresses should be printed alongside the senseless decisions they make. Safe in Surrey, I imagine, or the Chilterns and nowhere near the architectural rubbish tips they sanction.

The decision about Smithfield will presumably end up on the desk of the planning minister, Eric Pickles, a native of Bradford. In the 1960s Bradford, having already castrated itself via a motorway welcomed into its very guts, embarked on a programme of whole-sale destructions which included the delightful covered market in Kirkgate. Bradford's neighbour and rival, Leeds, was slightly more canny and did not demolish its own City Market, which is now, forty years later, one of the showplaces of the city. One might hope that Mr Pickles will have learned from experience but like the rest of the coalition he is doubtless in the grip of ideology and ideology drives out thought. [Except that Mr Pickles ended up making the right decision.]

16 August. I give R. a lift down to what Tristram P. calls The Square, the private garden (with a passage under the Marylebone Road) where the Powells played as children, as did Joan Collins. I like doing this and it's not a chore (which R. never quite believes) as en route we pass personal trainers and their clients working round the running track, then the giraffes and then (a relatively new addition) occasional glimpses of the reindeer. Both animals, particularly the giraffes, have a touch of melancholy – though whether theirs or mine I'm not sure. What I imagine they miss is 'the joy of living', waking every morning to the same enclosure and never running free.

17 August. Remember being rebuked when I was young for being impertinent. At Exeter by Dacre Balsdon, the senior tutor, for instance. I don't remember being especially wounded by this and it's only waking in the night that I realise anybody who accuses anyone of being impertinent is themselves stamped as pompous. Like 'disappointing' it's a schoolmasterish word.

'Pertinent' not the opposite of 'impertinent', which would rather be 'irrelevant' or 'inappropriate'. These are the kind of verbal and grammatical musings I at one point thought of giving to HMQ in *The Uncommon Reader*. I suppose she's of all people in a position to dismiss someone as 'impertinent'.

18 August. Watching the run-through of the touring version of *People* at the National I reflect that there isn't much swearing in my plays. I imagine the characters in a play by Mark Ravenhill, say, get through more 'fucks' in the first five minutes than there are in my entire oeuvre. The first time I wrote 'fuck' in a script was in my second play, *Getting On*, and Kenneth More, who was the star (and swore all the time himself), refused to say it on the understandable grounds that it would reduce the takings at the matinées, and since he was on a percentage this mattered.

9 September. When I was an undergraduate at Oxford i.e. 1954–7 we had a category (we were quite fond of pigeon-holing people) called merry. Merries were the sort of undergraduates who rode sitting up on the back seats of open cars, blew trumpets in the street and welcomed any occasion to dress up. Early fans of *Brideshead* toted teddy bears and the merries were always at their worst in a punt. Reminded of this long-forgotten category by the *Last Night of the Proms*, an overwhelmingly merry occasion – and licensed by the BBC to be so. Once it was tolerated, now it's catered for; in much the same way, the high jinks that for some signalled the end of Final Schools at Oxford, which were spontaneous and occasionally quite destructive with lawns, rooms, ancient surfaces trashed. Nowadays these too are licensed – and there is a photo in this time's Exeter College bulletin of candidates for the Final Schools being officially trashed afterwards with jinks and imprimatur both quite depressing.

Merries were undergraduates who entered more readily into the role of being an undergraduate.

23 September. Last night we watch Simon Schama's *Story of the Jews* – a series that has been consistently good and last night's episode superb – linking the yearning and optimism of 'Over the Rainbow' and *The Wizard of Oz* (1940) with the murder of the Jewish population of a small Lithuanian village around the same time who were cooped up in a barn and starved, many of them to death, with the survivors made to dig their own graves before being shot. I think it is the village of his mother's family but, whether or not, the film of him talking about it, seemingly in the place itself, was unbearable and comparable in intensity with Bronowski picking up the handful of mud at Auschwitz.

Gordon and I must have seen *The Wizard of Oz* at the Odeon in the Headrow in Leeds soon after it came out, taken, I imagine, by Aunty Kathleen or Aunty Myra, Mam and Dad not ones for going to the pictures 'in town'. I was terrified by it – particularly of course by the witch – but the whole set-up made me uneasy. Nearly thirty years later when *Forty Years On* was playing in the West End, a group of us went one Sunday night to the Talk of the Town, then in Cambridge Circus, to hear Judy Garland. She was at least half an hour late, maybe even longer, and we had almost given up on her when far away – it must have been – fifty yards from the stage we heard her start on 'Over the Rainbow'. Sentimental and I'm sure contrived though the moment was, it was magical.

1 October. That so much of what I've written has been in the valedictory mode ought to make these latter days seem nothing new. I was saying farewell to the world virtually in my teens and my first play (when I was aged thirty-four) was a lament for an England that has gone. My last play (aged seventy-nine) was still waving the same handkerchief. Better I suppose than always hailing a new dawn.

I was saying goodbye to the body before I'd even had a taste of it.

19 October. Back from Yorkshire on a Saturday for a change. We're used to repairs on the line on a Sunday but today they're so widespread that nobody at Leeds seems clear about the best way to get to London, one desk suggesting via Sheffield, another via York, so that we eventually get on a Newark train and get off at Doncaster. Here we wait for an hour but it's warm, and a Saturday afternoon at an empty railway station has seemed to me one well spent ever since I was a boy of fourteen with a Runabout ticket. When it finally arrives the train is from Aberdeen and chugs off at a stately pace with no hint of which way it's heading. About an hour later I look up to a wonderfully unexpected view as the train slides below the great mass of Lincoln Cathedral, looking like some city in the middle of France. Then as slowly as any little local train it ambles through Lincolnshire past Sleaford and Spalding to Peterborough when at last it puts on speed and we're back in London by six thirty. Not a wearisome journey at all.

27 October. All weekend TV and newspapers have been promising a huge storm, a hurricane like that of 1987 when so many trees were uprooted right across southern England. Accordingly airports have been closed, trains cancelled, movables battened down, with many people making no attempt to come into work. And certainly there have been rough seas and one sees the occasional tree down. But if there was wind in the night all it did was rattle the windows with this morning sunny and calm so that one is left feeling both cheated and let down. I was looking forward to a bit of chaos as I'm sure were the media. But nothing as yet and the sun shines in a sky of Mediterranean blue.

Some footage on the news that tries to make out there has been widespread disruption over the south-west but since the only branches that seem to have fallen across railways are so puny I could pull them off myself it doesn't convince. Another incident concerns a leylandii that has blown down in a suburban garden, burst the French windows and destroyed . . . a model train set.

1 November. Never having worked in the Olivier, coming in for the dress rehearsal for tonight and tomorrow night's National Theatre Gala I immediately get lost and end up clambering about in the band room. The dressing rooms, when I reach them, are cells arranged round a central well, with the actors often shouting across to one another from their uncurtained cubicles. Coming in this afternoon Maggie Smith said: 'Oh God. It's like a women's prison.' She didn't mean just any women's prison but the penitentiary that used to stand on the corner of Greenwich and Sixth Avenues in New York. Relations of the inmates used to gather on the sidewalk to shout up to their incarcerated loved ones in a performance that was a tourist attraction in itself.

Opposite my dressing room across the well is Judi Dench, one storey down are Alex Jennings and Penelope Wilton, with the next dressing room dark, the window slightly ajar and a thin skein of smoke ascending: Michael Gambon. I envy them all, since appearing regularly on the stage as most of them do this occasion is almost routine. I haven't acted on stage for twenty years and am petrified. That the extract from *The History Boys* isn't until ten minutes before the end makes it no easier. Still the dress rehearsal goes well, after which Nick Hytner rehearses an elaborate curtain call that grows out of Frances de la Tour's final stage manager's speech ('Plays, plays, plays') from *The Habit of Art*. I'm genuinely proud that it's my words that end this remarkable show even though I wish I didn't have to perform in it.

8 November, Leeds. Walking along Wellington Street towards City Square I pass the offices of the probation service, now plastered with protest leaflets and posters from NAPO against the selling off of the service, protests that in my view are wholly justified. The notion that probation, which is intended to help and support those who have fallen foul of the law, should make a profit for shareholders seems beyond satire. As indeed is the proposal to take the East Coast Line out of what is virtually public ownership and reprivatise it for the likes of the expatriate Branson. I never used to bother about capitalism. It was just a word. Not now.

27 November. We were supposed to be in New York this week but that falls through so instead we're on a roundabout progress north that takes us this morning to Tong, a tiny village off the M54. It's a treasure house of fifteenth- and sixteenth-century tombs. Stanleys,

Vernons, Pembrugges . . . some immaculate and unscribbled over, others with a patina of centuries of graffiti. Tong actually holds the secret of the English Reformation, as buried here is Sir Henry Vernon, guardian and treasurer to Arthur, Prince of Wales, the eldest son of Henry VII, who was married to Katherine of Aragon. Vernon was in the best position to know if his young charge had actually slept with his Spanish bride, as the boy claimed and Katherine later denied. The boy, of course, died and his brother Henry VIII succeeded him, with Vernon himself dying in 1515, ten years or more before his knowledge would have been crucial, though, courtier that he was, he would probably have had the sense to keep it to himself, his secret now entombed in this left luggage office of the dead.

28 November. Our appointment to see Debo is at eleven thirty. We're early at Edensor so we go in the church and look at the huge seventeenth-century Cavendish monument – a very late (I should have thought) cadaver tomb, with the body also shown in its shroud and flanking the tomb an empty suit of antique armour and a mourning figure. The village lady cleaning the church remembers me coming for the flower festival, 'Not that I could get a ticket, "You know who"' having sold them all beforehand.

'You know who' is sitting with her feet up on a chair by the drawing-room fire, a blanket over her and staring into space. Helen, her PA, shows us in, chatting throughout, though Her Grace, as D. still manages to be, gives no sign of recognition or awareness of anyone being here. Yet, Helen insists, she will be noting our presence and maybe later on if she manages a few words will say something to indicate that, like a stroke victim, she is not unaware.

No feeling that this is the home of, the room of an invalid – no sick-room smell, no old lady smell or anything different from the only time I was here before. An Atkinson Grimshaw on the wall and others of Bolton Abbey in the corner. Helen and Rupert fill in the space with cheerful talk which in a way I hope D. isn't noticing or being irritated by, though it's hard not to include her in the conversation without condescending to her at the same time – which one would never have dared to do when she was eighty-five, say.

Go to the silver-foil-lined downstairs loo with its memorials of Elvis and then we come away having talked, or just been there, for forty-five minutes or so.

1 December. On a slow and stopping journey southwards we call at Barnack near Stamford to have another look at its Saxon tower. Few churches we've seen have been without a food bank, which depresses, but today's visit is enlivened by two leafleting members of UKIP, whose campaign wagon is parked outside. They come in, inspect the church and quickly leave, and it's only when they've gone we discover pinned to the church noticeboard a UKIP leaflet with another on the bookstall. Any party using church premises for its propaganda seems to me out of order, particularly since the gist of the leaflet is how unwelcome immigrants are, hardly appropriate in an institution that purports to welcome all comers, even Romanians. We leave and I put both leaflets in the receptacle for dead flowers.

5 December. Debo D. apparently likes listening to my audiotapes, particularly *The Uncommon Reader*. Helen thinks she would like the Doctor Dolittle stories so I call Lucy at Chatto & Linnit to see if they are still available. It turns out they were marketed by BBC Audiobooks which then metamorphosed into AudioGO which was then sold off by the BBC. The firm to which this (huge) audio library was sold has now gone into administration: what happens to the tapes no one as yet knows. So much for [the healthy discipline of] the market. Needless to say this doesn't feature in the chancellor's budget statement today.

27 December. Home in Yorkshire after Christmas and Rupert brings out the fully dressed Christmas tree, exactly as it was put away (without being undressed) a year ago. Besides the lights one of its few ornaments is the battered celluloid fairy with a slit in her head for a glitterboard tiara, long since disappeared, and the bits of lampshade fringe Mam glued on as wings. She is my coeval, this fairy, bought I imagine when Gordon was born in 1931, three years after Mam and Dad were married. Now I look it's her skirt that is lampshade fringe, her wings are actually silver paper, probably pre-dating foil and made out of old sweet wrappings – these two weeks her brief sojourn in the light, the rest of the year spent in hibernation.

31 December. After the latest bulletin on the unconscious Michael Schumacher and the nation's rejoicing that Penelope Keith has at last been welcomed into the ranks of the dames, the evening news gets round to saying that John Fortune has died. I knew he was ill but no one I know had been in touch with him – Eleanor B., John Bird, Andrew Nickolds – and postcards went unanswered. We turn the TV off and I sit trying to remember him as he was when we used to do sketches together for Ned Sherrin, how helpless with laughter we would become off screen and on because, even though the shows were televised live, part of the game – and TV was still a game then – was to try and make each other laugh. His rage I remember at people's stupidity and at pretension and, like Peter Cook, his intolerance of boredom. Appropriately in view of his name he went through great vicissitudes of fortune: in the sixties when he was married to Susannah Waldo, he lived in a Scottish baronial castle at Blairgowrie, a precipitous drop outside the drawing-room window to a rushing torrent far below. The next I heard he was living in a poky basement flat in the Camden Road with Deborah Norton and together they then had a little house in Harlow. Then he married Emma Burge and lived in London and, I think, the New Forest. Like Peter C. he would ring up if any absurdity caught his eye, showbiz pretension always a delight. A lovely man.

2014

6 January. Though I've learned never entirely to believe in a film until it actually happens, it does seem likely that this autumn we will be shooting *The Lady in the Van*. This is the story of Miss Mary Shepherd, the elderly eccentric who took up residence in my garden in 1974, living there in a van until her death fifteen years later. Maggie Smith played Miss Shepherd on the stage in 1999 and all being well will star in the film with Nicholas Hytner directing. To date I've written two drafts of the script and am halfway through a third.

The house where the story happened, 23 Gloucester Crescent in Camden Town, is currently lived in by the photographer Antony Crolla though many of my belongings are still there. This afternoon I go round to start the lengthy process of clearing out some of the books and papers so that it can be used for the filming.

I first saw the house in 1968. Jonathan Miller lives in the same street and Rachel, his wife, saw the 'For Sale' sign go up. It belonged to an American woman who kept parrots and there were perches in the downstairs room and also in its small garden. Slightly older than the other houses in the crescent, like many of them it had been a lodging house, so every room had its own gas meter and some had washbasins. I did most of the decorating myself, picking out the blurred and whitewashed frieze in the drawing room with a nail file, a job that these days would be done by steam cleaning, though then I was helped by some of the actors in *Forty Years On*, which was running in the West End. One of the actors was George Fenton, who is doing the music for the film, and another was Keith McNally, the proprietor of Balthazar.

8 January. Trying to pep myself up I walk over to the shops for some milk and coming out see the always welcome Don Warrington. I tell him how I'm trying to find reasons not to go to John Fortune's funeral tomorrow – a predicament with which the deceased would be the first to sympathise. John was Stuart Burge's son-in-law and his funeral is at the same church near Lymington in Hampshire. It's a two-hour train journey and last time I remember it was followed by a bit of a wake in the village pub, which doesn't commend it either. 'Well,' says Don, 'at least you're coming back.' Which makes me laugh.

'We're all in the queue, dear.'

15 January. The police officer who shot Mark Duggan is to be returned to firearms duty just as was the officer who shot Jean Charles de Menezes. The Met doesn't seem to understand what is wrong with this. It's just one word. Tact.

25 January. House prices are on the rise and car production too – these are said to be 'encouraging signs'. For whom?

4 February. The betting shop on the corner of Chamberlain Street has gone. Not a great loss to me, who never went in there and wouldn't have known how to place a bet if I had. But it's to be replaced by yet another estate agent – another indicator of 'the recovery' though, I suppose, an estate agent is just a betting shop under a different name.

20 February. The walls of the sitting room and the study in Gloucester Crescent are just as I decorated them nearly half a century ago. I have always been quite proud of my efforts, though aware over the years that the finish I achieved has often been thought eccentric.

In 1969, having stripped the walls down to the plaster I stained the sitting room blue, using a polyurethane stain. The plaster was the original lime plaster put on when the house was built in 1840.

Lime plaster has many advantages: it's grainy and doesn't soak up the stain like blotting paper as modern plaster tends to do (and which is often brown or pink). All the blemishes of the lime plaster showed through, including the notes to themselves made by the builders and their occasional graffiti. None of this I minded, but blue was not a good colour; it was too cold and for a while I thought I had ruined the room and would have to paper it, which was the last thing I wanted. Then, as an experiment I tried some yellow stain on a small patch and this turned the wall a vibrant green, too strong I'm sure for many people but for me ideal, so that's how I did the whole room. The study next door I did differently using water-based stains and as the walls here were lime plaster too I painted them in a mixture of umber and orange, yellow and green. This I then washed down and sealed so that the room ended up far better than I could have imagined, taking on the warm shades of the walls of an Italian palazzo (I thought anyway). I am sure a competent scene painter would have been able to achieve the same effects with much less trouble but I'm happy I did it myself. And in the intervening years the colour has not faded and will I trust continue to glow as long as any new owner suffers the original plaster to remain, which is not long probably as there are few houses on the street left in their original trim, today's newcomers seldom moving in until they have ripped the guts out of these decent Victorian villas to turn them into models of white and modish minimalism.

28 February. Watch the last of the programmes about the celebrity architects – Foster, Grimshaw, Hopkins, Rogers and Farrell – Hopkins the most human but none of them betraying any kind of self-doubt and bankers apart a more arrogant and self-satisfied group one couldn't wish to meet. Friends to power all of them but none, so far as the programme went, showing much interest in people's ordinary living conditions (though there is a glimpse of a school by Foster) with all of them sublimely confident that what they are doing is for the good of humanity. Some of their work is rank bad – Farrell's often cheap and tawdry, and while I like Grimshaw's Lords (and his Waterloo as seen from above) his Camden Town Sainsbury's is grim and never fails to lower the heart. I remember still when its plans went on show, including the demolition of the art deco ABC bakery on the site and the young Grimshaw's architect smirking when I tackled him on this, ridiculing my concerns and saying it had all been decided. As I'm sure it had. With his Knightsbridge towers Rogers has long since forfeited any claim to moral authority but one would never guess it from the elevated notion he and the others have of themselves, a tone which the programme wholly endorsed.

Architecture – the bulldozer's friend.

5 March. On my walk I pass the Primrose Hill Community Library, which is closed to borrowers today but open for children, who throng the junior library, some of them sitting with an adult presumably learning to read, others in groups being told stories and at every table children reading on their own. This library is one of those institutions that Mark Littlewood, the head of the right-wing think tank the Institute of Economic Affairs, said would make 'a useful retail outlet', a facility and a building for which there was no longer a social purpose. Most of the children reading here are black or Asian, with Somali children in the majority. As a so-called economist Littlewood presumably thinks the place would be better used as a Pizza Hut.

26 March. Wake this morning thinking affectionately of the spring in the grounds of Jervaulx Abbey which bubbles up below a stone sill installed by the monks before scampering away underground somewhere as it has done for I suppose a thousand years. I'm cheered by this as I am, even if only in recollection, by the spring at the top of the Raikes near Wilsill in Nidderdale which I first saw aged six in 1940.

27 March. On Tuesday Mary-Kay rings to ask me to be interviewed by the *Shanghai Review of Books* and mentions a good piece on Auden by Edward Mendelson in the *NYRB*. I buy a copy and it is a revelation detailing some of Auden's almost obsessively secretive charities – two orphans to be supported all his life, the support transferred to a further two once a pair had grown up; kicking up a fuss over the prompt payment of a cheque from a publisher, the reason only becoming clear when the cheque was endorsed after payment showing it had gone towards keeping open a shelter for the homeless that would otherwise have closed. It's the kind of goodness one might meet in a Victorian novel and not, I think, figuring in any of Auden's various biographies and memoirs. Scrupulously secretive I suppose he was lest the motives for his charities were sullied by any hint of self-advertisement.

11 April. Sue Townsend dies, whom I count as a friend both on the strength of what she has written and because we were together part of a group of writers on a courtesy visit to the USSR, as it then was, in 1988, a party which included Craig Raine, Paul Bailey and Timothy Mo. I don't remember laughing more on any trip before or since; we were a very silly group, so much so that we often mystified our hosts and sometimes behaved disgracefully. Sue – and I even noticed this in the photo the *Guardian* used for her obituary – had something of Elsie Tanner about her. She looked battered by life, and presumably by love, to the extent that the men in the various literary groups entertaining us on our Soviet peregrinations invariably took her for an easy lay. On one occasion we were treated to a picnic, with one of our hosts bringing with him his teenage son plus a bottle of wine, hoping that Sue would take the young man into the woods and initiate him into the arts of love. None of them had any doubt that this was a woman of the world whereas Sue was actually quite shy and couldn't see that she had given them any cause to think otherwise. She hadn't; she just looked like a Scarlet Woman.

15 April. Watch five minutes of *Have I Got News for You* with Nigel Farage the guest and Ian Hislop and Paul Merton their usual genial selves. I never quite understand why they are happy to sit on a panel with Farage, Boris Johnson, Jeremy Clarkson et al. Their reasoning would, I imagine, be that this gives them the opportunity to have fun at the expense of Farage and co. And so they do. But the impression an audience comes away with is that actually nothing much matters and that these seemingly jokey demagogues are human and harmless and that their opinions are not really as pernicious as their opponents pretend. And even if they are what does it matter as politics is just a con anyway. Whereas Johnson, the bike apart, doesn't seem to have a moral bone in his body and the batrachoidal Farage likewise. 'So where's your sense of humour? It's only a joke.'

23 April. Remember Dad's homemade herb beer, which regularly used to explode. We'd be crouched round the wireless at 12 Halliday Place listening to *ITMA* when there would be a dull thud from the scullery as yet another bottle went up.

24 April. Coming back from Profile where I've been signing books and the cab takes me up Gray's Inn Road where sitting outside a café I see Lindsay Anderson or someone vaguely like him. I imagine the conversation.

'What's it like, Lindsay? Death?'

A heavy sigh. 'Death – well, it's like England. You'll love it.'

I nearly wrote 'You'll *probably* love it' but Lindsay would have struck out that 'probably', his mission with me (in which he never succeeded) to make my utterance less conditional, less moderated – all my 'quites' and 'possiblys' struck through in his futile crusade to make me epic.

7 May. On the TV news footage of Stuart Hall arriving for the first day of his trial at Preston Crown Court; he is seemingly handcuffed

with his hands held in front of him, but thus shackled has to negotiate the quite steep steps from the police van. At eighty-four, he
manages this without much help, which is more than I would be
able to do even with free hands and four years younger. But why is
he handcuffed in the first place? He's no danger to anyone; he is not
going to cut and run; it's simply part of his humiliation. Nothing is
too bad for him is the message.

A seven o'clock platform with Nick at the NT, the Olivier nearly
full with a row or two empty upstairs at the back. We do it better
than the BBC programme with both of us more relaxed though what
particularly strikes me is how unself-serving Nick is, sometimes
almost painting himself out of the picture. No other director I know
would defer to this degree even out of consideration for my birthday. And it's actually Nick's birthday too (fifty-eight) but we don't
mention that. I'm clearer on the subject of the Cambridge spies than
on TV and how treason these days is too narrowly defined. I say that
in my view Tony Blair was guilty of treason in 2002 (smattering of
applause) and that the present administration's policy of selling off
all our national assets without any mandate is also treason (much
louder applause).

8 May. Cheered this morning when Daniel, the young man from
Detroit who lives opposite, wishes me a happy eightieth birthday
for Friday, saying he'd read the stuff in the papers about the BBC
interview I did with Nicholas Hytner, the 'shocking' revelation that
I don't read much contemporary English fiction and all the tired old
stuff about treason that I've been saying since 1988 and *A Question
of Attribution*. 'It's great', says Daniel (who's off to Cuba next week),
'that you can still piss people off however old you are.'

18 May. Once upon a time when one saw an old couple walking
along holding hands the thought was of Darby and Joan. Nowadays
one just wonders which of them it is who has Alzheimer's.

21 May. Chairs in places now are crucial:

The chair in the chemist's

The chair by the post office counter

And no chair in the dry cleaner's.

1 June, Cambridge. On parade (on King's Parade in fact) just after ten, where the calming presence of Richard Lloyd Morgan, the chaplain of King's, waits to shepherd me to the Senior Common Room. It's already crowded with dons, some, since it's the university sermon, presumably heads of houses. I manage to avoid the chat by settling into a corner to con my already much conned text, though I'm still not sure that what I've written is what's expected or whether it's too long or even if I can make myself heard. ('You'll be in trouble,' the chaplain said, 'if you have a voice like a moth.') It's a hot morning and various dignitaries now await us outside the Gibbs Building, where there's a good deal of hat-doffing before we process along to the west door of the chapel – a nice sight, I imagine, if one is lucky enough not to have a part to play. Various tourists take pictures.

There's not a soul in the ante-chapel as Richard L. M. had warned would be the case, though the chapel itself is full. Rupert is in the next stall and Rowan Williams slips in beyond him in his capacity as Master of Magdalene. Comforting presence though he is, this means I will be preaching (*sic*) a few feet along from the ex-Archbishop of Canterbury. Still, at least he's not the dreadful Geoffrey Fisher who when I was young was for years synonymous with the office. R. has insisted that I keep sitting down for most of the service, which I do, the proceedings quite slow and choral and upstanding, the only time I feel I have to get to my feet, out of deference to my Anglican upbringing, during the Creed. Now after lengthy prayers from the dean I begin, thankful at least that the sun is pouring through the windows, making it easier to read my text than it was at the rehearsal last night.

The subject of the sermon is the unfairness of private education, hardly a tactful topic, particularly in King's with its historical connection with Eton. Whether it goes well I'm not sure. Used as I am to audiences that make their feelings felt, I'm slightly unnerved at being heard in such reverent silence. True there is the occasional guffaw and sometimes the congregation *mews* where in more secular circumstances people might have laughed. But when after twenty minutes or so I finish it still seems strange to sit down without applause. In the past I've managed to wheedle a clap out of a congregation in Westminster Abbey and various lesser places of worship, though nowhere, I suppose, as august as this. Still, as we process through the west door to the stirring strains of Walton's *Orb and Sceptre*, I'm just thankful it's over.

11 June. For years now I've been periodically sent press cuttings by someone unknown to me, his name and the note that accompanies them almost illegible. I take it I'm not the only beneficiary of this bounty, which must be quite costly in time and postage and indeed papers. Not that the cuttings are those one particularly wants to see; they're seldom from the 'posh papers' though frequently from the *Mail* and the *Radio Times*. So it is this morning, the bundle including various letters from the correspondence columns, so called, of the *Mail*, occasioned by my remarks in the television interview I did with Nicholas Hytner exculpating the Cambridge spies. All the sometimes almost incoherent correspondents take this to include Philby, which was not my intention and whom I have in the past both in print and in interviews taken care to distinguish from Burgess, Blunt and their associates. Cold-hearted, devious and supposedly a good chap, Philby has never appealed to me any more than Graham Greene does, who was his friend and admirer. It's ironical that even after his departure for Moscow Philby was always more sympathetically treated by journalists because he was a journalist himself, supposedly a good sort and of course he wasn't homosexual. Unsurprisingly, none of this has registered with the *Mail* or its readers, one of them so incensed that he suggests that had I been older and at Cambridge not Oxford I might have been a spy myself. Not so, though it wasn't age or university or sexual inclination that would have ruled me out. It was class.

23 June, Yorkshire. Sky slowly clearing of clouds, bars of cloud like the sand left by the tide, these correspondences in nature something I've never fathomed, the garden glittering and too hot to sit in. Up early because John, Bruce Mills's assistant, is here mending the radiator. Bees burrow in the borage by my rocking chair as I sit in the shade at the top of the garden. Half a dozen swallows – or martins maybe – twist and turn above the houses, our bedroom window open with Grandma's jug full of R.'s flowers. Everywhere so *full* – and busy.

5–6 July, Yorkshire. Watch various stages of the Tour de France on TV more out of an interest in the topography than the cycling itself, which is hardly a spectator sport and tedious to a degree. The route is thronged with spectators who seem highly excited and anxious to be part of the spectacle, leaning out in front of the bikers, flourishing flags in their faces and generally making the riding more hazardous than it has any need to be, so that when a rider comes off, as happens disastrously at the first day's finish, it's hard not to wonder how often the spectators are to blame. The countryside, particularly in Swaledale, is bathed in sunshine and looks spectacular, especially from a helicopter, though since part of the object of the exercise is to fetch more tourists in, I have mixed feelings about its attractions. Most memorable is the scene on Blubberhouses Moor when the cyclists stream over into Wharfedale watched by onlookers capping the most inaccessible crags.

15 July. Asked by Yorkshire Tea if I would like 'a quick jaunt to King's Cross Station' to have my face modelled in cake and put on a plinth in the forecourt. It's not a distinction that is to be conferred on me alone, though Yorkshire Tea does not specify who my fellow *modèles en gâteaux* might be – the late Freddie Trueman I would guess, Michael Parkinson possibly and Alan Titchmarsh (who's so amiable he might even do it). A candidate for patisserie posterity would once have been that son of Yorkshire Jimmy Savile, who seemed made for marzipan. But not now. No cake for James.

29 July. Hot and because Dr Posner has decreed I must take more exercise, bike included, I cycle round to Camden Town where for the purposes of the film, I have to have my identity authenticated at NatWest before I can receive any payment. What with the heat and feeling dishevelled I am put in mind of the European banks one used to have to go into when young and on holiday – in Italy or a French provincial town, a superior bank in Padua once and Cassa di Risparmio in Olbia. And always it was cool and elegant and the native customers who came in every day were treated deferentially by the clerks – who were generally male and never quite good-looking and, with us, offhand and condescending – students who carried all their belongings with them – in our boots and shorts, sandy and burnt, just wanted their measly traveller's cheques changing – the cheques themselves always treated with the utmost suspicion. Whereas what went on in the bank elsewhere was so cool and unquestioning, the notes so crisp and ungrubby it was hardly to do with money at all. An oasis of civilisation where we did not belong; we were interlopers.

As it is the Tories are behaving in their last term just as they did under John Major when he privatised everything in sight, particularly the railways. Today it's handing out wholesale fracking licences trusting that whatever happens they won't be rescindable without prohibitive compensation.

7 August. To Oxford and the Holywell Music Room where Bodley's librarian emeritus David Vaisey and I have a conversation about our time at Oxford in the 1950s. David and I were first aware of each other at the scholarship examination in Exeter College hall in January 1954. The hall was bitterly cold but both of us managed to bag places near the open fire where, sitting next to him, I envied his handwriting which unlike mine was already adult and fully formed; he just remembers how much I wrote. I was halfway through my National Service on the Russian course, David was a couple of years younger and having won an exhibition went off to Kenya as a second lieutenant in the King's African Rifles. As undergraduates neither of us was entirely happy, both remembering how inadequately we were taught and how long it took us to learn how to teach ourselves. I briefly became a fairly hopeless tutor myself, eking out my research grant with pupils from Exeter and Magdalen, where I was appointed a lowly junior lecturer and thus a member of Magdalen Senior Common Room. It was a daunting community, with A. J. P. Taylor, Gilbert Ryle and C. S. Lewis regularly met with on High Table. I didn't have much small talk but what was the point as one seldom got a word in with Taylor and had I had anything to chat to Ryle about it would have been like chatting to a figure on Easter Island.

The food was delicious but meals could be a nightmare. I remember once we had mince pie but not, of course, the common individual variety but a great dish of a pie from which, having been handed a silver trowel by the scout, one had to cut oneself a tranche and manoeuvre it onto one's plate. Next came another scout bearing a silver Bunsen burner and a ladle which a third scout filled with brandy which one then had to heat over the burner until it produced a wavering blue flame whereupon one poured it over the pie. A fourth scout then appeared carrying a pitcher of cream with which one doused the conflagration. It was a lengthy process and one which deprived me of all appetite for the end product, particularly since as the lowliest member of Common Room I was served last while Taylor, Ryle, Lewis et al. having long since finished looked on in unconcealed impatience. If anything cured me of wanting to be a don it was this.

9 August, Oxfordshire. We turn off the Burford road to look again at William Wilcote's tomb at North Leigh, knowing, though, from our last visit that some well-meaning vicar has desecrated the little masterpiece of a chapel by kitting it out with serpentine blue-up-holstered chairs and a garish triptych on the altar – the clergy so often no better custodians of their churches than farmers are of their fields. My supervisor Bruce McFarlane came out from Oxford to look at the church with A. L. Rowse in June 1944 and described the visit in a letter to his pupil Karl Leyser, then awaiting posting to Normandy just before D-Day. McFarlane knew a good deal about William Wilcote, describing his chapel as 'one of the most beautiful tombs of the fifteenth century and made by the most expensive mas-ter mason of the day' (who also built the Oxford Divinity School). Feeling himself on familiar terms with Wilcote, McFarlane 'startled even Rowse by giving his alabaster cheek a great smacking kiss'. I don't quite do this but touch his marble lips, an endearment meant as much for Bruce (who died in 1966) as for Richard II's chamber knight.

2 September. Because Dr Posner has told me I must take more exer-cise and with walking nowadays not easy I have taken to going for a daily therapeutic bike ride through the park down the Broad Walk as far as the inner circle where I turn round and cycle back. It's slight-ly tricky as there are always throngs of people and lots of children and the rules of the road not always seemingly applicable one weaves from side to side around both cyclists and pedestrians. It's interest-ing, though, and less tedious than I find walking and I'm not put off by the hazard that deters R.: there are always ball games being played alongside the Walk, soccer, baseball and what I would call rounders, so there's always the risk that a stray ball may come one's way, which one is expected to kick (or throw) back. Regardless of being thought a wimp (or a wuss) R. strides determinedly past, leaving whomever to fetch their own ball.

My exertions don't leave me tired or out of breath as they are ideally supposed to, even though my bike has no gears and is quite heavy. I wear a helmet which is both a precaution and a disguise. The only trouble nowadays being that I keep thinking, 'I am eighty.' There is no forgetting that.

3 September. Michael Hughes and his companion from the Bodleian come to Gloucester Crescent to take away what I hope will be the final consignment of my stuff there – I say to them that if I find anything else I'll just burn it. (They laugh nervously.) Of course there's loads of stuff here too – all the notes – copies of what I've written for instance and dozens more files. It's not affectation but I am truly ashamed to have written so much – or to have written so much besides what I've published.

In the afternoon comes Natalie, a nice woman from the film to look at photographs of me over the years if only to be convinced that I've been wearing pretty much the same outfit for forty years. Nick H. says this is a characteristic of Gloucester Crescent where Jonathan Miller, Michael Frayn and Colin Haycraft and me all went on dressing as we did as undergraduates. I branched out a bit in what Antony Crolla calls 'your Robert Redford period' – when my hair was longer – but otherwise it's my prep-school master look.

8 September. The growing likelihood of independence for Scotland is also lowering, though I don't altogether see why. I suppose I've always felt the Scots have been more sensible than we are – over Thatcher, education, politics and the law – and that with precious little common sense on offer in England we can ill afford to let them go.

10 September, Yorkshire. Up at six to catch the eight o'clock train to Leeds for Elaine Daniel's funeral. Elaine was the manageress of Hertz in Leeds and so we've known her for twenty years and more

– such a lovely funny *daft* woman who with her husband John, an ex-policeman, made a place for themselves in our lives. It's at Raw-don Crematorium down a long windy drive set in trees above the valley and insofar as these places ever are, quite pleasant, and I'm unsurprised by the numbers there – all in black and very formal in a way they wouldn't be in London. John on the other hand isn't, deliberately one imagines, without a jacket and ushering in the coffin in his shirtsleeves and stopping en route to embrace and shake hands with friends. The chapel is packed, with people standing all the way round and the service robustly secular – God never getting a look-in. It's taken by the undertaker, a Mr Crabtree, who's not much of a speaker (and who didn't know Elaine) but John's brother makes up for it by reading out not the letters but phrases from the letters John has had, in which seemingly many of her friends remarked on Elaine's delight in shopping, so 'shopping' keeps punctuating the list (and getting a laugh). Still, queuing up to speak to John I find myself filling up and when I come to hug him (this ex-policeman kissing everybody) I find myself unable to speak. To R. who's behind, whom he kisses, he says, 'Take care of him.'

As an occasion it was so *Leeds* – so serious which seems an odd thing to say about a funeral and heartfelt is I suppose what I mean. And so provincial – Elaine born and brought up in Leeds, like most of the people there, with many of them, I imagine, police or their connections – which isn't always Leeds at its most admirable – but here decent and humane. Glad to leave it there and not go over to the do afterwards at Drighlington Golf Club (where Elaine would have been in her element).

But she was a grand woman, a real light.

We get a taxi which (this lovely day) takes us to Ilkley where we have delicious kedgeree at Betty's before getting the 3.15 train back. This is another journey, though, ruined by a fellow passenger – a loud, complaining businessman, director of a printing firm, some of whose employees had managed to print some brochure upside down.

'I am so disappointed in you, Damian.' And still on the phone being disappointed when the train draws into King's Cross.

14 September, Yorkshire. By the field next to the organic shop Growing with Grace yesterday morning we stop and talk to some sheep – or rather rams, a score or so of them grazing. I think they are Jacob sheep and very distinguished-looking, the breed that Elizabeth I resembles on her tomb in Westminster Abbey. They are friendlier – or bolder – than sheep normally are and half a dozen of them come over to the gate where R. talks to them and scratches their heads as they try and nip his jacket. Their wool is a brownish colour and seems almost braided. Their dicks are just two-inch-long pipes and almost invisible whereas their balls are huge and heavy, ready for the flocks that they will be tupping. They belong to Mr Nelson, one of the farmers in the village, who presumably rents them out and over near Austwick we pass another field of (less distinguished) rams.

Later that afternoon, having had tea at Gardenmakers, we black-berry on the road to Black Bank. My intrepid blackberrying (Dad would call it 'blegging') days are over and I can only pick those that are within reach, not daring to venture over the ditch where the choicer fruit still hangs – because it's actually quite late to be picking, though there has as yet been no frost after which the devil is said to have pissed on them and they turn bitter.

Back in 1958 when I had been elected president of Exeter JCR I went off on my bike to Binsey (?) where I picked bagsful of black-berries, which were already (it must have been October) past their best. I stewed some of them on the gas ring in my room and with the rest I knocked on the door of the Lodgings and presented them to the rector's wife, Mrs Wheare. She professed herself very grateful though I must have been marked down as mildly eccentric.

18 September. I come out onto the steps of Cecil Sharp House to find Tom Stoppard having a cigarette prior to going up to do auditions for his new play that Nick will be directing in the new year – the first time T. can remember doing auditions for eight years. He is as always very flattering and courteous, saying how he's seen the book *Six Poets* in Agent Jones's office and how good it looks. I say that much of that is down to Dinah and I think as we chat how immensely distinguished he is: there is no way, seeing him in the street, that he could not be a person of some consequence. It's the hair, the eyes, the romantic look that he has – no one I know quite like him.

24 *September*. Open the paper this morning to find that Debo has died, 'has eventually died' I nearly wrote, since she was virtually turned to stone a few years ago and was only alive because of the loving care of her long-standing PA and friend Helen Marchant who kept her, smitten as she was, still looking as grand and handsome as ever with nothing of the invalid about her and – her silence apart – no hint of dementia. Nor did her home, the Old Vicarage at Edensor, the Old Vic as she called it, have anything of the sick room about it, with nothing to suggest anything was wrong. Everybody called her Debo but I was privileged not to do so, feeling when I first got to know her that our acquaintance was too brief for such familiarity so ending up calling her 'Ms Debo' while I was 'Mr Alan' or, later on, 'Nibs'. The darling of the *Spectator* and a stalwart of the Country-side Alliance she was hardly up my street, but when she wrote asking if I would write a preface for one of her books I could not have been more flattered had she been Virginia Woolf herself and I was soon eating out of her hand. Once the request was made I knew there was no refusing, saying that the only woman I had come across with a will of comparable iron was Miss Shepherd. Thereafter Debo signed all her letters to me 'D. Shepherd'. I favoured postcards, looking out for any of grubby back streets and sending them as 'yet another unsunned corner of the Cavendish estates'.

She was tough, kind and above all fun. The last time I saw her when she was still herself was in September 2010 at a reception at the

Garrick for the launch of her book *Wait for Me!*. She was ninety then but still sturdy and she could not be restrained from climbing onto a chair to address the party. And not a plain wooden chair either but an upholstered job on which she balanced precariously while she talked to a room which by that stage in her life she could no longer see.

By all accounts the funeral was as brisk and sensible as her life, with no elegy and the hymns old favourites that made for a good sing. Not wanting to set sail on a sea of cellophane she banned all wrappings for the flowers.

Unattributed, I lifted a detail of her life for my play *People*. Years ago a neighbour in London, Josie Baird, who had worked at the British Museum copying their jewellery, was asked by Chatsworth to do the same for them. Debo told her to nose around the house to see if she could find anything worth reproducing. Josie opened a drawer and found some beads wrapped in old newspaper. 'Oh yes,' said Debo (airily I'm sure). 'It's the rosary of Henry VIII.'

26 September, north Norfolk. In the late afternoon R. finds Bacons-thorpe Castle in the Shell Guide, which we manage to locate in a farmyard – the remains of a sixteenth-century fortified house with an intact gatehouse and two vast quadrangles and so looking not unlike Mount Grace (though minus the monastic cells). The house is moated, the moat leading off a mere on which float a dozen serene swans and in the evening light an enchanted place. A couple of other visitors stroll by and a village boy zooms through on his mountain bike but it's a perfect spot, the more so for being unexpected – with the mere so inviting I want uncharacteristically to sit down on the bank and *fish*.

We drive round the coast road to Salthouse. High above the village and serving once as a lighthouse, the church was being refurbished the last time we were here. It's now spick and span with the painted screen at the back of the nave defaced (literally) by iconoclasts but by the looks of it the paint so thin this can have taken very little doing.

In the chancel is another painted board, differently defaced as it's covered in graffiti of ships and names presumably done by the choir-boys. But the most poignant relic is more recent and in the porch, a dirt-encrusted memorial, possibly an ex-gravestone to a soldier presumably from the Norfolk Regiment killed in the Korean War. It's a rare feature in any church and seemingly as forgotten or as little regarded as that war itself. It's more poignant for me because, had I not as a national serviceman managed to get on the Russian course, it's a war I might have had to fight in myself like my fellow conscripts at Pontefract in 1952, some of whom were killed.

27 *September*. Increasingly deaf. In the friendly antique shop in Southwold a man with a camera round his neck wants to shake my hand. I ask if he is a photographer. 'Only in an amateur way. Ramsgate mostly.'

Me: 'Oh, I've never been to Ramsgate.'

'Not Ramsgate,' R. bellows from the other end of the shop. 'Landscapes. Landscapes.'

And I remember David Lodge's novel about his deafness which is full of such mishearings.

6 *October*. The first morning of filming for *The Lady in the Van* and I sit in what was once my study, the room now bare and cold, the walls plain plaster, just as it was when I first saw the house in 1968 though I've no memory of being shown it by the estate agent, which is an early shot in the film. Alex Jennings is playing me and looks remarkably like, with no hint of the outrageous blond there sometimes was in *Cocktail Sticks* when he played me on the stage.

Now Sam Anderson, ex-History Boy and a star of *Doctor Who*, does the opening shot as a Jehovah's Witness:

'Does Jesus Christ dwell in this house?'

Alex Jennings/A.B.: 'No. Try the van.'

14 October. A footnote. Nearly thirty years ago, in 1986 I wrote a piece for the *LRB* about my uncle Clarence, my mother's brother Clarence Eastwood Peel who was killed in the First War in 1917 at Passchendaele. Never having known where he was buried, I went to seek out the cemetery at Zillebeke, south-east of Ypres.

I wrote about his grave and the graves around, his companions in death who, as it were, are in the adjacent beds in this final barrack room, many of them from Leeds, and mentioned some of their names including a Private Mark Ruckledge. Today comes a letter from Helen Ruckledge, whose husband is this dead soldier's great-grand-son, who had happened to read the article in *Writing Home*. Until then, like our family, the Ruckledges had never known where their dead forebear was buried but now had sought him out just as we did.

17 October. On one occasion Miss Shepherd claimed to have seen a boa constrictor in Parkway 'and it looked as if it was heading for the van'. At the time I dismissed serpent sightings as just another of Miss S.'s not infrequent visions . . . boa constrictors, Mr Khrushchev and (putting in regular appearances) the Virgin Mary; the dramatis personae of her visions always rich and varied. It turned out, though, that on this particular occasion Palmer's, the old-fashioned pet shop on Parkway, had been broken into so a boa constrictor on the loose and gliding up the street wasn't entirely out of the question, though whether the glint in its eye meant that it was heading for the van was more debatable.

This morning we film the sighting of the snake in one of the Gloucester Crescent gardens. And a proper snake it is, too, a real boa constrictor, all of nine foot long and answering to the name of Ayesha, who has made the journey from Chipping Norton together with her slightly smaller friend and companion Clementine, both in the care of their handler.

I have had unfortunate experiences with animal handlers as indeed has Maggie Smith, who once had to vault over a stampeding porker during the shooting of *A Private Function*. Today's handler, though, seems sensible and (unlike the pig handler) unopinionated and since Ayesha doesn't have anything taxing to do in the way of acting, confines himself to making her and Clementine comfortable on a bed of hot-water bottles.

25 October. At noon comes Paul Hoggart to record some impressions of his father, Richard, whose memorial meeting is at Goldsmiths next week. He talks about his and his brother's childhood in the shadow of *The Uses of Literacy* and how anyone meeting them would generally kick off by remembering what an impression the book had made on them, reminding me that on first meeting Simon Hoggart I had done just that. I first read *The Uses of Literacy* (1957) in New York in 1963, not out of any sociological interest but from homesickness. Marooned on Broadway with *Beyond the Fringe*, for me the book was a taste of Yorkshire and more particularly of Leeds. It wasn't the Leeds I knew. We lived in Armley, which had some slums but was otherwise boring and comparatively genteel. Hoggart's Leeds was Hunslet, poorer, slummier and an altogether more straitened environment, with Hoggart brought up by his grandmother and various aunties – in that respect not dissimilar to the upbringing of Karl Miller. Forget P. G. Wodehouse, for a working-class boy aunties can be no bad thing. Before I read *The Uses of Literacy* had I had any thoughts of writing, my own childhood – safe, dull and in a loving family – was enough to discourage me. My life, it seemed to me, was not conducive to literature, but it was reading Hoggart's close account of his growing up in Hunslet that changed my mind.

Many years later Hoggart wrote asking to interview me for a TV series he was doing. To my lasting regret I turned him down, thinking as I often do with interviews, that I would at last be found out. So I wrote back saying how much his work meant to me, but we never met, though he would often send me copies of his books. Paul Hoggart tells me that late in life his father felt that he was a failure and that he ought to have been a novelist. Sad though this is, I can see why, and how a book as romantic as *The Uses of Literacy* could lead on to literature, as reading it did with me. It has some wonderful Hardyesque moments, Hoggart at one point standing on the edge of Hunslet Moor (the moors of Leeds, it should be said, as much cinder patches as haunts of heather) and looking across seeing the great bulk of his school, Cockburn High School, lit up in the dusk and freighted with all those hopeful souls like himself, passengers on a liner waiting to sail away to a better future. I quoted to Paul Hoggart something I had come across the day before in one of D. J. Enright's commonplace books, *Injury Time*. 'Richard Hoggart has written of the "scholarship boys" of his and my generation: "Like homing pigeons, to a loft we knew only from hearsay, we headed for the humanities and, above all, for literature."' I am happy to have been one of those pigeons.

27 *October*. Late going round to the unit this morning to find them about to film the scene when manure was being delivered to No. 23 whereupon Miss S. came hurrying over to complain about the stench and to ask me to put a notice up to tell passers-by that the smell was from the manure not her.

Having done one take we are about to go again when it occurs to me that the manure, if fresh, would probably be steaming, as I seem to recall it doing at the time. While this is generally agreed, no one can think of a way of making the (rather straw-orientated) manure we are using steam convincingly. Dry ice won't do it and kettles of hot water prove too laborious. So in the end we go with it unsteaming, the net result of my intervention being that whereas previously everybody was happy with the shot now thanks to me it doesn't seem quite satisfactory.

13 *November*. One of the small pleasures of living in Gloucester Crescent/NW1 and one which went unmentioned in the (ever more

lavish) brochures put out by the (ever more present) estate agents was waking around six in the morning to the sound of distant horses. Still in those days billeted in St John's Wood the King's Troop regularly exercised in Regent's Park, which would occasionally bring them along Oval Road and down the Crescent. The ancient sound of horsemen carried in the early morning air so one would hear the troop long before they cantered into view, twenty or thirty horses, with each khaki-clad soldier leading another riderless mount. The mood of this troop was often quite festive and carefree, in spring a rider plucking down a gout of cherry blossom and putting it in his hat, and in winter there would be some sly snowballing. I always got up to watch them go by and on occasion Miss Shepherd would observe her own stand-to, a young soldier once giving her a mock salute. In summer I fancy they were in shirtsleeve order, but even when they were more formally dressed it was a relaxed performance, which in winter was made more romantic as the riders materialised out of the gloom, preceded by a lone horseman with a lantern, another outrider with a lamp bringing up the rear. Somewhere in London I imagine this spectacle still goes on but St John's Wood Barracks has gone and it's Camden Town's loss – and since the Guards can't trek over from Hyde Park, the film's loss too.

28 November. We travel regularly on the East Coast Line. It's hugely expensive, as what line isn't, but that apart it's a very good service – generally punctual, the staff, some of whom we've got to know, cheerful and obliging and sometimes engagingly silly, making train travel as pleasant as it can be these days. For the last five years the line has virtually been nationalised with its profits going to the public purse and there is no economic reason why this state of affairs should not continue. But just as in the last months of his government John Major made haste to privatise (disastrously) the railways so this contemptible administration has sold off the line yet again, this time to Stagecoach and Virgin. There is no way this can be presented as being in the public interest: it's putting yet more money in private pockets already well lined from previous deals. It's ideology masquerading as pragmatism. I have always thought Branson a bit of a pillock and presumably (if they're as gay-unfriendly as they ever were) Stagecoach isn't much better. The prudes and the pillock. I look forward to the logo.

6 December. The nastification of England – pass on a short ride this afternoon umpteen houses e.g. at Sawley and beyond Wigglesworth that have been 'improved' or converted – all badly – bad windows, crude pointing, poor stonework – all *nastified*.

16 December. I've never much wanted a dog, feeling life is quite complicated enough. Rupert craves one, and other people's dogs always like him as they seldom do me. Today I'm coming along Regent's Park Road past the delicatessen when a woman stops me, wondering if I would mind holding her dog while she goes in and gets some pasta. It's a dachshund and harmless-looking, so I stand there, holding the lead of this (to me) entirely unsuitable dog as people go by, and whether they're being friendly to me or to the dog or to the pair of us together, stop and chat as I suppose dog owners do. Except I have to explain it's not my dog at all and should we ever get a dog it certainly wouldn't be a dachshund. Though actually the dog is sweet and affectionate, licking my hand and nuzzling me much in the way Hockney's famous Stanley does (or did). In a short story the owner would never come back, leaving me and the dog to make a life together, but here she is, having got her pasta, and duly grateful. 'I knew I could rely on you because you're from the North.' R., of course, is delighted by this incident, seeing it as a possible chink in my armour. I think not.

2015

7 *January*. Catch the last half hour of the film of *The History Boys* on Channel 4, presumably put on as a pendant to Mark Lawson's hour-long interview with Frances de la Tour that follows. Coming on it unexpectedly I'm surprised by its delicacy and how little of it is overdone which, considering when we made the film the cast had been doing the play for two and a half years, is no small achievement. In the interview afterwards Frankie (in the course of praising the film) says maybe it isn't as good as the play. Well, I think it is, the only casualty (which wasn't in the play) Penelope Wilton's beautiful cameo as the art mistress. Frankie remembers asking me why my dialogue isn't quite the way people speak. 'It's known as style,' I'm supposed to have (rather pompously) replied, though I've no recollection of it . . . and I'm not sure it is anyway. What I do remember is Russell Tovey in the wings murmuring to Ms de la Tour, 'Frankie, if I weren't gay would you shag me?' She looked him up and down before saying dubiously, 'I might.'

Jane Bown who died just before Christmas was a superb photographer and a nice, unassuming woman. I think, though, I was one of her failures, her pictures of me unremarkable and unrevealing to the extent that I don't think I even kept them. They were taken on the step outside Gloucester Crescent, her approach, presumably well tried, being a pretence of incompetence. It wasn't quite 'I don't really understand cameras' but I remember her saying at one point, as she was shooting both in black and white and colour, 'I'm never sure how to do colour.' This may have irritated me slightly, as I felt her disingenuous approach insulting to my intelligence. So maybe a hint of impatience showed in my face.

10 January. After supper at the NPG restaurant we slip next door to the National Gallery, still after all these years a great luxury to be able to go in after hours. Walking through the galleries with the lights springing on as one passes through each door it's always a temptation to turn aside and look at old favourites but we press on to the basement of the Sainsbury Wing and the Late Rembrandt show. Oddly arranged in that there are half a dozen of the great self-portraits at the start, which one somehow feels should be the climax of the show, but better for me as by the time we do get round this quite substantial exhibition I'm exhausted. As always with Rembrandt feel almost arraigned by the self-portraits and put on the spot. 'And?' he seems to be saying, 'So?' The self-disgust is there and the sadness but in a very contemporary way he's a celebrity, resenting being looked at while at the same time (and like any other celebrity) having put himself in the way of it in the first place. Bridget goes round pretty much at my pace, Rupert as always slower and taking more in . . . noting the tears brimming in Lucrezia's eye, for instance and how she has had to half slip herself out of her heavily brocaded dress the more easily to stab herself. He marvels at the oath of the Batavii which (it not having much colour) doesn't touch me in the same way though I wish I had some of the smaller dry-points . . . Christ preaching for instance . . . if only to examine the details . . . a child playing on the floor beneath Christ's feet, some of his hearers transfixed, others just bored . . . though apart from marvelling at Rembrandt's technical skill my appreciation doesn't get much beyond the 'people were the same then as they are now' level. I can see how touching the Jewish bride is, while always thinking it looks awkwardly posed ('Look, I'm permitted to touch her breast') and the moist sadness of Bathsheba is wonderful, (though R. of course notices as I don't the absurd hat the serving woman is wearing). One of the saints, Bartholomew in the penultimate room has always looked to me like Arnold Bennett (the author, not my cousin the policeman) but somehow I miss one of my favourites, the Kenwood self-portrait against its two circles, which is there but I pass it by. I also miss because it is not there at all *The Return of the Prodigal Son* from the Hermitage, which I have always wanted to see and about which I once wrote the rough outline of a script.

Shattered before the end and sometimes lying full length on one of the (relatively few) benches to ease my aching legs. The only other visitors we see are a couple of middle-aged ladies and a senior figure with four young people (which exactly describes them) all wearing *Clockwork Orange*-type bowler hats and seeming, we all agree afterwards, insufficiently awed by the privilege being accorded them. Which we decidedly are not, twenty years after it was bestowed still the greatest honour that could have come my way.

15 January. I'm reading the last volume of Isaiah Berlin's letters, *Building*, which is less interesting and less amusing than the earlier volumes as so much of it is to do with what his life became . . . fundraising, administration and setting up Wolfson. Two good quotes, though, one from Wodehouse and one (which I think I knew) from Pascal.

'As P. G. Wodehouse said (a quotation much loved by our friend Maurice Bowra, who brought it into many public utterances): "The trouble about you, old boy, is that you haven't a soul and it's the soul that delivers the goods."'

And Pascal: 'All men's unhappiness comes from not knowing how to remain peacefully in a room.'

28 January. Thoughts about *Wolf Hall* (TV 28 January):

Hilary Mantel, Niall Ferguson, Alan Taylor: History is a playground. The facts are Lego. Make of them what you will.

It's a sentiment I would happily have put into the mouth of Irwin in *The History Boys*.

15 February. Good reviews of Richard Wilson's production of Sarah Kane's *Blasted* at Sheffield. In such a violent play, though, I find myself spiked by my literalness (as I remember being by Mark Ravenhill's

Shopping and Fucking). If a character is mutilated on stage, blinded, say, or anally raped, or has his or her feet eaten off by rats, the pain of this (I nearly wrote 'the discomfort') must transcend anything else that happens on the stage. A character who has lost a limb cannot do other than nurse the wound . . . no other discussion is possible. Not to acknowledge this makes the play, however brutal and seemingly realistic, a romantic confection. If there is pain there must be suffering. (But, it occurs to me, Gloucester in *Lear*?) Other topics concerning me at the moment are Beckett's sanitisation of old age which, knowing so little of Beckett, I may have hopelessly wrong. But Beckett's old age is dry, musty, desiccated. Do Beckett's characters even smell their fingers? Who pisses? How does the woman in *Happy Days* shit?

When we went to see the Late Rembrandt the other week, I noticed that in none of the rooms at the National Gallery was there the usual chair for the warder. This was of personal concern to me who needs to keep sitting down and, with no warders on duty, I'll generally sit on their chairs. An article by Polly Toynbee in this morning's *Guardian* explains why. Presumably as part of the sponsorship deal for the exhibition the wardering of the exhibition was outsourced so the first casualty was the warders' chairs . . . and the warders' comfort. (I've a feeling that the warders in the Met in New York don't get to sit down either.) This outsourcing is presumably a prelude to outsourcing the wardering altogether with it being done by Serco or some similar organisation. Toynbee says the warders are not surprisingly opposed to this development and that the trustees are too, as I hope when I was a trustee I would have been. I'm mildly surprised that outsourcing still persists as these days it's so generally discredited.

26 February. In the afternoon come Martha Kearney and Julia Ross to record the Best of British piece for *The World at One*. No fuss about it, though it's not what they're expecting. Martha brings a jar of her own honey saying that bees are the best thing in her life, except that she's been stung so often she now has an allergy. A propos the bee skeps built into the walls in our village she says that bees don't mind the cold; it's damp they don't like (though in our village they'll get both).

We record the piece round the kitchen table and it's all done within half an hour. *The Best of British*.

I thought, why not Swaledale or medieval churches or even, with all its shortcomings, the National Trust. But what I think we are best at in England . . . I do not say Britain . . . what I think we are best at, better than all the rest, is hypocrisy.

Take London. We extol its beauty and its dignity while at the same time we are happy to sell it off to the highest bidder . . . or the highest builder.

We glory in Shakespeare yet we close our public libraries.

A substantial minority of our children receive a better education than the rest because of the social situation of the parents. Then we wonder why things at the top do not change or society improve. But we know why. It's because we are hypocrites.

Our policemen are wonderful provided you're white and middle-class and don't take to the streets. And dying in custody is what happens in South America. It doesn't happen here.

And it gets into the language. We think irony very English and are rather proud of it but in literary terms it's how we have it both ways, a refined hypocrisy. And in language these days words which start off as good and meaningful . . . terms like environment and energy-saving . . . rapidly lose any credence because converted into political or PR slogans, ending up the clichéd stuff of an estate agent's brochure . . . a manual for hypocrisy.

A memorable phrase in *Hamlet*, one of the few that hasn't been picked up as a quotation or a title for something else, is when Claudius is arranging for Hamlet to be arrested and executed when he gets to our shores. And in his letter he says, 'Do it, England.' And we say we do it or we're going to do it. But we don't. Scotland does it. And Wales. But not England. In England what we do best is lip service.

And before you stampede for the Basildon Bond or rather skitter for the Twitter I would say that I don't exempt myself from these strictures. How should I? I am English. I am a hypocrite.

10 March. Nationwide celebrations are apparently going on in connection with Barry Cryer's upcoming eightieth birthday. This was in connection with the Aardman Slapstick Comedy Legend Award:

> I have probably known Barry, if only by sight, as long as anyone here since both of us used to do our homework in Leeds Reference Library when we were schoolboys. Everybody, I'm sure, will say what fun he is which of course I endorse but he's also a great comforter. If one has had a bad notice or is being pilloried in the papers Barry is the first person to ring up with the most comfortable words in the language, namely 'Fuck 'em.'
>
> There'll be a joke to follow, generally parrot-based but it's the 'Fuck 'em' that counts.
>
> He's also full of surprises. I'm not authorised to bring greetings from beyond the grave but were he still with us someone who would surely stand up to be counted among Barry's friends and admirers would be that most austere and reticent of actors, Paul Scofield. It's an unlikely pairing but they were together in the fifties in the musical *Expresso Bongo*.

12 March. This last week I finish reading *Common Ground* by Rob Cowen and *The Places In Between* by Rory Stewart, both books about wildernesses, Stewart's in Afghanistan, Cowen's in almost comical contrast in and around Harrogate.

As he tells the story Stewart seems in regular peril of his life, Cowen less so as he just makes expeditions from his suburban home into the scrub and undergrowth that surrounds Bilton near Knaresborough. In a spell of unemployment and while his wife is pregnant Cowen goes native, lying out in the marginal areas around the town taking in the vegetation and the wildlife, some of it surprisingly copious . . . a large number of hares, for instance, owls, which he tracks,

Filming *The Lady in the Van*, October 2014

On the terrace, 16th Street, New York

Armley Public Library / By the beck, Yorkshire

En route to Leeds, 2016
With Dinah Wood and Eddie

Frances de la Tour and Linda Bassett whooping it up
in *People*, 2012

With Dominic Cooper and James Corden, *The History Boys*,
National Theatre Gala, 2013

Maggie Smith and Alex Jennings filming
The Lady in the Van, 2014

One of my dad's penguins, diary entry 6 December 2007

Plumber by Wilfrid Wood, diary entry 6 August 2015

My shoe depicted by Rupert as a birthday card, May 2010

Lynn's apartment, 16th Street, New York,
diary entry 31 October 2015

and roe deer which almost track him. It chronicles the inroads made by well-meaning planners and interest groups as they tidy up what they see as mess, laying a cycle path along an old railway line and with the threat of a new housing estate always looming. It ends on a positive note with the awkward birth of Cowen's baby vividly and movingly described, its eventual survival almost bringing tears to the eyes. Cowen writes very well and with none of the stylistic elaboration of some of the other nature writers.

It's hard to say why Stewart's book is so enthralling. It's partly the physical deprivation he puts himself through, cold most of the time and often soaking wet, regularly soiling his clothes with no mention of when he manages to wash them. Trudging across Afghanistan from Herat to Kabul it's rare he gets a square meal, his only regular companion a run-down mastiff that he adopts which, far from making life easier, requires more attention than a small child. Struck by his toughness and determination one wonders how he can stand his present-day Tory colleagues in the House of Commons. Both are cracking books so that having finished them I now feel deprived.

26 March. To Oxford where Nick Hytner and I are to speak at the Oxford Literary Festival. Rupert and I stay at the Old Parsonage where I have been staying now for thirty years, though it has recently been done up. It's showers now not baths and one can no longer make a cup of tea in the room. When I ask why, I'm told these are 'improvements'. Our talk is in the Sheldonian before which we have tea with Bodley's librarian, Richard Ovenden, who asks Nick (as I never have) what his plans are when he leaves the National tomorrow. This is the first I hear of the theatre he plans for Southwark. The audience in the Sheldonian is pretty star-studded, with Jessye Norman on the front row statuesque in a magnificent gown and scarlet turban. We get off to a good start by saying that we are undoubtedly destined for theatrical immortality if only because we were both stepping stones in the rise and rise of James Corden.

1 April. Almost out of piety and a respect for tradition I filch a couple of branches from the base of a balsam poplar on the north side of Regent's Park. The buds are hardly open and thus are briefly heavily scented. Now in a glass on the sitting-room mantelpiece they bring a flavour to the room as they have done every spring for the last forty years.

4 April, Easter Saturday, Yorkshire. With a bad ankle I edge my way carefully down the stairs and delicately round the garden. I still have the absurd notion that, as with any other ailment, age and infirmity will run its course and I will recover from it. That there is no recovery . . . or only one . . . doesn't always occur. Still the reopening of the village shop as a community enterprise means that I (and my stick) can once again trudge down there for the paper (as I do in London with much less effort on my bike).

12 April. Looking for a book to read while I'm in Paris I pick up *The Shepherd's Life* by James Rebanks, an account of the life and upbringing of a Lakeland shepherd. Sheep have never been of much interest to me, the only one to make an impression an affectionate and rather dog-like ram we encountered years ago at Thornton Priory in north Lincolnshire which must once have been a pet. Like Rory Stewart's book it's the hardship and deprivation of Rebanks's life that straight away enthrals. His initial absence of schooling (and an unattractive dislike of teachers) is coupled with a lack of interest in anything except the life of the farm and the love of working there. In the course of the book however (and almost without explanation) Rebanks starts to read and educate himself and (again without explanation) gets to Oxford and in due course (and not I think in the book) is awarded a First while remaining an almost emblematic hill farmer and, incidentally, a UNESCO representative. But hardship and husbandry lace themselves through his life even though I imagine he must now be a much sought-after author.

The whole thesis of the book celebrates or at least recognises the day-to-day labours of farmers such as Rebanks and their determination to maintain a way of life, though I imagine in his case that will these days be harder to do. I've only read one review of the book that's at all dubious though this shepherd's life can't be quite as straightforward as it seems.

The sheep round us have always seemed to me an unprepossessing lot, lank, shabby and not to be spruced up even for a show. What breed they are I've no idea though they're still brought down through the village to be sheared when the rams, haughty and disdainful, achieve a brief, even a Roman dignity. We have a narrow strip of front garden and at the first sound of the approaching flock my father used to rush out flapping his apron and shouting his head off to protect his precious plants.

13 April. Rereading *Portnoy's Complaint*, I'm not surprised at Dad's reaction when he found it in my bookcase at Wood Lane fifty years ago. In some misguided missionary zeal that makes me cringe even to remember I may actually have recommended it. Because if it shocked him then it shocks me now, though I don't imagine he read more than a few pages before putting it back and never mentioning it again. He'd probably have been hoping it was going to be more along the lines of Nancy Mitford who, slightly to my surprise, he found very funny. Fifty years later *Portnoy* still makes me laugh and to anyone shy or (an unlikely thought) thinking themselves wicked for wanking, the book is an emancipation, though without being in the least bit erotic. The style is still a delight.

30 April. A red kite low over suburban Bramhope, its forked tail plain against the sky. Two beats of its wings and it's away, the whole of Wharfedale spread out below. My unshared and unshareable despair at the likely outcome of the election.

5 May. In the evening to the Royal Free to see Owen, Rupert's brother, and Lucy and Freddy their new baby, born five weeks prematurely while we were in Paris and so now just ten days old. My inclination is simply to gaze, feeling like one of the Magi before this tiny, tiny thing who sleeps throughout while occasionally clenching his delicate fists and stretching. Awe is I suppose what I feel, and a huge clumsiness, though Rupert who at twelve had to nurse Owen when he was born is happy to hold Freddy throughout. There's a vast view of Parliament Hill from the window but one scarcely glances at it, this little scrap of humanity filling the room. The joy of Owen and Lucy at this safe deliverance is something to see. I don't think I've ever known a baby as newly born . . . and as safely born as this. It doesn't make me feel old, just huge. Rupert in raptures.

8 May. A feeling of bereavement in the streets. I shop for supper and unprompted a grey-haired woman in the fish shop bursts out, 'It means I shall have a Tory government for the rest of my life.'

In the library they say, 'Good morning . . . though we've just been trying to think what's good about it.'

I wanted a Labour government so that I could stop thinking about politics, knowing that the nation's affairs were in the hands of a party which, even if often foolish, was at least well-intentioned. Now we have another decade of the self-interested and the self-seeking, ready to sell off what's left of our liberal institutions and loot the rest to their own advantage. It's not a government of the nation but a government of half the nation, a true legacy of Mrs Thatcher. Work is the only escape, which fortunately moves along a little.

9 May. My birthday. A nice woman in a leopardskin coat who always speaks wishes me a happy birthday. I say that I wish it was.

'Why? What's happened?'

'Last Thursday. The election.'

'Oh, you don't want to worry about that. They're all the same.'

At which point (we are in Shepherd's grocers) I hear myself as very rarely shouting at the top of my voice. 'No, they are not all the same. This lot are self-seeking liars, the cabinet included, and we're landed with them for another five years.' She tries to calm me down but I tell her not to bother, with other customers peeping round the shelves to see who is making all this din.

She is waiting outside the shop with a cake she has bought me for my birthday and I kind of apologise. But as I walk back home I wonder how long it will be before this crew turn their attention to the BBC.

13 May. Talk to the (always cheering) Archie Powell. His four-year-old son Wilfred is learning chess and was recently taken to a Church of England confirmation service where the bishop officiating was Richard Charteris. Having ascertained that Charteris was a bishop Wilfred whispered, 'Does that mean he can only move diagonally?' Archie is 'easy' about religion but wife Jane, like Rupert, is fiercely atheist.

20 May, Yorkshire. Around seven R. shouts upstairs, 'Look out on the lawn. Now.' I look out of the bedroom window and there is something on the grass but I don't at first even recognise it as a bird. Then it becomes plain it's a hawk which has brought down an unspecifiable bird which is still feebly fluttering as the hawk rips into it. What is strange is that the hawk, possibly in order to give it purchase for its pecking, is spreading its wings over its prey and as it were cloaking it from view though never letting up from tearing strips off the now dead bird. Eventually R. opens the back door and the hawk – a white flash on its breast – flies off with (R. thinks) a blackbird in pursuit. All that it leaves on the grass is a smear and some feathers, everything else . . . beak, claws, legs . . . has been eaten. It's something neither of us has ever seen before, leaving us untalkative and slightly shocked.

23 May, Yorkshire. A glorious morning and for the first time in ten days, warm so that I can do my favourite thing, namely sit out in the rocking chair with my old straw hat on reading the paper and having my breakfast. This is after a now routine visit to the reopened village shop, a wholly delightful experience as it's busy, everybody working there a volunteer and far more of a social centre than it's been in twenty years. The pleasure begins at the (double) door itself, which was found abandoned in the attic and now reinstated and which as one pushes through feels like coming into a saloon in a western.

25 May. A woman in front of me in the greengrocer's:
    'I'll be ninety tomorrow. It's disgusting.'

27 May. Go through my papers looking for anything I may have overlooked about Miss Shepherd prior to the filming of *The Lady in the Van*. I find some notes on Miss S.'s costume in the 1980s plus a few of her odder remarks.

As I occasionally did I must have complained about the smell:
    Miss S.: Well there are mice, I know that and they make for a cheesy smell, possibly.

Miss S. today May 10 '76
    (the smell)
    It fair knocks you down
    Fawn Charlie Brown pitcher's hat
    or a golfing hat
    maroon
    turquoise

The mouse –
    She's made some little holes and one day a worm came in. Out of the rain, I think. Then it went out again.

This cough has thrown me back – I wouldn't give it to a dog.
    Steps are the problem.

ora soef's
hat.

(marmelk)
it faint knocks you
down

FAWN CHARLIE BROWN
PITCHERS HAT.

MRS'
TI-DAY
MAY 10 '76.

MAROON

TURQUOISE

[Sore awkward on
Mrs 5. finale 1980s]

The nature —
the's mare some little
holes
and one day a worm came in.
(out of the rain, I think)
then he walked you.

The devil gets people to say things and they don't know they say them.

There's not one in a thousand would do what you've done. (Not said by Miss Shepherd!)

Rabies is in the news:

Miss S. gets a severe pain in the back.

'I wonder if it could be rabies.'

I have builders in and knowing they must think I'm crazy to accommodate her feel I must complain about the stench of urine.

Miss S.: Well what can you expect when they rain bricks down on me all day.

*

To Hay-on-Wye with Nick Hytner and Dinah Wood, a much longer ride in time terms than the one to Leeds that I'm used to though it's much nearer. The set-up, a busy tented enclosure is like a county show with literature standing in for husbandry and authors being led about like pedigree cattle. Nick and I are interviewed by Francine Stock with a couple of clips from the film of *The Lady in the Van* which go down well. This is followed by Q&A with these days the questions having to be repeated for my benefit as, hearing aid or no hearing aid I still can't hear. I finish off with a paragraph I've written out in advance:

The story told by this film took place forty and more years ago and Miss Shepherd is long since dead. She was difficult and eccentric but above all she was poor and, these days particularly the poor don't get much of a look-in, poverty as much a moral failing today as it was under the Tudors. If the film has a point it's about fairness and tolerance and, however grudgingly, helping the less fortunate who are not well thought of these days and now likely to be even less so.

Tory heartland though this is, it produces continued applause and then I am given a medal, in accepting which I manage to weave in one of my favourite anecdotes told, I think, originally by Nigel Nicolson. He was at a launch of his big coffee-table book, *Great Houses of Britain* when he saw across the room a woman he thought he recognised and advanced towards her.

'Dear lady, may I congratulate you on having what is surely the most beautiful house in Britain.'

'Really? 47A Lansdowne Road?'

It's the 'A' that always makes me laugh.

28 May. Finish Adam Nicolson's book on Homer, *The Mighty Dead*, which is occasionally over-rich but very enjoyable. It ends as the *Odyssey* ends with Odysseus's return to Ithaca and the slaughter of Penelope's suitors and the hanging of her maids, scenes of such horror they alienate whatever sympathy one might have for the returning wanderer. Which is not much in my case as he seems a colossal bore . . . and likely to be more so as time goes on. If he and Penelope had an old age has anyone written about it? It would be like growing old alongside Field Marshal Montgomery.

Otherwise life at the moment is what my mother would have called 'a bit of a fullock', fullock meaning a hurry or a rush with fullocky its adjective. One thing piled on another.

29 May. Shortly after the East Coast franchise has been sold off to a tie-up between Virgin and Stagecoach I am sitting on Leeds Station waiting for Rupert when a notice is flashed up on the Sky screen:

'Hello Leeds. Meet Virgin Trains. We've just arrived and we can't wait to get to know you.'

And take you for every penny we can.

The last sentence mine.

27 June. What is particular to this time is that now we all have computers so we all have something to hide. Whereas once upon a time innocent boys kept their girlie mags under the mattress or on top of the wardrobe, now they – and their fathers and their sisters and their cousins and their aunts – have their stash or its location on their computers. So if disgrace should come the computer will compound it as it will be the first to be taken into custody. Whether the material has been downloaded or not the computer will reveal what pornography has been looked at and what sort and how often. We are all self-shamed.

4 July, Yorkshire. It's six in the evening and I'm sitting at the end of the garden in the warm sunshine and answering some of the letters I brought up with me yesterday, including one from Richard Hope, now in his last two weeks as Hector in a tour of *The History Boys*. He tells me that Sid Sagar, who plays Akhtar, has just got a First at Bristol, the last two terms of which must have overlapped with his being in the play. I write him a card of congratulations, hoping – though not saying – that the period after his graduation won't be as difficult as it often is . . . and as it certainly was with me.

7 July. Run into Philip and Kersti French in M&S with Philip bent tight over his trolley and using it as a walker. I ask him how he is.

'Dreadful.'

'Anything specific?'

'Knees. Legs. Lungs. Kidneys . . . shall I go on?' The recital so fluent it's partly a joke but looking at him it's hard not to believe every word. I come out not, I'm sure, having cheered them up, thankful that I can still at least mount my bike and cycle away. Sixty years since I first met him when he was a self-assured ex-paratrooper of an undergraduate at my college, his stutter used to emphasise his machine-gun wit . . . and already knowing everything there was to be known about films and quite definitely a man of the world.

18 July, Yorkshire. Not having a mortgage or being otherwise in hock to the bank I am not particularly perturbed when the governor of the Bank of England predicts a likely rise in the interest rate. What does bother me is that for no obvious reason that I've seen mentioned Mr Carney should have made his announcement in Lincoln Cathedral. Why there? And why in a cathedral at all? Are cathedrals for hire nowadays whatever the occasion? How long before one of Mr Osborne's rallying calls to the nation is embedded in Sung Eucharist?

The heron has been fishing in the beck every morning this weekend. I've never actually seen it catch anything or even to seemingly take much interest in what's going on in the water and it's so still that though quite a few walkers go across the packhorse bridge very few of them pick it out. An untidy Dickensian-looking bird, like a half-folded grey umbrella, if disturbed it unhurriedly takes off sailing languidly upstream towards the waterfall, as it flies never quite knowing what to do with its legs.

25 July. 'Your honesty will die.' This is a woman at the annual village street market when she sees Rupert buying an honesty plant. It will, of course which Rupert knows but he also knows that the dead flowers will then turn into translucent seed pods which are its attraction. As it is (and because she somehow comes up from below) she seems like the voice of doom and the phrase becomes a family joke (if the two of us constitute a family).

3 August (the day of Dad's death forty-one years ago). To Gosford Street behind the BBC to record Sue MacGregor's programme *The Reunion* about the writing and production of the two *Talking Heads* series in 1987 and 1998. The actors taking part are Penelope Wilton, Patricia Routledge and Stephanie Cole with Tristram Powell representing the direction. Stephanie, who has come up from Bath, is actually performing in *Talking Heads* at the Theatre Royal, though not *Soldiering On* which she did in the first series but *A Cream Cracker Under the Settee* in which Thora Hird had such a success. Sue MacGregor is a gentle, almost loving guide and commentator, teasing out anecdotes and generally getting some good stuff while making sure everybody gets a fair whack. There's a bit too much of the wondrousness of Alan Bennett's writing so that I almost feel it would have been easier had I not been present (and I ring this morning, 4 August, to tell the editor not to hesitate to cut some of the compliments) but though I'd been nervous about it (as had the others) I think it will make a good programme.

The best anecdote to come out of the first series was told me by Tony Cash, who heard *A Lady of Letters* translated on French radio. In the original version Miss Ruddock, talking about her dubious neighbours on whom she spies remarks, 'Couple opposite having their tea. No cloth on. Milk bottle stood there waiting.' This has been translated, 'Couple opposite having their tea. No clothes on. Milk bottle stood there waiting.' And it's the milk bottle that intrigues.

5 August. Watch guiltily over (and well beyond) my lunch an outstanding programme (*c.*2000) by David Attenborough in which by tracing the origins of a wooden figure he picked up in a New York auction house he unfolds the whole history and culture of Easter Island. Aside from it being such an instructive programme he also transmits some of the obsession and enthusiasm of the dedicated collector so that one ends up even envying him his little wooden figure.

6 August. Dinah Wood sends me a postcard à propos these diaries. The postcard is of a model of a plumber done by her brother Wilfrid and it's a cheerful figure all tooled up and girded with a belt of a plumber's typical accoutrements so dense and various that one doesn't immediately spot hanging among the ratchets, wrenches and spanners another plumber's tool, namely his dick. Nothing is done to draw attention to this personal hosepipe which to begin with I don't even notice and it's this (and the cheeriness of the plumber) that makes it very funny.

8 August. Sixty-three years since I went into the army when my biggest fear was having to take my clothes off whether for shower, medical examinations or whatever. In the event I managed never to have to go naked at any time during my National Service or indeed university that followed it. At Coulsdon where I was stationed to begin with I used to go for a shower (once a week) on a Saturday evening when the camp (and the showers) were empty. This was a dread that dogged me half my life.

11 August. A strike of warding staff at the National Gallery where it is planned to outsource the warding to Securitas, a firm supposedly with a wealth of experience in the field. No matter that the field also includes airports, car parks and whatever. I've seen no protests from the trustees or anyone making the point that the warders at the NG are a resource worth conserving, so various, interesting and eccentric they are that they don't just keep an eye on the visitors and the paintings but are themselves part of the NG's ecology. I don't know how the strike can succeed but I hope that it does. Not a good trustee myself I hope I would have made more of a public fuss than any that I've seen.

12 August. I'm not a member of the Labour Party and so can't vote. If I could, though, I'd vote for Jeremy Corbyn if only out of hope that the better part of salvation lies not in electoral calculation but in the aspirations of the people.

14 August. Bridget is cleaning the marble-topped chocolatier's table we bought four or five years ago at Spencer Swaffer's in Arundel when a piece of paper flutters out. It's a photograph of workmen in a chocolatier's, Cazenave in Bayonne, with a page of printing in French and another in a language I don't recognise but think (from its location) might be Basque or Catalan. We both get quite excited by this slip of paper and I can't wait until R. gets home to show him. While pleased at the light the slip of paper and photograph throw on the table's origins, R. thinks it's merely a page torn from a relatively modern guide book and that far from being Basque or whatever the language is modern Greek. Dampening though this is, it's still good to know more about this substantial piece of furniture which has been such a useful and dignified addition to our kitchen. It had an eventful beginning as the marble top is so heavy that in the course of getting it down the outside stairs it slipped and nearly disembowelled Rupert. Nor were we sure it would fit. But it does and our Cazenave refugee has proved ideal.

God is not a deity reverence for whom can be performance-related.

15 August. Rain stops me doing my usual half-hour cycle ride in Regent's Park and when I do go later on it's so busy I divert to the Nash terraces which are always deserted. Seats overlooking the (very dull) gardens would add to their amenity but since this would fetch more people in I imagine it's the last thing the well-to-do (and the well-to-do diplomatic) tenants would want. There are generally one or two cars parked with their engines running and the chauffeurs asleep but no other signs of life. In the evening I watch a programme about VE Day (though today has been marked by celebrations for the seventieth anniversary of VJ Day). Both of these I remember as I was aged eleven on 9 May 1945, i.e. VE Day + 1, but both VE and VJ Days are indistinguishable in memory, my lasting impression of both that of the sudden availability of *light*, shone on floodlit public buildings which I'd never seen before and streaming away prodigally into the night sky. This was a regular feature thereafter and still an object of wonder (as late as the Festival of Britain in 1951 and on into the early fifties). Those in the programme were often younger than me and didn't have much memorable to offer, far and away the best being David Attenborough, nineteen in 1945.

16 August. This aspect of things comes up again when I go round to the Millers this morning for coffee. Christina Noble is there who is working on some sort of family history and she treats me as a living witness to times past. Was venison ever on the ration? I think not, though Leeds butchers wouldn't in any case be its usual retail outlet and certainly not Bennett's High Class Meat Purveyors of Otley Road. What about trotters, were they on the ration? No and tripe certainly wasn't though even at eighty-one it still seems droll to me to be treated as a historical repository or the oldest inhabitant. The VE Day programme treated rationing as a national ordeal when it was nothing of the sort, butter short admittedly but the availability of food was seasonal and deliciously so as I've mentioned before, new potatoes, strawberries and all soft fruit tastier then than they have ever seemed since.

23 August. Countryfile touches on – it hardly tackles – the now permitted potash mine in the North Yorkshire National Park with John Craven posing against the idyllic landscape and asking some toothless questions. The usual justifications are put forward: local employment (no one says how much or how guaranteed it is); local prosperity, though with no questions as to who the shareholders are and where based – certainly not in the North Riding and probably not even in the country. No wonder Corbyn is ahead of the rest.

1 September. Oliver Sacks dies, my first memory of whom was as an undergraduate in his digs in Keble Road in Oxford when I was with Eric Korn and possibly, over from Cambridge, Michael Frayn. Oliver said that he had fried and eaten a placenta. At that time I don't think I knew what a placenta was except that I knew it didn't come with chips.

11 September. David Cameron has been in Leeds preaching to businessmen the virtues of what he calls 'the smart state'. This seems to be a state that gets away with doing as little as possible for its citizens and shuffling as many responsibilities as it can onto anyone who thinks they can make a profit out of them. I am glad there wasn't a smart state when I was being brought up in Leeds, a state that was unsmart enough to see me and others like me educated free of charge and sent on at the city's expense to university, provided with splendid libraries, cheap transport and a terrific art gallery, not, of course to mention the city's hospitals.

Smart to Mr Cameron seems to mean doing as little as one can get away with and calling it enterprise. Smart as in smart alec, smart of the smart answer, which I'm sure Mr Cameron has to hand. Dead smart.

14 September. Watch, though without intending to, J. B. Priestley's *An Inspector Calls*. Without intending to, I suppose, because I never feel Alastair Sim's performance in the film can be bettered. Tonight it's David Thewlis who's very, very good, bleak, unmannered and while I miss some of Sim's silkiness every bit as good. It's a play I'd dearly love to have written (as also his *When We Are Married*) and gives me a pang of conscience. Back in the nineties when I was doing some programmes on Westminster Abbey, the dean, Michael Mayne, talked to me about whether Larkin should be in Poets' Corner . . . an obvious yes on the strength of 'Church Going' let alone the rest. He also wanted my thoughts on another candidate, J. B. Priestley whom several supporters were pushing but on whom Michael M. wasn't keen. I hedged, I think, certainly not pressing Priestley's claim which on the evidence of tonight's *An Inspector Calls* fills me with regret and self-reproach.

23 September. A minor breakthrough today when I go to my barber's, Ossie's in Parkway, and for the first time in my life I allow Azakh, the barber to trim my eyebrows. It's a cosmetic refinement I've always resisted on the assumption that once cut the eyebrows would grow more luxuriantly and I feared I should end up looking like Bernard

Ingham. However I am getting on and there will scarcely be time for the development of comparable thickets so today I am tidied up. The last time I remember having related thoughts was when I was seventeen and had not yet started to shave. Though most of my contemporaries had been shaving for years, being fair and rather behind the rest in my case there was no need and I knew that once I started I should have to go on. A few months later I was in the army when the decision was taken out of my hands.

3 October. Denis Healey dies, whom I would have been happy to see prime minister. Met twice . . . once when I was cycling briefly (and slowly) on the pavement in Gower Street where he was waiting for a bus and he stopped me, saying, 'Now then, young Bennett' (I would have been fifty at the time). Then twenty years later we were both at a reception in Downing Street for Fanny Waterman, founder of the Leeds Pianoforte Competition. I was with Rupert and the joke was the same as at the bus stop as he shook hands with him before indicating me and saying to him, 'And is this your young man?'

11 October. In Primrose Hill Books I glance though Volume 2 of Charles Moore's biography of Mrs Thatcher, noting that it recycles Graham Turner's mendacious interview with me and other so-called artists and intellectuals in which we were supposed to have dismissed Mrs T. out of snobbery. This was the thesis Turner had come along anxious to prove and bore scant relation to the interview itself, which concentrated on her actual policies. It's only worth noting because it's an interview that often gets quoted e.g. in Noel Annan's *Our Age*. I did detest Mrs Thatcher and deplore her legacy. But she was a grocer's daughter as I am a butcher's son. Snobbery doesn't come into it.

13 October. As floor-covering the red carpet is pretty unprepossessing, threadbare, stabbed by too many high heels and, I imagine, weed on by dogs. It fronts the Odeon, Leicester Square for the premiere of *The Lady in the Van* and penned on its edges are dozens of reporters and photographers from the nation's press. I am put to begin at one end, Alex Jennings in the middle and Nick Hytner at the other and together we work the line, though the journalists, both newspaper and radio, are so jammed together that as one is questioned and photographed by one reporter the questions and one's answers are overheard by the next in line who often just puts them again. To begin with I try and vary my replies but invention soon flags and nobody seems to mind if I say the same thing three times over with three minutes max per interview. It's all very jolly, some of them shake hands and there are occasional selfies but even when we've been at it an hour we haven't reached the end of the line. Then we are called inside to be shepherded with Maggie Smith through the foyer, down the back stairs and onto the stage where we are introduced and shown to the audience by Nick. We don't have to speak and are a bit nonplussed with the audience just wanting to get on with the film. So by the time we get to our seats in the balcony the film has started. It goes well though as with other films I've done I worry that one laugh treads too closely on the heels of the next, which I've never managed to solve. Still people are crying at the end and seem to be happy.

23 October, Yorkshire. With the trip to New York looming I am unsurprised when on my way home I sprain my ankle, such avoidance mechanisms a not unusual prelude to major departures. I phone my GP who is concerned that it might be a clot and recommends going to A&E at Airedale Hospital where I should have an X-ray. It's early Saturday evening and Casualty very quiet, raising hopes we may be in and out quite quickly. We sit there slowly doing the *Guardian* Quick Crossword, noting as so often in institutions the presence of characters who seem habitués, knowing the procedures, familiar with the staff, A&E their scene. Quiet though it is, it's a couple of hours before we're seen by a youngish consultant who briskly disposes of any likelihood of there being a clot and sees no point in doing an

X-ray as it would just reveal wear and tear, 'the wear and tear of being . . .' and he glances at my form '. . . of being eighty-one'. He's not unfriendly but not chatty either and I wonder whether we are unwittingly contributing to one of the problems of the NHS, namely GPs referring patients to A&E just to be on the safe side. Out by nine o'clock we go the back way home, with an owl flying across the road near West Marton. Curry for supper after which I limp to bed, the hospital episode not as wearisome as might have been expected and R. even enjoying it.

27 October. To record *Private Passions*, Michael Berkeley's Radio 3 programme which I've always liked as more relaxed and less formulaic than *Desert Island Discs*, which was apt, particularly in the days of Sue Lawley, to bowl one a googly ('And would you say you were gay?'). Mind you I've always resisted *Private Passions* too if only because my musical appreciation is so adolescent and tied to memory with no specialist musical knowledge to it at all. Under Michael Berkeley's informed and benevolent eye the programme is a real contribution to the reputation of the BBC, or the old BBC anyway.

The studio is in a little house off Shepherd's Bush Green, putting me in mind of those days in the sixties when I worked two days a week for Ned Sherrin and *Not So Much a Programme* in Lime Grove. It's a nice group of people and a happy atmosphere and I'm grateful to the young assistant Oliver Soden whose opportune postcard persuaded me to do it. I talk about Dad playing his fiddle to the wireless on Sunday nights during the war and musical evenings at my grandma's on Gilpin Place when Aunt Eveline, a sometime pianist for the silent films, would regale us with the latest hits from Ivor Novello and latterly *Oklahoma*. I had wanted some Kathleen Ferrier but, with her recordings being relatively few, had had to settle for her singing part of Brahms's *Alto Rhapsody*, regretting that she had never recorded *Gerontius* or Strauss's *Four Last Songs*. My parents had heard her sing one winter night in 1947 in a concert she gave in Brunswick Chapel in Leeds but I thought I had never heard her. It was only when I was going through some old programmes that I came across the brochure for the 1950 Leeds Triennial Festival, tickets for which we had been given by a Mr Tansley who was the Corporation entertainments manager and a customer at Dad's shop. And good seats they were, Row B in the balcony of the Victoria Hall and, as we discovered, directly behind the royal party which consisted of the Princess Royal and the Harewoods, who were the festival's patrons. Everyone around us was in long dresses or dinner jackets. I was sixteen and in my school blazer with Mam in her best frock. Dad knew better than to go and wouldn't be persuaded, so to my acute embarrassment (of which at sixteen I was already a connoisseur), I had to escort Mam. I was no stranger to the Victoria Hall, going there every Saturday to hear the Yorkshire Symphony Orchestra but looking round at the cream of Leeds society I knew that they were seldom to be seen at a normal concert in the town hall unless as in this case it had the cachet of royalty.

It also had the cachet of Sir Thomas Beecham who made one of his witty speeches before embarking on a performance of Dvořák's *Stabat Mater* . . . to my mind (though I've never heard it since) a pretty dreary piece. So it was only years later that looking through my programmes I realised I had heard Kathleen Ferrier. She had been one of the singers. I've never forgotten that concert but it wasn't her performance that I remembered . . . or even noticed.

31 October, New York. Here yesterday in the lap of luxury as our first-class fare is paid partly by the New York Public Library, which is giving me an award and the rest by Sony which is producing *The Lady in the Van*. I wonder, though, looking at our fellow passengers, who is paying for them so ordinary do they look and even downright scruffy. Perhaps they're all in the music business in which case, this not being a private jet BA First Class is maybe a bit of a comedown. Most luxurious for me, though is that having sprained my ankle last week I get a wheelchair at both ends which, particularly at JFK, is a great blessing as in immigration we sidetrack the queue. There's a nasty bit of turbulence in mid-Atlantic though, which no amount of luxury can banish. It doesn't bother R. who sleeps throughout but has me gibbering, however smooth it is flying for me never other than an ordeal.

This morning we take a cab to the market in Union Square, a real pleasure. It's partly that though crowded with stalls selling farm produce, cheese, fruit and whatever it's resolutely ordinary with no hint of middle-class worthiness about it. Then too the places all the produce has been driven in from in the back of beyond of New York State reminds one how rural America is still and which one can detect in the faces of the people behind the stalls. Maybe I'm sentimental about this and maybe Borough Market (where I've never been) is much the same. But I find myself cheered by the diversity of New York as last time I was here. Then we happened to coincide with a march against the Iraq war, a march so big and close-knit we joined it simply in order to work our way across the street.

Then back to Lynn W.'s apartment on 16th Street where I sit out on the terrace in the sun.

2 *November*. Most of the day spent in a back room of the Four Seasons Hotel being interviewed with Nick Hytner and Alex Jennings by a succession of journalists and correspondents. They question us about the making of the film and the story behind it but most of all about Maggie Smith, who because she does so little publicity remains a creature of mystery. Alex like me is anecdotal, telling stories about the filming and Miss Shepherd whereas Nick, schooled by his time at the National, makes what would be called 'bullet points' about the film and how it came to be made and so is, I think a more useful interviewee. On the other hand if an interviewer bores him he finds it hard to hide so that Alex and I become absurdly over-animated just to compensate.

In the evening to the New York Public Library where I am to be made a Library Lion. When I said this to my friend David Vaisey, librarian emeritus of the Bodleian he remarked, 'Well I just hope you're not one of those aged lions that gets shot by a mid-western dentist', a welcome joke as he's just recovering from a stroke. It's a black tie affair which I only found out the day before we left so I stick to my Anderson and Sheppard suit (current record: four funerals and three memorial services). As I'm leaving my coat the attendant hands me what I take to be the coat check but in fact it's the lion itself on a red ribbon which I wear all evening. Spotted (also wearing his lion) is Salman Rushdie. There are half a dozen of us being lionised and we are lined up and photographed and made much of before going upstairs to a magnificent supper, getting home thoroughly knackered about eleven. How people lead a social life is beyond me.

13 November, Yorkshire. The film 'opens well' as they say and here in the village people have been going down to Skipton to see it. I don't even know where the cinema is. They show films occasionally in the village hall but whether *The Lady in the Van* will ever achieve such heights I doubt as none of my other stuff has. Years ago when I was still writing TV plays which didn't always go down well one of the village ladies complained: 'I can't understand how he writes the plays that he does with two such lovely parents as he had.'

2 December. Any day on which one has to spend time watching the House of Commons on TV will tend to depress and so it is with the Syrian bombing debate. Jeremy Corbyn gets no credit for his convictions or for respecting those of his party by licensing a free (i.e. unwhipped) vote. Instead he is ragged throughout his speech by loutish Tories, most of whom have no convictions to speak of but just do as they're told. Still at least nobody says it's the House of Commons at its best, which it decidedly isn't. Now if the campaigns in Kuwait and Iraq are anything to go by what will follow will be extensive coverage of our boys taking off from Cyprus and their happy fireworks in the desert.

And this is what happens, with the BBC commentator on the edge of the airfield at Akrotiri, counting them out and counting them back, though not the planes but rather the bombs they are carrying . . . and not bringing back.

9 December. Another session with Adam Low for next year's documentary. Note that though Adam positions himself beside the camera and I address what I have to say to him there is a definite difference between my ordinary conversational tone of voice and the tone in which I address the camera, which is never entirely 'natural' but always tinged with 'performance'. I am not talking to a person but to an audience. I don't know how to avoid this. If I had to say what is wrong I would simply say that the person talking isn't me. But whatever it is I do, I do it this morning from ten until one thirty when I have some soup and a piece of chocolate before going out for my therapeutic bike ride in Regent's Park.

27 December. I am reading *Anatomy of a Soldier* by Harry Parker whom I've met and who has sent me a pre-publication copy. It's hard to read and in every way with what is the hardest the knowledge that this is not just a novel written out of someone's head but a book written on his own body. It's about a soldier who is blown up by a roadside bomb as Parker himself was and who loses his legs just as he did. As the narrative comes up again and again to the moment of the explosion I find I can only read two or three pages at a time. So that is hard. Hard, too, is the way he has chosen to tell it through the items of equipment he carried . . . his phone, the camp bed on which he sleeps, the items of medical equipment used on the operating table and the plasma and the drugs that drip into him. Even the bacteria that get into his wounds have a voice. It's marvellously told and this way of telling it . . . giving the inanimate a voice . . . is both engrossing and distancing and I know of nothing quite like it. At the start there is something of Hardy's *The Convergence of the Twain* to the story, the young officer on patrol and the even younger tribesman planting the bomb and how they come together. Which they do again and again as the story is told and re-told. I'm so anxious to read it right and report it right as having finished it I must now write to him about what is in effect his own life. A year or so ago I got some stick for saying I seldom read contemporary English novels never feeling they had much to tell me. Now I am rebuked, though it is of course more than a novel and a tale of both sides, the ending unbearable.

28 December, Yorkshire. When I lie in the bath in London, some nights I can see the lights of planes stacking en route westwards to Heathrow. When I lie in the bath in Yorkshire I can see the moon and sometimes the lights in the milking shed on Coultherd's farm. I have never much cared for the look of my own body, particularly these days, and often take a bath in the dark. As an undergraduate I spent two of the vacations in my final year working at St Deiniol's, a residential library attached to Gladstone's home at Hawarden in North Wales. It was an Anglican institution, though staying there didn't oblige one to attend services in the local parish church, some of which were conducted by the warden of the library who was himself an Anglican clergyman. He and his wife were leaving for Evensong one Sunday when hearing a bath being run but seeing no lights on they postponed their religious observances and came belting up the stairs to bang on the bathroom door and enquire what was going on. I found it difficult to explain (I think I said I was saving electricity) and they took it, I'm sure, that I was engaged in some unmentionable immoral activity. Though the library, bathroom included, was way too cold for anything like that.

31 December, Yorkshire. Wanting to wind up this year with something resounding I am at a loss. It's that flat time after Christmas when nothing happens and on this last afternoon of 2015 little occurs. I am now eighty-one which, though it has been a long time coming, is still a bit of a surprise. I am comforted as I have been in the past by something I believe was said as he looked back on his life by the Argentinian author Borges: 'All the books I have ever written fill me only with a complex feeling of repentance.'

I take this to mean that he has never written the perfect book. As who has?

So we keep on, keeping on.

Postscript: *23 June 2016*. The day of the referendum, I spend sitting at the kitchen table correcting the proofs of these diaries, finishing them on Friday morning before going to Yorkshire in despair. I imagine this must have been what Munich was like in 1938 – half the nation rejoicing at a supposed deliverance, the other half stunned by the country's self-serving cowardice. Well, we shall see.

Baffled at a Bookcase

This piece was part of the continuing campaign to save local libraries including our own in Sharpleshall Street, Primrose Hill, which is now run as a community library.

I have always been happy in libraries, though without ever being entirely at ease there. A scene that seems to crop up regularly in plays that I have written has a character, often a young man, standing in front of a bookcase feeling baffled. He – and occasionally she – is overwhelmed by the amount of stuff that has been written and the ground to be covered. 'All these books. I'll never catch up,' wails the young Joe Orton in the film script of *Prick Up Your Ears* (1987), and in *The Old Country* (1977) another young man reacts more dramatically, by hurling half the books to the floor. In *Me, I'm Afraid of Virginia Woolf* (1978) someone else gives vent to their frustration with literature by drawing breasts on a photograph of Virginia Woolf and kitting out E. M. Forster with a big cigar. Orton himself notoriously defaced library books before starting to write books himself. This resentment, which was, I suppose, somewhere mine, had to do with feeling shut out. A library, I used to feel, was like a cocktail party with everybody standing with their back to me; I could not find a way in.

The first library I did find my way into was the Armley Public Library in Leeds where a reader's ticket cost tuppence in 1940; not tuppence a time or even tuppence a year but just tuppence; that was all you ever had to pay. It was rather a distinguished building, put up in 1901, the architect Percy Robinson, and amazingly for Leeds, which is and always has been demolition-crazy, it survives and is still used as a library, though whether it will survive the present troubles I don't like to think.

We would be there as a family, my mother and father, my brother and me, and it would be one of our regular weekly visits. I had learned to read quite early when I was five or six by dint, it seemed to me then, of watching my brother read. We both of us read comics but whereas I was still on picture-based comics like *Dandy* and *Beano*, my brother, who was three years older, had graduated to the more text-based *Hotspur* and *Wizard*. Having finished my *Dandy* I would lie down on the carpet beside him and gaze at what he was reading, asking him questions about it and generally making a nuisance of myself. Then – and it seemed as instantaneous as this – one day his comic made sense and I could read. I'm sure the process must have been more painstaking but not much more.

Having learned to read, other than comics there was nothing in the house on which to practise my newly acquired skill. My parents were both readers and Dad took the periodical *John Bull*, the books they generally favoured literature of escape, tales of ordinary folk like themselves who had thrown it all up for a life of mild adventure, a smallholding on the Wolds, say, or an island sanctuary, with both of them fans of the naturalist R. M. Lockley. There were a few volumes of self-help in the house but the only non-library book of autobiography was *I Haven't Unpacked* by William Holt, who had got away from the dark, satanic mills by buying a horse and riding through England.

The Armley Library was at the bottom of Wesley Road, the entrance up a flight of marble steps under open arches, through brass-railed swing doors panelled in stained glass which by 1941 was just beginning to buckle. Ahead was the Adults' Library, lofty, airy and inviting; to the right was the Junior Library, a low dark room made darker by the books which, regardless of their contents, had been bound in heavy boards of black, brown or maroon embossed with the stamp of Leeds Public Libraries. This grim packaging was discouraging to a small boy who had just begun to read, though more discouraging still was the huge and ill-tempered, walrus-moustached British Legion commissionaire who was permanently installed there. The image of General Hindenburg, who was pictured on the stamps in my brother's album, he had lost one or other of his limbs in the trenches, but since he seldom moved from his chair and just shouted it was difficult to tell which.

Such veterans of the First War were much in evidence well into the 1950s. As a child one encountered them in parks, sitting on benches and in shelters playing dominoes, generally grumpy and with reason to be, the war having robbed them of their youth and often their health. The luckier and less disabled ones manned lifts or were posted at the doors of public buildings, a uniformed and bemedalled conciergerie who were more often than not unhelpful, making the most of whatever petty authority they were invested with. And so it was here, the commissionaire's only concern to maintain absolute silence, and not at all the companion and friend novice readers needed on this, the threshold of literature.

Of the books themselves I remember little. Henty was well represented and Captain Marryat, books which, whenever I did manage to get into them, only brought home to me that I was not an entirely satisfactory version of the genus boy. I suppose there must somewhere have been Enid Blyton, but since she too would have been backed in the same funereal but immensely serviceable boards she passed me by. As it was, the books I best remember reading there were the Dr Dolittle stories of Hugh Lofting, which were well represented and (an important consideration) of which there were always more. I think I knew even at six years old that a doctor who could talk to animals was fiction but at the same time I thought the setting of the stories, Puddleby-on-the-Marsh, was a real place set in historical time with the doctor (and Lofting's own illustrations of the doctor) having some foundation in fact. Shreds of this belief clung on because when, years later, having recorded some of Lofting's stories for the BBC, I met his son, I found I still had the feeling that his father had been not quite an ordinary mortal.

Other mysteries persisted. What, for instance, was a cat's meat man? I had never come across one. Was the meat *of* cats or *for* cats? We didn't have a cat and even if we had with Dad being a Co-op butcher it would have been well catered for. And again it was when I was reading the stories on the radio and happened to mention this mysterious personage in my diary in the *LRB* that the small mystery was solved. A cat's meat man toured the streets (though not our street) with strips of meat suspended from a stick to be sold as pet food. One correspondent, her mother being out, remembered the stick of meat being put through the letterbox where she retrieved it from the doormat and, it being wartime, scoffed the lot.

In 1944, believing, as people in Leeds tended to do, that flying bombs or no flying bombs, things were better Down South, Dad threw up his job with the Co-op and we migrated to Guildford. It was a short-lived experiment and I don't remember ever finding the public library, but this was because a few doors down from the butcher's shop where Dad worked there was a little private library, costing 6d a week, which in the children's section had a whole run of Richmal Crompton's William books. I devoured them, reading practically one a day, happy in the knowledge that there would always be more. Years later when I first read Evelyn Waugh I had the same sense of discovery: here was a trove of books that was going to last. I wish I could say I felt the same about Dickens or Trollope or Proust even, but they seemed more of a labour than a prospect of delight.

The butcher for whom my dad worked also ran a horsemeat business, the meat strictly for non-human consumption and accordingly painted bright green. In his cattle truck Mr Banks would go out into the Surrey countryside to collect carcasses and sometimes, by dint of hanging around the lorry, I got to go with him. I would watch as the bloated cow or horse was winched on board and then we would drive to the slaughterhouse in Walnut Tree Close just by Guildford Station. While the carcass was dismembered I would sit in the corner absorbed in my latest William book. Richmal Crompton can seldom have been read in such grisly and uncongenial circumstances.

It wasn't long, though, before we ended up going back to Leeds where we now lived in Headingley, with the local public library on North Lane, a visit to which could be combined with seeing the film at the Lounge cinema opposite. I went to Leeds Modern School, a state school at Lawnswood (and now called Lawnswood). I spoke there a few months ago and, unlike Ofsted, was much impressed by it, its current disfavour a presumed punishment for its admirable headmistress, who is still managing to resist the siren charms of academy status and the wiles of Mr Gove. In those circumstances I am happy to boast that the school library has been named after me.

When I was in the sixth form at the Modern School I used to do my homework in the Leeds Central Library in the Headrow. At that time the municipal buildings housed not only the lending library and the reference library but also the education offices and the police department, which I suppose was handy for the courts, still functioning across the road in the town hall with the whole complex – town hall, library, courts – an expression of the confidence of the city and its belief in the value of reading and education, and where you might end up if they were neglected. It's a High Victorian building done throughout in polished Burmantofts brick, extravagantly tiled, the staircases of polished marble topped with brass rails, and carved at the head of each stair a slavering dog looking as if it's trying to stop itself sliding backwards down the banister.

The reference library itself proclaimed the substance of the city with its solid elbow chairs and long mahogany tables, grooved along the edge to hold a pen, and in the centre of each table a massive pewter inkwell. Arched and galleried and lined from floor to ceiling with books the reference library was grand yet unintimidating. Half the tables were filled with sixth-formers like myself, just doing their homework or studying for a scholarship; but there would also be university students home for the vacation, the Leeds students tending to work up the road in their own Brotherton Library. There was, too, the usual quota of eccentrics that haunt any reading room that is warm and handy and has somewhere to sit down. Old men would doze for hours over a magazine taken from the rack, though if they were caught nodding off an assistant would trip over from the counter and hiss, 'No sleeping!'

One regular, always with a pile of art books at his elbow, was the painter Jacob Kramer, some of whose paintings, with their Vorticist slant, hung in the art gallery next door. Dirty and half-tight there wasn't much to distinguish him from the other tramps whiling away their time before trailing along Victoria Street to spend the night in the refuge in the basement of St George's Church, where occasionally I would do night duty myself, sleeping on a camp bed in a room full of these sad, defeated, utterly unthreatening creatures.

With its mixture of readers and its excellent facilities (it was a first-rate library) and the knowledge that there would always be someone working there whom I knew and who would come out for coffee, I found some of the pleasure going to the reference library that, had I been less studious, I could have found in a pub. Over the next ten years while I still thought I might turn into a medieval historian I became something of a connoisseur of libraries, but the reference library in Leeds always seemed to me one of the most congenial. It was there, on leave from the army, that I discovered the library held a run of *Horizon*, the literary magazine started by Cyril Connolly in 1940, and that I eventually did get a scholarship to Oxford I put down to the smattering of culture I gleaned from its pages.

In my day, it was a predominantly male institution with the main tables dividing themselves almost on religious or ethnic lines. There was a Catholic table, patronised by boys from St Michael's College, the leading Catholic school, with blazers in bright Mary blue; there was a Jewish table where the boys came from Roundhay or the Grammar School, the Jewish boys even when they were not at the same school often knowing each other from the synagogue or other extra-curricular activities. If, like me, you were at the Modern School – and there were about half a dozen of us who were there regularly – you had no particular religious or racial affinities and indeed were not thought perhaps quite as clever, the school certainly not as good as Roundhay or the Grammar School. The few girls who braved this male citadel disrupted the formal division, leavened it, I'm sure for the better. And they worked harder than the boys and were seldom to be found on the landing outside where one adjourned for a smoke.

It had glamour, too, for me and getting in first at nine one morning I felt, opening my books, as I had when a small boy at Armley Baths and I had been first in there, the one to whom it fell to break the immaculate stillness of the water, shatter the straight lines tiled on the bottom of the bath and set the day on its way.

Of the boys who worked in the reference library a surprising number must have turned out to be lawyers, and I can count at least eight of my contemporaries who sat at those tables in the 1950s who became judges. A school – and certainly a state or provincial school – would consider that something to boast about, but libraries are facilities; a library has no honours board and takes no credit for what its readers go on to do but, remembering myself at nineteen, on leave from the army and calling up the copies of *Horizon* to get me through the general paper in the Oxford scholarship, I feel as much a debt to that library as I do to my school. It was a good library and though like everywhere else busier now than it was in my day, remains, unlike so much of Leeds, largely unaltered.

The library closed at nine and coming down in the lift (bevelled mirrors, mahogany panelling, little bench) the attendant, another British Legion figure, would stop and draw the gates at the floor below and in would get a covey of policemen and even the occasional miscreant en route for the cells. One of the policemen might be my cousin Arnold, who belonged to what my mother always felt was the slightly common wing of the Bennett family. Loud, burly and wonderfully genial, Arnold was a police photographer and he would regale me with the details of the latest murder he had been called on to snap: 'By, Alan, I've seen some stuff.' The stuff he'd seen included the corpse of the stripper Mary Millington, who had committed suicide. 'I can't understand why she committed suicide. She had a lovely body.'

To someone as prone to embarrassment as I was, these encounters, particularly in the presence of my schoolfriends, ought to have been shaming. That they never were was, I suppose, because Cousin Arnold was looked on as a creature from the real world, the world of prostitutes found dead on waste ground, corpses in copses and cars burned out down Lovers' Lane. This was Life where I knew even then that I was not likely to be headed or ever have much to do with.

There is no shortage of libraries in Oxford, some of them, of course, of great grandeur and beauty. The Radcliffe Camera seems to me one of the handsomest buildings in England and the square in which it stands a superb combination of styles. Crossing it on a moonlit winter's night lifted the heart, though that was often the trouble with Oxford – the architecture out-soared one's feelings, the sublime not always easy to match. There are in that one square three libraries, the Bodleian on the north side, on the east the Codrington, part of Hawksmoor's All Souls, and James Gibbs's Camera in the middle. Just off the square Brasenose has a seventeenth-century library and there's another more modest library, neo-Gothic in style, and built by George Gilbert Scott in 1856. It's over Exeter's garden wall in the north-west corner of Radcliffe Square, but you can't quite see that. This was where I worked, though it was possible if one was so inclined to get to study in the much more exclusive and architecturally splendid surroundings of the Codrington, and a few undergraduates did so. They tended, though, to set less store on what they were writing than on where they were writing it and I, with my narrow sympathies but who was just as foolish, despised them for it.

Staying on at Oxford after I'd taken my degree I did research in medieval history, the subject of my research Richard II's retinue in the last ten years of his reign. This took me twice a week to the Public Record Office then still in Chancery Lane and in particular to the Round Room, galleried, lined with books, a humbler version of the much grander Round Room in the British Museum. Presiding over the BM Round Room in his early days was Angus Wilson whereas at the PRO it was Noel Blakiston, friend of Cyril Connolly, hair as white as Wilson's and possibly the most distinguished-looking man I've ever seen.

Though I made copious notes on the manuscripts I studied (which were chiefly records of the medieval exchequer) I would have found it hard to say what it was I was looking for – imagining, I think, that having amassed sufficient material it would all suddenly fall into place and become clear. Failing that, I hoped to come upon some startling and unexpected fact, a very silly notion. Had it been Richard III I was researching rather than Richard II, it might have been something as relatively unambiguous as a note in the monarch's own hand saying: 'It was me that killed ye Princes in ye Tower, hee hee.' Historical research nowadays is a dull business: had I any sense I would have been collating the tax returns of the knights I was studying or the amount they borrowed or were owed, or sifting through material other historians had ignored or discarded; it is seldom at the frontier that discoveries are made but more often in the dustbin.

The Memoranda Rolls on which I spent much of my time were long thin swatches of parchment about five feet long and one foot wide and written on both sides. Thus to turn the page required the co-operation and forbearance of most of the other readers at the table, and what would sometimes look like the cast of the Mad Hatter's tea party struggling to put wallpaper up was just me trying to turn over. A side effect of reading these unwieldy documents was that one was straight away propelled into quite an intimate relationship with readers alongside and among those I got to know in this way was the historian Cecil Woodham-Smith.

The author of *The Great Hunger*, an account of the Irish Famine, and *The Reason Why*, about the events leading up to the Charge of the Light Brigade, Cecil was a frail woman with a tiny bird-like skull, looking more like Elizabeth I (in later life) than Edith Sitwell ever did (and minus her sheet-metal earrings). Irish, she had a Firbankian wit and a lovely turn of phrase. 'Do you know the Atlantic at all?' she once asked me and I put the line into *Habeas Corpus* (1973) and got a big laugh on it. From a grand Irish family she was quite snobbish; talking of someone she said: 'Then he married a Mitford . . . but that's a stage everybody goes through.' Even the most ordinary remark would be given her own particular twist and she could be quite camp. Conversation had once turned, as conversations will, to forklift trucks. Feeling that industrial machinery might be remote from Cecil's sphere of interest I said: 'Do you know what a forklift truck is?' She looked at me in her best Annie Walker manner. 'I do. To my cost.'

Books and bookcases cropping up in stuff that I've written means that they have to be reproduced on stage or on film. This isn't as straightforward as it might seem. A designer will either present you with shelves lined with gilt-tooled library sets, the sort of clubland books one can rent by the yard as decor, or he or she will send out for some junk books from the nearest second-hand bookshop and think that those will do. Another short cut is to order in a cargo of remaindered books so that you end up with a shelf so garish and lacking in character it bears about as much of a relationship to literature as a caravan site does to architecture. A bookshelf is as particular to its owner as are his or her clothes; a personality is stamped on a library just as a shoe is shaped by the foot.

That someone's working library has a particular tone, with some shelves more heterogeneous than others, for example, or (in the case of an art historian) filled with offprints and monographs or (with an old-fashioned literary figure for instance) lined with the faded covers and jackets of distinctive Faber or Cape editions, does not seem to occur to a designer. On several occasions I've had to bring my own books down to the theatre to give the right worn tone to the shelves.

In *The Old Country* the books (Auden, Spender, MacNeice) are of central importance to the plot. I wanted their faded buffs and blues and yellows bleached into a unity of tone that suggested long sun-lit Cambridge afternoons, the kind of books you might find lining Dadie Rylands's rooms, for instance. Anthony Blunt's bookshelves were crucial in *Single Spies (1988)*, the look of an art historian's bookshelves, as I've said, significantly different from those of a literary critic. All this tends to pass the designer by. One knows that designers seldom read, but they don't have much knowledge of Inca civilisation either or the Puritan settlement of New England and yet they seem to cope perfectly well reproducing them. An agglomeration of books as illustrating the character of their owner seems to defeat them.

When I first bought books for myself in the late 1940s they were still thought to be quite precious and in poor homes books might often be backed in brown paper. Paper itself was in short supply and such new books as there were often bore the imprint 'Produced in conformity with the Authorised Economy Standard'. The paper was mealy, slightly freckled and looked not unlike the texture of the ice cream of the period. It was, though, a notable period in book design and perhaps because they were among the first books I ever bought (one was C. V. Wedgwood's *William the Silent*) the books of that time have always seemed to me all that was necessary or desirable – simple, unfussy, wholesome and well designed.

They were not, though, to be left about at home. 'Books Do Furnish a Room', wrote Anthony Powell, but my mother never thought so and she'd always put them out of the way in the sideboard when you weren't looking. Books untidy, books upset, more her view. Though once a keen reader herself, particularly when she was younger, she always thought of library books as grubby and with a potential for infection – not intellectual infection either. Lurking among the municipally owned pages might be the germs of TB or scarlet fever, so one must never be seen to peer at a library book too closely or lick your finger before turning over still less read such a book in bed.

There were other perils to reading, but it was only when I hit middle age that I became aware of them. *Me, I'm Afraid of Virginia Woolf* was a television play written in 1978 and though it doesn't contain my usual scene of someone baffled at a bookcase the sense of being outfaced by books is a good description of what the play is about. 'Hopkins,' I wrote of the middle-aged lecturer who is the hero, 'Hopkins was never without a book. It wasn't that he was particularly fond of reading; he just liked to have somewhere to look. A book makes you safe. Shows you're not out to pick anybody up. Try it on. With a book you're harmless. Though Hopkins was harmless without a book.' Books as badges, books as shields; one doesn't think of libraries as perilous places where you can come to harm. Still, they do carry their own risks.

I have been discussing libraries as places and in the current struggle to preserve public libraries not enough stress has been laid on the library as a place not just a facility. To a child living in high flats, say, where space is at a premium and peace and quiet not always easy to find, a library is a haven. But, saying that, a library needs to be handy and local; it shouldn't require an expedition. Municipal authorities of all parties point to splendid new and scheduled central libraries as if this discharges them of their obligations. It doesn't. For a child a library needs to be round the corner. And if we lose local libraries it is children who will suffer. Of the libraries I have mentioned the most important for me was that first one, the dark and unprepossessing Armley Junior Library. I had just learned to read. I needed books. Add computers to that requirement maybe but a child from a poor family is today in exactly the same boat.

The business of closing libraries isn't a straightforward political fight. The local authorities shelter behind the demands of central government which in its turn pretends that local councils have a choice. It's shaming that, regardless of the party's proud tradition of popular education, Labour municipalities are not making more of a stand. For the Tories privatising the libraries has been on the agenda for far longer than they would currently like to admit. This is an extract from my diary:

> *22 February.* Switch on *Newsnight* to find some bright spark
> from, guess where, the Adam Smith Institute, proposing the
> privatisation of the public libraries. His name is Eamonn Butler
> and it's to be hoped he's no relation of the 1944 Education Act
> Butler. Smirking and pleased with himself as they generally are
> from that stable, he's pitted against a well-meaning but flustered
> woman who's an authority on children's books. Paxman looks
> on undissenting as this odious figure dismisses any defence
> of the tradition of free public libraries as 'the usual bleating
> of the middle classes'. I go to bed depressed only to wake and
> find Madsen Pirie, also from the Adam Smith Institute for the
> Criminally Insane, banging the same drum in the *Independent*.
> Not long ago John Bird and John Fortune did a sketch about the
> privatisation of air. These days it scarcely seems unthinkable.

That was written in 1996. It's hard not to think that like other Tory policies privatising the libraries has been lying dormant for fifteen years, just waiting for a convenient crisis to smuggle it through. Libraries are, after all, as another think-tank clown opined a few weeks ago, 'a valuable retail outlet'.

Speech delivered 15 June 2011 at St Mary's Church, Primrose Hill, London. First published in the *London Review of Books*, 28 July 2011.

Fair Play

I am grateful to the Chaplain of King's, Richard Lloyd Morgan, who persuaded me to do this sermon. It may not have been quite what he was expecting but to his great credit he never let me think so.

Preaching is a hazard when writing plays. One isn't supposed to preach and gets told off if one does. Poets are allowed to, but not playwrights, who if they have naked opinions, do better to clothe them in the decent ambiguities of their characters or conceal them in the sometimes all too thin thicket of the plot. Just don't speak to the audience.

I have always found this prohibition difficult. John Gielgud, who was in my first play, thought talking to the audience was vulgar. Then he was prevailed upon to try it and thereafter would seldom talk to anybody else. I understand this and even in my most naturalistic plays have contrived and relished the moments when a character unexpectedly turns and addresses the house and, in a word, preaches.

This may be because as a boy and a regular worshipper at St Michael's, Headingley I heard a lot of sermons. I also used to go to Saturday matinees at the Grand Theatre in Leeds, though on occasion the sermons were more dramatic than the plays. This was particularly so when they were preached, as they quite often were, by visiting fathers from the Community of the Resurrection at Mirfield who were almost revivalist in their fervour and the spell they cast over the congregation.

So when as a young man I first had thoughts about what nowadays is called stand-up it's not surprising it took the form of a sermon. Like all parodies it was born out of affection and familiarity and the Anglican services that were in my bones, and there is symmetry here as the first sermon I preached on a professional stage was in Cambridge fifty-odd years ago across the road at the Arts Theatre in the revue *Beyond the Fringe*. It was on the text, 'My brother Esau is an hairy man but I am a smooth man.' That sermon apart I have never formally preached since until this morning and here I am again in Cambridge.

This is where I came in.

I had first seen Cambridge ten years before when, as a boy of seventeen, I had come down from Leeds in December 1951 to sit the scholarship examination in history, staying the weekend, as one did in those days, in the college of my first choice, Sidney Sussex. The place and the university bowled me over. Leeds, where I had been born and brought up, was like the other great Northern cities still intact in 1951, but though I was not blind to its architectural splendours, unfashionable though at that time they were, it was a soot-blackened, wholly nineteenth-century city and as a boy, like Hector in *The History Boys*, I was famished for antiquity. I had never been in a place of such continuous and unfolding beauty as Cambridge and, December 1951 being exceptionally cold, the Cam was frozen over and a thick hoarfrost covered every court and quadrangle giving the whole city an unreal and celestial beauty. And it was empty, as provincial places in those days were.

I see my seventeen-year-old self roaming unrestricted through the colleges as one could in those unfranchised days, standing in Trinity Great Court in the moonlight thinking it inconceivable I could ever come to study in such blessed surroundings. And nor could I so far as Trinity was concerned. Sidney Sussex wasn't quite my taste in buildings, but you had to be cleverer than I was or higher up the social scale to have the real pick of the architecture. Still, we were examined in the Senate House, the interior of which, had it been in Leeds would have been sequestered behind red ropes, and I went to Evensong in King's, astonished that one could just walk in and be seated in the choir stalls. It was Advent, or what nowadays is called the countdown to Christmas, and one of the hymns was 'O Come, O Come Emmanuel', which is rather dirge-like but has stayed with me all my life since. Interviewed by the kindly dons at Sidney I was for the first time conscious of having a Northern accent.

If the dons were genial some of my fellow candidates were less so. That weekend was the first time I had come across public schoolboys in the mass and I was appalled. They were loud, self-confident and all seemed to know one another, shouting down the table to prove it while also being shockingly greedy. Public-school they might be but they were louts. Seated at long refectory tables beneath the mellow portraits of Tudor and Stuart grandees, neat, timorous and genteel we grammar-school boys were the interlopers; these slobs, as they seemed to me, the party in possession.

But it was a party, seemingly, that I was going to be allowed to join as, though I was a long way from getting a scholarship, Sidney Sussex offered me a place to read history, to come up after my National Service.

This, too, takes in Cambridge and if you're beginning to wonder whether, far from being a sermon, this is just a stroll down memory lane, take heart, because here is where a tentative homily begins to shove its nose above the horizon.

Having done basic training in the infantry I was then sent on a course to learn Russian, a year of which was spent out of uniform and in very relaxed circumstances in Cambridge. It was a heady atmosphere, more so in some ways than university proper, where many of my colleagues were headed after National Service. Some of them were disconcertingly clever, boys from public schools who, when they talked of their schooldays often had in the background a master whose teaching had been memorable and about whom they told anecdotes and whose sayings they remembered – teachers, I remember thinking bitterly, who had presumably played a part in getting them the scholarships most of them had at Oxford and Cambridge. For them the scholarship examination, from which I'd just managed to scrape a place, had almost been a formality. They had been schooled for it and groomed for the interviews that followed, with the scholarships and exhibitions that ensued almost to be taken for granted. This was Oxford and Cambridge after all; they were entitled.

If I felt this was wrong, which I did, it was not at that time an altruistic feeling. I was thinking of myself and how the odds were stacked against me and boys like me. And here I should apologise that this narrative is couched so continuously in single-sex terms, but then, so had my education been, my school, the army, my eventual college – all of them at that time male institutions.

As I say, I saw the odds as stacked against me but took some comfort, as I think educators did generally, in assuming that this situation must inevitably alter and that the proportion of undergraduates from state schools at Oxford and Cambridge would gradually overtake that from public schools until they were both properly and proportionately represented. It was only when as time passed this didn't happen that what in my case had begun as a selfish and even plaintive grievance hardened to take in not just entrance to Oxford and Cambridge but access to higher education in general, with the scramble for university places more desperate year by year. And this is to say nothing of the cost.

Better minds than mine have tackled this problem and continue to do so and I would be foolish if I claimed to have a solution. But I know what is part of the problem and that is private education. My objection to private education is simply put. It is not fair. And to say that nothing is fair is not an answer. Governments, even this one, exist to make the nation's circumstances more fair, but no government, whatever its complexion, has dared to tackle private education.

It might have been feasible at the time of the Butler reforms in 1944 but there were other things going on. The Labour government in 1945 could have tried but it had a great deal to do besides. There was not another chance until 1997 when Labour's huge majority would have at least allowed a start, except that the prime minister had been a public schoolboy himself and seemingly a happy one so that opportunity too went begging.

I am not altogether sure why. When the question comes up there is always talk of the social disruption that would result, as it might be the Dissolution of the Monasteries all over again. But would it? I am not after all suggesting that public schools should be abolished but a gradual reform which began with the amalgamation of state and public schools at sixth-form level, say, ought to be feasible and hardly revolutionary if the will is there. And that, of course, is the problem.

Some of this lack of will can be put down to the unfocused parental anxiety summed up, almost comically now, in Stephen Spender's 1930s poem:

> My parents kept me from children who were rough
> And who threw words like stones and wore torn clothes.

Class, in a word, still. Less forgivably, there is a reluctance to share more widely (and thus to dilute) the undoubted advantages of a private education: smaller classes, better facilities and still, seemingly, a greater chance of getting to university. Beyond that, though, I'm less sure of the long-term social advantages which once would have included the accent, but hardly today. Still, and this is not to discount the many excellent schools in the state sector, a child of average ability is likely to do better at a good public school. Otherwise why would they be sent there? Were reforms to happen I suspect that the ones who would be the least worried by such an amalgamation would be the boys and girls themselves.

It would be unsurprising if you were to discount these forthright opinions as the rantings of an old man. I am now eighty, an age that entitles one to be listened to though not necessarily heeded. I had never been much concerned with politics until the 1980s when they became difficult to avoid. Without ever having been particularly left-wing I am happy never to have trod that dreary safari from left to right which generally comes with age, a trip writers in particular seem drawn to, Amis, Osborne, Larkin, Iris Murdoch all ending up at the spectrum's crusty and clichéd end.

If I haven't, it's partly due to circumstances: there has been so little that has happened to England since the 1980s that I have been happy about or felt able to endorse. One has only had to stand still to become a radical. Though that, too, sounds like an old man talking. Still, I don't regret it and one thing it's always a pleasure to see on television is the occasional programme about ancient and persistent activists, old ladies recounting their early struggles for women's rights or battles for birth control, veteran campers from Greenham Common, cheerful, good-humoured and radical as they ever were, still – though it's not a word I care for – feisty after all these years. That to me is wisdom as disillusion is not.

Another reason why there is a lack of will and a reluctance to meddle – a reluctance, one has to say, that does not protect the state sector where scarcely a week passes without some new initiative being announced – is that private education is seemingly not to be touched. This I think is because the division between state and private education is now taken for granted. Which doesn't mean that it is thought to be fair, only that there is nothing that can or should be done about it.

But if, unlike the *Daily Mail*, one believes that the nation is still generous, magnanimous and above all fair it is hard not to think that we all know that to educate not according to ability but according to the social situation of the parents is both wrong and a waste. Private education is not fair. Those who provide it know it. Those who pay for it know it. Those who have to sacrifice in order to purchase it know it. And those who receive it know it, or should. And if their education ends without it dawning on them then that education has been wasted.

I would also suggest – hesitantly, as I am not adept enough to follow the ethical arguments involved – that if it is not fair then maybe it's not Christian either.

How much our ideas of fairness owe to Christianity I am not sure. Souls after all are equal in the sight of God and thus deserving of what these days is called a level playing field. This is certainly not the case in education and never has been but that doesn't mean we shouldn't go on trying. Isn't it time we made a proper start?

Unlike today's ideologues, whom I would call single-minded if mind came into it at all, I have no fear of the state. I was educated at the expense of the state both at school and university. My father's life was saved by the state as on one occasion was my own. This would be the nanny state, a sneering appellation that gets short shrift with me. Without the state I would not be standing here today. I have no time for the ideology masquerading as pragmatism that would strip the state of its benevolent functions and make them occasions for profit. And why roll back the state only to be rolled over by the corporate entities that have been allowed, nay encouraged, to take its place? I am uneasy when prisons are run for profit or health services either. The rewards of probation and the alleviation of suffering are human profits and nothing to do with balance sheets. And these days no institution is immune. In my last play the Church of England is planning to sell off Winchester Cathedral. 'Why not?' says a character. 'The school is private, why shouldn't the cathedral be also?' And it's a joke but it's no longer far-fetched.

With ideology masquerading as pragmatism, profit is now the sole yardstick against which all our institutions must be measured, a policy that comes not from experience but from assumptions – false assumptions – about human nature, with greed and self-interest taken to be its only reliable attributes. In pursuit of profit, the state and all that goes with it is sold from under us who are its rightful owners and with a frenzy and dedication that call up memories of an earlier iconoclasm.

Which brings me nearly to the end.

One pastime I had as a boy which, thanks to my partner, I resumed in middle age was looking at old churches, 'ruin-bibbing' Larkin dismissively called it though we perhaps have a little more expertise than Larkin disingenuously claimed he had. I do know what rood lofts were, for instance, though, like Larkin, I'm not always able to date a roof. The charm of most medieval churches consists in what history has left, and one learns to delight in little, the dregs of history: a few fifteenth-century bench ends, an alabaster tomb chest or, where glass is concerned, just the leavings of bigotry, with ideology weakening when it came to out-of-reach tracery – the hammer too heavy, the ladder too short – so that only fragments survive, a cluster of crockets and towers maybe, the glimpse of a golden city with a devil leering down.

In my bleaker moments these shards of history seem to me emblematic obviously of what has happened to England in the past but also a reminder and a warning of what in other respects is continuing to happen in the present, with the fabric of the state and the welfare state in particular stealthily dismantled as once the fabric of churches more rudely was, sold off, farmed out; another Dissolution, with profit taking precedence over any other consideration, and the perpetrators today as locked into their ideology and convinced of their own rightness as any of the devout louts who four and five hundred years ago stove in the windows and scratched out the faces of the saints as a passport to heaven.

I end with the last few lines of my first play, *Forty Years On*. It's set in a school with the headmaster on the verge of retirement and is what nowadays is called a play for England. It ends with the boys and staff singing the doxology 'All Creatures that on Earth Do Dwell', with before it, this advertisement for England:

> To let. A valuable site at the crossroads of the world.
> At present on offer to corporate clients. Outlying portions

of the estate already disposed of to sitting tenants. Of
some historical and period interest. Some alterations and
improvements necessary.

First published in the *London Review of Books*, 19 June 2014.

*

*Nervous about the length of my sermon and feeling also that its tone
might be too political for its surroundings, I edited it – redacted would be
the modish word – some of it, I remember, as I was actually delivering it.
I include these excised sections here.*

Perhaps one of the reasons why the chaplain has invited me here this
morning namely at eighty is to make a report on my life.

'Pass it on,' says the dead Hector at the end of *The History Boys*.
'Pass it on.'

But pass what on?

I don't actually seem to have much luggage and while I'd quite like
this to consist of decent old-fashioned leather suitcases such as one
sees nowadays in vintage shops I fear it's just an ancient backpack
and, more shamingly, a Tesco plastic bag, hardly fitting receptacles
for one's lessons from life . . . or maybe they are.

. . . Today's ideology masquerades as pragmatism with that pragmatism reduced to the simplistic assumption that the basis of
human nature is self-interest, a view which discounts philanthropy,
discredits altruism, with the only motive deserving of trust self-
promotion and self-advancement.

This so-called pragmatism is wicked and it is doubly so because it
is held up as being both realistic and a virtue. Whereas it is shallow,
shabby and all too often callous.

I also intended to quote a passage from an earlier piece, Hymn:

I am something of a parenthetical Anglican, my devotional brackets opening with my confirmation and the piety of adolescence which I later lost and the brackets closing, I hope not quite yet, with a continuing affection for the Church of England.

There are different ways of being English. Churches don't come into it much these days but that they're so often unregarded for me augments their appeal. Since I seldom attend a service this could be thought hypocrisy. But that's not un-English too.

Writing about hymns I have described a not especially remarkable church at Hubberholme in North Yorkshire. Unique in the West Riding its medieval rood loft survives and on a pillar, hung slightly askew is the roll of honour of the men of the parish who died in the First War and, unusually for England, their photographs. On another pillar is a plaque to say that J. B. Priestley had his ashes scattered in the churchyard.

'The rood, the roll of honour, the ashes of a writer . . . the remnants of history, the random trig points of time. I have never found it easy to belong. So much about England repels. Hymns help. They blur. And here among the tombs and tablets and vases of dead flowers and lists of the fallen it is less hard to feel, at least, tacked on to church and country.'

The History Boys, Film Diary

Having run for more than two years at the National Theatre and on Broadway The History Boys *was filmed in the summer of 2005.*

14 July 2005. Nick Hytner picks me up at 8.45 and by a roundabout route the bombed bus in Tavistock Place has made necessary, we go painfully through the traffic-choked streets down to the National and the first reading of the film script of *The History Boys*.

As always I'm startled by the size of the crew and the number of people in attendance, the beginning of a film like the conferences planning the Normandy landings. It's lovely to see all the cast again, though, and to hear the script read, what new jokes there are going down well. I read in for Frances de la Tour who's away on holiday and there's some talk of my playing a don in one of the Oxford scenes. But not if I can help it.

17 July. Yesterday to Broughton Castle where we filmed part of *The Madness of King George*. We have our sandwiches on the edge of a field of flax scattered with poppies, the earth of the cart track so rich and red the scene seems almost absurdly rural. So, too, does Broughton itself and though there are quite a few visitors, it's not besieged as it was when I first saw it ten years ago by all the trunks and tents and paraphernalia of a film crew.

The lady of the house, Marietta Say, is helping to show people around. She's cheerful and downright as ever, and when I tell her I'm about to start another film with Nicholas Hytner she says that though he's very clever as a director she secretly prefers directors who are less accomplished as they are more likely to overrun, in which case the estate will get more money.

There are good unseen bits in this lovely house, like a plain room at the top of a staircase tower where the campaign against Charles I is said to have been plotted and which gives onto the leads where one can walk, a privilege not accorded in any other country house that I've come across.

I am writing this up at a desk in a room at Watford Boys' Grammar School, which is dressed as Mrs Lintott's classroom for the filming of *The History Boys* which started this morning.

I feel a bit lost, as so often when filming, where the author has no ordained place or prescribed function and with nothing useful to do except gossip and make myself amiable; I succumb all too readily to the lure of conviviality and sociability's powerful drug and just sit around and watch. Our boys, with make-up, look satisfyingly younger than their real Watford Grammar School counterparts who are themselves part of 'directed action' and on cue play loudly (and quite violently) on the field outside.

I come away at three o'clock, my only contribution today to give Stephen Campbell Moore the correct pronunciation of prepuce.

21 July. A touch of writer's paranoia today. The trickiest and in some ways the most shocking scene in the play is the sixth-former Dakin's virtual seduction of Irwin, the young supply teacher. It's a difficult scene to play because Irwin, warned by the older schoolmaster, Hector, not to make a fool of himself over the boy, resists Dakin's (very specific) advances throughout the scene until he suddenly caves in and they fix up a date.

Why does he cave in? Partly because Dakin is, literally, irresistible: apart from being good-looking his will is much stronger than Irwin's and where sex is concerned he has all the know-how. On stage, though it was always a gripping scene, it wasn't always plain what prompted Irwin's surrender and so in the film script I have given this a physical trigger and at the point where Irwin is wavering I make Dakin touch him.

Chatting to Stephen Campbell Moore (Irwin) and Dominic Cooper (Dakin) yesterday I discover that having rehearsed the scene they are to do no touching. Normally Nick H. would tell me of any departure from the script and since it's seldom we disagree there's no problem. This time, though, he hasn't and I wonder if it's because he knows I feel quite strongly about it. At any rate it will have to be talked through before the scene is shot.

Waiting for my car to pick me up this morning I rehearse what I need to say about the scene, the only one in the play in which any-one comes even close to getting their heart's desire so that Dakin's hand on Irwin's chest or his belly as I've actually written it, is highly charged. The car is late and I know the scene will have been set up by now and perhaps even be shooting. I telephone to find no car has been ordered and one won't be free for half an hour. I sit there waiting, wondering if this is deliberate and a way of forestalling any objections I might have and avoiding the inevitable confrontation.

When I eventually get to the set they have indeed rehearsed the scene and done at least one take (with no touching). I say that some sort of physical contact seems to me essential, but the actors can't make it work though I still think that what I've suggested, Dakin's finger idly sliding inside Irwin's shirt would do it. What also works, though, is a much longer pause before Irwin surrenders and this, finally, is what we settle for . . . though whether the pause will survive in the editing I'm not sure.

Of course there has been no plot to keep me off the set while the scene is shot and I laugh about it afterwards. But I can think of other playwrights who would need more reassurance on that point than I do, and who would make more of a fuss about any divergence from what they've written.

The other lurking fear I have about scenes like this – and which ties in with Posner's view in the play – is that where sex is con-cerned, directors think I'm not that sort of writer (just as Posner is thought not that sort of boy) and so don't entirely trust what

I've written. It's one of the reasons I took to writing the occasional short story because in that form I could express myself without let or hindrance.

(It's interesting though, that when I later watch the dress rehearsal of the second cast doing the stage version I have exactly the same feeling about the scene, namely that it needs some sort of touch. Maybe that's what the audience is feeling also and it not happening is one reason why the scene works.)

Because of the shot Sam Anderson has to move his desk. 'Don't tell me. It's black boys to the back again.'

We eat our lunch on picnic tables outside the classroom in a huge tearing wind that topples the glasses and snatches away the plates. The school proper broke up at noon and the vast playing field is deserted, the high suburban trees roaring in the wind. I wander across the empty grass feeling as once I did fifty and more years ago when I was in my own last days at school. Meanwhile our boys play football against the playground wall with an openness and abandon I have never managed in all my life.

23 July. Though I knew there would not be time in the film to see the home lives of the boys I was hoping we would be able to include a brief collage of their various parents.

Lockwood, I thought, would come from a poor background; his mother is a single parent and while wanting him to go on to university doesn't know how it is to be paid for. Thus he is seen at the start of the film working in the holidays as a milkman; he goes up for the scholarship interview in his trainers and ends up enlisting in the army as this will pay for him to go to Oxford.

Whereas we never see Mrs Lockwood, we do get glimpses of some of the other parents, a few of whom were going to have a line or two. Mrs Scripps for instance, who is uncomfortable with her son's piety. ('I said to him, "Jesus is such a bad role model. You'd be better off with somebody like Paul McCartney."')

Mrs Dakin: He's full of this new master. Sexual intercourse seems to have taken a back seat.

And Mrs Crowther: He's a lovely-looking lad. Get him in a bathing costume and he'd walk it. And these posh places, black isn't necessarily a handicap. It can be a plus.

Mr Timms: (*waking up*) I went through Oxford once. Shocking traffic.

Significantly the only parents wholeheartedly in favour of their son going on to Oxford or Cambridge are the Asian Mr and Mrs Akhtar, though even there, not without reservations.

Mr Akhtar: I gather it is the centre court of English ideas.

Mrs A.: But we do not want a Mr Smart Arse.

Mr A.: Oh no, my love.

Mrs A.: We've got one of those already.

These scenes survived until the penultimate rewrite when they had to be cut on grounds of length. We get occasional glimpses (the Akhtars turning up in force for the posting of the A level results), but the film like the play is about school and the outside world scarcely figures.

24 July. Seeing Hector off on the bike for what turns out to be his last ride, the boys are not in school uniform but in their own clothes. It's no fault of the designer but it's curious how this blurs their characters. In school uniform, white shirts and ties, blazers and dark trousers, each character is clearly defined. Put into civvies they lose their edge and some of their attraction. James Corden in sweater and trousers looks, so he says, like White Van Man. Dominic, in white T-shirt and black leather jacket looks straight out of a sixties Cliff Richard movie and Posner, in sports coat and corduroys, seems to have been dressed like me . . . which I don't mind, though I'm not sure it suits him or his character.

What is certain is that all of them look better and more interesting in uniform than in their own clothes.

I've come across this once or twice before with orchestras for instance (better in evening dress) and with waiters. The staff of the Odeon in New York were dashing and aloof in their restaurant rig but catch them going home at two in the morning and they had shrunk to the drab, the camp and the ordinary creatures the uniform disguised.

28 July. Watch the first love scene between Dakin and Fiona, the Headmaster's secretary, shot in a suburban house just up the road from school. It is not especially intimate with no nudity at this stage, though I'd expected Dakin's trousers to be open as, since they're lying on the bed and it's quite heavy snogging, they presumably would be. However I don't suggest it as it seems prurient.

Later we film the second scene when Dakin, fully clothed, is talking about Irwin while Fiona waits for him to come to bed. This configuration came to me at a Sickert exhibition in the Abbot Hall Gallery in Kendal where there was a painting from the Camden Town murder series in which a clothed and threatening man, possibly a client, stands by the bed of a woman whom he is about to fuck or kill, or both.

Though hardly so dramatic our scene takes a long time to film but only because the sound of Dakin's falling trousers keeps obscuring the lines. I suggest to John Midgley on sound that Dominic be asked to hold the line until he's got his trousers off but John, who has obviously had some unfortunate experiences with actors, thinks this will only cause more problems. So we go to thirteen takes until the trousers just happen to come down before the line is said, the gate is checked and we go on to a scene on the football pitch. All rather wasted because the scene is eventually cut and with it the two lines which I like as, in half a dozen words, they wholly explain Dakin's relation to Irwin.

Dakin: I want him to rate me.

Fiona: Rape you?

Dakin: Rate. *Rate.*

1 August. A change of location. We film the first of Hector's class-room scenes at Watford Girls' Grammar School, an older estab-lishment than the boys' equivalent and one more appropriate to the piece. There are parquet floors not unlike the corridors of my own school, Leeds Modern, fifty years ago; the walls are lined with team photographs dating back to the 1920s and it's such a pleasing-ly old-fashioned place I imagine our set dressers must have been at work. In fact it's all the genuine article with some of the fixtures and fittings (the brass and Bakelite door handles for instance) so antique as to make it surprising they have survived.

2 August. Film the French class. Always the funniest scene in the theatre, it's hard to transfer its mischief to film. On stage one of the best moments is the arrival of Irwin and the Headmaster in the middle of Hector's class acting out a scene in a brothel with Dakin standing there in his shirt tails. The audience sees Hector and Irwin waiting to come in, while at the same time not being sure this is what they are meant to see. It gives them a stolen foretaste of what is to come and they begin laughing even before the Head-master has made his entrance. On film this can to some extent be achieved by cutting to the Headmaster and Irwin coming down the corridor, but what's lost is the furtive sneak preview sense you get on stage.

The days get hotter and a species of air conditioning is rigged up consisting of a noisy pump connected to a long coiling silver-foil-covered pipe, the opening of which is so huge it looks likely to suck in the unwary.

Sam Anderson is probably the handsomest and the most physical-ly perfect of all the boys and also the quietest, though without being the least bit shy or immune from the general piss taking. He came up to me today with a little screw he had found. 'Alan. Are your hips all right?'

3 August. A difficult day. We are filming a long corridor scene in which Mrs Lintott comes up the stairs and encounters Irwin with whom she stops to chat about Hector. Boys run up the stairs, who she absent-mindedly slows down (a hand on the shoulder, a touch on the head . . . all things teachers are not supposed to do nowadays) and they walk on together, the scene ending at the door of Hector's classroom with Mrs Lintott denouncing the Headmaster.

'Twat, twat, twat,' she says, the last 'twat' picked up by Timms (James Corden) who, taking it to refer to him, mumbles, 'Yes Miss,' and looks suitably sheepish.

With so many elements involved the shot takes most of the morning. Frances de la T. and Stephen C. M. sometimes get to the door too soon, the passing schoolboys are too animated or sometimes not animated enough. Made to troop up and down the corridor time and time again, they end up looking as grim as the creatures in Doré's version of a prison yard.

Another difficulty is that today Archie Powell and his camera crew are here to pick up shots for my *South Bank Show*. Someone sensible and less self-conscious than I am would manufacture an opportunity to catch me in conversation with Nick H. over some point arising out of the shot. But nothing occurs so half the time they have nothing to film, or nothing to film involving me anyway.

Later on the boys are playing football and, the cameras nowhere in sight, I wander round the field, glad to be outside. By the time, though, I've got to the border of trees, the camera has materialised from nowhere, filming the football and me lonely as a cloud-ing in the background. And that will, I fear, be how the story will be told . . . solitary ageing author a spectator at the games of the young.

4 August. Today we film the heart of the play, the scene between Hector and Posner in which the boy recites Hardy's 'Drummer Hodge' and Hector talks about the poem. Richard Griffiths and Sam B. rehearse the scene for the benefit of Andrew Dunn and the camera crew but so quietly I can scarcely hear what they are saying. It is shorter than on the stage (all the references to Larkin, for instance, omitted) but uncut are the lines, 'The best moments in reading are when you come across something – a thought, a feeling, a way of looking at things – which you had thought special and particular to you. Now here it is, set down by someone else, a person you have never met, someone even who is long dead. And it is as if a hand has come out and taken yours.'

This speech I only put in as an afterthought as I'd had it written for nearly thirty years, first delivering it one December night in 1977 as part of the radio programme *With Great Pleasure*. It was recorded at a parish hall somewhere in the depths of Somerset on a very foggy night and the audience so small that canned applause had to be added at the editing.

9 August. What music we should use is decided initially by Nick H. reading out a list of songs for the boys to approve. The Smiths they like (whom at least I have heard of) and anything by Kate Bush; any songs that have been in *Billy Elliot* are automatically ruled out and Madness too (whom I also like). But whereas most of the songs I have never heard of, the boys have only to hear the title before they can reel off the words with an accompanying routine as it's the music they've grown up with.

This morning *Vogue* comes to take a photograph of the cast and they pose, unnaturally still and stern with one shot on their own, another with Frances de la Tour and a final one with me.

I first had my photograph in *Vogue* in 1960 when Peter Cook, Jonathan Miller, Dudley Moore and I were put in a Daimler (the first I had ever been in) and taken out to Acton where we were pictured with our coat collars up against a power station in Park Royal . . . a fashionably gritty photograph that made us look more like a pop group than young men putting on a revue.

No better at having my picture taken now than I was then, and never having learned to put it on (as the boys do as a matter of course), instead I still endeavour to look like myself, whatever that is. Somehow sincere, I suppose.

As I sit outside the Arts block writing this the school groundsman brings me a bowl of mulberries from a two-hundred-year-old tree in the garden.

11 August. The car comes early so I'm in time to see Dom and Jamie doing the corridor scene in which Jamie tells Dom that just because he's grateful to Irwin for getting him through the examination doesn't mean he should offer Irwin unfettered access to his dick. Jamie is peaking too soon in the sequence 'give him a subscription to the *Spectator* or a box of Black Magic', both over-emphasised, with the dick a bit of an anticlimax. So I'm able to point this out and feel, as so seldom, that I've been of some use.

15 August. Hector's memorial service with the boys singing 'Bye Bye Blackbird' against a screen showing Hector at various stages of his life. I first saw this scene on stage at the play's dress rehearsal when the conjunction of the song and the (unexpected) photographs brought me close to tears and whenever I saw it during the run it retained its pathos. On screen, though, this may be hard to recapture as it must depend on when the pictures of the young Hector are seen or cut to.

The memorial service is hard to shoot not least because the school hall is filled with schoolboy extras, who chatter and are soon bored and though Nick H. does his best to damp them down the boys' natural exuberance, inappropriate in the circumstances, keeps breaking through.

The scene is tricky, too, in that it involves talking to the camera. This is easily done on the stage but much harder to bring off on film: sometimes it works, sometimes not, though without it always being obvious why. Nick shoots an alternative version in which most of the talking to camera (and the information thus conveyed) is done as dialogue and this seems to work better.

Still it's a lengthy job and as we do more and more takes the schoolboys, not understanding why they are having to do it again, start groaning when another take is announced and applauding when it's finished. The PAs are powerless to control them and what we need, I suppose, is a figure like that of the Headmaster in the film who can scare the shit out of them.

16 August. The actors are normally picked up first thing by car and taken out to Watford and then, when we have finished shooting, taken home. It's easy enough in a morning but the journey home can be much slower and so some of them have taken to going by train, as I do, Watford to Euston only a twenty-minute ride.

Sacha Dhawan is an Asian actor from Manchester and Sam Anderson from London is of mixed race. Coming home together this last week they were both stopped and searched at Euston. Quite cool about it they also found it funny, though Sacha says that having to spread and be searched as commuters hurried by was a bit shy-making. Nor did the police seem to know what they were looking for. Sacha writes poetry and has kept a diary of the filming, and having been told that they were actors, the police went through his diary and questioned them about the film though less in the interests of counter-terrorism, Sacha felt, than as readers of *Hello* magazine.

Today I travelled to Euston with Sacha, rather hoping he would be stopped again so that I could see the process at first hand. But for the first time in a fortnight there were no policemen at the station.

On another day (and not with Sacha, fortunately) I overhear a genial looking middle-aged workman, a builder possibly, chatting on his mobile. 'No, we're moving, hadn't you heard? Well, we're getting outnumbered where we are, know what I mean?'

17 August. A scene in the school gymnasium, the girls' gymnasium not the boys', as, like the rest of the school, it's more old-fashioned, so much so that even the equipment, 'the apparatus' as it was always called, has scarcely changed since I was a boy. It's like revisiting the chamber in which one was tortured years ago: here are the long, brightly varnished forms, the ropes, the wall bars, the tiered box . . . always a bad moment when another tier was added . . . against the unyielding side of which I invariably thumped my crotch.

But of course it's also toys, and before and between takes the boys swing on the ropes and vault over the horse though they can't do what the script actually requires them to do, namely to hang upside down on the wall bars. So PE master Adrian Scarborough's line, 'They won't want you at Oxford University if you can't hang upside down on the wall bars,' has to be cut. The boys get some teen-movie mileage out of being in a girls' shower room, the changing rooms to me as a boy as much a place of torment as the gym itself.

The gym at my school was the province of an oldish master, Mr King, not quite a thorough-going sadist (he played the viola in the school orchestra) but an expert at catching you on the side of the head with a well-aimed gym shoe. Early in 1952 the rumour went round that Mr King had died very suddenly. Hope turned to exultation when the whole school was summoned to an extraordinary afternoon assembly. However hearts sank when there, large as life, at his music stand and sawing away at the National Anthem was Mr King. Whereupon the headmaster stood up to announce the death not of Mr King but, far less excitingly, of the King himself. I suppose we were sorry but George VI was always a shadowy figure and not much loved, though this at least could be said for His Majesty: he wasn't wont to catch you unexpectedly on the side of the head with a well-aimed gym shoe.

18 August. En route through Wembley yesterday to the location at Harrow we kept passing schools and colleges with the pupils standing about waiting, or, in one case, just having received their A level results. Today we film the same scene for our own school, Cutlers' Grammar School, Sheffield with the boys crowding round the noticeboard and exulting in their success.

No such scene occurred in my youth as the results came by post and were slightly mysterious when they did. Whereas I had done well in the earlier exam, School Certificate, in Higher School Certificate, the equivalent of A levels, I did well enough in History but indifferently in English and not at all well in Latin. They were just good enough, though, to get me a scholarship from Leeds City Council though not a State scholarship which was thought to be superior. There was none of the over-excitement that attends the posting of such results these days as it was easier to get to university (and to be paid for there), and so wasn't made such a fuss of as nowadays (not that there isn't anything that is not made a fuss of nowadays). I can't imagine my fellow sixth-formers behaving like ours do on film, embracing one another, jumping on each other's backs in the manner of goal-scoring footballers.

With us a gloomy satisfaction was more the order of the day; this was one examination, but there were going to be others and more hurdles to come. And before all that the worst hurdle of all, the army.

And, of course, what nobody tells you, then or now, is that it won't matter. Nobody has ever asked me what my results were at school or since. I have never had to say what class of degree I got or even where I was educated. Did anybody go to university on the unit? Nick apart, I have no idea. But what examinations did procure was time. The vague promissory capabilities of A levels and degrees count for very little except that they give you a breathing space. Life can be put off.

19 August. Sacha Dhawan has been auditioning for one of the films being made about 9/11. He does the speech he's been given very well only then the director says, 'Now do it in Arabic.' Sacha is English, born and bred in Manchester, and can no more speak Arabic than he can Serbo-Croat. He points this out whereupon an Arab speaker is procured whom Sacha is supposed to imitate. He does his best but ends up just making Arabic-type noises at which the director professes himself well satisfied. Luvvies nothing: actors are both saints and heroes.

22 August. When I ask myself why the filming has been so easy and good-tempered I think, well that's how the whole play has been, right from the start. This is partly thanks to Nick H.'s temperament (or lack of it) and also to the fact that we get on well.

A film, though, is different. Schedules these days are horrendously tight, with an enormous amount crammed into each day. So that even when, as with us, lighting is kept to a minimum we're always working against the clock.

That nobody feels this particularly or gets obviously ratty is, I suspect, more down to the cameraman, Andrew Dunn, than one realises. He's quiet, shy and self-effacing and looks like a kindlier Wittgenstein. Good temper starts with him and spreads through the crew. I don't think I've ever worked on an easier, more relaxed film than this . . . and obviously there are other factors (the cast knowing the play so well, for a start) . . . but Andrew is at the centre of it.

24 August. Fountains Abbey. Been here before, I keep thinking, though not just about Fountains which I've known all my life. No, it's the filming that is the same. I first filmed here in 1972 with Stephen Frears when we were making *A Day Out*. Today we set up camp with our rugs and chairs on the same spot and at one point we are waiting for the sun for a shot identical with one we framed all of thirty years ago.

I show Sam Barnett and Russell Tovey and Justine from costumes the echo under the cliff at the east end of the nave, something I put in the script of *A Day Out* and had David Waller testing out. That was the first film I ever did. Now I'm back at Fountains and maybe this will be my last film. Still not a bad place to start and not a bad place to finish either. This time, though, we can shoot in the nave which we couldn't then as Abbot Huby's tower was covered in scaffolding. 'Great production values,' someone says, and so they are, particularly when we get the occasional flash of late sunshine. The film ends with Hector saying his 'Pass the parcel' speech as they all line up on the high altar for a class photograph.

1 November. In the earliest draft of *The History Boys*, which we for a time rehearsed, one of the many quotations Hector bandied about (cut when it was slimmed down) was from Jowett, the nineteenth-century Master of Balliol.

'We have sought the truth, and sometimes perhaps we have found it. But have we had any *fun*?'

Well, one thing that can be said about the play and the film is, yes, we have had fun, and lots of it.

Introduction to *The Habit of Art*

By the time Auden came to live in the Brewhouse, a cottage in the grounds of Christ Church, in 1972, I had long since left Oxford, and in any case would never have had the nerve to speak to him. I'd first heard his voice in Exeter College hall some time in 1955. The lower end of the scholars' table where I was sitting was only a yard or two from High Table where the dons dined and, hearing those harsh, quacking tones without knowing whose they were, I said to my neighbour that it sounded like the voice of the devil. Someone better informed put me right. It was Auden, at that time still with blondish hair and the face yet to go under the harrow.

I don't think I'd read much of his poetry or would have understood it if I had, but when Auden gave his inaugural lecture as Professor of Poetry the following year I dutifully went along, knowing, though not quite why, that he was some sort of celebrity. At that time I still harboured thoughts of becoming a Writer (and I thought of it in capital letters), so when Auden outlined what he took to be the prerequisites of a literary life, or at any rate a life devoted to poetry, I was properly dismayed. Besides favourite books, essential seemed to be an ideal landscape (Leeds?), a knowledge of metre and scansion, and (this was the clincher) a passion for the Icelandic sagas. If writing meant passing this kind of kit inspection, I'd better forget it. What Auden was saying (and he said it pretty regularly) was, 'All do as I do,' which is what unhelpful writers often say when asked about their profession, though few with such seeming conviction and authority as the newly inaugurated Professor of Poetry.

He used to hold court in the Cadena, but it wasn't a café I cared for. There were undergraduates I knew at whom Auden made passes, though I was still young and innocent enough to find a pass as remarkable as the person making it.

When he died in 1973 his death seemed to me less a loss to poetry – the poetry was largely over – than a loss to knowledge. Auden was a library in himself and now all this store – the reading, the categories, the associations – had gone down with that great listing clay-coloured hulk. And though much of what he knew he had written down and published, either as lectures or in reviews, there was always more: the flurry of memoirs and reminiscences of the poet and his talk that began almost immediately on his death, not only a testament to his life but an attempt to salvage some of the wisdom he had discarded in conversation – and some of the unwisdom, too.

In *The Hunting of the Snark*, Lewis Carroll, a Christ Church don, wrote: 'What I tell you three times is true.' With Auden, also at Christ Church, it was the opposite. What Auden said three times you would begin to doubt, and when he'd said it a dozen times nobody cared anyway. Auden somewhere makes the distinction between being boring and being a bore. He was never boring – he was too extraordinary for that – but by the time he came back to live in Oxford he had become a bore. His discourse was persistently pedagogic; he was never not teaching and/or showing off how much he knew, always able to make a long arm and reach for references unavailable to his less well-read hearers. As he got towards the end of his life his conversation and his pedagogy got more and more repetitive, which must have been a particular disappointment to his colleagues at Christ Church where, when he had been briefly resident in the past, he had been an enlivening member of the common room. Now he was just infuriating.

What they had been hoping for was, understandably, some form of enlightenment and entertainment. This was made plain early on in *The Habit of Art*, in a speech by the Dean which had to be cut, as favourite bits of my scripts often are:

The Brewhouse is not a garret, quite – say sheltered accommodation rather. A granny flat. But mark this. If the college is minded to provide this accommodation it's for nothing so vulgar as a poet in residence. This isn't Keele, still less is it East Anglia. No. We see it as providing a niche – young persons nowadays might even call it a pad – for one of our most renowned graduates. If it is a touch spartan, blame the Bursar, but then the point of Parnassus was never the upholstery. Besides, the hope is that undergraduates will find their way up the stairs to sit not in the chairs but at these famous feet. But remember, we are not asking the great man to do. His doing after all is mostly done. No. We are asking him to be. Count the poet's presence here as one of those extra-curricular plums that only Oxford has to offer. Fame in the flesh can be a part of education and in the person of this most celebrated poet the word is made flesh and dwells among us, full of grace and truth.

But to everyone's disappointment – the college, the students, Auden himself – it didn't turn out like that. But say it had been Larkin at the same stage of his life – he wasn't much fun either at the finish.

In 1972, when Auden arrived in Oxford, Britten was well advanced in the writing of *Death in Venice*, his last opera. Neither poet nor composer was in good health, with Auden six years older than Britten. I never met or even saw Britten, but find I wrote about him in my diary in June 2006:

> *16 June.* Having seen the TV programme on which it was based, I've been reading *Britten's Children* by John Bridcut. Glamorous though he must have been and a superb teacher, I find Britten a difficult man to like. He had his favourites, children and adults, but both Britten and Pears were notorious for cutting people out of their lives (Eric Crozier is mentioned here, and Charles Mackerras), friends and acquaintances suddenly turned into living corpses if they overstepped the mark. A joke would do it,

and though Britten seems to have had plenty of childish jokes with his boy singers, his sense of humour isn't much in evidence elsewhere. And it was not merely adults that were cut off. A boy whose voice suddenly broke could find himself no longer invited to the Red House or part of the group – a fate which the boys Bridcut quotes here seem to have taken philosophically but which would seem potentially far more damaging to a child's psychology than too much attention. One thinks, too, of the boys who were not part of the charmed circle. There were presumably fat boys and ugly boys or just plain dull boys who could, nevertheless, sing like angels. What of them?

Britten and Peter Pears came disastrously to *Beyond the Fringe* some time in 1961. Included in the show was a parody of Britten written by Dudley Moore, in which he sang and accompanied himself in 'Little Miss Muffet' done in a Pears-and-Britten-like way. I'm not sure that this in itself would have caused offence: it shouldn't have as, like all successful parodies, there was a good deal of affection in it and it was funny in its own right. But Dudley (who may have known them slightly and certainly had met them) unthinkingly entitled the piece 'Little Miss Britten'. Now Dudley was not malicious nor had he any reason to mock their homosexuality, of which indeed he may have been unaware (I don't think I knew of it at the time). But with the offending title printed in the programme, they were reported to be deeply upset and Dudley went into outer darkness as probably did the rest of us.

There's a story told in Tony Palmer's superb film about Britten, *A Time There Was*, of how when Kathleen Ferrier was working with the composer on *The Rape of Lucretia* there was quite a serious quarrel (though not with her). Britten tells the story against himself of how Ferrier took him on one side and said: 'Oh Ben. Do try and be nice.' And he says, slightly surprised: 'And it worked.' Both Britten and

Auden's works were in better taste than their lives. 'Real artists are not nice people,' Auden wrote. 'All their best feelings go into their work and life has the residue.'

The Habit of Art was not easy to write, though its form is quite simple, because so much information had to be passed over to the audience about Auden and his life and about Britten and his and about their earlier association. Thinking of *Beyond the Fringe*, now nearly half a century ago, makes me realise how I have projected onto Britten particularly some of the feelings I had when I was a young man, not much older than he was and thrust into collaboration (which was also competition) with colleagues every bit as daunting as Auden. Recalling their early collaborations (in another passage from the play since cut), Britten remembers his slightly desperate attempts to keep up with Auden and make a contribution besides the musical one:

> In those days I used to bring along a few carefully worked out notions I'd had for the film shots and sequences, but it was no good. Wystan, you see, could never admit that I'd thought of anything first.
>
> 'Oh yes,' he'd say, as if I was just reminding him of something he'd thought of earlier. You could never tell Wystan anything, just remind him of it.
>
> Either that or he'd scamper off with your idea and make it his own . . . and not merely an idea. A whole country.
>
> Wystan was the first person to go to Iceland, did you know that? And Christopher Columbus didn't discover America. Wystan did.

While this seems to me a true assessment of Britten's early relationship with Auden, it also chimes with my experiences in 1960. So, though in some ways I find Britten unsympathetic he, much more than Auden, is the character I identify with.

When I started writing the play I made much use of the biographies of both Auden and Britten written by Humphrey Carpenter and both are models of their kind. Indeed I was consulting his books so much that eventually Carpenter found his way into the play. His widow, Mari Prichard, was more than helpful over this, though feeling – and I'm sure rightly – that I hadn't done justice to him as a biographer or as a personality. I had had the same problem in *The Madness of George III* (1991) when trying to fit in another character who was larger than life, namely Charles James Fox. To have given him his proper due would have meant him taking over the play. And so it is with Humphrey Carpenter, my only excuse being that he would have been the first to understand this and to be unsentimental about it. When he turned up on the stage he tended to hang about and act as commentator, often speaking directly to the audience. This was useful as he could explain points of fact and saved the main characters from telling each other stuff both of them knew already but the audience didn't. Even so, there was still a good deal of explaining left to be done. It's a perennial problem for dramatists and one which Ibsen, for instance, never satisfactorily solved, or, so far as I can see, ever tried to.

Towards the end of the play Carpenter mildly reproves Auden and Britten for being so concerned about their reputations, when their audience, Auden's readers, Britten's hearers, are anxious simply to draw a line under them both. They don't want more poetry; they don't want more music; they want – as they say nowadays – closure. Guilty at occasionally entertaining such thoughts myself à propos Updike's relentless output, for instance, I was reassured to find myself not alone in feeling like this. On the death of Crabbe, Lord Melbourne wrote: 'I am always glad when one of those fellows dies for then I know I have the whole of him on my shelf.' Which is, of course, the cue for biography.

This is the fifth play on which Nicholas Hytner and I have collaborated, not counting two films. Asked, as one inevitably is in Question and Answer sessions, what this collaboration consists in,

I can describe it in general terms: discussion on various drafts of the script, for instance, decisions on casting and suchlike, but I can seldom be satisfyingly precise and nor can he. There are no rows or even arguments; neither of us, that I remember, ever sulks. It's so amicable that directors or authors of a more abrasive or histrionic turn of mind might think that the creative process was being short-changed. However, believers in creative conflict will be reassured to hear that this play has been different.

If Ibsen couldn't explain things it's not surprising that I found it hard, so, whereas Nicholas Hytner had liked the first draft, he was less keen on the second, the script returned neatly annotated with remarks like 'Do we need to know this?', 'Too much information' and 'Haven't we had this already?'

At this point (though not as a result), in April 2008 I had to go into hospital. This knocked me back a bit and the last thing I wanted to be worrying about was the play. I therefore asked for it to be taken out of the National Theatre schedule (it had been slated for October 2008) until further notice. When I took it up again I found the problems to do with too much information had not gone away, but it occurred to me that the business of conveying the facts could be largely solved if a frame were put round the play by setting it in a rehearsal room. Queries about the text and any objections to it could then be put in the mouths of the actors who (along with the audience) could have their questions answered in the course of the rehearsal.

There was an unexpected bonus to this in that when, as happened on the next couple of drafts, Nicholas Hytner raised objections, these queries, too, could just be passed on to the actors. 'Do we need this?' N.H. would write in the margin. And on the next draft he would find 'Do we need this?' (his own query) given to the actor. At one point he suggested cutting a pretty tortuous section on Auden's (to me) impenetrable poem *The Sea and the Mirror*. We had a discussion about it and I duly cut it but then introduced the author as a character complaining about the cut. I found all this quite enjoyable, but it happened so often I began to feel the director almost deserved an author's credit.

Less of this, more of that, the director is in the first instance an editor and so it is with Nicholas Hytner and myself. He likes action more than he does discussion so it's often the more reflective passages that get cut, though they're not always lost. Sometimes they end up in the introduction or, greatly condensed, I manage to smuggle them back into the text – even though this may have to wait until another play comes along: the fractured speech about biography, for instance, that begins the play was actually a casualty from *Kafka's Dick*, written more than twenty years ago. Still, it's a pragmatic process and I'm thankful never to have reached that eminence which would endow every sentence I write with significance and make it untouchable.

There is some talk in the play about Auden's propensity to edit his poems, with his older self censoring what in his younger self he found dishonest or embarrassing. I think he was mistaken, but provided the original survives, which it does both in print and in his readers' heads, it doesn't seem to me to matter much, and just gives editors and bibliophiles something to talk about. To censor one's work is tempting, though. While I was writing *The Habit of Art* an earlier play of mine, *Enjoy* (1980), was revived. At its first outing it wasn't well received, and were I writing it today there are things I wouldn't include and dialogue I would do differently. That I didn't cut it or alter it I would like to think was from reading about Auden falling into a similar time trap. But if I left the play as it was, it was just through laziness and a feeling that by this time the director and the cast probably knew more about it than I did.

The stylistic oddities in *The Habit of Art* – rhyming furniture, neighbourly wrinkles, and words and music comparing notes – may just be an attempt to smuggle something not altogether factual past the literalist probation officer who's had me in his charge for longer than I like to think and who I would have hoped might have retired by now. Or it may be that whatever oddities there are come under

Edward Said's category of Late Style. Feeling I'd scarcely arrived at a style, I now find I'm near the end of it. I'm not quite sure what Late Style means except that it's some sort of licence, a permit for ageing practitioners to kick their heels up. I don't always need that and I'm often mildly surprised when something I've included in a script almost as a joke gets treated in production as seriously as the rest. 'Gracie Fields?' I jotted in the margin of *The History Boys* (2004) and the next thing I knew they were rehearsing 'Sing as We Go'.

The probation officer or the internal censor one is always trying to outflank chimes with Britten's plea on behalf of constraint which, while true to his character, is also not unsympathetic to mine. With Britten, censorship was home-grown, his personal policeman never off duty. Stage censorship itself was abolished in 1968, the year of my first play, so I've never been seriously incommoded by it. On the other hand, I regretted its abolition insofar as it seemed to me to deplete significantly the armoury of the dramatist. With censorship there was a line between what one could and couldn't say and the nearer one got to this line the greater the tension: how candid did one dare to be? Would the men kiss or the women fondle? After censorship went, the dramatist had to manufacture tension of his/her own.

An author is sometimes surprised by what he or she has written. A play or a novel may start off as having nothing seemingly to do with his or her earlier work, and then as it progresses, or even long after it is finished, it can be seen to relate to themes or persons written about in previous books or plays. It was only when I was finishing the play that I realised that Stuart, the rent boy, is only the latest of a succession of not always similar characters who have found their way into my plays, beginning with my second play, *Getting On* (1971), where he's related to the young jobbing carpenter, Geoff, who is another young man who feels himself shut out (and sees sex as a way in). He in turn is fellow to the rather pathetic young man, Eric, in *The Old Country* (1977), whose complaint is similar to Stuart's (and to

Leonard Bast's in *Howards End*). He's less obviously out of the same box as Coral Browne, who, visiting Guy Burgess in his seedy flat in Moscow in *An Englishman Abroad* (1983), pauses by a bookshelf (oh, those bookshelves!) obviously baffled by most of its contents and even more so by Burgess's questions about Harold Nicolson, Cyril Connolly and London literary life. The wife in *Kafka's Dick* (1986) is another unmetropolitan waif, and the sports-mad Rudge in *The History Boys*, rather than the sensitive Posner, is the real outsider.

I ought to be embarrassed by these recurrences and did I feel they had anything to do with me I might be. But these personages slip in through the back door or disguised as somebody else altogether and it's only when, like Stuart, they want their say and make a plea for recognition and acknowledgement that I realise the uninvited guest is here again.

I ought to know who this figure is, but I'm not sure that I do. Is he myself as a young man at Oxford baffled by the academic world? Is he one of the young actors in my first play, *Forty Years On* (1968), many of whom I feared would have wasted lives? Is he even one of the procession of young actors who have auditioned over the years to play such parts and who have had to be sent away disappointed?

Some of the yearning felt in this play by Stuart in the houses of his clientele reflects my own wonder as an undergraduate going to tutorials in the vast Victorian houses of north Oxford. I was there on a different, and more legitimate, errand from Stuart, but to see a wall covered in books was an education in itself, though visual and aesthetic as much as intellectual. Books do furnish a room and some of these rooms had little else, and there in a corner the don under a lamp. Sometimes though, there would be paintings, and occasionally more pictures than I'd ever seen on one wall, together with vases, urns, pottery and other relics – real nests of a scholarly life. And there were wonders, too: drinking soup, once, from fifteenth-century Apostle spoons, medieval embroideries thrown over chair backs, a plaque in the hall that might be by Della Robbia.

These days I think of such houses when I go to museums like the Ashmolean or the Fitzwilliam, where the great masterpieces are plumped out with the fruits of bequests from umpteen academic households: paintings (particularly in the Fitzwilliam), antiquities, treasures brought back from Egypt and Italy in more franchised days than ours, squirrelled away up Norham Road and Park Town, the components of what Stuart rightly sees as a world from which he will forever be excluded – and from which I felt excluded too, though with less reason.

Introduction to *Hymn*

That I wrote *Hymn* is entirely thanks to the composer George Fenton, whom I've known since he appeared as a schoolboy in my first play, *Forty Years On*, and who has written music for many of the plays since. In 2001 the Medici Quartet commissioned him to write a piece commemorating their thirtieth anniversary and he asked me to collaborate. *Hymn* was the result. First performed at the Harrogate Festival in August 2001, it is a series of memoirs with music. Besides purely instrumental passages for the quartet, many of the speeches are underscored, incorporating some of the hymns and music I remember from my childhood and youth.

At the first performance, in a later one at the Buxton Festival and in the live recording we made for the BBC, I played myself. Though I'd never appeared with musicians on a concert platform I didn't anticipate any difficulty. Having to memorise a script is what gives me stage fright, but here it was entirely in order to read the words; the musicians were reading from a score and so was I.

What I'd not anticipated was how in a concert situation the narrator is just one element in the composition, with timing to some extent taken out of his or her hands. There was a moment in the first performance when I stood up for my first speech, saw George cue me in and thought, just for a split second, 'If I don't speak now the whole thing falls apart.' I did speak, though my hesitation was enough to make it a slightly rough passage. It was enough, too, to make me more nervous than I had been . . . which was probably a good thing. That apart, the performance went off well. It was on the stage of the Royal Hall in Harrogate, an auditorium designed by the Edwardian theatre architect Frank Matcham and a riot of exuberant plasterwork. This was in August 2001. Ten days later the roof fell in and the theatre was closed for the next five years.

Never having worked with a string quartet before, rehearsals for me were something of an eye-opener. What astonished me was the freedom with which members of the quartet felt entitled to comment on each other's performances, speaking up when they felt one or other of them was too loud, say, or not incisive enough, comments which the player in question either took in good part or which provoked a reasoned defence. At no point, though, did I detect any animosity.

At first I explained this to myself by thinking that this particular quartet had been playing together for thirty years and it was familiarity, bred out of friendship and working together, that made them so magnanimous and forgiving. But no, I was told; string quartets and chamber music groups in general were most often like this.

I kept thinking of actors in a comparable situation where, should one actor venture to criticise or comment on the performance of a colleague, it would provoke resentment and sulks and certainly an appeal to the director. If an actor does have any opinions to offer on another actor's performance, the etiquette, the ironclad etiquette, is that such comments should be made to the director, who will then relay them to the actor in question in the form of direction and with no hint as to their source. Actors, one is always told, need to be loved. Quartet players are seemingly thicker-skinned.

Of course I am not the first to have noted the musicians' resilience, and indeed the string quartet has been used as a model in business schools to exemplify a readiness to accept constructive criticism without hurt feelings. What players do quarrel about, if they ever do, I'm not sure.

It has always been a mystery to me how it was my father came to learn the violin, though, like so many things about my parents' early life, I never thought to ask him while I still could. It's an unrewarding instrument for a beginner, the more so in his case because he received scant encouragement at home. His mother died when he was a child, leaving his father with four sons to bring up. He quickly married again, this time a sour-faced woman, a stalwart of the chapel whose name I have never known as she was always referred to in the family as 'The Gimmer', a gimmer being a sheep that has had no lambs. Though my father was allowed to practise the violin in the front room, it was only by the light of the street lamp that came in through the window. But still he persisted, perhaps knowing that he had perfect pitch and could name the notes if he heard someone else playing.

How he knew so much orchestral music is another question I never asked him. If there were orchestral concerts in Leeds when he was a young man I doubt that he could have afforded to go, and it would have been with his first and only girlfriend, my mother, and she never mentioned it. Brass bands are a possibility and it's true some of the music he knew – *Poet and Peasant*, *Ruy Blas* and Rossini's *Semiramide* – was the kind of showpiece stuff that bands went in for. It was only in middle age that my parents would have had a wireless, when he started playing along to that.

As time went on it became increasingly difficult to question him about the past as he took the interrogation to mean he was coming to the end of his life, which at that time he wasn't, his relatively early death wholly unexpected. Still, remembering what a struggle he'd had to acquire his skill, it must have been galling when he tried to pass it on to my brother and me how unserious we were about it and how reluctant to practise. He had practised with no encouragement at all; his pampered sons couldn't even be bothered. 'Now the Day Is Over' isn't a hymn one hears very often nowadays, but if ever I do it transports me to the attic at 92A Otley Road where I am scraping it out on the half-size violin.

These days, though, hymns are changing. Gone are the days when I could sing them without looking at the book. The standards these days – 'Make Me a Channel of Thy Peace', 'Amazing Grace' and

'Lord of the Dance' – have me glued to the hymn book and not all that sure of the tune. Even with the old standards – 'Praise My Soul the King of Heaven', 'O Worship the King' – they've sometimes been amended to suit the taste of the time and it's like missing a step on the stair.

Hubberholme, the church at the very tip of the West Riding where *Hymn* finishes up, isn't an especially beautiful church inside, scraped as so many churches were in the nineteenth century and the plaster taken off to reveal the unlovely stonework underneath. Still, it has its rood loft and a nice atmosphere. It also has pews made by Thompson of Kilburn, the famous Mouseman, and on the occasions when I've called at the church to look at the rood loft the only other visitors have been Thompson fans scouring the pews for the trade-mark mouse. They never give the rood loft a second glance, making me feel somewhat superior, though between Larkin's 'ruin-bibber, randy for antique' and the mousehunters I don't suppose there's much to choose.

There are different ways of being English. Churches don't come into it much these days and that they're so often unregarded for me augments their appeal. Since I seldom attend a service this could be thought hypocrisy. But that's not un-English either.

Introduction to *Cocktail Sticks*

From time to time at literary festivals and suchlike I do readings, mainly of extracts from my published diaries, which are generally followed by a question-and-answer session. One of the questions that regularly comes up is whether I have any misgivings or regrets about having written so much about my parents. 'No' is the short answer, and I certainly don't feel, as the questioner sometimes implies, that there is any need for apology. 'Why do you write about Yorkshire when half the time you don't live there?' is the question in a different form. 'Why do you write about your parents when they're no longer around?'

Distance is one answer – perspective. But I will often quote the American writer Flannery O'Connor who, in *Mystery and Manners* (1969), said that anyone who survives their childhood has enough material to last them the rest of their days.

But I don't quite see it like that either, as in my case (and this is partly what *Cocktail Sticks* is about) I had hardly written about them readily, and it took me a while before in a formal way I did, as my first volume of autobiography, *Writing Home*, wasn't published until 1994, while the second, *Untold Stories*, was ten years or so later. It's true that many of the TV plays I have written about the North owe a good deal to my parents' way of talking and looking at things, which is what my mother means when she remarks in *Cocktail Sticks*, 'By, I've given you some script!' But I don't think that is what the question implies, which is more that my parents were a shy and retiring couple, so to write about them even after their deaths is to violate their privacy, with autobiography a kind of betrayal. Not surprisingly, I don't buy this at all.

Both my parents felt constrained, even imprisoned, by their lack of education, though it was as much temperament that held them back. That needed talking about, it seemed to me, just as my mother's depression needed to be brought into the open, if only because this was a more common experience than is (or was then) generally admitted. That it seemed to me was no betrayal. And no betrayal to dramatise it either. And I'm not sure they wouldn't agree. Flannery O'Connor again: 'I once had the feeling I would dig my mother's grave with my writing, too, but I later discovered this was vanity on my part. They are hardier than we think.'

That said, it can be no fun having a writer in the family, always on the make, never happy to let things lie undescribed or leave them unremembered, and ready, too, to tweak experience if the drama or the narrative demands it. Philip Roth, keeping watch at his father's deathbed, knows that he is there out of affection but also because, as he admits, he will one day write about it. 'It is', he says, 'an unseemly profession.'

Had I had any thoughts of 'being a writer' (which is not the same as writing), I would have been discouraged when I looked at my family, so ordinary did they seem and so empty the landscape. To be brought up in Leeds in the forties was to learn early on the quite useful lesson that life is generally something that happens elsewhere. True, I was around in time for the Second World War, but so far as Leeds was concerned that was certainly something that happened elsewhere. From time to time the sirens went and my brother and I were wrapped in blankets and hustled out to the air-raid shelter that stood outside our suburban front door, there to await the longed-for rain of bombs. Sheffield caught it, Liverpool caught it, but Leeds never. 'Why should it? I live here,' was my reasoning, though there was a more objective explanation. The city specialised in the manufacture of ready-made suits and the cultivation of rhubarb, and though the war aims of the German High Command were notoriously quixotic, I imagine a line had to be drawn somewhere. Thus in the whole course of hostilities very few bombs fell on Leeds and those that did were promptly torn apart by schoolboys starved of shrapnel.

All through the war there was a slogan painted on a wall in Wellington Street: 'Start the Second Front Now'. What this injunction meant I never knew at the time . . . It was still there in the early sixties, when it fell, as most things eventually do in Leeds, to the bulldozer. When with the invasion of Normandy the Second Front actually did start it still remained a mystery. We were told that particular day was D-Day and I'm not sure we weren't given a holiday, but I still managed to feel cheated. If this was D-Day, I reasoned that logically there must already have been an A-Day, a B-Day and a C-Day, and me being me and Leeds being Leeds we had, of course, missed them. I note at the age of ten a fully developed ability not quite to enjoy myself, a capacity I have retained intact ever since. I think this is one of the things that *Cocktail Sticks* is about.

It's also about finding something to write about. As I've said, childhood is always high on a writer's list but in the 1940s it was as if childhood itself was on the ration, dull, without frills and done up like the groceries of the time in plain utility packets. We were not well off but nor were we poor, and we were, I imagine, happy. Home – and this is *Cocktail Sticks* – was nothing to write home about. Larkin says that they fuck you up, your mum and dad. And if you end up writing, then that's fine because if they have, then you've got something to write about. But if they haven't fucked you up, you don't have anything to write about, so then they've fucked you up good and proper.

Leeds at that time was an almost wholly nineteenth-century city which, like most Northern cities before the clean air campaign, was black as soot. Growing up, I could see some of its Victorian grandeur, but I was like Hector in *The History Boys*, 'famished for antiquity'. As a boy in a provincial city I was famished for celebrity too and famished, if the truth be told, for a good deal else besides, but which, being a religious boy, I wasn't supposed to think about.

Northern writers like to have it both ways. They set their achievements against the sometimes imaginary squalor of their origins
and gain points for transcendence while at the same time implying
that Northern life is richer and in some undefined way truer and
more honest than a life of southern comfort. 'Look, we have come
through' is the stock version of it, though why a childhood in the
(ex-) industrial North should be thought a handicap as distinct from
some featureless suburb in South London isn't plain. True, if you're
born in Barnsley and set your sights on being Virginia Woolf, it isn't
going to be roses all the way. And had she been born in Doncaster I
can't imagine Ivy Compton-Burnett coming to much. Though she
could have written *A Pit and its Pitfalls*.

Still, education was movement; it was departure. Towering above
the mean streets from which many of their pupils came, the schools
of Leeds were like liners, their rows of windows lit up on winter
afternoons as if great ships of learning, waiting to bear their passengers away from the dirt and fog of this smoking city to the promise
of another life, or at least a more distant one. Because though that
other life might only mean an office or the counter of a better class
of shop, it was at least elsewhere, not Leeds. So, like the steam trains
loading up in the city's City and Central Stations, these schools were
conveyances. Education was a way out.

There was another way out. The Infirmary behind the town hall
was a way out, too, with the first-class passengers berthed round the
corner in the Brotherton Wing, and up Beckett Street a poorer ship,
St James's, where everyone travelled steerage, though some got no
further than the cemetery they could see from the windows. Ships
of hope; ships of fear.

All of which is better put by Richard Hoggart, writing about his
own education at Cockburn High School.

Walking home at about 4.15 or so in the middle of winter when
the street lights have already begun to come on I would look

448

round as I finished crossing the clinkered 'Moor' and still see
over the house-tops, half a mile away, the pale yellow glow of
its classrooms and corridors and its cupolas standing up half
silvery-grey in the near-darkness. It exercised as powerful a pull
on my imagination as Oxford's dreaming spires on Matthew
Arnold's or Christminster on Jude the Obscure's.

(*A Local Habitation*, pp. 182–3)

The year I graduated at Oxford happened to be the year Richard
Hoggart published *The Uses of Literacy*, which was both a celebration of and a lament for working-class culture. Since much of it was
about Leeds, it rang all sorts of bells, but partly because Hoggart was
writing about Hunslet and not Headingley and because I thought
him closer to my parents' generation than my own, I saw his book
as a description of their lives rather than mine. Hunslet was nearer
both topographically and socially to the mean streets of my grandmother's Wortley than it was to the more salubrious suburb of Armley where I'd been brought up. So, not for the first time – and it's a
recurring theme in *Cocktail Sticks* – I felt our family wasn't typical;
we no more made the lower grade than we did a higher one.

It was a time when much was being made in fiction and social commentary of the gulf that higher education opened up between working-class parents and their studious offspring. It was one of Dennis
Potter's early themes and is the central concern of Brian Jackson and
Dennis Marsden's *Education and the Working Class*, a book, judging
from my pencilled notes on the end papers, that I seem to have studied quite carefully when I was in New York with *Beyond the Fringe* in
1962, partly, I suppose, because it was also a breath of home.

There seemed to be agreement that a working-class child educated at university found it difficult thereafter to come to terms with
– relate to if you like (which I didn't much) – his or her parents who
looked on bewildered at this graduate cuckoo they had reared in their
back-to-back nest. I never found this the case . . . or my case anyway.

University was my sphere, home was theirs, and far from wanting my parents to adapt their way of going on to my 'university outlook' (whatever that was), what I wanted, once I'd stopped being embarrassed by them, was that they should remain the same as they had always been, or as I imagined them to have been. That this was as false in its own way as wanting them to defer to my newly acquired sophistication I did not yet see. I just knew I wasn't like the characters I read about in novels – *Sons and Lovers* I suppose a classic example – or some of the disillusioned graduates in Jackson and Marsden.

Once upon a time, as I say in the play, I had longed for my parents to be socially accomplished and anonymously middle-class, unfazed by the occasional glass of sherry or, when coming to Oxford, going out to supper at the Randolph as other parents did. University – and more significantly show business – meant that I had changed tack and, being more socially at ease myself, what I was requiring of them now was that in a parody of conservation they should preserve their old-fashioned down-to-earth character as I recalled (and sometimes imagined) it from when I was a child.

Thus my letters home from Oxford and later from New York were written in a self-consciously homely tone which revived the extremes of dialect and 'Leeds talk' long after my parents had begun to discard them themselves. It's true that Dad for instance used to refer to the August bank holiday as 'Banky' as in 'Where are we off for Banky?' but that had been in the forties and casual conversation. To find the phrase resurrected and set down in one of my letters in the sixties together with other similar outmoded expressions seems self-conscious and condescending. To read my letters home now is shaming. What can they have thought? I had been seven years at Oxford and was now appearing on Broadway, and yet I still affected to address them as if we were all in a dialect farce.

It must have been around this time, too, that I stopped bothering about my Northern accent. I never had much, though I'd made some attempt at Oxford to iron out its worst excesses, with vowels always the problem, though whether one said 'bath' or 'barth' of less moment (and less of a giveaway) than if you came out with 'batcher' instead of 'butcher'.

But of course accents didn't matter any more – not because the class structure had altered; it hadn't particularly – it was thanks, in large measure, to the Beatles. By the mid-sixties a provincial accent (with the possible exception of Wolverhampton) had become not unfashionable, an attribute one need not strive to get rid of or even tone down. Sexual intercourse may have begun in 1963 but so did freedom of speech.

By this time I was performing on the stage in *Beyond the Fringe* and beginning to write, though I detect there a progression in my writing voice corresponding to that of my speaking one. My first play, *Forty Years On* (1968), was entirely metropolitan and not written, any bit of it, in the voice with which I'd been born and brought up, but in the one which I had (if a little patchily) acquired. Set in a public school, the play provided a potted cultural history of England from 1900 to 1940, seen through the eyes of an upper-class couple in an air-raid shelter in Claridge's, a far cry from the streets of Upper Armley where I'd spent the war and even further from the streets of Tong Road. My second play, *Getting On*, was metropolitan too, though less lofty, and it was not until 1971, ten years after I'd first gone on the stage, that with my first TV film, *A Day Out*, I began to write plays in the voice with which I'd been born.

That I should have ended up in the theatre hardly seemed to surprise my parents. 'Folks did clap,' Mam said, after they had seen the opening performance of *Beyond the Fringe* in Edinburgh in August 1960, but there was no surprise in the remark, theatre, like university, another sphere in which they could not nor wanted to follow me. It had never been one of my own ambitions, though I'd been going to the theatre since I was a small child, taken there first by my grandmother who every year would give us an outing to the pantomime at the Theatre Royal in Lands Lane. It was never the Grand or the

Empire, still less the much more disreputable City Varieties. It was always the blue and gold Theatre Royal where, long after Christmas, and even in May, the panto would still be running and we would toil up the scrubbed wooden stairs and come out on what at first seemed the almost sheer face of the gallery.

Invariably produced by Francis Laidler, it seemed a spectacular show and would, I think, seem so even today with transformation scenes, a flying ballet and a troupe of Tiller Girls. The star of the show would be a famous name from the music hall – Norman Evans, Frank Randle or Albert Modley – and these were always the bits Grandma enjoyed best.

These early visits to the pantomime stopped with the death of Grandma and the demolition of the Theatre Royal which came not long afterwards. My theatregoing then was confined to Saturday afternoons and the matinees at the Grand, nowadays the home of Opera North. By London standards it was a huge theatre and, sitting in the gods and already short-sighted but still without glasses, I could never see the actors' faces (nor even knew that one was meant to). And they were distinguished actors too, as in those days shows toured before and after they went into the West End still with their original cast. So I saw Edith Evans in James Bridie's *Daphne Laureola*, Flora Robson playing a troubled shoplifter in *Black Chiffon*, Eric Portman as a Labour colonial governor in *His Excellency* and dozens of plays where the furnishings were by the Old Times Furnishing Company and the cigarettes were by Abdulla and nylons by Kayser Bondor.

Cracks began to appear in this safe little world when later in the fifties I saw *Waiting for Godot* here, Olivier in *The Entertainer* and Dennis Lotis in the pre-London try-out of Osborne's *The World of Paul Slickey*. Even Olivier didn't draw the crowds, the theatre virtually empty, but so the theatre always was on a Saturday matinee and I took this as a matter of course, theatres like churches not meant to be full.

It was a shock when in 1951 I went to my first London theatre, the shortly to be demolished St James's. I could not get over how small it was. Laurence Olivier and Vivien Leigh were alternating *Antony and Cleopatra* and *Caesar and Cleopatra* and I saw the Shaw, remembering now only my wonder that, though I was in the cheapest seats, for the first time in my life I could see the faces of the actors.

There was no difficulty in that department the first time I appeared on the London stage, as it was in *Beyond the Fringe* at the Fortune, one of the smallest (as well as the steepest) of the London theatres and opposite the stage door of Drury Lane where *My Fair Lady* was still playing. We met everybody at that time and I wish I'd kept more of a diary, though it would just have been a list of celebrities who had come backstage and who I dutifully listed in my weekly letters home.

Harold Macmillan, the prime minister, came to be harangued by Peter Cook, imitating Harold Macmillan on the stage. In Washington we were taken along to the press conference when President Kennedy first revealed the existence of the Cuban missiles. My chief recollection of which is how briskly Kennedy strode to the podium and got on with the proceedings and how he flirted with and charmed the older women journalists.

The Cuban crisis was brewing all the time we were on tour with the revue, and the night it opened on Broadway was the night the Soviet ships were intercepted and turned back. At one point during the first night a siren sounded and the audience went utterly silent, only for it to turn out to be just a fire engine. And I remember lying awake at night listening for the sound of breaking glass, because it was thought if war were going to come the first signs of it would be looting and rioting in the streets.

In due course after the crisis, the Kennedys themselves came to the show, the red telephone was installed in the box office and backstage thronged with Secret Servicemen, who, ironically in view of what was to happen the following year, were deeply suspicious of the wooden rifle we used in one of our sketches. The Kennedys came backstage, as did Adlai Stevenson along with fabled stars of the movies, but I've no memories of anything that was said. Like so many occasions in one's life, including some of its most intimate moments, one would like to have been there without being actually present, a fly, as it were on one's own wall, just watching.

So much of *Cocktail Sticks* is to do with class, it's appropriate I should end fairly high up the social scale in Downing Street. Several years after *Beyond the Fringe*, when Harold Wilson was prime minister, I was invited to a dinner at Downing Street for Canadian Prime Minister Pierre Trudeau. It was during the period when Harold Wilson imagined himself an English Kennedy, and when figures from the world of show business and entertainment began to be allowed in at the front door.

My welcome wasn't all that auspicious. Mr and Mrs Wilson were lined up with Prime Minister Trudeau at the top of the stairs, and when Trudeau asked me what I did, I said I was a playwright, but had started off as an actor, in revue. Mary Wilson frowned. 'I hope it wasn't one of those revues where there is no scenery and they just wear black sweaters and so on.' I had to admit that it was, in fact, *Beyond the Fringe*. Now it was Mr Wilson's turn to frown. He looked at me suspiciously. '*Beyond the Fringe*? But you weren't one of the original four.' I said, 'Yes.' 'Well, I don't remember you. Are you sure?' So, feeling like Trotsky must have felt when he was cut out of the history of the Revolution, I then went in to dinner, where the guest opposite, a noted London publisher, had the seating altered so that he could be opposite someone of more importance, and at a later stage in the meal one of the legs of my chair came off.

September 2012

Introduction to *People*

I sometimes think that my plays are just an excuse for the introductions with which they are generally accompanied. These preambles, while often gossipy and with sidelights on the rehearsal process, also provide me with a soapbox from which I can address, sometimes more directly than I've managed in the play itself, some of the themes that crop up in the text. In *The History Boys* it was private education; in *The Habit of Art* biography; in *People*, though, I'm not sure.

Rehearsals aren't just for the actors; they are also a first opportunity for the author to hear the play and find out what he or she has written. But since this introduction is being put together in August 2012, nearly two months before rehearsals begin, I am still to some extent in the dark about the play or what (if anything) it adds up to.

Some plays seem to start with an itch, an irritation, something one can't solve or a feeling one can't locate. With *People* it was a sense of unease when going round a National Trust house and being required to buy into the role of reverential visitor. I knew this irritated me, but, like the hapless visitors whom Dorothy confronts as they are leaving, I still found it hard to say what it was I had expected to find and whether I had found it.

National Trust guides more conventional than Dorothy (and for whom I almost invariably feel slightly sorry) assume that one wishes to be informed about the room or its furniture and pictures, which I don't always. Sometimes I just want to look and occasionally (eighteenth-century porcelain, Chinoiserie and most tapestries) prefer to walk straight through. Sometimes I actively dislike what I'm seeing: yet another table massively laid for a banquet, for instance, or massed ranks of the family photos ranged on top of a grand piano with royal visitors given some prominence. Even when I am interested but want to be left alone with the pictures or whatever, I have learned not to show too much interest as this invariably fetches the guide over, wanting to share his or her expertise. I know this is bad behaviour and it's another reason why I'll often come away as dissatisfied with myself as I am with the house.

The first stately home I can remember visiting was Temple Newsam, a handsome early sixteenth-century house given to Leeds by the Earl of Halifax. We often used to go on outings there when I was a child, taking the tram from outside the City Market up through Halton and past the municipal golf course to the terminus at Temple Newsam House. An adjunct of Leeds Art Gallery, it had a good collection of furniture, a long gallery without which no country house was complete, besides housing some of the city's collection of Cotman drawings and watercolours. While aged nine or ten I didn't wholly appreciate its contents, I saw Temple Newsam as a wonderfully ancient and romantic place, which it wasn't really, having been heavily restored and remodelled in the nineteenth century. Still, it gave me a lifelong taste for enfiladed rooms and for Leeds pottery (particularly the horses) neither of which life has enabled me to indulge. As a boy, though, for me its most numinous holding was a large felt hat reputed to be that of Oliver Cromwell with a bullet hole in the crown to prove it.

Visiting Temple Newsam was always a treat, as it still is more than half a century later. Back in 1947, though, with the country in the throes of the post-war economic crisis, the push was on for more coal, and the whole of the park in front of the house was given over to open-cast mining, the excavations for which came right up to the terrace. From the state rooms you looked out on a landscape as bleak and blasted as a view of the Somme, an idyll, as it seemed to me then, irretrievably lost, and young though I was I knew this.

But of course I was wrong. It wasn't irretrievable and to look at the grounds today one would have no idea that such a violation had ever occurred. And it had occurred, too, with even greater devastation at other country houses south of Leeds: Nostell Priory was similarly beleaguered, as was Wentworth Woodhouse, both, like the Stacpooles' house, smack in the middle of coal-bearing country and where the notion as in the play of a country house with a mine in the immediate vicinity is far from far-fetched.

Nostell Priory is full of Adam furniture, and both Nostell and Temple Newsam have Chippendale desks like the one referred to in the play, that at Temple Newsam bought by Leeds Corporation from the Harewoods at Harewood House – another outing from Leeds, and a mansion, incidentally, that was once on the National Trust's wish list but which happily still remains with the family that built it. It is, though, one of those reprobate mansions cited by June in the play, Harewood having been built from the profits of eighteenth-century sugar and slaves . . . from one of whom is descended one of the National Theatre's noted actors, David Harewood.

Previous productions of my plays at the National Theatre have generally been accompanied by a Platform evening, very often shared with Nicholas Hytner, when we talk about the play and answer questions from the audience. We did one of these evenings in 2009 after the opening of *The Habit of Art*, and at the end of the session Nick thanked the audience, saying that my plays seemed to turn up (and be put through his letterbox) at roughly four-year intervals. He felt this was a bit long to wait and if the audience agreed and wanted something sooner he asked them to put their hands together. This they gratifyingly did. It was a Tinkerbell moment, and not having known what he was planning to say I found myself uncharacteristically choked up. But it did the trick, this play clocking in at three years after its predecessor.

When I first showed it to Nick he remarked that it wasn't like anything else I'd done . . . or anything else I'd done with him. The play, though, that does have hints of it is *Getting On* (1971), which, like *People*, is what has since become known as a 'play for England', sort of, anyway. In those days when I had less compassion for the audience (and for the actors) I went in for much longer speeches than I would venture to do nowadays. But some of the diatribes I put into the mouth of George Oliver, a right-wing Labour MP, are echoes of the complaints more succinctly expressed by Dorothy in *People*, the complaints generally being about 'England'.

Enjoy (1980) is another play with which *People* has similarities in that both, while ostensibly contemporary in setting, have a slightly fanciful notion of the future. At least I thought of it as fanciful, but what I was writing about in *Enjoy* – the decay and preservation of a working-class quarter in a Northern town and the last back-to-back in Leeds – all came true much quicker than I could have imagined in the decades that followed. The same threatens to be the case with *People*.

Privacy or at any rate exclusivity is increasingly for hire, instances of which make some of Bevan's proposals in the play not even outlandish. I had written the play when I read that Liechtenstein in its entirety could be hired for the relatively modest sum of £40,000 per night. Around the same time I read that Lancaster Castle, which once housed the County Court and the prison that often went with such institutions, was up for sale. That it had also hosted the execution of condemned prisoners probably increased the estimate. At one point in 2011 the Merchant Navy War Memorial at Tower Hill was to have been hired out for some banker's junket. That a Methodist church in Bournemouth has been bought and reopened as a Tesco is hardly worth mentioning. So what is? Everywhere nowadays has its price and the more inappropriate the setting the better. I scarcely dare suggest that Pentonville or Wormwood Scrubs be marketed as fun venues lest it has already happened.

When it came to giving offence, there too I kept finding that I had been if not timid, at least over-scrupulous. In the management and presentation of their newly acquired property of Stacpole House I imagined the Trust as entirely without inhibition, ready to exploit any aspect of the property's recent history to draw in the public, wholly unembarrassed by the seedy or the disreputable. I envisaged a series of events I took to be wildly implausible, but in the light of recent developments they turn out to be almost tame.

I read for instance that the audio guide to the National Trust house at Hughenden, once lived in by Disraeli, is voiced by Jeffrey Archer, euphemistically described by the Trust as 'a provocative figure'. And in the matter of pornography the Trust has recently sponsored a tape to accompany a tour round London's Soho, the highlights of which are not architectural. It is apparently selling very well.

My objections to this level of marketing are not to do with morals but to do with taste. In another connection, though, and nothing to do with the Trust, I found life had outstripped my paltry imagination. I have no reference for this other than what the *DNB* used to call 'personal knowledge', but talking to someone about what I still thought of as the outrageousness of a country house being made the venue for a porn film, I was told that there was (and maybe still is) an entrepreneur who does just that, arranging similar (and equally chilly) filming in country houses north of the border.

So, writing the play and imagining I was ahead of my times, I then found I was scarcely even abreast of them. Had the play not been produced when it was (in November 2012), in six months' time it might have seemed hopelessly out of date.

As is made plain in the play, Dorothy is not shocked by porn being filmed under her (leaking) roof. As she points out, she is a peeress in her own right. 'The middle class . . . they're the respectable ones.' Which is a cliché but I'd have thought no less true for all that. But then, what do I know?

My experience of high life is limited, but years ago, I think through George Melly, I used to be invited to parties given by Geoffrey Bennison, the fashionable interior decorator. He lived in Golden Square ('Above Glorex Woollens, dear') and there one would find Geoffrey in full drag, and very convincing drag it was, too, as he made no attempt to seem glamorous, instead coming across as a middle-aged duchess not unlike Lady Montdore in Nancy Mitford's *Love in a Cold Climate*. It would be a very mixed bag of high life and low life – Diana Duff Cooper dancing with a well-known burglar sticks in the mind – respectability and the middle classes nowhere.

'Now that I'm eighty there are two things I no longer have to do,' said another grand lady of my acquaintance. 'Tell the truth and wear knickers.' What Dorothy is or is not wearing under her fur coat I don't like to think.

That said, I have never been entirely confident that the glimpses one is allowed in stately homes of the family's 'real life' always ring true. Years ago I was filming at Penshurst Place, the home of Lord de L'Isle and Dudley, and I wrote in my diary (15 December 1984):

> The house is everything one imagines an English country house should be . . . a hotchpotch of different periods – mediaeval hall, eighteenth-century courtyards, Gothick front, solid green walls of yew and parterres of box. We film in a gallery adjoining the drawing room, part of the private wing, with photographs of Lord D. at Cambridge, in India as a young man and ADC to Wavell and now standing beside Macmillan as he unveils a plaque to Lord Gort. On a coffee table are back numbers of the *Economist*, *Country Life* and the *TLS* with drinks on the side.
>
> 'Ah,' one thinks. 'A glimpse here of the private life.' But is it? Is this really a private room or just a private room for public consumption? These drinks (and the bottle of vitamin pills beside them), have they been artfully arranged to suggest a private life? Is there somewhere else, another flat which is more private? And so on. And so on. The impression is confirmed by the hall table, on which are all the Viscount's hats: his green Guards trilbies, his bowler, his lumberjack's hat that was plainly presented to him on some sort of ceremonial visit. Surely, all this is meant to be seen?

(Writing Home)

No soiled underwear in the state bedroom at least . . . but even voicing the thought I can see it coming one day soon. The links between such unworthy musings and what happens in the play are obvious.

Plays have buds, points at which something is mentioned in one play though not dwelt on but which turns up in a later play. Never sure of the significance of what one writes or the continuity of one's concerns, I find these recurrences reassuring as pointing if nothing else to consistency. They can, though, be shaming.

In *The History Boys* Irwin is a dynamic supply teacher who ends up as a TV historian and government special adviser. Televised in the latrine passage below the reredorter at Rievaulx Abbey, he speculates on those scraps of cloth on which the monks wiped their bums, some of which have been recovered and are in the abbey museum. Could it be shown that one of these fragments had actually been used by St Aelred of Rievaulx, would that scrap of cloth, Irwin wonders, then constitute a sacred relic? It's an unsavoury preoccupation, but unnoticed by me a related concept has smuggled itself into *People*, where the notion of historical and celebrity urine is a branch grown from Irwin's bud.

On a different level the discussion of the Holocaust in *The History Boys* relates to Hector's dismay that Auschwitz has become just another station on the tourist trail, with Hector concerned about the proportion of reverence to prurience among the visitors. This recurs – and to my mind more harshly – in *People*, with Lumsden's comment that there is 'nowhere that is not visitable. That at least the Holocaust has taught us.'

Dorothy's comments about the graffiti done by the Canadian troops billeted in the house during the war echo similar speculations in James Lees-Milne's *Ancestral Voices*:

Wednesday 7 January 1942. [At Brocket] I walked across a
stile and down a footpath to the James Paine bridge, which the
Canadian troops have disfigured by cutting their names, with

463

addresses in Canada, and personal numbers, all complete and inches deep – the vandals. Yet, I thought, what an interesting memorial this will be in years to come and quite traditional, like the German mercenaries' names scrawled in 1530 on the Palazzo Ducale in Urbino.

He might have added the Viking inscriptions cut centuries earlier into the lions outside the Arsenale in Venice.

It was in Lees-Milne, too, that I read about the Jungman sisters, who in their youth were Bright Young Things and contemporaries of Evelyn Waugh. In later life they turned reclusive, stockpiled the newspaper (the *Telegraph*, I suspect), reading one a day still but years behind the times.

It has been said (by Kathryn Hughes in the *Guardian*) that nowadays 'it is the demotic and the diurnal that matter to us when thinking about the past' and what are generally called 'bygones' make a brief appearance in the play, as they regularly do in the below-stairs rooms of country houses. Fortunate in having had a relatively long life, I have grown used to seeing everyday items from my childhood featuring in folk museums or even as items on *The Antiques Roadshow*, a brass and pewter gill measure from a milk pail, for instance (wielded at the Bennett family back door by the milkman, Mr Keen, his horse and trap waiting in the street); a posser for the clothes wash and jelly moulds galore.

Even so I was surprised this summer when going round Blickling to see a young man rapt in contemplation of a perfectly ordinary aluminium pan. Still, he was doubtless a dab hand at the computer, which I'm not, even though to me aluminium pans are commonplace. Other vintage items which were in common use when I was young would be:

A wicker carpet beater.
A wooden clothes horse.
A tidy betty.

A flat iron.
Pottery eggs.
Spats.
Black lead.
Virol.

The danger of making such a list is that one will in due course figure on it.

Curiously it was only when I'd finished the play that I realised I'd managed to avoid giving the house a name. I suppose it ought to be the family name and so Stacpoole, except that one proof of aristocracy is to subtly distinguish the name of the house from the name of its location. Thus in a minor snobbery Harewood, the home of the Lascelles family and their earldom, is pronounced Harwood, whereas the village of Harewood, its location near Leeds, is pronounced as it's spelled, Harewood. So on a similar principle I've called the house Stacpole but it's pronounced Stacpool.

In the play Bevan sings the praises of solitude with his slogan 'P-S-T . . . people spoil things.' While Bevan hardly carries the moral burden of the play he has a point . . . and some authorial sympathy.

I have tasted the pleasures of singularity myself, having been lucky enough to be in Westminster Abbey at midnight and virtually alone. As an ex-trustee I am permitted to visit the National Gallery after hours, and filming has meant that I have often been in well-loved places like Fountains Abbey almost on my own.

So, while it is to be hoped that such privileged privacies are never marketed in the way Bevan and 'The Concern' would like, the heady delights of exclusion are these days touted commercially more and more and without apology.

The notion that the eighties in England marked a turning point keeps recurring – a time when, as Dorothy is told, we ceased to take things for granted and self-interest and self-servingness took over. Some of this alteration in public life can be put down to the pushing back of the boundaries of the state as begun under Mrs Thatcher and pursued even more disastrously thereafter, though in regretting this (and not being able to be more specific about it) Dorothy in her fur coat and gym shoes is thought by her sister the archdeacon to be pitiably naive as perhaps I am, who feels much the same. The state has never frightened me. Why should it? It gave me my education (and in those days it was a gift); it saved my father's life as it has on occasion saved mine by services we are now told have to be paid for.

What is harder to put one's finger on is the growth of surliness in public behaviour and the sour taste of public life. There has been a diminution of magnanimity in government both central and local, with the public finding itself rebranded as 'customers', supposedly to dignify our requirements but in effect to make us available for easier exploitation. The faith – which like most ideologies has only a tangential connection with reason – is that everything must make a profit and that there is nothing that cannot be bought and sold.

These thoughts are so obvious that I hesitate to put them down, still less make them specific in the play. Dorothy is asking what is different about England, saying how she misses things being taken for granted. We were told in the eighties and pretty constantly since that we can't afford to take anything for granted, whereas to my mind in a truly civilised state the more that can be taken for granted in terms of health, education, employment and welfare the better we are for it. Less and less are we a nation and more and more just a captive market to be exploited. 'I hate it,' says Dorothy, and she doesn't just mean showing people round the house.

A propos the closet with the ancient chamber pots: having finished the play, we went for a short holiday in Norfolk in the course of which we went round Felbrigg Hall, the family home of R. W. Ketton-Cremer, who willed it to the National Trust on his death in 1969. Ketton-Cremer was an historian and had a well-stocked Gothick library which, as distinct from other such rooms in country houses, was a place of work, as Ketton-Cremer produced many books. Set in the thickness of the wall behind a pivoting bookcase was a closet with, on a table, a chamber pot. It was, alas, empty.

I end as I have ended the introductions to the previous five plays on which we've worked together with my heartfelt thanks to Nicholas Hytner. He brings to life what to me on the page often seems dull. I write plays; he turns them into theatre. His productions of the plays are always a pleasure to work on and he emboldens me in writing them. And it's always fun. 'Plays is work,' said Ellen Terry. 'No play about it.' But then she never worked with Nicholas Hytner.

Thanks too to another encourager, Dinah Wood, my editor at Faber, and of course to all the cast of the play and the staff of the National. To turn up every few years with a play and still find oneself welcome is a great pleasure. It has its moments though. When I went in on the first day of rehearsal for *People* someone at the stage door said, 'Still hanging on then?'

Foreword to *The Coder Special Archive*

Having in 1952 got a place at university I was required by my college before taking up residence to do my two years' National Service. Dreading National Service though I did, even I could see I wasn't ready for university. School was Leeds Modern School, a state school where even though I was in the sixth form I was very young for my age and at seventeen it was a toss-up which would come first, puberty or the call-up. At eighteen I had never been in a pub or had a cigarette or a girlfriend. I was an innocent and if I was unsuited for university I was even more so for the army.

However there was a lifeline. We all of us in the sixth form knew about the Russian course, a cushy number (as I learned to call it) available if one persisted to boys like me who had got O levels or A levels (School Certificate or Higher School Certificate as they were then.) When I came to registering I opted for the navy, a choice of service dictated in part by aesthetic considerations – I thought a coder's uniform looked more becoming. At the same time at seventeen I saw the three services, navy, air force and army as approximating to, corresponding with, the class system – navy as upper class, air force as middle, the army as working. So putting down for the navy I knew I was being over-aspirational, and it was no surprise at all when I ended up in the army where I belonged.

Some of my classmates did manage to get into the navy, though: one of my closest friends John Totterdill becoming a midshipman where he had, it seemed to me, an ideal life swanning around the Mediterranean as office-boy cum valet to Admiral Sir Philip Vian. My classmates John Scaife and Tony Cash both became coders so I knew it could be done. But not by me, and when my papers came and

I found I hadn't got into the navy I also found it was far from certain I was going to be able to do Russian. Certainly nobody seemed to have heard of the course at Pontefract Barracks where I did my basic training with the York and Lancaster Regiment. But though not by nature tenacious I persisted so that when at the end of six weeks most of my platoon were drafted into the Duke of Wellington's Regiment for eventual transfer to Korea I kicked my heels at Pontefract with another would-be Russian course candidate, Thomas Pearce, both of us eventually ending up at Coulsdon where we embarked on our study of the Russian language.

In memoirs that I've read by others on the course much has been made of how hard one had to work. While this was hardly true of the later stages it was certainly the case during those first six weeks at Coulsdon. This was when one was learning the alphabet and the basic grammar and coming to terms with the daily word lists that one had to master and on which one was tested at the end of each week.

The pressure, though, was to some extent self-imposed. We knew that the course at Coulsdon would end in an examination, with the top twenty-five per cent going on to Cambridge. The prospect of Cambridge would have been incentive enough but what made it seem almost beyond imagining was that did we get into the top twenty-five per cent at Cambridge we would no longer have to wear uniform, do drill or bull our kit – all the irksome and sometimes humiliating burdens that had been visited upon us would fall away. No more guard duty or the threat of jankers or being put on a charge. One would be a person again not a soldier. No wonder we worked.

I am told that I am by nature competitive but I have never since been in a situation where one had to compete so directly with one's fellows and so relentlessly that it coloured sociability and almost ruled out friendship. This was certainly true of the first pre-university period of the course and continued for some time afterwards though less unremittingly – or maybe one just got used to it. Hanging over us was always the threat of being RTU'd – returned to one's unit, in my case Pontefract. I can't recall this ever happening to anybody however poorly they did in the weekly tests, but it was perhaps because existence was to some extent precarious that I remember it as in many ways the most idyllic period of my life, and much more so than university proper which came a year or two later.

We were housed to begin with at Cecil Lodge in Newmarket from which we were bussed every morning to the course HQ in Salisbury Villas on Station Road in Cambridge. At the end of the first term the lucky ones were allocated a house in Newnham Terrace in the centre of Cambridge (and subsequently part of New Hall). The rest of us were relegated to Foxton Hall, a square lavatory-bricked villa just outside Cambridge on the main line to King's Cross. Gone now, it was where I had my first gin and tonic and my first cigarette and used to stand on the lawn at dusk listening to the bats.

Finally we were all reunited at Douglas House on Trumpington Road, both Foxton and Douglas House having an afterlife as convalescent homes before being demolished. If I dwell on these houses it's because they rather than Salisbury Villas are what remain in the memory, so much so that walking up the road to the station a few weeks ago I couldn't even pick out which villa it was where we'd studied half a century ago.

After Cambridge it was back to uniform and six months at Bodmin, living in the Spider, a conglomeration of Nissen huts heated only by coke stoves. Morning parades were a shambles with pyjamas worn under uniforms the weather was so bitter and classrooms so cold. Again it's the extra-curricular activities I remember most vividly – the poker fever that gripped the camp for a few months then ceased as abruptly as it had started; swimming at a surely insanitary waterhole on the moors followed by stupendous farmhouse teas at Mrs Penhaligon's. Cornwall then was criss-crossed by railways so there were trips to Fowey and Lostwithiel with weekends spent at St Columb Minor and Polzeath, surfing yet to be discovered.

Bodmin was also a reunion with the navy students who to me remained as enviable and out of reach as they'd been when I first tried to join their number at the start of National Service. Huddled on the parade ground in army fatigues one saw these lofty and elegant creatures – Mark Frankland, Jeremy Wolfenden, Robin Hope – sauntering to their places, their social and academic skills making me feel still the uncouth squaddie I'd been in basic training.

It was around this time we all sat the Civil Service exam in Russian, a hurdle I failed ignominiously. This was a surprise as I'd earlier got a distinction in the A-level exam but then the army hadn't bothered to explain that doing well in the Civil Service exam would mean a pay increase, so there was no incentive. The hectic competition of the first months of the course was long forgotten.

At some point, too, we went off to take the WOSB, the board that would decide whether having been officer cadets for the last year we really were proper officer material. To my surprise (and already being something of an actor) I passed this first hurdle, the second being two weeks at Mons, the officer training unit at Aldershot. This proved more of a trial and I was failed. It dismayed me then and shames me now how much I wanted to pass. It was the first failure I'd ever had, but it was salutary. I had begun my National Service as a committed Christian, a Conservative and, I'm sure, a prig. Now, priggishness apart, I was none of these things quite, and though I didn't know it at the time it had cured me for life of any desire to join. It's this rather than the Russian word for 'rolling barrage', say, that sixty years later remains with me.

Adapted from the Foreword to *The Coder Special Archive: The Untold Story of Naval National Servicemen Learning and Using Russian During the Cold War* by Tony Cash and Mike Gerrard, Hodgson Press, 2012.

Art and Yorkshire: From Turner to Hockney

This is a preface I wrote for an exhibition at the Mercer Gallery in Harrogate in 2014. When I write about art it's generally in extenuation of my own shortcomings and how little I know, and so it is here.

When I was a child growing up in Leeds art was quite thin on the ground. It was wartime and though we were regularly in the art gallery on school trips it was seldom to look at the pictures most of which had been put away for the duration or altogether evacuated. In London the National Gallery's collection had been glamorously spirited away to a cave in the depths of Wales. In Leeds, with glamour as usual not on the agenda, our pictures had just been put on a tram and taken up through Halton past the golf course to Temple Newsam.

So if we came down from Armley to the art gallery in the Headrow it was not to be uplifted by art (difficult anyway for me aged six) but to be given a dose of propaganda, exhorted to Dig for Victory! or to Save the *Ark Royal*! in a series of exhibitions which included at one point a mock-up of a coal mine. If art did get a look-in it was only via the paintings we had to do when we got back to school with the promise, never made good, that the best of them might end up in the art gallery themselves.

More satisfying was to be taken by my grandma, as we regularly were, on the same journey as the city's paintings up to Temple Newsam House where some of the braver paintings could still be seen. Not that I was much interested. Far more fascinating was the broad-brimmed felt hat that was on display all through my childhood and which purported to be that of Oliver Cromwell, with a bullet hole in the crown to prove it.

I can see, though, that simply for want of anywhere more exciting to go one did as a child begin to acquire the habit of art, without . . . and this was important . . . necessarily thinking art was anything special. And this persisted, so that when as I got older I used to do my homework in the City Reference Library I often took a break in the art gallery next door, where quite early on art in Yorkshire began to rub off.

The most notable artist in this book is, of course, Turner though it's not the Turner of the huge stormy canvases of his later years. These are kinder paintings and of views we can still recognise. What makes the Yorkshire Turners immediately accessible is that they are so topographical. Here is Kirkstall Abbey, pretty much as we know it today (though not quite as black). Here is Bolton and the transept at Fountains with the setting at this stage of Turner's development not subordinated to some vast meteorological drama or a battle between darkness and light which reduces the ostensible subject to a corner of the canvas and even there seen through a fitful haze. They aren't picture postcards either but they are views, prospects and works that Turner's patrons at Farnley and Harewood could readily appreciate. They are . . . dare one say it . . . down to earth.

Down to earth, too, in a different way is Henry Moore, much lauded now in his home county . . . his home Riding one should say . . . though it was not always so. When in 1951 the Festival of Britain included one of Moore's reclining figures outside Leeds Art Gallery it was regularly defaced and was the subject of acrimonious correspondence in the local papers. Nowadays it's hard to see what people got so upset about but that's simply because the public has caught up with him, with some, glibly, even claiming to have left him behind.

Moore's thoughts are said to have been turned to sculpture when, as a boy, he was taken to services at Methley Church where there is indeed plenty of stonework to occupy a boy's attention during a boring sermon. One would like to think it was something so ordinary and so local but I'm never sure that one can pin down the source of an artist's inspiration as precisely as this even when the attribution comes from the actual artist. It's certainly not true of literature where characters, however vivid, are rarely based on one particular person, and seldom yanked out of life into art as readily as readers think. Art is a mystery even to its practitioners, a sculptor's inspiration in the hand as much as the eye.

I remember when we were on holiday in Bridlington in the late forties going with my mother to Burton Agnes Hall which we were enchanted by ('It's like somewhere Down South,' said my mother). Less enchanting then were Marcus Wickham-Boynton's Post-Impressionists which I can remember visitors, myself included, being shocked by. The comments were as they say nowadays 'robust' with 'I wouldn't give that thing house room' a typical remark. I think, even at fourteen, I had enough sense to keep my mouth shut, knowing instinctively that with art it was often a case of catching up.

Besides, reputations come and go. The virtues of Atkinson Grimshaw nowadays go without saying whereas even as late as the 1950s he was taken to be old hat. I've always liked his pictures if not for purely aesthetic reasons. All too often he brings back what we have lost and his painting of Park Row in Leeds Art Gallery is a sad reminder of what Leeds used to look like before the developers got to work, his painting of Boar Lane similarly. Then too his studies of suburban Roundhay and Shadwell recall my lonely teenage walks through Woodhouse and Headingley, their leaf-covered lanes redolent of my youth. In the early sixties Grimshaw used to be recommended in the colour supplements as a good investment, an artist whose stock was going to rise. And so he was, if that is what you were after. But at his best he captures Leeds and Harrogate as I can remember them, nostalgia as fitting a response to paintings as an appreciation that is more purely aesthetic.

Where pictures are concerned I have always found my appreciation is linked far too closely to possession. I know if I like a painting when my instinct is to walk out of the gallery with it under my raincoat. It stamps me as aesthetically immature, I can see that, and not being a Russian billionaire it's not a craving I can indulge. But if I did own even the modest pictures I've fancied it would be both a distinguished and pleasing collection numbering, among others, the Camden Town paintings I first saw in Leeds Art Gallery, the Cotmans I saw at Temple Newsam and the aforesaid Grimshaws of Park Row and Boar Lane. There would also be the odd Pompeo Batoni, which figure in so many country house collections, quite silly though some of them are and a bit big for the raincoat. I'd also like one of the early drawings of Lucian Freud and the Patrick Heron portrait of Herbert Read that figured in the celebratory exhibition about Read a few years ago.

This desire for possession is ignoble, particularly if possession involves as it so often does a large degree of showing off, though if the showing off includes admitting the public to the collection as it does in so many country houses it can perhaps be forgiven. What recommends ownership of even the most modest painting is that it allows the virtues and the beauty of the picture to creep into one's affections. It's another reason to visit and revisit galleries as a reminder of one's old friends. Many of these pictures we know so we don't have to cudgel our sensibilities into some sort of response; this is not a fresh encounter, it's a reunion. Here is Fountains as Turner saw it and we remember him seeing it from last time. Here are Grimshaw's autumnal lanes and on the Tube platform Moore's sleepers cuddle up as the Blitz rages above.

I had too many cold, wet holidays at Bridlington as a child readily to succumb to that locality's undoubted charm and the latest phase of David Hockney's development. I prefer (only once having been there) his California or his paintings done in Paris. They are the ones that would go under the raincoat. No room for his circumambient trees anyway.

The weather in Katharine Holmes's pictures is what rings a bell as she lives not far from us in Craven and we share the often grim climate of the Western Pennines which she seems to brave on a daily basis. Simon Palmer's Yorkshire is a more idyllic landscape though I can't say he idealises it any more than Katharine Holmes does hers. The corner of North Yorkshire round Jervaulx, Masham and Coverham is indeed blessed and with his evocative titles Palmer invests it with an additional layer of mystery. I can congratulate myself on having acquired two of his pictures when I'd never heard of him. This was thirty years ago in a print shop in Camden Town. My two pictures are entitled *Between Lane and Field* (which isn't very exciting) and *After a Late Breakfast* with on the edge of the picture a spectral figure who looks as if she has strayed from a novel by Barbara Pym. One could almost dramatise Palmer's world; they would be small dramas . . . women waiting on the edge of woods, solitary figures at bus stops . . . but always in this rapturous landscape, poems in paint with life almost stopping but going on.

Rather than bare white rooms I like domesticity in the presentation of art, which few galleries go in for. I like paintings in rooms and even behind a vase of flowers. It's a notion of pictures as furniture which art historians would deplore but suits me because, liking pictures to rub off, I'm happy to catch them out of the corner of my eye. Leading on from that, I don't think it goes against the spirit of a book of this kind if I put in a plea for art to be more taken for granted.

Not long ago I wrote a play, *People*, in which Dorothy Stacpoole is the aristocratic owner of a run-down Yorkshire country house which the National Trust and other interested parties are anxious to acquire. Dorothy wants things left as they are, reconciled to a degree of decay and neglect as preferable to having the place, its pictures and its furniture spruced up and made a showcase. There are masterpieces here, she admits that but she shrugs them off as they are what she has grown up with. It's Art, yes but she doesn't want her nose rubbed in it. She'd rather go on as she always has, taking it for granted.

It's a point of view with which many people found it difficult to sympathise but I think (an author not always the best person to know what he or she has written) I was putting in a plea for the ordinariness of art as opposed to the superstardom of pictures in particular that has been wished upon them by the great auction houses. Any one of the Turners in this book, the one of Fountains for instance, would sell for many hundreds of thousands of pounds but to the casual viewer it's a familiar prospect of a well-loved place. It's good but it's also ordinary. Is it a masterpiece? I don't know and I don't much care because that gets in the way. Here where we know these paintings and often know the places they depict we can and should ignore the rest. Paintings can be friends.

You may not agree but still, I hope you'll enjoy the pictures.

Foreword to *Art and Yorkshire: From Turner to Hockney* by Jane Sellars, Great Northern Books Ltd, 2014.

Nights at the Opera

The Clothes They Stood Up In is a play I failed to write. I had the idea years ago and had several goes at writing it but never got beyond twenty minutes into the first act. This is always a critical point with me; it's when questions like 'Haven't we been here before?' and 'Whom do you think you're kidding?' become too insistent to ignore. If I can get past this twenty-minute barrier I can generally write the play but in this case not.

Since I'm now at the stage where I'm beginning to tidy up a bit I decided to forget the play and try and write it as a short story for the *London Review of Books*. This turned out to be altogether easier and I even hit on a reasonable explanation for the total disappearance of the Ransomes' possessions, the result of which is to leave them, as the title suggests, just with the clothes they stood up in.

Sending the Ransomes to Covent Garden was a bit of naughtiness as it enabled me to parade some of my misgivings about opera though these, it has to be said, are based on very little knowledge. I have seen few operas, most of them before I was twenty. Except for three quarters of a production of *Tristan* and half a dress rehearsal of *Eugene Onegin* I have never seen an opera at Covent Garden nor have I been to the Coliseum. Most of the operas I have seen . . . and they include oddities like Vaughan Williams's *Pilgrim's Progress* and Walton's *Troilus and Cressida* . . . I saw as a boy at the Grand Theatre in Leeds. This was in the early fifties and long before it became the home of Opera North, though it occasionally put on a season by the Carl Rosa Opera Company or hosted touring versions from Covent Garden. So there I saw *Bohème*, *Tosca*, *Flying Dutchman* and the Walton and the Vaughan Williams, the last two part of the celebrations to do with the Festival of Britain in 1951. But no touring productions of Mozart came to Leeds in those days so other than Bergman's production of *Magic Flute* on television I have never seen a Mozart opera. I realise this is a shocking admission, though better to have seen too little than too much. There are undoubtedly people who see too much opera and let you know it too.

Far and away the most memorable of the productions I saw at the Grand in that Festival year was *Der Rosenkavalier*. Sylvia Fisher was the Marschallin, Otakar Kraus Baron Ochs but who sang Sophie or Octavian I don't remember. I was an odd boy, though, because I understood almost instinctively the renunciation and regret poured forth in the final trio by the Marschallin (with whom I utterly identified) while in other ways being a total innocent. The opera opens in the Marschallin's bedroom as she and her lover Octavian have breakfast. I had no notion at seventeen that anything might have been going on or that Octavian might have stopped the night: I just thought that he/she had come round for tea and toast.

Still the music has stayed with me all my life and I have never forgotten that production. There was standing room only. The side gallery had recently been painted so when I came out entranced on that July evening I found my hands, which had been gripping the rails, covered with gold. I have never seen *Der Rosenkavalier* since, nor wanted to, preferring the memory of that summer of 1951 unblurred.

The operas I have seen since have been a pretty mixed bag. Filming in Ljubljana in 1986 I saw *Nabucco* at the local opera house and found it delightful, though the rumty-tum music hardly seemed to sort with the biblical subject and it was not until the chorus glumly filed on halfway through that I realised this was the source of that old *Housewives' Choice* standard, the chorus of Hebrew slaves. The stage was so small that by the end of the big number the first line of the chorus were filing off while the last row were still waiting to get on. I didn't see that much of the action, though, as I was sitting in the front row right above the orchestra, which to me is the best place in the house, catching the glances between the players and wondering who is sleeping with whom, far more interesting than the goings-on on the stage.

Then there was a production of *Un ballo in maschera* in the Arena at Verona where a sudden thunderstorm sent the orchestra scuttling off, followed soon after by the chorus until finally only the principals and the conductor were left doing the whole thing as an unaccompanied oratorio. I suppose, though, it is one of the charms of opera that, comprising several elements more things are therefore likely to go wrong . . . which is what one always wants to see. Needless to say I never saw Trevor Nunn's Covent Garden production of *Katya Kabanova*, which figures in the documentary *The House*, but my expectations would have risen at the sight of the live horses. If only a night at the opera was more often like *A Night at the Opera* I might be persuaded to go.

First published in the *Radio Times*.

Bruce McFarlane 1903–1966

_____

K. B. McFarlane was one of the most influential medieval historians of post-war Britain but his name is unknown outside academic circles. This would have pleased him. He grew up in Dulwich, the son of a civil servant in the Admiralty. A day boy at Dulwich College, he won an open scholarship to Exeter College, Oxford, followed by a senior demyship at Magdalen College where in 1928 he became a fellow and where the rest of his life was spent. In terms of published output his career might not seem to amount to much; there is a small book on Wyclif and a handful of scholarly articles in historical periodicals although most of his work, notably his Ford Lectures, 'The Nobility of Medieval England', was published after his death. Through his teaching and lecturing and the supervision of a large number of graduate students he was undoubtedly the leading medieval historian of his time. A perfectionist in both research and writing he shunned popularity and publicity and was feared for his acerbic and deflational comments. But those who broke through his reserve knew him as a gentle and companionable man.

I first met Bruce McFarlane at Oxford late in Michaelmas term 1957. I had read history at Exeter College and in Final Schools the previous term, rather to my own surprise (and very much to the surprise of my college), had just scraped into the first class. So instead of being thrust out into the world as I had expected I was offered the chance of putting Life off a little longer by staying on, as I thought vaguely, 'to do research', though into what I had no idea. In quest of a supervisor and also a subject I paid a disastrous visit to Beryl Smalley at St Hilda's, thinking I might do something on the Franciscans. There had been a torrential thunderstorm and forgetting to wipe my feet I trailed wet footsteps all across her white carpet, thus putting paid to any hope of research into the friars, barefoot or otherwise. I then went to see K. B. McFarlane.

My special subject in Schools was Richard II so I had been to McFarlane's lectures on the Lollard Knights; I also had a copy of some notes on his 1953 Ford Lectures that was passed down from year to year in Exeter. I knew of his austere reputation and of his reluctance to publish from David Marquand, who was at Magdalen and who told me how he had been scared out of his wits one dark night in the cloisters when Bruce had swept past him in his Spanish cloak.

I must have written to him and been told to come down to Magdalen. I remember nothing of that first meeting except that Bruce was sitting in his armchair, possibly with a cat on his knee, and that I marched awkwardly into the room, stood on the hearthrug and said, 'I'm Bennett,' at which he laughed. And the laughter and the angle of his head and the smile that was so often in his eyes is how I recall him now. Freesias bring him back too, as there were always some in a glass scenting the whole room, with its collection of keys hung on the plain plaster wall, the bleached oak, the thirties paintings and bits of brocade. But as one came in the last smell was always the fish that was put out in the vestibule for the cats.

We settled on 'The Royal Retinue of Richard II 1388–99' as my research subject and thereafter I used to go down and see him pretty regularly, not in my recollection talking much about work; these visits, very often around tea time, gradually became less tutorial and more social. I'd generally take with me a cake from Fuller's or some establishment in the Covered Market, cakes that can have done him no good but which he ate with relish, meringues particularly.

I had never come up against as strong a personality as this before and I found without any conscious effort that my handwriting now began to resemble his. He always wrote Esq. with the superscription re and I found myself doing that too. It's rare enough nowadays to write Esq. at all but I still write it Esqre and note that others of his former pupils do the same.

Bruce was very set in his ways, though perhaps no more than I am now. At Stonor once I was helping him change some sheets and had put the bottom sheet on with the crease folding down, not up . . . the fact that I find my mistake hard to describe indicates how finicky I found it. Bruce reproved me, explaining that the creases should go the other way. I thought this pedantic and probably said so but I have observed his method ever since.

Stonor, his pied-à-terre in the country, was hardly the cottage I had imagined but a sizeable house with an extensive garden tended largely by Helena Wright, the pioneer of birth control with whom he shared the house, who was often knelt there working, planting out the beds, with her radio (a source of irritation to Bruce) always beside her. Brudenell House at Quainton, to which he subsequently moved, was more imposing but I never stayed there. Food was fairly simple with lots of soups and salads, the soup in the evening drunk with a set of sixteenth-century silver Apostle spoons. In those more expansive days one took elaborate table silver for granted, under-graduates at my own college regularly drinking beer in hall from eighteenth- and nineteenth-century silver tankards. But the spoons I knew were in a different class and indeed they had to be deposited in the bank between visits. Bruce enjoyed food and was quite funny and snobbish about it. Dining once with him at the Randolph (a more intimidating experience then than it is now) I chose scampi, which I'd never eaten. Bruce sniffed, 'Commercial traveller's food.'

McFarlane has figured in accounts of the period chiefly as the col-league and opponent of A. J. P. Taylor with whom he shared the his-tory teaching at Magdalen. Taylor achieved the kind of fame Bruce wanted none of but, unlike Taylor, Bruce managed without effort to acquire a body of pupils who were both friends and disciples and who carried on his work and cherished his memory. Anyone who was supervised by McFarlane must have been aware that they had a

long way to travel before they reached the frontier of his own knowledge and there was very little any of his students could tell him that
he didn't already know, though this didn't stop one trying. Having
come under his spell I wanted very much to please him even though
it gradually became apparent to me that I was pretty hopeless at
research and not much better as a teacher. Still he steered a number of his surplus pupils my way which financially was a great help,
finally getting me appointed a junior lecturer in history at Magdalen.

He did too much teaching himself and grumbled about it but never treated it as a chore; what takes me by surprise in his letters is how
much his happiness and well-being was bound up with the progress
and responsiveness of his pupils – and not just the cleverest ones
either. A good tutorial even with an average pupil put him in a good
mood and was thought worth mentioning in a letter. This dedication
to teaching could make him intolerant of what he saw as laziness and
he was harsh with pupils who, it seemed to him, were performing
below their capacity. His zeal was tempered by his relish for oddity
and his interest in the personalities of those whom he taught but it
could make him seem unfeeling.

It wasn't that he measured intellectual worth by success in examinations, though he did believe that one had to play the system and
that if a good degree bought you time or opened doors and gave
you the opportunity to do what you wanted, you were a fool not to
take examinations seriously. This comes out in one of his letters to
Michael Wheeler-Booth, a letter I find encouraging because it deals
to some extent with the stratagems necessary to get through Finals. I
had used stratagems myself and felt a bit shabby for doing so, though
mine were probably cruder (artful quotations, a selection of facts
learned by rote) than anything Bruce was advocating. Still they did
the trick, but his friend and colleague Karl Leyser having been one
of my examiners, Bruce would have known that it was a close-run
thing, so I always felt intellectually I was on very thin ice.

I knew that Bruce was fond of me but did not let on that I knew, flattered that he should be glad of my company but embarrassed when he gave any hint of it. I've always regretted this, reproaching myself for not acknowledging his affection and managing things better.

I ended up quarrelling, as I'm reassured, reading his letters, to find that several of his friends and pupils did, though I'm glad I made it up with him before he died. I called to see him one afternoon at Quainton and we sat in the garden talking. Suddenly he said, à propos of nothing, 'I think I'm going to retire.' I thought he meant into the house and so stood up abruptly and this made him laugh. So I'm happy to think that our friendship both began and ended with his laughing.

First published in the *London Review of Books* in 1997.

John Schlesinger 1926–2003

It's not often that one can reprise or indeed recycle a speech made at a memorial service but I'm in that happy or unhappy position this evening. A few weeks ago I had to speak at Thora Hird's memorial service and began by talking about a scene from *A Kind of Loving*, John's film of Stan Barstow's novel, made in 1962. Thora played the sour-faced Mrs Rothwell, straitlaced, houseproud and wary mother of the beautiful Ingrid. At Thora's service I told the story from her p.o.v. This evening, I suppose, I'm doing the reverse angle.

Woken late one night Mrs Rothwell comes downstairs to find Alan Bates's Vic drunk and snogging the beautiful Ingrid in the parlour. Bates is about to apologise when he is abruptly and copiously sick behind the sofa.

John took a great deal of pleasure in this scene, calling initially for much more sick (probably Crosse and Blackwell's Scotch Broth) and even stirring it himself. It was quite a long scene, Bates throwing up at least twice but the Waterhouse and Hall script only gave Thora one line, 'You filthy, disgusting pig.' It was a line admirably suited to her talents but not enough to cover what went on so John told Thora to improvise.

This was not a technique Thora had ever had any occasion to acquire, her job to say the words not make them up. However she did her best and having a text, 'You filthy disgusting pig,' she proceeded to play variations on it.

'You . . . pig. You're filthy . . . you. Disgusting.' Then, looking over the back of the sofa, 'You . . . you're . . . a pig!'

Thora thought that would be all that would be required of her but John with what in every sense was gay abandon, kept the camera rolling with Thora forced to weave more and more variations on the four words the script had allotted her. Alan remembers that she said the magic phrase no less than eleven times, with all her frustration at not being able to think of anything better feeding into the anger she was supposed to feel as the character. And it's a wonderful scene.

But it demonstrates the first thing you could expect when working with John, namely that there would always be a good deal of fun and sheer mischief.

I first became aware of John with that film, *A Kind of Loving*, which, together with Lindsay Anderson's *This Sporting Life* and Karel Reisz's *Saturday Night and Sunday Morning* were all defining films of the early sixties . . . and part of a new anatomy of England that was being put together in the films and plays of that time.

A Kind of Loving and *Billy Liar*, both scripted by Keith Waterhouse and Willis Hall, were funnier than the others, less grim and with a fondness for the North. John begins *Billy Liar* with a long sequence in which the camera pans across an estate of council houses at nine o'clock in the morning, every house tuned to *Housewives' Choice* on the radio, the snatches of music you hear so right . . . Litolff's Scherzo, the 'Chorus of the Hebrew Slaves' from *Nabucco* . . . that they were practically a joke in themselves and you know at once you're in the hands of a sceptical and amused observer of the English scene and that it's going to be fun.

When eventually I came to work with John on *An Englishman Abroad* I was frightened that it wasn't going to be fun at all, simply because I'd never worked with anyone who had such a short fuse, or whose moods could change so dramatically. Coral Browne, though, reassured me. 'Don't worry, dear. John can always drag the crown of thorns out from under the bed whenever it suits him.'

Like Lindsay Anderson (though not), part of the dynamic of film-making with John was to have someone to blame. He needed a villain. Film-making put him instinctively on the defensive though it was so instinctive it was almost a joke. It was like Old Mother Riley getting her corsets out of the oven and going into pugilistic mode.

Sometimes it was the costume department, sometimes it was even the writer . . . John, for instance, didn't get on at all with Penelope Gilliatt on *Sunday, Bloody Sunday* . . . and routinely, of course, it was the front office and the money.

But the films I did with him were for the BBC and were produced by Innes Lloyd, the most emollient of producers and a saintly man with whom even John at his most choleric could find no fault. And with Innes on hand it was hard to blame the BBC so John . . . like Lindsay again . . . would go into terrible rages about the shortcomings of England. The advantage of blaming England rather than the wardrobe being that England isn't found two hours later weeping in the loo.

But his ambiguous attitude to England I always found deeply sympathetic and I wish he'd had the opportunities to work it out more in films or on television. Too often, landed with an unsympathetic project he was himself the Englishman abroad and one would get calls from some location hotel on the other side of the world to hear John say sadly, 'No jokes, dear. No jokes at all.'

John was very much a family man. He revered his parents and after *An Englishman Abroad* asked me to write a film based partly on the book of tributes to his parents that was put together at the time of their golden wedding.

So we had talks about it and tried to rough out a plot. And I began to turn up again at Victoria Road with treatments and pages but unusually for John, who was always bold and didn't worry about treading on toes . . . with this project he was tentative. He was anxious not to upset anyone in the family, which sometimes my treatments might unwittingly have done . . . and above all he wanted to do his parents justice and properly to celebrate them.

Gradually it became clear that we were getting nowhere and so it was never written. But in a sense this was right, too, and evidence of his affection and respect, the fact that he couldn't make a film about his family as much a tribute to them as if he had.

It's impossible to talk about John even in these circumstances without referring to sex. Being gay determined his life and much of his work. It informs, of course, one of his best films, *Sunday, Bloody Sunday*, the moment when only a few frames from the end Peter Finch turns and talks to the camera one of the great moments in cinema and still as fresh and startling when you see it today.

He was so aware of his sexuality that he contrived to find a corresponding awareness in the unlikeliest of places. At his investiture with the CBE the Queen had a momentary difficulty getting the ribbon round his neck.

'Now, Mr Schlesinger,' she said, 'let us see. We must try and get this *straight*.' Which John chose to take as both a coded acknowledgement and a seal of royal approval.

I owe John an immense amount. *An Englishman Abroad* was one of the happiest films I've ever worked on and one that thanks to John far exceeded my expectations. We shot it largely in Dundee and our hotel was next door to a housing estate and after supper every night Alan Bates, John and I used to take a stroll round these rather genteel streets when we would speculate about the lives lived there.

Someone looking through the curtains would have seen three middle-aged men, entirely sober but helpless with laughter, night after night for no apparent cause.

It was such a happy time and that's how I will always remember him, full of joy and fun.

The National Theatre at Fifty:
What the National Means to Me

The first time I set foot on the stage at the National was in November 1987 at the Cottesloe. It was an inauspicious debut. Patrick Garland had put together an evening of Philip Larkin's poetry and prose entitled *Down Cemetery Road*, done as a two-hander with Alan Bates as Larkin. This was then revived at short notice for some extra performances but Alan wasn't available and I agreed to substitute. The change of cast hadn't been advertised and many of the audience, having come along expecting to see Alan Bates, must have thought he'd gone downhill a bit since they last saw him wrestling naked on a rug with Oliver Reed. I was also in the middle of some extensive dentistry, which involved the removal of several bridges and, though the dentist had assured me that the effects of the anaesthetic would have worn off long before the evening's performance, I often took the stage feeling as if large sections of my mouth were coned off. The anaesthetic did indeed wear off during the course of the performance so that when I hit a suddenly tender spot there was an agonised yelp uncatered for in Larkin's muted verse. Even at the best of times the poet didn't care for the public performance of his works so it was perhaps fortunate he had died two years previously.

What the audience felt I tried not to think though I remember coming off at the interval and en route for my dressing room meeting Judi Dench and her attendants bound for the Olivier stage. 'Not many laughs tonight,' I said. 'None at all with us,' she replied but since she was appearing in *Antony and Cleopatra* this was hardly surprising. They had one unscheduled laugh, though, as it was while she was giving her Cleopatra that Judi was made a dame. On the evening in question Michael Bryant, playing Enobarbus, turned upstage and muttered en passant, 'Well I suppose a fuck's quite out of the question now,' an extra-textual remark, such was Michael's never other than immaculate diction, that was heard by the first ten rows.

About the NT building itself I've always had reservations. It's better inside than out with the foyers, in particular, interesting and lively and even living up to those fanciful illustrations with which architects populate their constructions with idly gossiping creatures who seem to have all the time in the world. They always have oval heads and are wholly intent on using the space the architect has so thoughtfully provided. Oval heads apart, the foyer of the National is a bit like that and works, just as Denys Lasdun envisaged it should.

Nor are the three theatres too bad, with the Olivier, to my mind, the best. From an actor's point of view (or that of someone with a weak bladder) the huge central block of seats of the Lyttelton is daunting. The Olivier is more broken up, though it, too, has its drawbacks and it's said that Michael Gambon got so accustomed to playing the vast space that even in private conversation he would still slowly move through the necessary arc.

A few years after the building had opened the late Ronald Eyre, having directed one or two productions here, said that it would be better for all concerned if the National Theatre could straight away close again and be converted into an ice rink and/or dance hall . . . the Olivier, I suppose most suited for the ice rink, the Lyttelton for the *palais de danse*. Then, after twenty years or so, when the corners had been rubbed off the building and it had acquired its own shabby and disreputable history, all the cultural stuffing long since knocked out of it and every breath of Art dispersed, it would be time for it to be reclaimed for theatre. As it was it was too much of a temple for him and altogether too worthy; somewhere ordinary was what he wanted and with no pretensions. I remembered this and years later included it as part of the stage manager's final speech in *The Habit of Art* (2009).

It's certainly true that audiences (and critics in particular) come to the National Theatre in a different frame of mind from when they go to see a play on Shaftesbury Avenue. They're more reverential, more inclined to invest what they're seeing with significance (or deplore its absence). It's all in capital letters: Art, Theatre; it's never just a play. I first noticed this twenty-five years ago in the Lyttelton. It was the second night of the opening week and the play was John Osborne's *Watch It Come Down*. It wasn't one of his best but, as always with Osborne, even when I disliked the play I found his tone sympathetic. I was in a minority. To give a flavour of the audience, Edward Heath was sitting in front, Alec Douglas-Home behind and the rest looked as if they'd come on reluctantly after the Lord Mayor's Banquet. Of course, audiences were bound to get better and broader and they have but there's still a feeling that this is Something Special; it's not yet the community-minded place that subsidised theatres (those that survive) manage to be in the provinces.

Nor is it particularly comforting. When I was acting in *Single Spies* (1988) I never got over the nightly walk along the corridor from my dressing room, pushing through the swing door and suddenly being hit by the amplified roar of the audience. They were just chatting before curtain up but to me they sounded like the crowd at the Colosseum waiting for the massacre to begin.

Mind you, this is not peculiar to the National Theatre. All theatre is theatre of blood. I once had to give a talk at the West Yorkshire Playhouse and was accosted on my way in by two sabre-toothed pensioners.

'It had better be good,' warned one of them. 'We're big fans of yours.'

Still, whatever its shortcomings or the fear that stalks its corridors, the bleakness of the building has always been compensated for by the cheerfulness of the staff and I have never felt other than welcome here and with all my grumblings, I am thankful to have had a small part in the National's history. *The Wind in the Willows* (1990) and *The Madness of George III* (1991), both directed by Nicholas Hytner, were two of the happiest plays I have ever worked on and when I recall the ending of the first part of *Wind in the Willows* with the snow coming down and the mice singing 'In the Bleak Midwinter' and the wonderful bravura opening of *The Madness of George III* when the whole cast comes over the crest of the hill and down onto the stage, I am glad to have been at least the occasion for such a spectacle.

Of *Single Spies* my memories are only less fond because the cast was quite small and looming up at the end of rehearsal there was the awful prospect of having to go on stage and do it. Also, though the technical side of it wasn't particularly complicated, things did tend to go wrong. In the scene in Buckingham Palace where the Queen comes upon Anthony Blunt hanging a picture, there were two console tables trucked in from stage left and stage right. On the tables were various *objets d'art* which the Queen would pick up and comment on as she chatted to her Keeper of Pictures. These tables had a life of their own, only occasionally trucking on submissively as they were meant to do, but more often coming on, taking one look at the audience and then retreating shyly into the wings. This meant that Prunella Scales, playing the Queen, instead of idly fingering an object and discoursing on its origins ('This ostrich egg was a present from the people of Zambia') had instead to dive offstage, locate the item in question and fetch it on for Sir Anthony to admire, so that she looked less like the monarch than one of those beady ladies queuing up with their treasures on *Antiques Roadshow*.

The success of *The History Boys* (2004) was wholly unexpected. We'd had such a good time rehearsing it I don't recall ever wondering how well it would go down. Nicholas Hytner has said that on first reading the script he thought it would perhaps make eighty performances. As it was the reception of the play at its first preview took us both by surprise. It wasn't so much the laughter – though at least twice it brought the show to a halt – but it was the hush in the audience just before the curtain when the boys talk of their future lives and Hector comes back from the dead to give them his last message. When the curtain came down there was a moment's silence and then the house went up like a furnace.

Which is an unfortunate image in the circumstances as days later, half an hour before the curtain was due to go up for the press night in the Lyttelton, a fire was discovered in the flies. It wasn't a serious blaze but the sprinklers flooding the stage was what held the job up. After twenty-five years at the National I still get lost backstage so when I came across a lone fireman wandering the corridors who said, 'Where is this Lyttelton theatre?' I knew what he meant.

After the success of *The History Boys* I found my next play much harder to write. This was *The Habit of Art*, an account of an imaginary meeting between Benjamin Britten and W. H. Auden, and it was only when I set it as a rehearsal of a play that it began to work. It takes place in Rehearsal Room 2 in the National, the room reproduced so exactly by Bob Crowley that one had to keep reminding oneself this was not the real thing.

Playing Britten, Alex Jennings was well placed to perfect an imitation of me, which I suspect he had long been doing on the quiet but which he was able to put to legitimate use in *Hymn* and *Cocktail Sticks* (2013), two short autobiographical pieces which began life in the Platform slot before transferring to the Duchess. Prior to this, though, was *People* (2012), a tour round the question of conservation and which, when the National Trust laid on tours of the Big Brother household, turned out to be mildly prophetic; art as so often limping way behind life.

Nobody would call the National Theatre a homely place but it has been my artistic home for twenty-five years and for that I count myself very lucky. I have met nothing but kindness and co-operation not least, of course, from Nicholas Hytner but at every level. It has enabled me to go on working much longer than I could have imagined through turning up with a play every three or four years. I am happy not to have acquired any dignity in the process. When I came in for the first rehearsal of *People* someone at the stage door said, 'Oh hello. Still hanging on then?'

First published in the *Observer*, Sunday 20 October 2013.

On Nicholas Hytner

'Don't worry. Just write it and I'll make it work.'

This was Nicholas Hytner, whom I'd not previously met when, in 1989, I was baffled by *The Wind in the Willows* which, at Richard Eyre's suggestion, Nick was asking me to adapt. And for the next twenty-five years 'Just write it, I'll make it work' has stood me in good stead and given me the confidence I always need.

I don't know how Nick works with other playwrights – typically he hasn't ever said – but special to me is his ability to gauge the encouragement one wants and the degree of criticism. Too much enthusiasm on his part means I don't feel there's much more to do; too little and I feel it's not worth doing anyway. I'm not sure if this makes him my muse but certainly in the early stages what matters to me is his approval. Putting a script through his door in Primrose Hill, I'm like a pupil turning up with his homework.

To a playwright, what immediately commends him is the amount of work he puts in. Directing can be quite a lazy profession with the play once roughed out and in preview left to coast along or settle down. Not with Nick; he never lets up. Nor does he just direct the principals; he directs around the edges with no one left out. And he likes actors (it's surprising the directors who don't) and he's loyal to them. Nor is the production a stage on which to play the virtuoso director. He's never the star of his own productions. Modest and unassuming, he often goes unrecognised in his own foyer.

Some thoughts:

His rehearsals are sometimes lessons; they are never lectures.

He has no sense of entitlement. As Director of the National Theatre he has found himself drafted onto prestigious committees and in quite august company. He doesn't take this as his due but is delighted by it.

He likes risk and is always up for it. The dodgiest parts of my stuff – the talking furniture in *The Habit of Art*, the porn scene in *People* – are what gets him going.

He delights in spectacle and is not afraid of being popular. I'm not sure if I said this or someone else (I hope a well-wisher) but there is in his character an iron streak of tinsel.

And he gives lovely parties and is, I imagine, a very nice uncle.

I will always be grateful to Richard Eyre, who brought Nick and me together. It's been twenty-five years of fun and fellowship with so many moments I will never forget: the end of the first part of *Wind in the Willows* with the snow falling and the field mice singing 'In the Bleak Midwinter'; George III clamped into the restraining chair just as the chorus bursts out with 'Zadok the Priest'; and the silence at the end of *The History Boys* as Mrs Lintott calls up the boys one by one and tells us what will become of them.

At the end of the Fiftieth Anniversary Gala in 2013, the actors who have played at the National came forward year by year and took their bows, followed by the backstage staff and everyone who works here who could crowd onto the Olivier stage. It was a scene that might have taken days to rehearse but Nick had put it together in the brief gap between the end of the dress rehearsal and the half-hour call. There was, of course, a tumultuous reception, but I don't even know whether he was himself on the stage.

First published as a National Theatre programme note, January 2014.

Epilogue

I still occasionally speak at literary festivals and suchlike, doing readings from my diaries and short extracts from my plays. These are generally followed by a Q&A session and this winds up the proceedings. Except that all too often it doesn't, quite, the questions dribbling to a stop with me or the chairperson waiting in mild embarrassment for a final question which doesn't come. So the evening ends rather lamely. I've learned over the years not to conclude with Q&A but to finish with a final reminiscence of my childhood coupled with a speech from an early play, *Enjoy*, that relates to it. And that's how I'll end this book.

As a child in Leeds in the forties I often go down on a Saturday afternoon to see my grandma in Gilpin Place off Tong Road in Wortley. If I am with my brother we will sometimes put up our tent on the grass in Grandma's tiny garden, the space so small that the tent pegs for the guy ropes have to be stuck in the cracks between the paving stones of the path. Grandma is in her seventies and, though I don't altogether understand this, is beginning to fail. While she dozes by the fire in the kitchen I go into the front room and investigate the always fascinating contents of the sideboard, a bright chestnut-varnished many-mirrored piece of furniture crammed with the relics and evidences of Grandma's life . . . glossy, deckle-edged postcards from Bangor or Dunoon, photograph albums with snaps of Grandma and her friends in their duster coats and cloche hats striding along the promenade at Morecambe or Cleveleys on the bowling club outing. There are sadder evidences, too . . . a silk bookmark printed with a photo of Clarence, her only son, killed at Ypres in 1917, a picture of Aunty Myra in the WAAFs in India and occasional pictures on stiff card of a kindly-looking moustached man who I gather was my grandfather. Sometimes Grandma wakes up and calls out, 'What are you doing in there? Are you rooting?' (which she pronounces 'roo-i-ting'). 'I'm reading,' I lie, 'I'm reading my comic,' though if I am reading it's as clandestine as the rooting because it will be Aunty Kathleen's brown paper-backed copy of *Forever Amber*.

Later on we have our tea, toasting some of Grandma's homemade flat bread in a twisted wire roasting fork against the fire. The clock on the mantelpiece chimes five and the *Yorkshire Evening Post* struggles in through the letterbox, which is always blocked with coats. Now in the fading light Grandma sits in the easy chair and strains to read it . . . strains because she has an exaggerated notion of the cost of the electric and never puts the light on until she has to and so holding up the *Evening Post* to the last of the sun coming through the kitchen window. In a ritual that never varies she reads out items that catch her eye . . . and as the years pass and she loses her memory reads them out twice or three times. 'Blackburn gripped by bread hysteria. Pensioner cleared of teacake theft.' 'I see the President of Rumania's mother's died. There's always trouble for somebody.'

This perusal of the paper always ends in the same way with her reading out the Deaths and In Memoriams. The In Memoriams are always chosen from a big ledger in the *Evening Post* offices on Commercial Street in Leeds and adapted, not always successfully to the requirements of the deceased, my favourite (which isn't apocryphal) ending up:

> Down the lanes of memory
> The lights are never dim.
> Until the stars forget to shine
> We shall remember her.

This ceremony takes place in front of the fire and beneath the kitchen mantelpiece and in *Enjoy* (a play which would have been better entitled *Endure*) one of the characters describes it and catalogues its contents. Part of the play though it is I have read this speech so often in public it has become almost a parlour recitation so I'm happy to have it here as the conclusion to this book.

One clock in light oak, presented to Mam's father after forty years with Greenwood and Batley. Stopped; the key lost.

A wooden candlestick that's never seen a candle. A tube of ointment for a skin complaint that cleared up after one application. An airmail letter, two years old, announcing the death of a cousin in Perth, Western Australia, the stamp torn off. Two half-crowns not cashed at decimalisation because Mam read in the *Evening Post* that one day they would be priceless. Four old halfpennies kept on the same principle. A dry Biro.

Various reminders on the backs of envelopes. 'Pension, Thursday', 'Dad's pills', 'Gone down the road. Dinner on'. And, starkly, 'Gas'. A rubber band. Three plastic clips from the package of a new shirt, kept by Dad with the idea it will save wasting money on paper clips. Not that he ever does waste money on paper clips.

Three tuppenny-halfpenny stamps.

A packet of nasturtium seeds on offer with some custard powder. A newspaper cutting recording the conviction for shoplifting of the wife of the local vicar, saved to send to relatives in Canada. Dad's last appointment card at the Infirmary and two grey aspirins.

Altar, noticeboard, medicine chest, cemetery. A shrine laden with the relics of the recent past and a testimonial to the faith that one day the world will turn and the past come back into its own and there will be a restoration. The coinage will make sense once more, letters again cost twopence halfpenny and life return to its old ways. On that day the nasturtiums will be planted, the half-crowns spent, the skin complaint will recur and the ointment be applied once more to the affected part. The Biro will flow again, the second cousin in Toronto will be informed at last of the conviction of the vicar's wife and on that day the key will be found and the clock strike.

Acknowledgements

In a book that chiefly comprises a collection of diaries I perhaps ought to acknowledge the help, unwitting though it is, of anybody who happens to turn up there. The first reader of these accounts is always Sue Powell, who has been transcribing my diaries now for twenty-five years and in the process has become adept at deciphering my handwriting, undaunted by the odd bits of paper . . . backs of envelopes the least of it . . . on which I choose to write. Her diligence is only equalled by her discretion.

Once transcribed, an edited version of the diaries is published in the *London Review of Books*, to which I've been a contributor since its inception in 1979. With the editorial staff both young and bright it's a fierce filter to pass through but Mary-Kay Wilmers, whom I've known all my writing life, has always made me welcome. Besides which, computer illiterate as I am the *LRB* will always Google for me on request.

Plays apart, I'm published by Faber and Profile in tandem, an arrangement which Stephen Page at Faber and Andrew Franklin at Profile make work admirably. I am not always an easily marketable product but Rebecca Gray tactfully guides me through the publishing maze while Dinah Wood edits me at Faber.

One of the pleasures of doing plays at the National Theatre was to have the programmes compiled by Lyn Haill, then Head of Publications, and I see her touch in the prefaces of the plays and other writings to do with the NT that are included here. My gratitude to Nicholas Hytner is everywhere apparent and repeatedly acknowledged. Thanks too to Niamh Dilworth who so often has smoothed my path.

My debt to my editor at Faber, Dinah Wood, is overwhelming. Patient, meticulous and always cheerful she has made putting the book together a pleasure. I am lucky to have her as my editor.

It will be obvious from the text how much I owe to my partner Rupert Thomas. I don't think I'm a particularly moody author though I probably wouldn't know if I was. Rupert tends not to bring work home and I'm seldom at my desk after 7.30 so we don't tread on one another's toes. He's a great help with questions of design and the look of a book and wise to any attempts to bump me into deadlines or unnecessary publicity. Writing isn't always fun but without him there would be no fun at all.

TEXT PERMISSIONS:

The publishers gratefully acknowledge permission to reprint copyright material in this book as follows:

Extracts from 'Bestiaries Are Out', 'The Sea and the Mirror' and 'Epistle to a Godson' by W. H. Auden taken from *Collected Poems*, edited by Edward Mendelson. Copyright © 1976 and 1991 by the Estate of W. H. Auden. Reprinted by permission of Random House, Inc.

Extract from *The Power of Delight: A Lifetime in Literature, Essays 1962–2002* by John Bayley (Duckworth Overlook, 2005). Courtesy of Gerald Duckworth & Co Ltd and W. W. Norton & Company, Inc.

Extract from *Building: Letters, 1960–1975* by Isaiah Berlin (Chatto & Windus, 2013). © The Isaiah Berlin Literary Trust. Reprinted by permission of Curtis Brown Group Ltd.

Excerpt from 'He Resigns' from *Collected Poems: 1937–1971* by John Berryman. Copyright © 1989 by Kate Donahue Berryman. Reprinted by permission of Faber & Faber Ltd and Farrar, Straus and Giroux, LLC.

Extract from *Borderland: Continuity and Change in the Countryside, a Country Diary* by Ronald Blythe (Hymns Ancient & Modern Ltd, 2005). Reprinted courtesy of Canterbury Press.

Extract from *The End of the Line* by Richard Cobb (John Murray, 1997). © The Estate of Richard Cobb. Reprinted by permission of Christopher Sinclair-Stevenson.

Extract from *Injury Time: A Memoir* by D. J. Enright (Pimlico, 2003). © The Estate of D. J. Enright. Reproduced by permission of Watson, Little Ltd.

Extract from *Poems and Poets* by Geoffrey Grigson (Macmillan, 1969). © The Estate of Geoffrey Grigson. Reprinted courtesy Chatto & Windus and Macmillan.

Extract from *Against Oblivion: Some Lives of the Twentieth-Century Poets* (Viking, 2002). © The Ian Hamilton Estate, with the kind permission of Aitken Alexander Associates Ltd.

'Goodbye to the Villa Piranha' by Francis Hope taken from *Instead of a Poet and Other Poems* (The Bodley Head, 1965). © The Estate of Francis Hope and The Bodley Head, an imprint of Penguin Random House UK.

Extract from *The Sixties: Volume Two, 1960–1969* by Christopher Isherwood (Chatto & Windus, 2010). © The Estate of Christopher Isherwood with the kind permission of The Wylie Agency.

'A War' from *The Complete Poems by Randall Jarrell*. Copyright © 1969, renewed 1997 by Mary von S. Jarrell. Reprinted by permission of Faber & Faber Ltd and Farrar, Straus and Giroux, LLC.

Extract from 'High Windows' from *The Complete Poems by Philip Larkin*. © Estate of Philip Larkin. Reprinted by permission of Faber & Faber Ltd.

Extract taken from October 1967, *Letters to Monica* by Philip Larkin. © Estate of Philip Larkin. Reprinted by permission of Faber & Faber Ltd.

Extract from *Mysteries and Manners* by Flannery O'Connor reprinted by permission of Faber & Faber Ltd and Peters Fraser & Dunlop (www.petersfraserdunlop.com) on behalf of the Estate of Flannery O'Connor.

Extract from 'My Parents', taken from *New Collected Poems* by Stephen Spender, © 2004. Reprinted by kind permission of the Estate of Stephen Spender.

Extract from 'Song' by R. S. Thomas, *Stones of the Field* (Druid Press, 1946). © The Estate of R. S. Thomas.

Extract from *New Ways to Kill Your Mother: Writers and Their Families* by Colm Tóibín. Published by Viking, 2012. Copyright © Colm Tóibín. Reproduced by permission of the author c/o Rogers, Coleridge & White Ltd, 20 Powis Mews, London W11 1JN.

Extract from *A Streetcar Named Desire* by Tennessee Williams, published by Methuen Drama © 1947 the Estate of the late Tennessee Williams, © 1947, 1953 by The University of The South. Reproduced by permission of Sheil Land Associates Ltd and Georges Borchardt, Inc. for the Estate of Tennessee Williams. All rights reserved.

PICTURE PERMISSIONS:

All photographs courtesy of Rupert Thomas except:

With Rupert en route to our civil partnership 2006 © Tom Miller; Outside the Spider, Bodmin © Adrian Bedson; Alex Jennings as Britten, *The Habit of Art* © Johan Persson/ArenaPAL; With Nicholas Hytner, *The Habit of Art* © Johan Persson/ArenaPAL; Richard Griffiths as Auden, *The Habit of Art* © Johan Persson/ArenaPAL; Jeff Rawle and Gabrielle Lloyd, *Cocktail Sticks* © Jayne West; George Fenton, *Hymn* © Jayne West; Filming *The Lady in the Van*, Gloucester Crescent © Antony Crolla; Filming *The Lady in the Van* © Antony Crolla; On the terrace, 16th Street, New York, courtesy of Lone Star Productions; Armley Public Library, courtesy of Lone Star Productions; By the beck, Yorkshire, courtesy of Lone Star Productions; With Dinah Wood and Eddie © Olly Lambert; Frances de la Tour and Linda Bassett in *People*, 2012 © Catherine Ashmore; With Dominic Cooper and James Corden, *The History Boys*, National Theatre Gala © Catherine Ashmore; Maggie Smith and Alex Jennings filming *The Lady in the Van*, Nicola Dove © Van Productions; One of my dad's penguins © Antony Crolla; *Plumber* by Wilfrid Wood, photo by Stephen Lenthall; My shoe depicted by Rupert as a birthday card © Antony Crolla; AB © Antony Crolla.

Index